Study Guide

for

Weiten's

Psychology
Themes and Variations

Seventh Edition

Richard B. Stalling
Bradley University

Ronald E. Wasden
Bradley University

THOMSON
WADSWORTH

Australia • Brazil • Canada • Mexico • Singapore • Spain • United Kingdom • United States

Printer: Thomson West

ISBN: 0-495-17034-8
Credit image: main image © Walter Hodges/Corbis (small images from left to right) © Bryan F. Peterson/Corbis; © K. Hackenberg/zefa/Corbis; © Josh Westrich/zefa/Corbis; © Andersen Ross/Blend Images/Alamy

Thomson Higher Education
10 Davis Drive
Belmont, CA 94002-3098
USA

For more information about our products,
contact us at:
Thomson Learning Academic Resource Center
1-800-423-0563

For permission to use material from this text or product, submit a request online at
http://www.thomsonrights.com.
Any additional questions about permissions can be submitted by email to **thomsonrights@thomson.com.**

Contents

To the Student iv

Chapter 1   The Evolution of Psychology 1

Chapter 2   The Research Enterprise in Psychology 19

Chapter 3   The Biological Bases of Behavior 37

Chapter 4   Sensation and Perception 57

Chapter 5   Variations in Consciousness 77

Chapter 6   Learning 93

Chapter 7   Human Memory 117

Chapter 8   Language and Thought 135

Chapter 9   Intelligence and Psychological Testing 153

Chapter 10   Motivation and Emotion 169

Chapter 11   Human Development Across the Life Span 189

Chapter 12   Personality: Theory, Research, and Assessment 213

Chapter 13   Stress, Coping, and Health 235

Chapter 14   Psychological Disorders 251

Chapter 15   Treatment of Psychological Disorders 273

Chapter 16   Social Behavior 289

Appendix B   Statistical Methods 313

Appendix C   Industrial/Organizational Psychology 319

Appendix D   Careers in Psychology 327

To the Student

In Wayne Weiten's *Psychology: Themes and Variations* you will encounter a truly remarkable book. Across seven editions of this text we have noted Wayne's extraordinary ability to create vivid, self-relevant examples. We continue to be amazed at the breadth and the beauty of this text.

So, what is there left for us to do? It turns out that the concepts in an introductory course are complex. It is also the case that understanding and memory are not automatic. How does one process information and put things into memory? We remember more easily if we can relate concepts to our selves, the self-reference effect. And we also remember through the process of elaboration, thinking of examples and links to information already in memory (described in Chapter 7, Human Memory). So that is what we've tried to do in this study guide, provide examples and practice, with the goal in mind of helping the student remember, both for practical reasons now (e.g., tests) and for use in the future after the course is over.

What's the best way to work with this study guide? There are four parts of each chapter: the *Review of Key Ideas* (comprising most of each Study Guide chapter), the *Review of Key Terms* (a matching exercise involving important concepts), the *Review of Key People* (matching confined to major researchers in each area), and a *Self-Quiz*. We suggest that you try this: Work on each learning objective one at a time. Read each objective, then read the part of the textbook that relates to it, and then complete the exercises and check your answers. Then do the matching exercises and take the Self-Quiz.

You may find it more useful to select only certain parts of the study guide that provide practice with particular concepts. (For example, if you are having difficulty understanding the Freudian defense mechanisms, or the difference between operant and classical conditioning, do the practice exercises relating to these specific topics.) Whatever method you use, the learning objectives will serve as an excellent review. At the end of your study of a particular chapter you can quiz yourself by reading over the learning objectives, reciting answers aloud, and checking your answers. This procedure roughly parallels the SQ3R study technique introduced in the Personal Application section of Chapter 1.

Who is Wayne Weiten, anyway? For one thing, he is a graduate of Bradley University, where the two of us are professors. In fact, we were Wayne's professors many years ago. He was a particularly memorable student, remarkable for his writing ability, as a member of our forensics' team, and as the radio announcer for Bradley men's basketball. Since those years, and after completing his Ph. D. at the University of Illinois at Chicago, Wayne has received many honors, including recognition by the American Psychological Association as one of America's outstanding teachers and a post as president of the Society for the Teaching of Psychology.

We wish to acknowledge the help of a few people. First, we thank Wayne Weiten, the author of your textbook and our former student, to whom we owe any success that this study guide achieves. Wayne wrote the learning objectives and set out the basic organization, and he has been our teacher in this project. We acknowledge the help of others as well. Jane helped Ron, Judy listened to Rick's examples, Nancy Schwartz and student Anjuli Paroo made useful comments, Gail Reynolds transformed our copy, and Jennifer Keever of Wadsworth cheerfully kept us on task. Rick would like to thank his parents, who tolerated his changes; Tom Brownell, who taught him that sentences with blanks could flow; Jim Lester, his first psychology teacher, who interested him in cognition; and W. F. Oakes, Art Staats, and Lou Herman, who interested him in philosophy of science, human behavior, and dolphin behavior, respectively.

Finally, if you have any comments, suggestions, or find any errors we would truly appreciate your sending these to us (c/o Psychology Department, Bradley University, 1501 W. Bradley Ave., Peoria, IL 61625).

Rick Stalling and Ron Wasden

Chapter One
THE EVOLUTION OF PSYCHOLOGY

Review of Key Ideas

FROM SPECULATION TO SCIENCE: HOW PSYCHOLOGY DEVELOPED

1. **Summarize Wundt's accomplishments and contributions to psychology.**

    1-1.   If you ask most college graduates to name the founder of psychology they might mention the name of a famous psychologist (for example, maybe Sigmund Freud), but they almost certainly would *not* say Wilhelm Wundt. Yet among psychologists Wundt is generally acknowledged to be the "_____" of our field.

    1-2.   Wundt established the first experimental psychology _____, in Leipzig, Germany, in 1879. He also established the first _____ devoted to publishing psychological research.

    1-3.   The subject matter of Wundt's psychology was (<u>consciousness/behavior</u>).

    1-4.   Wundt's major contributions to the evolution of psychology may be summarized as follows: He is the _____ of psychology as an independent academic field, and he insisted that psychology can and must use the _____ method.

    Answers: 1-1. founder **1-2.** laboratory, journal **1-3.** consciousness **1-4.** founder, scientific (experimental). (Personal note from RS: Shortly after East Germany opened its barriers to the West I visited Leipzig and looked for the famous founding laboratory. It wasn't there! I found Wundt Street, but no lab. An English-U.S. bombing raid destroyed the laboratory in 1943.)

2. **Summarize Hall's accomplishments and contributions to psychology.**

    2-1.   Wundt had many important students, among them the G. Stanley Hall, an American. Hall established the first American psychological _____ at Johns Hopkins and the first _____ devoted to publishing psychological research.

2-2. In 1892, with 26 of his colleagues, Hall began the American Psychological Association, known by the initials _____. Hall also became the first _____ of the Association. The APA now includes more than 155,000 members and affiliates.

Answers: **2-1.** laboratory, journal **2-2.** APA, president.

3. Describe structuralism and its impact on the subsequent development of psychology.

3-1. Another of Wundt's students, Edward Titchener, developed the school of psychology known as _____. The major tenet of this viewpoint was that psychology should follow the model of the physical sciences–by breaking phenomena (in this case, consciousness) into basic _____.

3-2. The basic elements of consciousness were thought to be the sensations (or images or feelings) that people reported when they observed some object. Subjects were first trained to observe (or listen to) something and then, through introspection, report on their conscious experience. Thus, the subject matter of structuralism was _____, and its method involved training observers in the technique of _____.

Answers: **3-1.** structuralism, elements **3-2.** consciousness, introspection.

4. Describe functionalism and its impact on the subsequent development of psychology.

4-1. Rather than breaking down consciousness into basic elements, the _____ school emphasized determining the _____ or purpose of consciousness.

4-2. The origins of functionalism are associated with William James. Influenced by the Darwin's concept of natural selection, James concluded that psychology should study the basic (elements/purpose) of consciousness.

4-3. Which "school" is characterized by each of the following descriptions? Place an "S" for structuralism or "F" for functionalism in the appropriate blanks.

_____ Concerned with the purpose (or function) of consciousness.

_____ Trained observers to introspect about consciousness.

_____ Assumed that consciousness could be broken down into basic elements (in the same way that physical matter is comprised of atoms).

_____ Interested in the flow of consciousness.

_____ Focused on the adaptive (evolutionary) value of consciousness.

_____ Emphasized sensation and perception in vision, hearing, and touch.

4-4. While neither structuralism nor functionalism survived as viable theories of psychology, functionalism had a more lasting impact. The emphasis of functionalism on the practical (or the adaptive or purposeful) led to the development of these two areas of modern psychology: _____ and _____ psychology.

5. **Summarize Freud's principal ideas and why they inspired controversy.**

   5-1. For Wundt, the subject matter of psychology was human consciousness. For Freud, the major subject matter was what he termed the _____. With this concept, Freud asserted that human beings are (aware/unaware) of most of the factors that influence their thoughts and behavior.

   5-2. There is a word beginning with *s* that means the same thing as feces. This word, however, may be more likely to cause laughter, embarrassment, or anger than the word feces. Why do two words that mean the same thing produce such differing reactions? For Freud, such irrationalities in language and other aspects of human behavior reflect the influence of the _____.

   5-3. Although generally not accessible to us, the unconscious is revealed in several ways, according to Freud. Freud thought, for example, that the unconscious is revealed in mistakes, such as "_____ of the tongue," or the symbolism in _____ that occur during sleep.

   5-4. Freud's ideas were (and still are) considered quite controversial. The general public tended to find Freud's ideas unacceptable because of his emphasis on _____. Scientific psychologists, with an emphasis on observable events, rejected Freud's notion that we are controlled by _____ (and unobservable) forces. Nonetheless, Freud's theory gradually gained prominence and survives today as an influential theoretical perspective.

6. **Summarize Watson's view on the appropriate subject matter of psychology, nature versus nurture, and animal research.**

   6-1. A literal translation of the root words of psychology (*psyche* and *logos*) suggests that psychology is the study of the _____. For both Wundt and James, this was the case: they studied human _____. For Watson, however, the subject matter of psychology was _____.

   6-2. Watson believed that psychology could not be a science unless it, like the other sciences, concentrated on _____ rather than unobservable events.

   6-3. Which of the following are observable behaviors–capable of being seen by someone other than the performer of the act? Place an "O" in the blank if the event is observable and an "N" if it is not.

   _____ writing a letter

   _____ feeling angry

   _____ saying "Please pass the salt"

   _____ passing the salt

   _____ perceiving a round object

_____ experiencing hunger

_____ walking rapidly

6-4. Watson largely discounted the importance of genetic inheritance. For Watson, behavior was governed by the _____.

6-5. Watson also made a shift away from human introspection by using _____ as the subjects for research. Why the change in orientation? First, animal behavior is observable; human consciousness is not. Second, the environment of laboratory animals, in contrast to that of humans, is subject to much more _____.

6-6. Let's briefly review structuralism and behaviorism:

(a) As defined by the structuralists, what was the <u>subject matter</u> of psychology?

(b) For behaviorists, what was the subject matter of psychology?

(c) While structuralists and behaviorists differed in their views of the subject matter of psychology, their approach to the new field was similar in one major respect. In what way were the two systems similar?

Answers: **6-1.** soul (or mind), consciousness, behavior **6-2.** observable (behavior) **6-3.** O, N (you can't see or hear your own or another person's feelings of anger; you may see the results of anger), O, O, N (you can't see or hear perception), N (you can't see or hear hunger), O **6-4.** environment **6-5.** animals, control (manipulation) **6-6.** (a) conscious experience (consciousness), (b) animal or human behavior, (c) They studied "parts" rather than "wholes." Both systems believed that the task of psychology was to break down psychological phenomena into their smallest elements. (For the structuralists the smaller elements were the sensations or images that made up consciousness; for the behaviorists the elements were the stimulus-response bonds thought to make up behavior.)

7. Summarize Skinner's work, views, and influence.

7-1. While he did not deny their existence, Skinner said that (<u>mental/environmental</u>) events are not observable and cannot be studied scientifically.

7-2. The fundamental principle of behavior, according to Skinner, is that organisms will tend to _____ behaviors that lead to positive outcome (and tend not to repeat responses that lead to neutral or negative outcomes).

7-3. Skinner asserted that because behavior is under the lawful control of external events, our feeling of _____ is an illusion.

7-4. According to Skinner, to adequately account for and predict behavior psychologists must understand

a. the relationship between thinking and behavior

b. the physiological basis of action

c. the way environmental factors affect behavior

d. all of the above

8. **Summarize Rogers's and Maslow's ideas and the contributions of humanistic psychology.**

   8-1. The ideas of the _____ psychologists, which include the writings of Rogers and Maslow, emphasize the extent to which human beings are (similar to/different from) the other animals.

   8-2. While Freud and Skinner stressed the way in which behavior is *determined* (by unconscious forces or by the environment), Rogers and Maslow emphasized human beings' _____ to determine their own actions.

   8-3. Rogers and Maslow also asserted that human beings have a drive to express their inner potential, a drive toward personal _____.

   8-4. Perhaps the greatest contribution of the humanistic movement has been in producing (scientific findings/new approaches) in psychotherapy.

9. **Explain how historical events have contributed to the emergence of psychology as a profession.**

   9-1. Applied psychology is the part of psychology that is concerned with (research issues/practical problems). Prominent among the applied areas of psychology is the field of _____ psychology, which deals with the treatment of psychological disorders.

   9-2. Clinical psychologists were relatively rare in a field devoted primarily to research. One of the historical events that changed this picture was the advent of _____. With the increased need for screening recruits and treating emotional casualties, the Veterans Administration began funding many new training programs in the field of _____ psychology.

   9-3. Other applied areas followed, including the fields of industrial, counseling, and school psychology. The growth of applied (especially clinical) psychology within the APA caused a rift that resulted in the birth of a new organization devoted exclusively to (research/application) in psychology. This organization, founded in 1988, is the American Psychological Society or _____.

10. **Describe two recent trends in research in psychology that reflect a return to psychology's intellectual roots.**

    10-1. Think about sucking on a lemon. When you do, the amount of saliva in your mouth will increase measurably. While it would be enough to describe your observable response as a function of my observable instruction, it is also obvious that thinking, or cognition, is involved: My instruction changed your _____ image. Thus, psychologists have returned to an interest in thinking or cognition, especially with regard to research on imagery, problem solving, and decision making.

10-2. The second recent trend involves a different kind of "internal" process and includes research on electrical stimulation of the brain, brain specialization, and visual signals. These are _____ processes. Thus, the two recent trends in research in psychology involve the reemergence of the fields of _____ psychology and _____ psychology.

Answers: **10-1.** mental (cognitive) **10-2.** physiological (biological), cognitive, physiological.

11. Explain why Western psychology traditionally had scant interest in other cultures and why this situation has begun to change.

11-1. Several factors contributed to the narrow focus of Western, and especially United States, psychology:

(a) First, studying other cultures is expensive and time consuming. It's much _____ for researchers to study people in their own country (and especially middle-class students at their own schools).

(b) Second, some psychologists worry that study of diverse groups may inadvertently foster _____, especially of groups that have historically been the objects of prejudice.

(c) Third, there may be a tendency among Western psychologists to view their own group as superior, the group tendency referred to as _____.

11-2. The situation has begun to change in recent years for two primary reasons: (1) increased communication and trade worldwide, the so-called _____ economy or global interdependence; and (2) increased diversity of ethnic groups within the countries of the Western World, including the _____ mosaic characteristic of the United States.

Answers: **11-1.** (a) cheaper (easier), (b) stereotypes, (c) ethnocentrism **11-2.** global; multicultural.

12. Summarize the basic tenets of evolutionary psychology.

12-1. According to evolutionary psychologists, human behavior—including not only aggression and mate selection but perception, language, personality, and cognition—are strongly influenced by the _____ value that these factors have had for the human species.

12-2. While Darwin's influence is clear in other psychological theories (e.g., James, Freud, and Skinner), the new emphasis on natural selection is (less/more) comprehensive and widely researched than the earlier versions.

12-3. The viewpoint has its critics. Some charge that evolutionary conceptions are simply post hoc accounts rather than explanations and that the theory is not subject to scientific _____. Nonetheless, the viewpoint has gained a high degree of acceptance and is clearly a major new perspective in contemporary psychology.

Answers: **12-1.** survival (adaptive) **12-2.** more **12-3.** test (evaluation, disconfirmation, proof).

13. **Discuss the growth of psychology and the most common work settings for contemporary psychologists.**

13-1. Psychology is a thriving field that has experienced a remarkable growth since its founding in 1879. Nationwide it is the second most popular undergraduate major, and about ___% of doctoral degrees in the sciences and humanities are in psychology.

13-2. Psychology was founded in a University, and earlier in this century almost all psychologists were employed as academics. Today, however, more than two-thirds of psychologists are employed in (<u>university/non-academic</u>) settings that include hospitals, business and industry, schools, and government agencies.

Answers: **13-1.** 9 **13-2.** non-academic.

14. **List and describe seven major research areas in psychology.**

14-1. Read over the descriptions of the research areas in Figure 1.9. Then match the names of the areas with the sampled research topics by placing the appropriate letters in the blanks. (Note that the separation between these areas is not always perfect. For example, a personality theorist might also be a psychometrician who has a physiological focus in explaining behavior. Nonetheless, the following topics have been chosen so that one answer is correct for each.)

A. Experimental _____ attitude change, group behavior

B. Physiological _____ personality and intelligence assessment, test design, new statistical procedures

C. Cognitive _____ personality assessment, personality description

D. Developmental _____ "core" topics (e.g., perception, conditioning, motivation)

E. Psychometrics _____ influence of the brain, bodily chemicals, genetics

F. Personality _____ child, adolescent, and adult development

G. Social _____ memory, decision making, thinking

Answers: **14-1.** G, E, F, A, B, D, C.

15. **List and describe the four professional specialties in psychology.**

15-1. Review Figure 1.10. Then match the following specialties with the descriptions by placing the appropriate letter in the blanks.

A. Clinical _____ Treatment of less severe problems and problems involving family, marital, and career difficulties.

B. Counseling _____ Treatment of psychological disorders, behavioral and emotional problems.

C. Educational and school _____ Involves work on curriculum design and achievement testing in school settings.

D. Industrial and organizational _____ Psychology applied to business settings; deals with personnel, job satisfaction, etc.

15-2. What is the difference between psychology and psychiatry? The major difference is a matter of degree (this is a pun, folks). Psychiatrists have _____ degrees. Clinical psychologists generally have _____ degrees (although some clinical psychologists have Ed.D. or Psy.D. degrees).

15-3. The major portion of psychiatrists' training occurs in _____ schools and in the residency programs in psychiatry that follow medical school. Clinical psychologists' training occurs in _____ schools.

15-4. While clinical psychologists and psychiatrists frequently use the same psychotherapeutic treatment procedures, _____ is a branch of medicine. Psychology generally takes a nonmedical approach to treatment.

Answers: **15-1.** B, A, C, D **15-2.** medical (M.D.), Ph.D. **15-3.** medical, graduate **15-4.** psychiatry.

SEVEN UNIFYING THEMES

16. Summarize the text's three unifying themes relating to psychology as a field of study.

16-1. When my (R. S.'s) older daughter Samantha was about three years old, she pulled a sugar bowl off a shelf and broke it while I was not present. Later, when I surveyed the damage, I said, "I see you've broken something." She said, "How do yer know, did yer see me do it?" I was amused, because while it was obvious who had broken it, her comment reflected psychology's foundation in direct observation. **Theme 1** is that psychology is _____. Empiricism is the point of view that knowledge should be acquired through _____.

16-2. My daughter's comment caused me to think about one other aspect of empiricism: she expressed *doubt* (albeit somewhat self-serving with regard to the sugar bowl). One can describe belief systems along a continuum from *credulity*, which means ready to believe, to *skepticism*, which means disposed toward doubt. Psychology, and the empirical approach, is more disposed toward the _____ end of the continuum.

16-3. We would ordinarily think that if one theory is correct, any other theory used to explain the same data must be wrong. While scientists do pit theories against each other, it is also the case that apparently contradictory theories may both be correct—as with the explanation of light in terms of both wave and particle theories. Thus, **Theme 2** indicates that psychology is theoretically _____.

16-4. Psychology tolerates (and in fact encourages) different theoretical explanations because:

16-5. As is the case with science in general, psychology does not evolve in a vacuum. It is influenced by and influences our society. For example, the current interest in cultural diversity has prompted increased interest in cross-cultural research, which in turn affects the viewpoints in our society. As stated in **Theme 3**, psychology evolves in a _____ context.

Answers: **16-1.** empirical, observation **16-2.** skepticism **16-3.** diverse **16-4.** more than one theory may be correct; or, one theory may not adequately explain all of the observations **16-5.** sociohistorical.

17. Summarize the text's four unifying themes relating to psychology's subject matter.

17-1. When looking for an explanation of a particular behavior, someone might ask: "Well, why did he do it? Was it greed or ignorance?" The question implies the very human tendency to reason in terms of (<u>one cause/multiple causes</u>) for each event.

17-2. What influences the course of a ball rolled down an inclined plane? Gravity. And also friction. And the presence of other objects, and a number of other factors. That is the point of **Theme 4**: even more than is the case for physical events, behavior is determined by _____ _____.

17-3. Among the multiple causes of human behavior is the category of causes referred to as *culture*. Cultural factors include the customs, beliefs, and values that we transmit across generations—what we eat, how we walk, what we wear, what we say, what we think, and so on. **Theme 5** indicates that our behavior is shaped by our _____ heritage.

17-4. For example, I have observed that many American students traveling abroad initially think that their European lecturers talk down to them; the lecturers, in turn, may regard our students as spoiled and insolent. Perhaps closer to the truth is that there is a clash of customs invisible to both cultures. While we are shaped by our cultural _____ we are often _____ (<u>aware/unaware</u>) of the precise rules and customs that affect us.

17-5. **Theme 6** relates to the influence of heredity and environment. What is the consensus among psychologists about the effect of heredity and environment on behavior?

17-6. The scientific method relies on observation, but observation by itself isn't sufficient. Why isn't it?

17-7. **Theme 7** indicates that our experience is subjective. What does this mean?

Answers: **17-1.** one cause **17-2.** multiple causes **17-3.** cultural **17-4.** heritage, unaware **17-5.** Theme 6 states that heredity and environment *jointly* affect behavior. While the relative influence of each is still debated, theorists no longer assert that behavior is entirely a function of one or the other. **17-6.** Because (Theme 7) people's experience of the world is highly subjective. **17-7.** Different people experience different things; even if we observe the same event at the same time, we do not "see" the same things; we selectively focus on some events and ignore others.

18. Discuss three important considerations in designing a program to promote adequate studying.

18-1.   Three features of successful studying are listed below. Elaborate on them by providing some of the details asked for.

(a) A schedule: When should you plan your study schedule? Should you write it down? Should you do the simpler tasks first or begin the major assignments? What is a major difference between successful and unsuccessful students regarding time management?

(b) A place: What are the major characteristics of a good study place?

(c) A reward: When should you reward yourself? What kinds of rewards are suggested?

Answers: 18-1. (a) It's probably useful to set up a general schedule for a particular semester and then, at the beginning of each week, plan the specific assignments for each study session. Put your plans in writing. People tend to put off the larger tasks, but it's usually getter to tackle the major assignments first, breaking them into smaller components as needed. (b) Find a place to study with minimal distractions: little noise, few interruptions. (c) Reward yourself shortly after you finish a particular amount of studying; snacking, watching TV, or calling a friend are suggested. **Suggestion:** You are studying now. Is this a good time for you? If it is, why not write out your weekly schedule now. Include schedule preparation as part of your study time.

19. Describe the SQ3R method and explain what makes it effective.

19-1.   Below are descriptions of an individual applying the five steps of the SQ3R method to Chapter 1 of your text. The steps are not in the correct order. Label each of the steps and place a number in the parentheses to indicate the correct order.

(   ) _____ Vanessa is taking introductory psychology using this book. She looks at the title of the first subsection of the chapter. After wondering briefly what it means for psychology to have "parents," she formulates this question: How was the field of psychology influenced by philosophy and physiology?

(   ) _____ She turns to the back of Chapter 1 and notes that there is a chapter review. She turns back to the first page of the chapter, sees that the outline on that page matches the review at the end, and browses through some of the other parts of the chapter. She has a rough idea that the chapter is going to define the field and discuss its history.

(   ) _____ Keeping in mind the question she has posed, she reads the section about the meeting of psychology's "parents" and formulates a tentative answer to her question. She also asks some additional questions: "Who was Descartes?" and "What method did philosophers use?"

( )   _____ She answers her first question as follows: "Philosophy (one of the parents) posed questions about the mind that made the study of human thinking and actions acceptable; physiology (the other parent) contributed the scientific method." She decides to note down her answer for later review.

( )   _____ When she has finished steps 2 through 4 for all sections, Vanessa looks over the entire chapter, section by section. She repeats the questions for each section and attempts to answer each one.

19-2. What makes the SQ3R technique so effective?

Answers: 19-1. (2) Question (1) Survey (3) Read (4) Recite (5) Review **19-2.** It requires active processing and identifying key ideas.

20. Summarize advice provided on how to get more out of lectures.

20-1. Indicate T or F for the following statements.

_____ Poor class attendance is associated with poor grades.

_____ Research has shown that the average student records less than 40% of the crucial ideas in lectures.

20-2. Using a few words for each point, summarize the four points on getting more out of lectures.

Answers: 20-1. T, T **20-2.** Listen actively; focus full attention on the speaker and try to anticipate what's coming. For complex material, read ahead. Take notes in your own words and attend to clues about what is most important. Consider asking questions during lectures (to keep involved and to clarify points presented).

21. Summarize advice provided on improving test-taking strategies.

21-1. True or false.

_____ On a multiple-choice test, it's better to go with one's first hunch than to change answers.

21-2. Following are situations you might encounter while taking a test. Reread the section on general test-taking tips and then indicate what you would do in each situation.

(a) You run into a particularly difficult item:

(b) The answer seems to be simple, but you think you may be missing something:

(c) The test is a timed test:

(d) You have some time left at the end of the test:

21-3. Following are samples of the situations mentioned under the discussion of tips for multiple-choice and essay exam questions. Based on the suggestions, what would you do?

(a) In a multiple-choice test, item *c* seems to be correct, but you have not yet read items *d* and *e*. What would you do next?

(b) You know that items *a* and *b* are correct, are unsure of items *c* and *d*, and item *e* is an "all of the above" option. Which alternative (a, b, c, d, or e) would you choose?

(c) You have no idea which multiple-choice alternative is correct. You note that option *a* has the word "always" in it, items *b* and *c* use the word "never," and item *d* says "frequently."

(d) You have read the stem of a multiple-choice item but you have not yet looked at the options.

(e) Faced with an essay, you wonder whether to simply begin writing and let the ideas flow or to spend a few minutes in organization.

Answers: 21-1. False(!). In general, changing answers seems to be better. Available research indicates that people are more than twice as likely to go from a wrong answer to a right one as from a right answer to a wrong one. **21-2.** (a) Skip it and come back to it if time permits. (b) Maybe the answer is simple! Don't make the question more complex than it was intended to be. (c) Budget your time, checking the proportion of the test completed against the time available. (d) Review, reconsider, check over your answers. **21-3.** (a) Read all options. (b) Answer *e*. (c) Answer *d*. (Still good advice and generally the best procedure to follow. But note that some professors, aware of the strategy, may throw in an item in which "always" is part of a correct answer! It's sort of like radar detectors: someone builds a better detector and someone else tries to build radar that can't be detected.) (d) Try to anticipate the correct answer *before* reading the options. (e) Spend a few minutes looking over the questions and allocating time, planning, organizing, and possibly even outlining. Many examiners will appreciate your use of headings or numbers to identify points made.

22. Explain the nature of critical thinking skills and why they need to be taught.

22-1.   The previous section on test-taking strategies asked whether or not it is better to change answers or go with one's first hunch. Actually, that is a critical thinking question. While our hunches are often pretty good, sometimes they don't lead to desired outcomes. When we think critically we use the same principles that we would use in conducting a _____ investigation. We also use formal and informal rules of _____ and analyze the soundness of a proposed conclusions. As with scientific investigations, we also consider conflicting or alternative _____ of data.

22-2.   Critical thinking is not something that we come by naturally, and it (is/is not) a normal part of instruction in most subject areas. So, in most cases, if people are to develop the ability to think critically, critical thinking skills must be deliberately and consciously _____.

Answers: **22-1.** Scientific, logic, interpretations (explanations) **22-2.** is not, taught.

23. Discuss some weaknesses in evolutionary explanations for gender differences in spatial abilities.

23-1.   Some evidence suggests that males tend to have better visual-spatial perception than females and that females have better memories for locations. The reason for these gender differences, according to evolutionary psychologists, is that in our evolutionary past natural selection favored a division of labor in which men were _____ and women were _____. Hunting (aiming a spear, traveling long distances) required _____ perception, while gathering required _____ for locations of food.

23-2.   As previously discussed, evolutionary psychology is a major new theoretical perspective in psychology. While the interpretation of the evolutionary psychologists is certainly plausible, critical thinking urges us to consider the following two questions when assessing a truth claim: (1) Are there _____ explanations for these results? And, (2) are data available that _____ the evidence provided?

23-3.   It turns out that the answer to both of these questions is a qualified "yes." For example, it may be that most cultures encourage male children to engage in visual-spatial activities (e.g., playing with blocks) that would provide an _____ interpretation to one based on evolutionary principles. In addition, some scholars have suggested that women in early hunter-gatherer societies often did, in fact, travel long distances to obtain food and were also involved in hunting. While certainly not "disproving" evolutionary theory, this type of evidence would _____ some of the data presented by evolutionary psychologists.

Answers: **23-1.** hunters, gatherers, visual-spatial, memory **23-2.** alternative, contradicts **23-3.** alternative, contradict (challenge, dispute, weaken).

Review of Key Terms

Applied psychology
Behavior
Behaviorism
Clinical psychology
Cognition
Critical thinking
Culture
Empiricism
Ethnocentrism

Evolutionary psychology
Functionalism
Humanism
Introspection
Natural selection
Phi phenomenon
Positive psychology
Psychiatry

Psychoanalytic theory
Psychology
SQ3R
Stimulus
Structuralism
Testwiseness
Theory
Unconscious

_____ 1. A reaction against a negative emphasis in psychology; a new focus on positive, adaptive, and creative aspects of human existence.

_____ 2. The branch of psychology concerned with practical problems.

_____ 3. School of thought based on notion that the task of psychology is to analyze consciousness into its basic elements.

_____ 4. Observation of one's own conscious experience.

_____ 5. School of thought asserting that psychology's major purpose was to investigate the function or purpose of consciousness.

_____ 6. The theoretical orientation asserting that scientific psychology should study only observable behavior.

_____ 7. An observable activity or response by an organism.

_____ 8. Examines behavioral processes in terms of their adaptive or survival value for a species.

_____ 9. The use of cognitive skills and strategies to increase the probability of a desirable outcome.

_____ 10. The Darwinian principle that characteristics that have a survival advantage for a species are more likely to be passed on to subsequent generations.

_____ 11. Freudian theory that explains personality and abnormal behavior in terms of unconscious processes.

_____ 12. According to psychoanalytic theory, that portion of the mind containing thoughts, memories, and wishes not in awareness but nonetheless exerting a strong effect on human behavior.

_____ 13. The psychological theory asserting that human beings are unique and fundamentally different from other animals.

_____ 14. The tendency to view one's own group as superior to other groups.

_____ 15. Widely shared customs, beliefs, values, norms, and institutions that are transmitted socially across generations.

_____ 16. The branch of psychology concerned with the diagnosis and treatment of psychological disorders.

_____ 17. Mental processes or thinking.

_____ 18. The science that studies behavior and the physiological and cognitive processes that underlie it, and it is the profession that applies this knowledge to solving various practical problems.

_____ 19. The branch of medicine concerned with the diagnosis and treatment of psychological problems and disorders.

_____ 20. The point of view that knowledge should be based on observation.

_____ 21. A system of ideas used to link together or explain a set of observations.

_____ 22. A five-step procedure designed to improve study skills.

_____ 23. Ability to use the characteristics and formats of a test to maximize one's score.

Answers: 1. positive psychology **2.** applied psychology **3.** structuralism **4.** introspection **5.** functionalism **6.** behaviorism **7.** behavior **8.** evolutionary psychology **9.** critical thinking **10.** natural selection **11.** psychoanalytic theory **12.** unconscious **13.** humanism **14.** ethnocentrism **15.** culture **16.** clinical psychology **17.** cognition **18.** psychology **19.** psychiatry **20.** empiricism **21.** theory **22.** SQ3R **23.** testwiseness.

Review of Key People

Sigmund Freud   Carl Rogers   John B. Watson
G. Stanley Hall   B. F. Skinner   Wilhelm Wundt
William James

_____ 1. Founded experimental psychology and the first experimental psychology laboratory.

_____ 2. Established the first American research laboratory, launched America's first psychological journal, was first president of the APA.

_____ 3. Chief architect of functionalism; described a "stream of consciousness."

_____ 4. Founded behaviorism.

_____ 5. Devised the theory and technique known as psychoanalysis.

_____ 6. Identified operant conditioning.

_____ 7. A major proponent of "humanistic" psychology.

Answers: 1. Wundt **2.** Hall **3.** James **4.** Watson **5.** Freud **6.** Skinner **7.** Rogers.

Self-Quiz

1. Structuralism is the historical school of psychology that asserted that the purpose of psychology was to:
   a. study behavior
   b. discover the smaller elements that comprise consciousness
   c. explore the unconscious
   d. examine the purposes of conscious processes

2. Of the two parents of psychology, physiology and philosophy, which provided the method? What is the method?
   a. philosophy; logic, reasoning
   b. philosophy; intuition, introspection
   c. physiology; observation, science
   d. physiology; anatomy, surgery

3. Who is Wilhelm Wundt?
   a. He founded the first experimental laboratory.
   b. He founded the American Psychological Association.
   c. He discovered the classically conditioned salivary reflex.
   d. He founded behaviorism.

4. For John B. Watson, the appropriate subject matter of psychology was:
   a. animal behavior
   b. the unconscious
   c. consciousness
   d. human physiology

5. Which of the following represents a major breakthrough in the development of applied psychology?
   a. the use of the method of introspection
   b. Binet's development of the intelligence test
   c. establishment of the first animal laboratory
   d. Wundt's founding of experimental psychology

6. Within academic psychology, Freud's ideas initially encountered resistance because he emphasized:
   a. human consciousness
   b. human behavior
   c. introspection
   d. the unconscious

7. Which of the following would be considered the major principle of operant conditioning?
   a. Human behavior derives in part from free will; animal behavior is determined by the environment.
   b. Humans and other animals tend to repeat responses followed by positive outcomes.
   c. The majority of human behavior is based on thoughts, feelings, and wishes of which we are unaware.
   d. Human beings are fundamentally different from other animals.

8. Which of the following theorists would tend to emphasize explanations in terms of freedom and potential for personal growth?
   a. Carl Rogers
   b. Sigmund Freud
   c. B. F. Skinner
   d. all of the above

9. Recent research trends in psychology involve two areas largely ignored by early behaviorists. These two areas are:
   a. observable and measurable responses
   b. cognition (thinking) and physiological processes
   c. classical and operant conditioning
   d. the effect of environmental events and the behavior of lower animals

10. Which core psychological research area is primarily devoted to the study of such topics as memory, problem solving, and thinking?
    a. physiological
    b. social
    c. cognitive
    d. personality

11. Critical thinking includes:
    a. analysis of problems in terms of scientific principles
    b. making decisions based on formal and informal logic
    c. thinking that includes consideration of conflicting interpretations
    d. all of the above

12. The assertion that "psychology is empirical" means that psychology is based on:
    a. introspection
    b. logic
    c. observation
    d. mathematics

13. In looking for the causes of a particular behavior, psychologists assume:
    a. one cause or factor
    b. multifactorial causation
    c. free will
    d. infinite causation

14. Contemporary psychologists generally assume that human behavior is determined by:
    a. heredity
    b. environment
    c. heredity and environment acting jointly
    d. heredity, environment, and free will

15. What does SQ3R stand for?
    a. search, question, research, recommend, reconstitute
    b. silence, quietude, reading, writing, arithmetic
    c. summarize, quickly, read, research, reread
    d. survey, question, read, recite, review

Answers: 1. b **2.** c **3.** a **4.** a **5.** b **6.** d **7.** b **8.** a **9.** b **10.** c **11.** d **12.** c **13.** b **14.** c **15.** d.

InfoTrac Keywords

Applied Psychology
Behaviorism
Critical Thinking

Clinical Psychology
Humanism

Natural Selection
Psychoanalytic Theory

Chapter Two
THE RESEARCH ENTERPRISE IN PSYCHOLOGY

Review of Key Ideas

LOOKING FOR LAWS: THE SCIENTIFIC APPROACH TO BEHAVIOR

1. **Explain science's main assumption and describe the goals of the scientific enterprise in psychology.**

   1-1. A major assumption of science is that events occur in a(an) _____ manner.

   1-2. The three interrelated goals of psychology and the other sciences are: (a) measurement and description, (b) understanding and prediction, and (c) application and control. Match each of the following descriptions with the goal it represents by placing the appropriate letters in the blanks. (There is considerable overlap among these goals; pick the closest match.)

   _____ Muscle relaxation techniques are found to be useful in reducing anxiety and improving concentration and memory.

   _____ A psychologist develops a test or procedure that measures anxiety.

   _____ Researchers find that participants in an experiment conform more to the judgments of someone similar to themselves than to someone who is dissimilar.

   Answers: **1-1.** lawful (predictable, consistent, regular, orderly) **1-2.** c, a, b.

2. **Explain the relations between theory, hypotheses, and research.**

   2-1. A theory is a system of ideas used to explain a set of observations. One could devise an exhaustive description of human behavior, but the description wouldn't be a theory unless it also included concepts that would _____ why the behavior occurs.

   2-2. Researchers can't test a theory all at once, but they can test one or two hypotheses derived from a theory. For example, evolutionary theory asserts that humans form groups because this behavioral tendency has had survival value. To reflect on this idea, one could test the _____ that certain specific aspects of group-oriented behavior occur in all cultures.

2-3. The relationship between theory, hypothesis, and research is this: theories suggest _____ (questions or predictions), which are then tested in _____. If the hypotheses are supported, confidence in the _____ is strengthened. If the findings fail to support the hypothesis, confidence in the theory decreases and the theory may be revised or discarded. In this way theory building is a gradual process with the result that over time theories (remain fixed/are subject to revision).

Answers: 2-1. explain **2-2.** hypothesis **2-3.** hypotheses, experiments (research), theory, are subject to revision.

3. Outline the steps in a scientific investigation.

3-1. Following are the five steps generally used in performing a scientific investigation. Fill in the missing key words.

a. Formulate a testable _____.

b. Select the research _____ and design the study.

c. _____ the data.

d. _____ the data and draw conclusions.

e. _____ the findings.

3-2. Following are descriptions of various phases in the study by Cole and his co-workers (Cole et al., 1996). Indicate which step of this study is being described by placing a letter from the previous question (1, 2, 3, 4, or 5) in the appropriate blank.

_____ Sherman and his co-workers thought that disagreement on one topic, affirmative action, might cause people to assumed that they disagree on a more general dimension, such as liberalism-conservatism.

_____ The researchers decided to use a survey procedure and rating scales. One of the items, concerning agreement with an affirmative action issue at their college, permitted the groups to be divided into those who were in favor and those who were opposed to the statement.

_____ The researchers collected data by administering the surveys to students in their dorm rooms.

_____ Analysis of the data indicated that subjects who disagreed on the issue of affirmative action overestimated the extent to which they would disagree on the general dimension of liberalism-conservatism.

_____ The authors prepared a report of their findings that was accepted for publication in a technical journal.

Answers: 3-1. (a) hypothesis (b) method (c) collect (d) analyze (e) report (publish, write up) **3-2.** a, b, c, d, e.

4. Discuss the advantages of the scientific approach.

4-1. We all tend to agree with the idea that "haste makes waste." We are also likely to agree with a commonsense saying that has the opposite implication: "a stitch in time saves nine." What are the two major advantages of the scientific approach over the commonsense approach?

Answers: 4-1. First, scientific descriptions generally have a clarity and precision lacking in commonsense proverbs. While we have a general idea about the meaning of haste, for example, we don't know precisely when or in what way or how much haste we should avoid. Second, science has an intolerance for error or for contradictory conclusions; commonsense sayings are likely to be contradictory. (Note that the proverbs in our example have contradictory messages: one says to slow down, the other says to hurry up.)

LOOKING FOR CAUSES: EXPERIMENTAL RESEARCH

5. **Describe the experimental method, explaining independent and dependent variables, experimental and control groups, and extraneous variables.**

   5-1.   Schachter proposed that *affiliation* is caused (in part) by level of *anxiety*. What was his independent variable? _____ Dependent variable? _____

   5-2.   The variable that is manipulated or varied by the experimenter is termed the _____ variable. The variable that is affected by, or is dependent on, the manipulation is termed the _____ variable.

   5-3.   What is the name of the variable that *results from* the manipulation? _____ What is the name of the variable that *produces* the effect? _____

   5-4.   The group of subjects that receives the experimental treatment is known as the _____ group; the group that does not is known as the _____ group.

   5-5.   Control and experimental groups are quite similar in most respects. They differ in that the experimental group receives the experimental _____ and the control group does not. Thus, any differences found in the measure of the _____ variable are assumed to be due to differences in manipulation of the _____ variable.

   5-6.   In Schachter's study, the experimental group was given instructions that produced a high level of _____. Results were that the experimental group, the high anxiety group, had a greater tendency to _____ with others than did the control group.

   5-7.   An extraneous variable is any variable other than the _____ variable that seems likely to cause a difference between groups as measured by the _____ variable.

   5-8.   To review the parts of an experiment: Suppose a researcher is interested in the effect of a drug on the running speed of rats. The _____ group is injected with the drug and the _____ group is not. Whether or not the rats received the drug would be the _____ variable, and running speed would be the _____ variable.

   5-9.   Suppose also that the average age of the experimental rats is two years while the average age of the control rats is 3 months. What is the extraneous variable in this experiment? _____ Why does this variable present a problem?

   5-10. Researchers generally control for extraneous variables through random _____ of subjects to groups. Write a definition of this procedure:

5-11. Research design may get complicated! For example, (true-false):

_____ While we frequently speak of two group designs (experimental and control), a single group is sometimes used in both procedures.

_____ There may be more than one independent variable, and there may be more than dependent variable.

Answers: 5-1. anxiety, affiliation **5-2.** independent, dependent **5-3.** dependent, independent **5-4.** experimental, control **5-5.** treatment, dependent, independent **5-6.** anxiety, affiliation **5-7.** independent, dependent **5-8.** experimental, control, independent, dependent **5-9.** age. Any difference between groups could be due to age rather than the independent variable **5-10.** assignment. All subjects have an equal chance of being assigned to any group or condition **5-11.** T, T.

6. Describe the Featured Study on how expectations influence reactions to positive and negative outcomes.

6-1. The featured study examined the effect of expectations on emotional reactions. In which of the following cases, according to the hypothesis of the study, would people have a more negative emotional reaction (be more sad)?

a. They expect something positive to happen, and something positive does happen.

b. They expect something negative to happen, and something positive happens.

6-2. In the featured study, half of the subjects expected good news–that they did not have the "enzyme deficiency" –and half expected bad new, that they did have the deficiency. These two groups were further divided: half of each group was given good news (no deficiency) and half bad (deficiency). Thus, the featured study manipulated two independent variables, so it actually involved _____ treatment groups.

6-3. In the results, which of these groups felt a more positive emotional reaction?

a. The group that expected good news and received good news.

b. The group that expected bad news and received good news.

6-4. And which of these groups felt a more positive (less negative) reaction?

a. The group that expected bad news and received bad news.

b. The group that expected good news and received bad news.

6-5. The study illustrates the use of two independent variables, and it also points up one of the unifying themes, that we are not objective observers of reality, that people's experience of the world is highly _____.

Answers: 6-1. b **6-2.** four **6-3.** b **6-4.** a **6-5.** subjective.

7. Explain the major advantages and disadvantages of the experimental method.

7-1. What is the major advantage of the experimental method?

7-2.   What are the two major disadvantages of the experimental method?

7-3.   Suppose a researcher is interested in the effect of drinking large amounts of coffee on health (e.g., 30 cups per day over an extended period of time). What would be a major disadvantage of the experimental method in examining this particular question?

Answers: 7-1. The major advantage is that it permits researchers to make cause-effect conclusions. **7-2.** The major disadvantages are that (a) precise experimental control may make the situation so artificial that it does not apply to the real world, and (b) ethical or practical considerations may prevent one from manipulating independent variables of interest. **7-3.** To the extent that excessive coffee drinking is a suspected factor in health problems, it would be unethical and perhaps impossible to require an experimental group to drink that much per day.

LOOKING FOR LINKS: DESCRIPTIVE/CORRELATIONAL RESEARCH

8.   Discuss three descriptive/correlational methods: naturalistic observation, case studies, and surveys.

8-1.   Naturalistic observation involves study of human beings or animals in their natural environments conducted (<u>with/without</u>) direct intervention from the observer.

8-2.   A case study is an in-depth and generally highly subjective or impressionistic report on (<u>a group of people/a single individual</u>) that may be based on interviews, psychological testing, and so on.

8-3.   The third descriptive procedure is the survey technique. Surveys use _____ to find out about specific aspects of human attitudes or opinions.

8-4.   List the three descriptive/correlational methods in the space below.

Answers: 8-1. without **8-2.** a single individual **8-3.** questionnaires (or interviews) **8-4.** naturalistic observation, case studies, surveys.

9.   Explain the major advantages and disadvantages of descriptive/correlational research.

9-1.   While descriptive/correlational methods extend the scope of psychological research, they do not permit scientists to manipulate variables. Consequently, these methods do not permit one to demonstrate conclusively a _____ relationship among variables.

9-2.   For example, suppose you have data indicating that people who happen to drink a lot of coffee tend to have cardiovascular problems. Is this experimental or descriptive/correlational research? _____ Would it be correct to conclude (from these data) that coffee drinking causes cardiovascular problems? _____

9-3. An advantage of the descriptive/correlational methods is that they allow researchers to study phenomena that they could not study with experimental methods. Thus, the descriptive/correlational methods (narrow/broaden) the scope of phenomena studied. A major disadvantage of these techniques is that one generally cannot make _____ conclusions from the resulting data.

Answers: 9-1. cause-effect (causal) **9-2.** descriptive/correlational (because the variables are not manipulated by the experimenter), no **9-3.** broaden, cause-effect (causal).

LOOKING FOR CONCLUSIONS: STATISTICS AND RESEARCH

10. Describe three measures of central tendency and one measure of variability.

10-1. To review the meaning of the three measures of central tendency, determine the mean, median, and mode of the following scores: 3, 5, 5, 5, 6, 6, 7, 9, 80.

Mean: _____

Median: _____

Mode: _____

10-2. One can describe a group of data with a single number by using one of the measures of central tendency. In the blanks below indicate which measure of central tendency is being described.

_____ The score that occurs most frequently.

_____ The sum of all scores divided by the total number of scores.

_____ Half the scores fall above this measure and half below.

_____ Very sensitive to extreme scores.

_____ Usually the most useful because it may be used in further statistical manipulations.

_____ The middle score.

10-3. What is the median of data set A, below? _____ of set B? _____ Which of these sets is more variable, A or B? _____

A. 30, 40, 50, 60, 70   B. 10, 30, 50, 70, 90

10-4. What is the name of the major statistic used to represent variability? _____ _____.

Answers: 10-1. 14, 6, 5 **10-2.** mode, mean, median, mean, mean, median **10-3.** 50, 50, B **10-4.** standard deviation.

11. Distinguish between positive and negative correlations.

11-1. Which of the following relationships are positive and which are negative? (Indicate with a + or − sign.)

_____ The better students' grades are in high school, the better their grades tend to be in college.

_____ The more alcohol one has drunk, the lower their scores on tests of reaction time.

_____ The higher the anxiety, the worse the test performance.

_____ The greater the fear, the greater the need for affiliation.

11-2. Which of the following indicates the *strongest correlational relationship*?

a. 1.12

b. −.92

c. .58

d. .87

Answers: 11-1. +, −, −, + **11-2.** b (not *a*, because correlations cannot exceed +1.00 or −1.00).

12. Discuss correlation in relation to prediction and causation.

12-1. Suppose you have data indicating that the more money people make the less depressed they report being on a mood survey. Thus, if you know the incomes of people in a comparable group, you should be able to _____, with some degree of accuracy, their self-reported depressed mood.

12-2. The accuracy of your prediction will depend on the size of the correlation coefficient. Which of the following correlation coefficients would allow you to predict with the greatest accuracy?

a. +.41

b. +.54

c. −.65

12-3. What kind of conclusion is justified on the basis of the previous relationship, a conclusion involving prediction or one involving a statement about causation? _____

12-4. Consider the relationship described in an earlier question: You discover that the more money people make, the greater their happiness. Which of the following conclusions is justified? Explain why.

a. Money makes people happy.

b. Happiness causes people to earn more money.

c. Both happiness and money result from some unknown third factor.

d. any of the above

12-5. Again consider the relationship between money and happiness. Assume that money does not cause happiness and happiness does not cause money. What possible *third factor* can you think of that could cause both? (I'm asking you to make a wild speculation here just to get the idea of how third variables may operate.)

12-6. We aren't justified in making causal conclusions from a correlation, but we can predict. Let's examine what prediction means in the case of our hypothetical example. If the relationship really exists, what prediction would you make about people who are rich? What prediction would you make concerning people who are unhappy?

Answers: 12-1. predict 12-2. c 12-3. prediction (Generally, one can't make causal conclusions from a correlation.)
12-4. d. Any of the statements is a possible *causal* explanation of the relationship, but we don't know which one(s) may be correct because the data are correlational. Therefore, *no causal conclusions* are justified. 12-5. For example, poor health might cause one to be both unhappy *and* poverty stricken (while good health would cause one to be both happy and wealthy). Intelligence or aggressiveness or stubbornness or a number of other physiological or behavioral factors could be causally related *both* to income and to happiness without those two factors being causes of one another.
12-6. You would predict that a group that was rich would also be happy and that a group that was unhappy would be poor. No causation is implied in these statements.

13. Explain the meaning of statistical significance.

13-1. In the hypothetical experiment described in your text there are two groups, largely equivalent except that the _____ group receives the computerized tutoring sessions and the _____ group does not. What is the hypothesis of this experiment?

13-2. Researchers statistically evaluate the hypothesis by comparing means and determining the likelihood or probability that a difference between means of the size obtained (or larger) would occur by _____. If the probability that such a difference would occur by chance is very low, say less than 5 times in 100, the researchers would conclude that the difference (is/is not) due to chance. They would declare the difference statistically _____ at the _____ level of significance.

13-3. Statistically significant does not mean important or significant in the usual sense of that word. What does statistically significant mean?

Answers: **13-1.** experimental, control. The hypothesis is that special tutoring would increase reading scores.
13-2. chance, is not, significant, .05 **13-3.** It means that a difference that large would be rare on a chance basis, so it is assumed *not* to be due to chance. Or, more simply, it is assumed that the difference between means is due to treatment.

LOOKING FOR FLAWS: EVALUATING RESEARCH

14. Explain what makes a sample representative and discuss the problem of sampling bias.

14-1. Sampling bias exists when the sample is not representative of the _____ from which it was drawn.

14-2. Dr. Brutalbaum distributes a questionnaire in an attempt to find out how the students in a particular course react to his teaching. Unfortunately, the day he selects for the evaluation is the day before a scheduled vacation, and about half the students are absent. He knows, however, that he does not have to test the entire class, and the sample that remains is large enough. Is the sample representative? Define the concept representative sample. Which of the four common flaws is illustrated?

Answers: **14-1.** population **14-2.** Probably not representative. A representative sample is one that is similar in composition to the population from which it is drawn. In this case, it seems likely that students who attend are different from those who do not (e.g., perhaps more enthusiastic, harder working, etc.). Thus, the flaw illustrated is *sampling bias*.

15. **Explain when placebo effects are likely to be a problem.**

15-1.   A student in Brutalbaum's class orders some audio tapes that promise to produce sleep learning. (Brutalbaum is dubious, because from his observations students sleep a lot in class but still don't seem to learn very much.) The student runs the experiment in Brutalbaum's class. She describes the anticipated sleep-learning benefits to the class and then *gives the sleep tapes to a random half of the students and nothing to the other half*. After the next test she analyzes the results. The mean test score of the experimental group is statistically significantly higher than that of the control group. What is the flaw in this experiment?

a. sampling bias

b. possible placebo effects

c. time of day

d. none of the above

15-2.   What are placebo effects?

15-3.   How would you change the study described above to reduce or eliminate the possibility of placebo effects?

Answers: 15-1. b **15-2.** Placebo effects: the tendency for people's behavior to change because of their expectation that the treatment will have an effect **15-3.** Include a placebo treatment. For example, the experimenter might have given the control group a placebo tape that was the same as the sleep tape in every respect except for the supposedly critical information. (And if the experiment were double-blind, see below, it would also be much improved.)

16. **Describe the typical kinds of distortions that occur in self-report data.**

16-1.   Brutalbaum is now concerned about class attendance and decides to find out what proportion of students miss class regularly. He distributes a questionnaire asking students to indicate how many classes they have missed. Which of the four common flaws is he likely to encounter? _____

16-2.   For a number of reasons, people may not answer questions correctly, including the fact that they may not understand the question or may not remember accurately. Respondents also frequently want to create a favorable impression, the response tendency known as the social _____ bias. People may also be predisposed to respond in particular ways regardless of the question, for example, to agree or disagree regardless of content. This type of response tendency is known as a response _____.

Answers: 16-1. distortions in self-report **16-2.** desirability, set.

17. Describe Rosenthal's research on experimenter bias.

17-1. When we ask a question, we frequently expect a particular answer. When scientists form a hypothesis, they also may expect a particular answer, and in some cases the scientist's hypotheses or expectations may influence the answers that they obtain. When a researcher's expectations about the outcome of a study influence the results, then the flaw in procedure known as _____ has occurred.

17-2. Experimenter bias or influence may occur in subtle ways. Rosenthal has repeatedly demonstrated that when the experimenter merely knows which treatment condition a subject is in, the fact of that knowledge or expectation alone may influence the subject's behavior. For this reason it is extremely important in research to maintain the _____ procedure, in which neither subjects nor experimenters know which treatment condition the subject is in.

Answers: **17-1.** experimenter bias **17-2.** double-blind.

LOOKING AT ETHICS: DO THE ENDS JUSTIFY THE MEANS?

18. Discuss the pros and cons of deception in research with human subjects.

18-1. In the space below present one or two of the arguments in favor of using deception and one or two arguments against.

Answers: **18-1.** On the con side, deception is, after all, lying; it may undermine people's trust in others; it may cause distress. On the pro side, many research issues could not be investigated without deception; the "white lies" involved are generally harmless; research indicates that deception studies are not actually harmful to subjects; the advances in knowledge obtained may improve human well-being. Despite these positive aspects, the issue of deception creates a moral dilemma that will continue to be debated.

19. Discuss the controversy about the use of animals as research subjects.

19-1. What is the major reason that some people object to using animal subjects in research? In view of this objection, what moral considerations are raised by those who favor using animals in research?

Answers: **19-1.** Many people believe that it is morally wrong to use animals in research, especially in painful or harmful treatments that would be unacceptable for human subjects. In defense of the practice, others cite the significant advances in treatment of a variety of mental and physical disorders that have resulted from animal research. The question to some degree involves the issue of whether or not saving human lives or finding remedies for human illnesses and disabilities justifies the sacrifice of, or pain inflicted on, research animals.

20. **Summarize the major ethical principles governing psychological research.**

20-1.   Among the APA's guidelines for research are the following (true-false):

_____ 1. Participation should be voluntary and subjects should be allowed to withdraw from the study at any time.

_____ 2. Participants should not be subjected to dangerous or harmful treatments.

_____ 3. If a study requires deception, participants should be debriefed as soon as possible

_____ 4. Participants' right to privacy should be assured.

20-2.   Concerning research with animals (true-false):

_____ 1. Harmful or painful procedures can never be used.

_____ 2. Research animals are entitle to decent living conditions.

Answers: 20-1. T, T, T, T, T **20-2.** F (If potential benefits of the research are substantial, the guidelines permit the use of harmful or painful procedures in animal research), T.

REFLECTING ON THE CHAPTER'S THEMES

21. **Explain how this chapter highlighted two of the text's unifying themes.**

21-1.   One of the text's unifying themes is that psychology is _____ , which means that its conclusions are based on systematic _____ and that it tends to be (skeptical/credulous).

21-2.   In what way did the discussion of methodology suggest that psychology tends to be skeptical of its results?

21-3.   People's experience of the world is highly subjective. Which of the methodological problems discussed point up psychology's awareness of the subjective nature of our experience?

Answers: 21-1. empirical, observation (research), skeptical **21-2.** Researchers constantly look for methodological flaws and subject their results to critical scrutiny by other scientists. **21-3.** Behavioral scientists try to guard against subjective reactions by building in appropriate experimental controls for *placebo effects* and *experimenter bias*. The Featured Study also illustrates the effect of expectations on reaction to an event.

PERSONAL APPLICATION • FINDING AND READING JOURNAL ARTICLES

22. **Describe the nature of technical journals.**

22-1.   A journal publishes technical material in a field, generally the results of research or other scholarly activity. Since journal articles are written primarily for (the layman/other professionals), they frequently contain technical language that makes it difficult for people outside the field to understand.

22-2. In psychology, most journal articles are reports of research or other empirical studies. Some journals also publish articles that summarize findings from a large number of studies; these articles are known as _____ articles.

Answers: **22-1.** other professionals **22-2.** review.

23. Explain how to use *PsychINFO* and discuss the advantages of computerized literature searches.

23-1. PsychINFO is a computerized database that contains abstracts or concise _____ of articles published in psychological journals.

23-2. To find information about a particular journal article referred to in the popular press, for example, you could begin your search by entering the name of the _____. If you have an idea of when the article was published you could further narrow your search by entering the approximate _____ in which the article might have been published.

23-3. You can also search under topic. To further reduce your search, enter _____ topics (e.g., insomnia and mood). By pairing two topics you are more likely to find articles relevant to your particular question.

23-4. The advantages of computerized over manual searches (in the print journal Psychological Abstracts) include:

a. speed or power

b. decreased likelihood of missing relevant articles

c. the option of pairing topics in a search

d. all of the above

Answers: **23-1.** summaries **23-2.** author, years (dates, time period) **23-3.** two **23-4.** d.

24. Describe the standard organization of journal articles reporting on empirical research.

24-1. In the blanks below list the six parts of the standard journal article in the order in which they occur. (The initial letters of each section are listed on the left.)

A _____

I _____

M _____

R _____

D _____

R _____

24-2. In the blanks below match the name of the sections of the standard journal article with the descriptions.

_____ States the hypothesis and reviews the literature relevant to the hypothesis.

_____ A list of all the sources referred to in the paper.

_____ A summary.

_____ Presents the data; may include statistical analyses, graphs, and tables.

_____ Describes what the researchers did in the study; includes participants, procedures, and data collection techniques.

_____ Interprets or evaluates the data and presents conclusions.

Answers: 24-1. abstract, introduction, method, results, discussion, references **24-2.** introduction, references, abstract, results, method, discussion.

CRITICAL THINKING APPLICATION • THE PERILS OF ANECDOTAL EVIDENCE: "I HAVE A FRIEND WHO..."

25. Explain why anecdotal evidence is flawed and unreliable.

25-1. Anecdotal evidence consists of personal stories that support a particular point of view. Anecdotes are frequently persuasive because they are concrete and vivid and, therefore, easy to _____.

25-2. What's wrong with anecdotal evidence? First, one cannot generalize from a single case. Although a political candidate's story about a coal minor named Bob (or a physician named Alice, etc.) may be memorable, Bob's experiences cannot be _____ to other people or situations.

25-3. Second, people tend to represent themselves in the most favorable light. To the extent that Bob is the source of the anecdote, Bob's self-report data may reflect the social _____ bias.

25-4. In addition, stories change with the telling, so that later versions may bear little resemblance to the original event. Stories one has heard second- or third-hand, so-called _____ evidence, are likely to be particularly unreliable.

25-5. Nor is it likely that Bob, or the story about Bob, was picked randomly. The candidate selects an anecdote to make a particular point, a process similar to _____ bias in a research setting. The clear alternative to anecdotal evidence is to solve problems based on solid evidence, the so-called _____-based decision-making process.

Answers: 25-1. remember **25-2.** generalized **25-3.** desirability **25-4.** hearsay **25-5.** sampling, evidence.

Review of Key Terms

Anecdotal evidence
Case study
Confounding of variables
Control group
Correlation
Correlation coefficient
Data collection techniques
Dependent variable
Descriptive statistics
Double-blind procedure
Experiment
Experimental group
Experimenter bias
Extraneous variables

Hypothesis
Independent variable
Inferential statistics
Journal
Mean
Median
Meta-analysis
Mode
Naturalistic observation
Operational definition
Participants
Placebo effects
Population
Random assignment

Replication
Research methods
Response set
Sample
Sampling bias
Social desirability bias
Standard deviation
Statistical significance
Statistics
Subjects
Survey
Theory
Variability
Variables

_____   1.   Any of the factors in an experiment that are controlled or observed by an experimenter or that in some other way affect the outcome.

_____   2.   A tentative statement about the expected relationship between two or more variables.

_____   3.   Precisely defines each variable in a study in terms of the operations needed to produce or measure that variable.

_____   4.   Persons or animals whose behavior is being studied; means the same thing as *participants*.

_____   5.   Differing ways of conducting research, which include experiments, case studies, surveys, and naturalistic observation.

_____   6.   A research method in which independent variables are manipulated and which permits causal interpretations.

_____   7.   A condition or event that an experimenter varies in order to observe its impact.

_____   8.   The variable that results from the manipulation in an experiment.

_____   9.   The group in an experiment that receives a treatment as part of the independent variable manipulation.

_____ 10.   The group in an experiment that does not receive the treatment.

_____ 11.   Any variables other than the independent variables that seem likely to influence the dependent measure in an experiment.

_____ 12.   Distribution of subjects in an experiment in which each subject has an equal chance of being assigned to any group or condition.

_____ 13.   A link or association between variables such that one can be predicted from the other.

_____ 14.   The statistic that indicates the degree of relationship between variables.

_____ 15.   A research method in which the researcher observes behavior in the natural environment without directly intervening.

_____ 16.   An in-depth, generally subjective, investigation of an individual subject.

_____ 17.   A questionnaire or interview used to gather information about specific aspects of subjects' behavior.

_____ 18. Procedures for making empirical observations, including questionnaires, interviews, psychological tests, and physiological recordings.

_____ 19. Mathematical techniques that help in organizing, summarizing, and interpreting numerical data.

_____ 20. Statistics helpful in organizing and summarizing (but not interpreting) data.

_____ 21. Statistical procedures used to interpret data in an experiment and draw conclusions.

_____ 22. A statistical procedure that combines the results of many studies.

_____ 23. A descriptive statistic and measure of central tendency that always falls in the exact half-way point of a distribution of data.

_____ 24. The arithmetic average.

_____ 25. The score that occurs most frequently.

_____ 26. The spread or dispersion of data, including the extent to which scores vary from the mean.

_____ 27. A measure of variability in data.

_____ 28. A judgment inferred from statistics that the probability of the observed findings occurring by chance is very low.

_____ 29. A repetition of a study to determine whether the previously obtained results can be duplicated.

_____ 30. A group of subjects taken from a population.

_____ 31. A larger group from which a sample is drawn and to which the researcher wishes to generalize.

_____ 32. Exists when a sample is not representative of the population from which it was drawn.

_____ 33. Also known as subjects, the individuals whose behavior is systematically observed in a study.

_____ 34. Occurs when a researcher's expectations influence the results of the study.

_____ 35. Effects that occur when subjects experience a change due to their expectations (or to a "fake" treatment).

_____ 36. The tendency to respond in a particular way (e.g., agreeing) that is unrelated to the content of questions asked.

_____ 37. Occurs when an extraneous variable makes it difficult to sort out the effects of the independent variable.

_____ 38. The tendency to answer questions about oneself in a socially approved manner.

_____ 39. A research strategy in which neither the subjects nor experimenters know which condition or treatment the subjects are in.

_____ 40. A periodical that publishes technical and scholarly material within a discipline.

_____ 41. A system of interrelated ideas used to explain a set of observations.

_____ 42. Support for a particular point of view through the use of personal (and frequently vivid) stories.

Review of Key People

Neal Miller   Robert Rosenthal   Stanley Schachter

_____   1.   Studied the effect of anxiety on affiliation.

_____   2.   Studied experimenter bias, a researcher's unintended influence on the behavior of subjects.

_____   3.   Asserted that the benefits of animal research (e.g., the resulting treatments for mental and physical disorders) far outweigh the harm done.

Self-Quiz

1. Which of the following is a major assumption of science?
    a. Events occur in a relatively orderly or predictable manner.
    b. Cause and effect is indicated by correlational relationships.
    c. In contrast to the behavior of lower animals, human behavior is in part a function of free will.
    d. Events are largely randomly determined.

2. An experimenter tests the hypothesis that physical exercise helps people's mood (makes them happier). Subjects in the experimental group participate on Monday and Tuesday and those in the control group on Wednesday and Thursday. What is the *independent* variable?
    a. the hypothesis
    b. day of the week
    c. the exercise
    d. the mood (degree of happiness)

3. Regarding the experiment described in the previous question: What is the *dependent* variable?
    a. the hypothesis
    b. day of the week
    c. the exercise
    d. the mood (degree of happiness)

4. Regarding the experiment described above: What is an *extraneous* (confounding) variable?
    a. the hypothesis
    b. day of the week
    c. the exercise
    d. the mood (degree of happiness)

5. The major advantage of the experimental method over the correlational approach is that the experimental method:
   a. permits one to make causal conclusions
   b. allows for prediction
   c. is generally less artificial than correlational procedures
   d. permits the study of people in groups

6. In looking through some medical records you find that there is a strong relationship between depression and chronic pain: the stronger the physical pain that people report, the higher their scores on an inventory that measures depression. Which of the following conclusions are justified?
   a. Depression tends to produce chronic pain.
   b. Chronic pain tends to produce depression.
   c. Both chronic pain and depression result from some unknown third factor.
   d. any of the above could be true

7. What is the mode of the following data? 2, 3, 3, 3, 5, 5, 7, 12
   a. 3
   b. 4
   c. 5
   d. 6

8. What is the median of the following data? 1, 3, 4, 4, 5, 6, 9
   a. 3
   b. 4
   c. 4.57
   d. 6

9. Researchers find a negative relationship between alcohol consumption and speed of response: the more alcohol consumed, the slower the response speed. Which of the following fictitious statistics could possibly represent that correlation?
   a. −4.57
   b. −.87
   c. .91
   d. .05

10. The term *statistical significance* refers to:
    a. how important the data are for future research on the topic
    b. the conclusion that there are no reasonable alternative explanations
    c. the inference that the observed effects are unlikely to be due to chance
    d. the representativeness of the sample

11. An instructor wishes to find out whether a new teaching method is superior to his usual procedures, so he conducts an experiment. Everyone in his classes is quite excited about the prospect of learning under the new procedure, but of course he cannot administer the new teaching method to everyone, so some students are disappointed. A random half of the students receive the new method and the remaining half receive the old. What is the most obvious flaw in this experiment?
    a. Subjects should have been systematically assigned to groups.
    b. The sample is not representative of the population.
    c. Placebo effects or experimenter bias are likely to affect results.
    d. Distortions in self-report will affect results.

12. What procedure helps correct for experimenter bias?
    a. extraneous or confounding variables
    b. sleep learning or hypnosis
    c. a higher standard for statistical significance
    d. use of the double-blind procedure

13. With regard to the topic of deception in research with human subjects, which of the following is true?
   a. Researchers are careful to avoid deceiving subjects.
   b. Some topics can not be investigated unless deception is used.
   c. It has been empirically demonstrated that deception causes severe distress.
   d. All psychological research must involve some deception.

14. Which of the following is one of the six standard parts of a psychological journal article?
   a. conclusions
   b. bibliography
   c. data summary
   d. discussion

15. PsychINFO is a computerized database containing:
   a. standard diagnostic information for classifying behavior disorders
   b. abstracts of and bibliographic references for journal articles
   c. psychological profiles of known felons
   d. names of authors who specialize in abstractions

Answers: 1. a **2.** c **3.** d **4.** b **5.** a **6.** d **7.** a **8.** b **9.** b **10.** c **11.** c **12.** d **13.** b **14.** d **15.** b.

InfoTrac Keywords

Correlation   Experimenter Bias   Placebo Effects

Chapter Three
THE BIOLOGICAL BASES OF BEHAVIOR

Review of Key Ideas

COMMUNICATION IN THE NERVOUS SYSTEM

1. **Describe the various parts of the neuron and their functions.**

   1-1. The neuron has three basic parts: the dendrites, the cell body or soma, and the axon. The major mission of the average neuron is to receive information from one neuron and pass it on to the next neuron. The receiving part is the job of the branch-like parts called _____. They then pass the message along to the nucleus of the cell, called the cell body, or _____. From there the message is sent down the _____to be passed along to other neurons.

   1-2. Many axons are wrapped in a fatty jacket called the _____ _____, which permits for faster transmission of information and prevents messages from getting on the wrong track. Like the covering on an electrical cord, myelin acts as an _____ material.

   1-3. When the neural message reaches the end of the axon it excites projections called terminal _____, which then release a chemical substance into the junction that separates them from other neurons. This junction between neurons is called the _____.

   1-4. Identify the major parts of a neuron in the figure below. Note that the arrow indicates the direction of the flow of information.

   (a) _____ (b) _____ (c) _____ (d) _____

2. Describe the main functions of glia cells

2-1. In addition to supplying nourishment to neurons, removing their waste products, and providing insulation, what other recently discovered function might glia serve?

3. Describe the neural impulse.

3-1. When it is at rest, the neuron is like a tiny battery in that it contains a weak (negative/positive) charge. When the neuron is stimulated, the cell membrane becomes more permeable. This allows positively charged _____ ions to flow into the cell, thus lessening the cell's negative charge.

3-2. The change in the charge of the cell caused by the inflow of positively charged sodium ions, called an _____ potential, travels down the _____ of the neuron. After the firing of an action potential, there is a brief period in which no further action potentials can be generated. This brief period is called the absolute _____ period.

3-3. The text likens the neuron to a gun in that it either fires or it does not fire. This property of the neuron is called the _____ law. Neurons transmit information about the strength of a stimulus by variations in the number of action potentials generated. For example, in comparison to a weak stimulus, a strong stimulus will generate a (higher/lower) rate of action potentials.

4. Describe how neurons communicate at chemical synapses.

4-1. A neuron passes its message on to another neuron by releasing a chemical messenger into the gap or _____ that separates it from other neurons. The sending neuron, called the _____, releases a chemical messenger into the synaptic cleft, which then excites the _____ neuron.

4-2. The chemical messenger that provides this transmitting service is called a _____. The chemical binds with specifically tuned receptor sites on the postsynaptic neurons. In other words, the receptor sites accept some neurotransmitters and reject _____.

5. **Describe the two types of postsynaptic potentials and how neurons integrate and form neural circuits.**

5-1. When the neurotransmitter combines with a molecule at the receptor site it causes a voltage change at the receptor site called a _____ potential (PSP). One type of PSP is excitatory and (increases/decreases) the probability of producing an action potential in the receiving neuron. The other type is inhibitory and _____ the probability of producing an action potential.

5-2. Whether or not a neuron fires depends on the number of excitatory PSPs it is receiving and the number of _____ PSPs it is receiving. PSPs (do/do not) follow the all or none law.

5-3. Put the five steps of communication at the synapse in their correct order (by using the numbers 1 through 5):

_____ (a) The reuptake of transmitters by the presynaptic neuron.

_____ (b) The enzyme inactivation or drifting away of transmitters in the synapse.

_____ (c) The synthesis and storage of transmitters.

_____ (d) The binding of transmitters at receptor sites on the postsynaptic membrane.

_____ (e) The release of transmitters into the synaptic cleft.

5-4. Whether or not a neuron fires depends upon the balance between excitatory PSPs and _____ PSPs.

5-5. Most neurons are interlocked in complex networks that are constantly changing, eliminating old networks and adding new ones. Which process, adding networks or pruning, plays the larger role in molding the neural networks?

Answers: **5-1.** postsynaptic, increases, decreases **5-2.** inhibitory, do not **5-3.** (a) 5, (b) 4, (c) 1, (d) 3, (e) 2 **5-4.** inhibitory **5-5.** pruning.

6. **Discuss some of the functions of acetylcholine and the monoamine neurotransmitters.**

6-1. Our moods, thoughts, and actions all depend on the action of neurotransmitters. For example, the movement of all muscles depends on _____ (ACh). Like other neurotransmitters, ACh can only bind to specific sites, much like a lock and _____. However, other chemical substances can fool the receptor sites. For example, an agonist like nicotine can (block/mimic) the action of ACh, while an antagonist like curare can (block/mimic) the action of ACh.

6-2. Three neurotransmitters, dopamine, norepinephrine, and serotonin, are collectively known as _____. Both Parkinson's and schizophrenia have been linked with alterations in _____ activity, while the mood changes found in depression have been linked to receptor sites for norepinephrine and _____. Serotonin also plays a key role in the regulation of _____ and wakefulness and perhaps _____ behavior in animals.

Answers: **6-1.** Acetylcholine, key, mimic, block **6-2.** monoamines, dopamine, serotonin, sleep, aggressive.

7. Discuss how GABA and endorphins are related to behavior.

7-1. GABA and its partner glycine are peculiar in that they appear to produce only (<u>excitatory/inhibitory</u>) PSPs.

7-2. Endorphins are chemicals internally produced by the body that have effects similar to those produced by the drug _____ and its derivatives. That is, they are able to reduce pain and also induce _____, such as the "runner's high" sometimes experienced by joggers.

Answers: 7-1. inhibitory **7-2.** opium, pleasure (or euphoria).

ORGANIZATION OF THE NERVOUS SYSTEM

8. Provide an overview of the peripheral nervous system, including its subdivisions.

With approximately 85 to 180 billion individual neurons to control, it is important that the central nervous system has some kind of organizational structure. This organizational structure is depicted in Figure 3.6 of the text, and it will prove helpful if you have this figure in front of you while answering the following questions.

8-1. Answer the following questions regarding the organization of the peripheral nervous system:

(a) What constitutes the peripheral nervous system?

(b) What two subdivisions make up the peripheral nervous system?

(c) What is the role of the afferent and efferent nerve fibers?

(d) What two subdivisions make up the autonomic nervous system?

(e) Describe the opposing roles of the sympathetic and parasympathetic nervous systems.

Answers: 8-1. (a) All of the nerves that lie outside of the brain and spinal cord. (b) The somatic nervous system and the autonomic nervous system. (c) Afferent fibers carry information inward from the periphery, while efferent fibers carry information outward to the periphery. (d) The sympathetic nervous system and the parasympathetic nervous system. (e) The sympathetic system prepares the body for fight or flight, and the parasympathetic system conserves the body's resources.

9. **Distinguish between the central nervous system and the peripheral nervous system.**

    9-1.   What are the two parts of the central nervous system?

    9-2.   What is the name given to all of the nerves that lie outside of the central nervous system?

    Answers: 9-1. The brain and the spinal cord. **9-2.** The peripheral nervous system.

LOOKING INSIDE THE BRAIN: RESEARCH METHODS

10. **Describe how the EEG, lesioning, and ESB are used to investigate brain function.**

    10-1.   The electroencephalograph, or _____, is a device that can measure the brain's _____ activity. Electrodes are placed on the scalp, and the brain's electrical activity is then monitored by the EEG machine and transformed into line tracings called _____ waves.

    10-2.   Answer the following questions regarding the use of lesioning and ESB to investigate brain function:

        (a) What technique involves the actual destruction of brain tissue in order to examine the resulting effect on behavior?

        (b) What technique would most likely be employed by a neurosurgeon to map the brain of a patient?

        (c) Which techniques employ the use of electrodes and electrical currents?

        (d) In what fundamental way does lesioning differ from ESB?

    Answers: 10-1. EEG, electrical, brain **10-2.** (a) lesioning, (b) ESB, (c) lesioning and ESB, (d) Lesioning is used to actually destroy tissue, whereas ESB is used to merely elicit behavior.

11. **Describe transcranial stimulation and various brain imaging procedures.**

    11-1.   Scientists can use transcranial magnetic stimulation to create "virtual lesions" in the human brain. What does this mean?

11-2. Three kinds of brain-imaging procedures are widely used. One of these procedures consists of a computer enhanced X-ray machine that compiles multiple X-rays of the brain into a single vivid picture. The resulting images are called _____ scans. An even newer device that produces clearer three-dimensional images of the brain goes by the name of magnetic resonance imaging scanner, and the images it produces are known as _____ scans.

11-3. Unlike CT and MRI scans, which can only show the structure of the brain, the positron emission tomography scanner can portray the brain's actual _____ across time. The images produced by this procedure are called _____ scans. Newer variations of MRI scans can also monitor brain activity, such as blood and oxygen flow, and thus provide both functional and structural information. These scans are called _____ magnetic images (fMRI).

Answers: 11-1. They can either increase or decrease the excitability of neurons in a particular area. **11-2.** CT, MRI **11-3.** activity, PET, functional.

THE BRAIN AND BEHAVIOR

12. **Summarize the key functions of the medulla, pons, cerebellum, and midbrain.**

12-1. Three separate structures make up the hindbrain: the cerebellum, the pons, and the medulla. Identify these structures from the descriptions given below.

(a) This structure is essential for executing and coordinating physical movement.

(b) This structure attaches to the top of the spinal cord and controls many essential functions such as breathing and circulation.

(c) This structure forms a bridge of fibers between the brainstem and cerebellum and plays an important role in both sleep and arousal.

12-2. Helping to locate objects in space is one of the major roles of the _____. In addition, dopamine releasing neurons originate here and help to regulate the performance of _____ movements carried out by higher brain centers. It also shares a structure with the hindbrain that is essential for the regulation of sleep and wakefulness as well as modulation of muscular reflexes, breathing, and pain perception. This structure is called the _____ formation.

Answers: 12-1. (a) cerebellum, (b) medulla, (c) pons **12-2.** midbrain, voluntary, reticular.

13. Summarize the key functions of the thalamus and hypothalamus.

13-1. The structure that serves as a way station for all sensory information headed for the brain is called the _____. The thalamus also appears to play an active role in _____ sensory information.

13-2. In addition to its role in controlling the autonomic nervous system and linking the brain to the endocrine system, the hypothalamus also plays a major role in regulating basic biological drives such as fighting, _____, feeding, and _____.

Answers: **13-1.** thalamus, integrating **13-2.** fleeing, mating.

14. Describe the nature and location of the limbic system, and summarize some of its key functions.

14-1. An interconnected network of structures involved in the control of emotion, motivation, and memory are collectively known as the _____ system. The hippocampus, for example, appears to play a key role in the formation of _____. However, the limbic system is best known for its role as the seat of _____. Electrical stimulation of particular areas of the limbic system in rats (particularly in the medial forebrain bundle) appears to produce intense _____. These "pleasure centers" actually appear to be neural circuits that release the neurotransmitter _____.

Answers: **14-1.** limbic, memories, emotion, pleasure, dopamine.

15. Name the four lobes in the cerebral cortex, and identify some of their key functions.

15-1. The cerebrum is the brain structure that is responsible for our most complex _____ activities. Its folded outer surface is called the _____ cortex. The cerebrum is divided into two halves, known as the right and _____ cerebral hemispheres. The two hemispheres communicate with each other by means of a wide band of fibers called the _____ _____.

15-2. Each cerebral hemisphere is divided into four parts called lobes. Match these four lobes (occipital, parietal, temporal, and frontal) with their key function:

_____ (a) Contains the primary motor cortex that controls the movement of muscles.

_____ (b) Contains the primary visual cortex which initiates the processing of visual information.

_____ (c) Contains the primary auditory cortex which initiates the processing of auditory information.

_____ (d) Contains the primary somatosensory cortex that registers the sense of touch.

15-3. The prefrontal cortex seems to play an active role in higher order functions involving working memory and relational reasoning, suggesting to some that it serves an "executive _____ system".

Answers: **15-1.** mental, cerebral, left, corpus callosum **15-2.** (a) frontal, (b) occipital, (c) temporal, (d) parietal **15-3.** control.

16. Summarize evidence on the brains plasticity.

16-1. Research shows that the brain (is/is not) hardwired in the manner of computers. Rather, both children and adults can generate new neurons, and the wiring of the brain itself is flexible. This brain plasticity (increases/decreases) with age.

Answers: 16-1. is not, decreases.

RIGHT BRAIN/LEFT BRAIN: CEREBRAL LATERALITY

17. **Explain why scientists viewed the left hemisphere as the dominant hemisphere, and describe how split-brain research changed this view.**

17-1. Until recent years, it was believed that the left hemisphere dominated a submissive right hemisphere. Evidence for this belief came from several sources which all seemed to indicate that the left hemisphere played the dominant role with respect to the use of _____. For example, damage to an area in the frontal lobe known as _____ area was associated with speech deficits. Also, damage to another area located in the temporal lobe was found to be associated with difficulty in speech comprehension. This area is called _____ area. Both of these areas are located in the _____ cerebral hemisphere.

17-2. Answer the following questions regarding split-brain research:

(a) What was the result of severing the corpus callosum in these patients?

(b) Which hemisphere was found to be primarily responsible for verbal and language tasks in general?

(c) Which hemisphere was found to be primarily responsible for visual and spatial tasks?

17-3. What can be concluded with respect to hemispheric domination from split-brain studies?

Answers: 17-1. language, Broca's, Wernicke's, left **17-2.** (a) The two cerebral hemispheres could no longer communicate with each other. (b) The left cerebral hemisphere. (c) The right cerebral hemisphere. **17-3.** Neither hemisphere dominates, rather each has its own specialized tasks.

18. **Describe how neuroscientists conduct research on cerebral specialization in normal subjects and what this research has revealed.**

18-1. Researchers have looked at left-right imbalances in the speed of visual or auditory processing in the two hemispheres and (<u>have/have not</u>) observed perceptual asymmetries in normal subjects.

18-2. Answer the following questions regarding the conclusions that can be drawn from the research on hemispheric asymmetry:

(a) Are you more likely to identify verbal stimuli quickly and accurately when presented to the right visual field (left hemisphere), or when presented to the left visual field (right hemisphere)?

(b) Are you more likely to identify visual-spatial information quickly and accurately, such as recognizing a face, when the stimuli are presented to the right visual field (left hemisphere) or when presented to the left visual field (right hemisphere)?

(c) What conclusions can be drawn from the research on normal subjects regarding hemispheric specialization with respect to cognitive tasks?

Answers: 18-1. have **18-2.** (a) When presented to the right visual field (left hemisphere). (b) When presented to the left visual field (right hemisphere). (c) The two hemispheres are specialized to handle different cognitive tasks.

THE ENDOCRINE SYSTEM: ANOTHER WAY TO COMMUNICATE

19. Describe some of the ways in which hormones regulate behavior.

19-1. Answer the following questions regarding the workings of the endocrine system:

(a) What is the role played by the hormones in the endocrine system?

(b) While many glands comprise the endocrine system, which one functions as a master gland to control the others?

(c) What structure is the real power behind the throne here?

19-2. Fill in the boxes in the diagram below showing the role of the pituitary gland in the "fight or flight" response to stress.

| Hypothalamus | → | | → | ACTH hormone | → | |

19-3. The communication between the brain and the endrocrine system (<u>is/is not</u>) a one-way street. The levels of many hormones are regulated through (<u>positive/negative</u>) feedback systems.

19-4. What is the role of sexual hormones:

(a) Prior to birth?

(b) At puberty?

HEREDITY AND BEHAVIOR: IS IT ALL IN THE GENES?

20. Describe the structures and processes involved in genetic transmission.

20-1. When a human sperm and egg unite at conception they form a one-celled organism called a _____. This cell contains 46 chromosomes, half of which are contributed by each _____, thus making 23 pairs. Each member of a pair operates in conjunction with its _____ member. The zygote then evolves to form all of the cells in the body, each of which have _____ pairs of chromosomes.

20-2. Each chromosome is actually a threadlike strand of a _____ molecule, and along this threadlike structure are found the individual units of information, called _____, that determine our biological makeup. Like chromosomes, genes operate in _____. For example, type of ear lobe is determined by a pair of genes. If both parents contribute a gene for the same type, the child will inherit this type, and the two genes are said to be _____. If the parents contribute two different genes for the type of ear lobe, the genes are said to be _____, and the child will inherit the type carried by the dominant gene. When heterozygous genes are paired, the dominant gene masks the _____ gene.

21. Explain the difference between genotype and phenotype and the meaning of polygenic inheritance.

21-1. Answer the following questions about the difference between genotype and phenotype:

(a) What are the two genes that make up your ear lobe type said to be?

(b) What is your resulting ear lobe type said to be?

(c) Can your genotype or phenotype change over time?

21-2. What is meant when it is said that most human traits are polygenic?

Answers: 21-1. (a) your genotype, (b) your phenotype, (c) only your phenotype can change **21-2.** They are determined by two or more pairs of genes.

22. Explain the special methods used to investigate the influence of heredity on behavior.

22-1. If a trait is due to heredity, then more closely related members of a family should show (lesser/greater) resemblance on this trait than less closely related family members. Studies using this method are called _____ studies. Data gathered from family studies (can/cannot) furnish conclusive proof as to the heritability of a specific trait. Even when it is demonstrated that a particular trait is highly related to the degree of family relationship, the cause for this relationship could be either heredity or _____.

22-2. A second method in this line of investigation is to compare specific traits across identical twins and fraternal twins. This method, called _____ studies, assumes that inherited traits are much more likely to be found among (identical/fraternal) twins. These studies do in fact show that for many characteristics, such as intelligence and extraversion, the resemblance is closest for _____ twins. However, since identical twins are far from identical on these characteristics, _____ factors must also play a role here.

22-3. A third method in this line of investigation is to study children who have been separated from their biological parents at a very early age and raised by adoptive parents. The idea behind these _____ studies is that if the adoptive children more closely resemble their biological parents with respect to a specific trait, then it can be assumed that _____ plays a major role. On the other hand, if the adoptive children more closely resemble their adoptive parents with respect to a specific trait it would indicate that _____ plays a major role. Studies using this method to study the heritabilty of intelligence have found that adoptive children _____ resemble their biological and adoptive parents on this particular trait. This would indicate that a trait such as intelligence is influenced by both heredity and _____.

Answers: 22-1. greater, family, cannot, environment **22-2.** twin, identical, identical, environmental **22-3.** adoption, heredity, environment, equally, environment.

THE EVOLUTIONARY BASES OF BEHAVIOR

23. Explain the four key insights that represent the essence of Darwin's theory.

23-1. Darwin's four key insights are listed below. Match each one with the statement that best reflects the essence of the insight.

1. Organisms vary in endless ways.

2. Some of these characteristics are heritable.

3. Organisms tend to reproduce faster than the available resources necessary for their survival.

4. If a specific heritable trait contributes to survival or reproductive fitness its prevalence will increase over generations.

_____ (a) The gazelle that runs the fastest is most likely to leave offspring behind.

_____ (b) The members of most species die from starvation or other side effects of overcrowding.

_____ (c) Birds fly, fish swim, and lions roar.

_____ (d) We all have some traits that are very similar to our grandparents.

Answers: 23-1. 1 (c), 2 (d), 3 (b), 4 (a).

24. Describe some subsequent refinements to evolutionary theory.

24-1. Although contemporary theorists accept Darwin's basic theory of natural selection, they have found that natural selection operates on a gene pool that is also influenced by genetic drift, mutations, and gene flow. Match these terms with the definitions given below.

(a) Spontaneous, heritable changes in a piece of DNA can occur in an individual organism.
_____

(b) Gene frequencies in a population can shift because of emigration (out flow) and immigration (in flow). _____

(c) There can be random fluctuations in a gene pool. _____

Answers: 24-1. (a) mutation (b) gene flow (c) genetic drift.

25. Provide some examples of animal behavior that represent adaptations.

25-1. Answer the following questions about behavioral adaptations:

(a) What advantage do gazelles that stot (we humans call it mooning) gain when spotting a cheetah?

(b) What advantage do rats gain by only eating a small amount when they encounter a new food?

Answers: 25-1. (a) It increases their chances of escaping. (b) It decreases their chances of being poisoned.

REFLECTING ON THE CHAPTER'S THEMES

26. Explain how this chapter highlighted three of the texts unifying themes.

26-1. Indicate which of the three unifying themes (heredity and environment jointly influence behavior, behavior is determined by multiple causes, and psychology is empirical) is particularly illustrated in each of the following situations:

(a) The discovery of the factors that lead to the development of schizophrenic disorders.

(b) The development of many new techniques and instruments that led to the discovery of cerebral specialization.

(c) A new look at the two major factors that influence the development of personal characteristics such as intelligence and temperament.

Answers: 26-1. (a) Behavior is determined by multiple causes. (b) Psychology is empirical. (c) Heredity and environment jointly influence behavior.

EVALUATING THE CONCEPT OF "TWO MINDS IN ONE"

27. **Critically evaluate the five ideas on cerebral specialization and cognitive processes discussed in the chapter.**

   27-1.   Your text lists five popular ideas that have found support among some neuroscientists and psychologists. These ideas are:

   (a) The two hemispheres are _____ to process different cognitive tasks.

   (b) Each hemisphere has its own independent stream of _____.

   (c) The two hemispheres have _____ modes of thinking.

   (d) People vary in their _____ on one hemisphere as opposed to the other.

Answers: 27-1. (a) specialized (b) consciousness (c) different (d) reliance (dependence).

   27-2.   We will now proceed through each of these five assumptions to show how each has to be qualified in light of currently available evidence.

   (a) The idea that the left and right brains are specialized to handle different kinds of information (is/is not) supported by research. However, there is evidence that this specialization hardly occurs in some persons, while in other persons the specialization is reversed, particularly among _____ handed persons. Moreover, most tasks require the ongoing cooperation of _____ hemispheres.

   (b) The evidence that each hemisphere has its own mind, or stream of consciousness, is actually very weak, except for persons who have undergone _____-_____ surgery. The resulting "two minds" in these patients appears to be a byproduct of the surgery.

(c) The assertion that each hemisphere has its own mode of thinking is (plausible/confirmed). A big problem here, however, is that mode of thinking, or cognitive style, has proven difficult to both define and _____.

(d) The assertion that some people are left-brained while others are right-brained (is/is not) conclusive at this time. Abilities and personality characteristics (do/do not) appear to be influenced by brainedness.

(e) The notion that most schooling overlooks the education of the right brain (does/does not) really make sense. Since both hemispheres are almost always sharing in accomplishing an ongoing task, it would be _____ to teach only one hemisphere at a time.

Answers: 27-2. (a) is, left, both (b) split-brain (c) plausible, measure (d) is not, do not (e) does not, impossible.

28. **Explain how neuroscience research has been overextrapolated by some education and child care advocates who have campaigned for infant schooling.**

28-1. Answer the following questions regarding neuroscience research:

(a) What happened to kittens deprived of light to one eye for the first 4-6 weeks of life?

(b) What happened to kittens deprived of light to one eye for the same amount of time after four months of age?

(c) What is the name given to that early period in the kitten's life when light is essential for the normal development of vision?

(d) What difference was found in synapses in rats that were raised in "enriched" environments when compared to rats raised in "impoverished" environments?

28-2. Answer the following questions regarding the overextrapolation of neuroscience findings:

(a) What findings argue against the notion that brain development is more malleable during the first three years of life?

(b) There are findings that argue against the notion that greater synaptic density is associated with greater intelligence. Which of the following is correct?

1. Infant animals and human beings begin life with an overabundance of synaptic connections.

2. Infant animals and human beings begin life with an insufficient number of synaptic connections.

3. Learning involves the pruning of inactive synapses and reinforcing heavily used neural pathways.

Review of Key Terms

Afferent nerve fibers
Agonist
Antagonist
Autonomic nervous system (ANS)
Axon
Behavioral genetics
Central nervous system (CNS)
Cerebral cortex
Cerebral hemispheres
Cerebrospinal fluid (CSF)
Chromosomes
Corpus callosum
Critical period
Dendrites
Dominant gene
Efferent nerve fibers
Electrical stimulation of the brain (ESB)
Electroencephalograph (EEG)
Endocrine System
Endorphins
Excitatory PSP
Family studies

Fitness
Forebrain
Fraternal (dizygotic) twins
Genes
Genetic mapping
Genotype
Heterozygous condition
Hindbrain
Homozygous condition
Hormones
Hypothalamus
Identical (monozygotic) twins
Inclusive fitness
Inhibitory PSP
Lesioning
Limbic system
Midbrain
Myelin sheath
Natural selection
Nerves
Neurons
Neurotransmitters

Parasympathetic division
Perceptual asymmetries
Peripheral nervous system
Phenotype
Pituitary gland
Polygenic traits
Postsynaptic potential (PSP)
Recessive gene
Resting potential
Reuptake
Soma
Somatic nervous system
Split-brain surgery
Sympathetic division
Synapse
Synaptic cleft
Terminal buttons
Thalamus
Transcranial magnetic stimulation (TMS)
Twin studies
Zygote

_____ 1. A technique that temporarily enhances or depresses neural activity in a specific area of the brain.

_____ 2. A limited time span for the development of an organism that is optimal for certain capacities to emerge because the organism is especially responsive to certain experiences.

_____ 3. Refers to the reproductive success of an individual organism relative to the average reproductive success in the population.

_____ 4. Individual cells in the nervous system that receive, integrate, and transmit information.

_____ 5. Neuron part that contains the cell nucleus and much of the chemical machinery common to most cells.

_____ 6. Branchlike parts of a neuron that are specialized to receive information.

_____ 7. A long, thin fiber that transmits signals away from the soma to other neurons, or to muscles or glands.

_____ 8. An insulating jacket, derived from glia cells that encases some axons.

_____ 9. Small knobs at the end of the axon that secrete chemicals called neurotransmitters.

_____ 10. A junction where information is transmitted between neurons.

_____ 11. The stable, negative charge of an inactive neuron.

_____ 12. A process in which neurotransmitters are sponged up from the synaptic cleft by the presynaptic neuron.

_____ 13. Posits that heritable characteristics that provide a survival or reproductive advantage are more likely than alternative characteristics to be passed on to subsequent generations and thus come to be "selected" over time.

_____ 14. A microscopic gap between the terminal buttons of the sending neuron and the cell membrane of another cell.

_____ 15. Chemicals that transmit information from one neuron to another.

_____ 16. A voltage change at the receptor site of a neuron.

_____ 17. An electric potential that increases the likelihood that a postsynaptic neuron will fire action potentials.

_____ 18. An electric potential that decreases the likelihood that a postsynaptic neuron will fire action potentials.

_____ 19. A technique for assessing hereditary influence by examining blood relatives to see how much they resemble each other on a specific trait.

_____ 20. A chemical that mimics the action of a neurotransmitter.

_____ 21. A chemical that opposes the action of a neurotransmitter.

_____ 22. An entire family of internally produced chemicals that resemble opiates in structure and effects.

_____ 23. System that includes all those nerves that lie outside the brain and spinal cord.

_____ 24. Bundles of neuron fibers (axons) that travel together in the peripheral nervous system.

_____ 25. System made up of the nerves that connect to voluntary skeletal muscles and sensory receptors.

_____ 26. Axons that carry information inward to the central nervous system from the periphery of the body.

_____ 27. Axons that carry information outward from the central nervous system to the periphery of the body.

_____ 28. System made up of the nerves that connect to the heart, blood vessels, smooth muscles, and glands.

_____ 29. The branch of the autonomic nervous system that mobilizes the body's resources for emergencies.

_____ 30. The branch of the autonomic nervous system that generally conserves bodily resources.

_____ 31. System that consists of the brain and spinal cord.

_____ 32. A solution that fills the hollow cavities (ventricles) of the brain and circulates around the brain and spinal cord.

_____ 33. A device that monitors the electrical activity of the brain over time by means of recording electrodes attached to the surface of the scalp.

_____ 34. Assessing hereditary influence by comparing the resemblance of identical twins and fraternal twins on a trait.

_____ 35. Method that involves destroying a piece of the brain by means of a strong electric current delivered through an electrode.

_____ 36. Method that involves sending a weak electric current into a brain structure to stimulate (activate) it.

_____ 37. Part of the brain that includes the cerebellum and two structures found in the lower part of the brainstem, the medulla and the pons.

_____ 38. The segment of the brainstem that lies between the hindbrain and the forebrain.

_____ 39. Part of the brain encompassing the thalamus, hypothalamus, limbic system, and cerebrum.

_____ 40. A structure in the forebrain through which all sensory information (except smell) must pass to get to the cerebral cortex.

_____ 41. A structure found near the base of the forebrain that is involved in the regulation of basic biological needs.

_____ 42. A densely connected network of structures located beneath the cerebral cortex, involved in the control of emotion, motivation, and memory.

_____ 43. The convoluted outer layer of the cerebrum.

_____ 44. The right and left halves of the cerebrum.

_____ 45. The structure that connects the two cerebral hemispheres.

_____ 46. The process of determining the location and chemical sequence of specific genes or chromosones.

_____ 47. Surgery in which the corpus callosum is severed to reduce the severity of epileptic seizures.

_____ 48. System of glands that secrete chemicals into the bloodstream that help control bodily functioning.

_____ 49. The chemical substances released by the endocrine glands.

_____ 50. The "master gland" of the endocrine system.

_____ 51. Threadlike strands of DNA molecules that carry genetic information.

_____ 52. A one-celled organism formed by the union of a sperm and an egg.

_____ 53. DNA segments that serve as the key functional units in hereditary transmission.

_____ 54. A gene that is expressed when the paired genes are different (heterozygous).

_____ 55. A gene that is masked when paired genes are heterozygous.

_____ 56. A person's genetic makeup.

_____ 57. The ways in which a person's genotype is manifested in observable characteristics.

_____ 58. Characteristics that are influenced by more than one pair of genes.

_____ 59. The sum of an individuals' own reproductive success, plus the effects the organism has on the reproductive success of related others.

_____ 60. Twins that result when two eggs are fertilized simultaneously by different sperm cells, forming two separate zygotes.

_____ 61. Left-right imbalances between the cerebral hemispheres in the speed of visual or auditory processing.

_____ 62. Twins that emerge from one zygote that splits.

_____ 63. An interdisciplinary field that studies the influence of genetic factors on behavioral traits.

_____ 64. The two genes in a specific pair are the same.

_____ 65. The two genes in a specific pair are different.

Answers: 1. transcranial magnetic stimulation **2.** critical period **3.** fitness **4.** neurons **5.** soma **6.** dendrites **7.** axon **8.** myelin sheath **9.** terminal buttons **10.** synapse **11.** resting potential **12.** reuptake **13.** natural selection **14.** synaptic cleft **15.** neurotransmitters **16.** postsynaptic potential (PSP) **17.** excitatory PSP **18.** inhibitory PSP **19.** family studies **20.** agonist **21.** antagonist **22.** endorphins **23.** peripheral nervous system **24.** nerves **25.** somatic nervous system **26.** afferent nerve fibers **27.** efferent fibers **28.** autonomic nervous system (ANS) **29.** sympathetic division **30.** parasympathetic division **31.** central nervous system (CNS) **32.** cerebrospinal fluid (CSF) **33.** electroencephalograph (EEG)

34. twin studies 35. lesioning 36. electrical stimulation of the brain (ESB) 37. hindbrain 38. midbrain 39. forebrain 40. thalamus 41. hypothalamus 42. limbic system 43. cerebral cortex 44. cerebral hemispheres 45. corpus callosum 46. adoption studies 47. split-brain surgery 48. endocrine system 49. hormones 50. pituitary gland 51. chromosomes 52. zygote 53. genes 54. dominant gene 55. recessive gene 56. genotype 57. phenotype 58. polygenic traits 59. inclusive fitness 60. fraternal (dizygotic) twins 61. perceptual asymmetries 62. identical (monozygotic) twins 63. behavioral genetics 64. monozygous condition 65. heterozygous condition.

Review of Key People

Charles Darwin
Alan Hodgkin & Andrew Huxley

James Olds & Peter Milner
Candice Pert & Solomon Snyder

Robert Plomin
Roger Sperry & Michael Garzzaniga

_____ **1.** Unlocked the mystery of the neural impulse.

_____ **2.** Known for their work with the split-brain.

_____ **3.** Showed that morphine works by binding to specific receptors.

_____ **4.** Discovered "pleasure-centers" in the limbic system.

_____ **5.** One of the leading behavior genetics researchers in the last decade.

_____ **6.** Identified natural selection as the mechanism that orchestrates the process of evolution.

Answers: 1. Hodgkin & Huxley **2.** Sperry & Garzzaniga **3.** Pert & Snyder **4.** Olds & Milner **5.** Plomin **6.** Darwin.

Self-Quiz

1. Most neurons are involved in transmitting information:
a. from one neuron to another
b. from the outside world to the brain
c. from the brain to the muscles
d. from the brain to the glands

2. Which part of the neuron has the responsibility for receiving information from other neurons?
a. the cell body
b. the soma
c. the axon
d. the dendrites

3. The myelin sheath serves to:
a. permit faster transmission of the neural impulse
b. keep neural impulses on the right track
c. add structural strength
d. permit faster transmission and keep neural impulses on track

4. The change in the polarity of a neuron that results from the inflow of positively charged ions and the outflow of negatively charged ions is called the:
a. presynaptic potential
b. postsynaptic potential
c. synaptic potential
d. action potential

5. The task of passing a message from one neuron to another is actually carried out by:
   a. the myelin sheath
   b. the glia cells
   c. the action potential
   d. neurotransmitters

6. Which of the following techniques is often used by neurosurgeons to map the brain when performing brain surgery?
   a. EEG recordings
   b. ESB
   c. lesioning
   d. all of the above

7. The seat of emotion is to be found in the:
   a. reticular formation
   b. hindbrain
   c. limbic system
   d. forebrain

8. Persons having difficulty with language and speech following an accident that resulted in injury to the brain are most likely to have sustained damage in the:
   a. right cerebral hemisphere
   b. left cerebral hemisphere
   c. right cerebral hemisphere if they are a male and left cerebral hemisphere if they are a female
   d. I have no idea what you are talking about

9. In carrying out the "fight or flight" response, the role of supervisor is assigned to the:
   a. adrenal gland
   b. pituitary gland
   c. hypothalamus
   d. parasympathetic nervous system

10. A person's current weight and height could be said to exemplify his or her:
    a. genotype
    b. phenotype
    c. both of the above
    d. none of the above

11. Which of the following kinds of studies can truly demonstrate that specific traits are indeed inherited?
    a. family studies
    b. twin studies
    c. adoption studies
    d. none of the above

12. Current evidence indicates that schizophrenia results from:
    a. genetic factors
    b. environmental factors
    c. multiple causes that involve both genetic and environmental factors
    d. completely unknown factors

13. Psychology as a science can be said to be:
    a. empirical
    b. rational
    c. analytic
    d. both b and c

14. Which of the following statements is/are correct?
    a. The right side of the brain is the creative side.
    b. The right and left brains are specialized to handle different kinds of information.
    c. The left side of the brain always handles language tasks.
    d. Most schooling overlooks the education or the right brain.

15. Which of the following is not one of Darwin's four key insights?
    a. Some characteristics are heritable.
    b. Organisms vary in endless ways.
    c. Genetic drift is a major factor in the evolution of species.
    d. Organisms tend to reproduce faster than available resources.

16. The evolution of species is:
    a. a fact
    b. a theory with a few flaws
    c. a theory with many flaws
    d. a speculation not open to empirical verification

17. Which of the following is correct?
    a. Human beings begin life with an insufficient number of synapses.
    b. Human beings begin life with an overabundance off synapses.
    c. Synaptic density is associated with intelligence.
    d. Brain development is only malleable during the first 3 years of life.

Answers: 1. a **2.** d **3.** c **4.** d **5.** d **6.** b **7.** c **8.** b **9.** c **10.** b **11.** d **12.** c **13.** a **14.** b **15.** c **16.** a **17.** b

InfoTrac Keywords

Family studies   Twin Studies

Chapter Four
SENSATION AND PERCEPTION

Review of Key Ideas

PSYCHOPHYSICS: BASIC CONCEPTS AND ISSUES

1. **Explain how stimulus intensity is related to absolute thresholds.**

    1-1.   You are sitting on a secluded beach at sundown with a good friend. You make a bet as to who can detect the first evening star. Since you have just recently covered this chapter in your text, you explain to your friend that doing so involves the detection of a stimulus threshold. In this case, the first star that provides the minimal amount of stimulation which can be detected is said to have crossed the _____. All of our senses have thresholds, but research clearly shows that the minimal amount of stimulation necessary to be detected by any one of our senses (is/is not) always the same. Therefore, the absolute threshold is defined as the stimulus intensity that can be detected _____ percent of the time.

    Answers: **1-1.** threshold, is not, 50.

2. **Describe the JND and explain Weber's law.**

    2-1.   The smallest difference in stimulus intensity that a specific sense can detect is called the _____. Weber's law states that the size of a just noticeable difference (JND) is a constant proportion of the intensity (size) of the initial stimulus. This means that as a stimulus increases in intensity, the JND increases proportionally as well. Therefore, it would be more difficult to detect a slight increase in the length of a (1-inch/20-inch) line, a slight decrease in a (quiet/loud) tone, or a slight increase in the weight of a (30-ounce/90-ounce) object.

    Answers: **2-1.** JND (just noticeable difference) 20-inch, loud, 90-ounce.

3. **Explain the basic thrust of signal-detection theory.**

3-1.   The major idea behind signal detection theory is that our ability to detect signals depends not only on the initial intensity of a stimulus, but also on other sensory and decision processes as well. One factor that is particularly important here is the criterion you set for how certain you must feel before you react (what are the gains from being correct and what are the losses from being incorrect). What other factor is particularly important here?

3-2.   Thus, according to signal detection theory, the concepts of absolute thresholds and JNDs need to be replaced by the notion that the probability of detecting any given stimulus will depend on all of the above factors; this is called the concept of _____.

Answers: 3-1. background noise **3-2.** detectability.

4. **Summarize evidence on perception without awareness, and discuss the practical implications of subliminal perception.**

4-1.   Answer the following questions about the study conducted by Jon Krosnick and his colleagues:

(a) What two different kinds of emotion arousing subliminal stimuli accompanied the slides of the target person?

(b) Which group rated the target group in a more favorable manner?

4-2.   What general conclusions can be drawn from the research on subliminal perception with respect to its potential persuasive effects?

Answers: 4-1. (a) Stimuli that would elicit either positive or negative emotions. (b) The group exposed to positive emotional stimuli. **4-2.** The effects are very weak.

5. **Discuss the meaning and significance of sensory adaptation.**

5-1.   Which of the following examples best illustrates what is meant by sensory adaptation?

(a) You are unable to clearly hear the conversation at the next table even though it sounds intriguing, and you are straining to listen.

(b) The strawberries you eat at grandma's farm at the age of 20 seem not to taste as good as when you ate them at the age of six.

(c) The wonderful smell you encounter upon first entering the bakery seems to have declined considerably by the time you make your purchase and leave.

5-2. If you answered c to the above question you are right on track and understand that sensory adaptation involves a gradual _____ in sensitivity to prolonged stimulation. This automatic process means that we are not as likely to be as sensitive to the constants in our sensory environments as we are to the _____.

Answers: 5-1. c **5-2.** decrease, changes.

OUR SENSE OF SIGHT: THE VISUAL SYSTEM

6. List the three properties of light and the aspects of visual perception that they influence.

6-1. Before we can see anything, _____ must be present. There are three characteristics of lightwaves that directly effect how we perceive visual objects; match each of these characteristics with its psychological effect.

_____ (a) wavelength   1. color

_____ (b) amplitude   2. saturation (or richness)

_____ (c) purity   3. brightness

Answers: 6-1. lightwaves or light, (a) 1, (b) 3, (c) 2.

7. Describe the role of the lens and pupil in the functioning of the eye.

7-1. Getting light rays entering the eye to properly focus on the retina is the job of the _____. It accomplishes this task by either thickening or flattening its curvature, a process called _____. Controlling the amount of light entering the eye is the job of the _____. It accomplishes this task by opening or closing the opening in the center of the eye called the _____.

Answers: 7-1. lens, accommodation, iris, pupil.

8. Describe the role of the retina in light sensitivity and in visual information processing.

8-1. The structure that transforms the information contained in light rays into neural impulses that are then sent to the brain is called the _____. All of the axons carrying these neural impulses exit the eye at a single opening in the retina called the optic _____. Since the optic disk is actually a hole in the retina, this part of the retina cannot sense incoming visual information, and for this reason it is called the _____ spot.

8-2. The specialized receptor cells that are primarily responsible for visual acuity and color vision are called the _____. The cones are mainly located in the center of the retina in a tiny spot called the _____. The specialized receptor cells that lie outside of the fovea and towards the periphery of the retina are called the _____. The rods are primarily responsible for peripheral vision and for _____vision.

8-3. Both dark and light adaptation are primarily accomplished through _____ reactions in the rods and cones. This chemical reaction occurs more quickly in the _____, so they are quicker to show both dark adaptation and light adaptation.

8-4. Light rays striking the rods and cones initiate neural impulses that are then transmitted to _____ cells and then to _____ cells. From here the visual information is transmitted to the brain via the axons running from the retina to the brain, collectively known as the _____ nerve.

8-5. The processing of visual information begins within the receiving area of a retinal cell called the _____ field. Stimulation of the receptive field of a cell causes signals to be sent inward towards the brain and sideways, or _____, to nearby cells, thus allowing them to interact with one another. The most basic of these interactive effects, lateral antagonism, allows the retina to compare light falling in a specific area against the general lighting. This allows the visual system to compute the (<u>relative/absolute</u>) levels of light.

Answers: **8-1.** retina, disk, blind **8-2.** cones, fovea, rods, night **8-3.** chemical, cones **8-4.** bipolar, ganglion, optic **8-5.** receptive, laterally, relative.

9. Describe the routing of signals from the eye to the brain and the brain's role in visual information processing.

9-1. Visual information from the right side of the visual field (Figure 4-13 in the text) exits from the retinas of both eyes via the optic nerves and meet at the _____ chiasm, where it is combined and sent to the _____ side of the brain. Visual information from the left side of the visual field follows a similar pattern, meeting at the optic chiasm, and then on to the _____ side of the brain.

9-2. After leaving the optic chiasm on their way to the visual cortex, the optic nerve fibers diverge along two pathways. Fill in the missing parts of the pathways below.

Main pathway

(a) Optic chiasm _____ Visual cortex _____

Secondary pathway

(b) Optic chiasm _____ Visual cortex _____

9-3. The main pathway is subdivided into the magnocellular and parvocellular pathways that simultaneously extract _____ kinds of information from the same input.

(a) Which channel handles the perception of color?

(b) Which channel handles the perception of brightness?

9-4.   Because the cells in the visual cortex respond very selectively to specific features of complex stimuli, they have been described as _____ detectors. There are two major types of cells in the visual cortex: simple cells and complex cells. Identify them from their descriptions below.

(a) These cells are particular about the width and orientation of a line but respond to any position in their receptive field.

(b) These cells are very particular about the width, orientation, and position of a line.

9-5.   After processing in the primary visual cortex, the signals diverge into two separate streams. The ventral stream processes the details of _____ objects are out there and the dorsal stream processes _____ the objects are located.

9-6.   As signals move further along in the visual processing system the neurons become (less/more) specialized as to what turns them on, and the stimuli that will activate them become (less/more) complex. For example, cells in the temporal lobe along the "what" pathway best respond to pictures of human _____.

Answers: 9-1. optic, left, right **9-2.** (a) thalamus, lateral geniculate nucleus (b) superior colliculus, thalamus **9-3.** different, (a) parvocellular (b) magnocellular **9-4.** feature, (a) complex cells (b) simple cells **9-5.** what, where **9-6.** more, more, faces.

10. Describe the two types of color mixing and discuss the trichromatic and opponent process theories of color vision, as well as their reconciliation.

10-1.   Removing some wavelengths of light, leaving less light than was originally there is called _____ color mixing. Superimposing lights, putting more light in the mixture than exists in any one light by itself is called _____ color mixing.

10-2.   The trichromatic theory of color vision, as its name suggests, proposes three different kinds of receptors (channels) for the three primary colors: red, _____, and _____. The opponent process theory of color vision also proposes three channels for color vision, but these channels are red versus _____, yellow versus _____, and black versus _____.

10-3.   These two theories of color vision can be used to explain different phenomenon. Use T (trichromatic) or O (opponent process) to indicate which theory best explains the following phenomena.

_____ (a) The color of an afterimage is the complement of the original color.

_____ (b) The different kinds of color blindness suggest three different kinds of receptors.

_____ (c) Any three appropriately spaced colors can produce all other colors.

_____ (d) People describing colors often require at least four different names.

10-4. The evidence is now clear that both theories are (<u>incorrect/correct</u>). Each is needed to explain all of the phenomena associated with color vision. Three different kinds of cones have been found in the retina which are sensitive to each of the three primary colors; this supports the _____ theory. It has also been found that visual cells in the retina, the LGN, and the visual cortex respond in opposite (antagonistic) ways to complementary colors, thus supporting the _____ theory.

Answers: 10-1. subtractive, additive **10-2.** green, blue, green, blue, white **10-3.** (a) O (b) T (c) T (d) O **10-4.** correct, trichromatic, opponent process.

11. Discuss the subjectivity of your perception, explain the concept of feature analysis, and distinguish between top-down and bottom-up processing.

11-1. The same visual stimulus can result in radically different perceptions, and thus our perceptions of the world are (<u>subjective/objective</u>). We perceive what we expect to perceive (perceptual set) and we may not perceive the unexpected, a phenomenon called _____ blindness.

11-2. The process of detecting specific elements in visual input and assembling them into a more complex form is known as _____ _____.

11-3. Answer the following questions regarding top-down and bottom-up processing:

(a) Which process appears to assume feature analysis?

(b) Which process appears to account for our ability to rapidly recognize and read long strings of words?

(c) What does the text conclude about which theory is correct?

Answers: 11-1. subjective, inattentional **11-2.** feature analysis **11-3.** (a) bottom-up processing, (b) top-down processing, (c) Both theories have a place in form perception.

12. **Explain the basic premise of Gestalt psychology, and describe Gestalt principles of visual perception.**

12-1. The Gestalt view of form perception assumes that form perception is not constructed out of individual elements; rather the form, or whole, is said to be _____ than the sum of its individual elements. The illusion of movement, called the _____ phenomenon, is used to support the Gestalt view of form perception because the illusion of movement (is/is not) completely contained in the individual chunks of stimuli that give rise to it. In other words, the illusion, or whole, appears to be _____ than the sum of its parts.

12-2. Five Gestalt principles of visual perception are illustrated below. Match each illustration with its correct name.

Proximity

Similarity

Continuity

Closure

Simplicity

(a) _____

(b) _____

(c) _____

(d) _____

(e) _____

12-3. What Gestalt principle is illustrated by:

(a) The words printed on this page appear to stand out from the white paper they are printed on?

(b) Things moving in the same direction together get grouped together?

Answers: **12-1.** greater (more), phi, is not, greater (more) **12-2.** (a) proximity, (b) closure, (c) similarity, (d) simplicity, (e) continuity **12-3.** (a) figure and ground (b) common fate.

13. **Explain how form perception can be a matter of formulating perceptual hypotheses.**

13-1. The objects that surround us in the world outside of our bodies are called _____ stimuli; the images the objects project on our retinas are called _____ stimuli. When perceived from different angles or distances, the same distal stimulus projects (similar/different) proximal images on the retina. This forces us to make perceptual _____ about the distal stimulus.

Answers: **13-1.** distal, proximal, different, hypotheses or guesses.

14. Describe the monocular and binocular cues employed in depth perception and cultural variations in depth perception.

14-1. There are two general kinds of cues that allow us to perceive depth. They are easy to remember because one kind involves the use of both eyes and is called _____ cues; the other kind requires the use of only one of the eyes and is called _____ cues. Depth perception (<u>does/does not</u>) require the use of both binocular and monocular cues.

14-2. Here are examples of two different kinds of binocular cues, retinal disparity and convergence. Identify each from these examples:

(a) As a person walks towards you your eyes turn inward.

(b) The images are slightly different on each retina and the differences change with distance.

14-3. There are two general kinds of monocular cues. One kind involves the active use of the eye, such as the accommodation used for focusing the eye. The other general kind is used to indicate depth in flat pictures and thus is called _____ depth cues.

14-4. Identify the following pictorial cues:

(a) Parallel lines grow closer as they recede into the distance.

(b) More distant objects are higher in the field than nearer objects.

(c) When objects appear to be of the same size, closer ones appear larger than more distant ones.

(d) Near objects block or overlap more distant ones.

(e) Texture appears to grow finer as viewing distance increases.

(f) Patterns of light and dark suggest shadows that can create an impression of three-dimensional space.

14-5. What differences have been found in a few cultures without previous experience in viewing two-dimensional figures and photographs?

Answers: 14-1. binocular, monocular, does not **14-2.** (a) convergence (b) retinal disparity **14-3.** pictorial **14-4.** (a) linear perspective, (b) height in plane, (c) relative size, (d) interposition, (e) texture gradients, (f) light and shadow **14-5.** They have difficulty in perceiving depth (using only pictorial depth cues).

15. **Summarize the Featured Study and follow-up research on the perception of geographical slant.**

    15-1. After reading the Featured Study you should be able to answer the following questions:

        (a) Which method of judgment of geographical slant, verbal, visual, or haptic (based on touch), was the most accurate?

        (b) In what way might overestimates of geographical slant by the visual and verbal methods be of value?

        (c) In what way might the better accuracy of haptic estimates be of value?

    15-2. Answer the following questions regarding the follow-up research.

        (a) The overestimates of geographical slant were even more pronounced when the hills were viewed from the top than from the bottom. What functional purpose would this serve?

        (b) What effect did fatigue have on the overestimation bias?

Answers: 15-1. (a) haptic, (b) They prevent people from undertaking climbs they are not equipped to handle. (c) It prevents stumbling (when climbing or descending a geographical slant). **15-2.** (a) Steep hills are harder to descend than ascend. (b) It increased the bias.

16. **Describe perceptual constancies and illusions in vision, and discuss cultural variations in susceptibility to certain illusions.**

    16-1. The tendency to experience stable perceptions in spite of constantly changing sensory input is called perceptual _____. For example, even though the retinal image shrinks as a friend walks away, she continues to appear her usual height. This is an example of _____ constancy.

    16-2. Being fooled by the discrepancy between the appearance of a visual stimulus and its physical reality is what is meant by an optical _____. Both perceptual constancies and optical illusions illustrate the point that we are continually formulating _____ about what we perceive and also that these perceptions can be quite (subjective/objective).

16-3. What do the variations in cultural susceptibility to certain illusions tell us about our perceptual inferences?

Answers: 16-1. constancy, size **16-2.** illusion, hypotheses, subjective **16-3.** They can be shaped by our experience.

OUR SENSE OF HEARING: THE AUDITORY SYSTEM

17. List the three properties of sound and the aspects of auditory perception that they influence.

17-1. Name the perceived qualities that are associated with the following properties of sound waves.

Physical property	Description	Perceived Quality
(a) purity	kind of mixture	_____
(b) amplitude	wave height	_____
(c) wavelength	wave frequency	_____

Answers: 17-1. (a) timbre, (b) loudness, (c) pitch.

18. Summarize the information on human hearing capacities, and describe how sensory processing occurs in the ear.

18-1. Below are questions concerning human hearing capacities. Match the questions with their correct answers.

Answers	Questions
1. 90 to 120 decibels (dB).	____ (a) What is the frequency range of human hearing?
2. 1,000 to 5,000 Hz.	____ (b) How loud do sounds have to be to cause damage to human hearing?
3. 20 to 20,000 Hz.	____ (c) To what frequency range is human hearing the most sensitive?

18-2. Below is a scrambled sequence of events that occurs when a sound wave strikes the ear. Put these events in their correct order using the numbers 1 through 4.

_____ Fluid waves travel down the cochlea causing the hair cells on the basilar membrane to vibrate.

_____ The pinna directs air to the eardrum.

_____ The hair cells convert fluid motion into neural impulses and send them to the brain.

_____ The motion of the vibrating eardrum is converted to fluid motion by the ossicles.

Answers: 18-1. (a) 3, (b) 1, (c) 2 **18-2.** 3, 1, 4, 2.

19. **Compare and contrast the place and frequency theories of pitch perception, and discuss the resolution of the debate.**

19-1.   One theory of pitch perception assumes that the hair cells respond differentially to pitch depending on their location along the basilar membrane. This is the main idea of the _____ theory of pitch perception. A second theory assumes a one to one correspondence between the actual frequency of the sound wave and the frequency at which the entire basilar membrane vibrates. This is the main idea of the _____ theory of pitch perception.

19-2.   Below are several facts uncovered by research. Tell which theory of pitch is supported by each of these facts.

   (a) The hair cells vibrate in unison and not independently.

   (b) Even when they fire in volleys, auditory nerves can only handle up to 5000 Hz.

   (c) A wave pattern caused by the vibrating basilar membrane peaks at a particular place along the membrane.

19-3.   The above facts mean that the perception of pitch depends on both _____ and _____ coding.

Answers: 19-1. place, frequency **19-2.** (a) frequency theory, (b) place theory, (c) place theory **19-3.** place, frequency.

20. **Discuss the cues employed in auditory localization.**

20-1.   The sound shadow cast by the head is in a large part responsible for enhancing two important cues used for auditory localization. What are these two cues?

Answers: 20-1. The differences in the intensity and time of arrival of sound waves reaching each ear.

OUR CHEMICAL SENSES: TASTE AND SMELL

21. **Describe the stimuli and receptors for taste, and discuss individual differences in taste perception.**

21-1.   The stimuli for taste perception are _____ absorbed in the saliva that stimulate taste cells located in the tongue's _____ _____. It is generally thought that there are four fundamental tastes; these are: _____, _____, _____, and _____.

21-2.   What accounts for much of the wide variations in taste preferences among people?

21-3.   What appears to account for the difference between supertasters and nontasters (is it a learned or genetic characteristic)?

Answers: **21-1.** chemicals, taste buds, sweet, sour, salty, bitter (in any order). **21-2.** What they have been exposed to. **21-3.** It is a genetic characteristic.

22. **Describe the stimuli and receptors for smell, and discuss how well people perform in odor identification tasks.**

    22-1.   The stimuli for the sense of smell are _____ molecules floating in the air. The receptors for smell are hairlike structures located in the nasal passages called _____ _____. If there are any primary odors, they must be (large/small) in number. Human sensitivity to smell (does/does not) compare favorably with that of many other animals, although some animals surpass us in this respect.

    Answers: **22-1.** chemical, olfactory cilia, large, does.

OUR SENSE OF TOUCH: SENSORY SYSTEMS IN THE SKIN

23. **Describe the processes involved in the perception of pressure on the skin.**

    23-1.   Cells in the somatosensory cortex that respond to pressure are sensitive to specific patches on the _____. Tactile localizstion of pressure depends on _____ _____ similar to those seen for vision.

    Answers: **23-1.** skin, feature detectors.

24. **Describe the two pathways along which pain signals travel, and discuss evidence that the perception of pain is subjective.**

    24-1.   Pain signals travel to the brain by two slightly different pathways. One pathway sends signals directly and immediately through myelinated neurons to the cortex and is called the _____ pathway. The other sends signals to the cortex through unmyelinated neurons and is called the _____ pathway. The _____ pathway mediates lingering, less localized pain.

    24-2.   Many studies have demonstrated that the perception of pain can be affected by factors such as mood, ethnicity, and culture. Thus, the perception of pain is _____.

    Answers: **24-1.** fast, slow, slow **24-2.** subjective.

25. **Explain the gate-control theory of pain perception and recent findings related to it.**

    25-1.   Answer the following questions regarding the perception of pain:

    (a) What phenomenon did the gate-control theory of pain perception attempt to explain?

    (b) What effect do endorphins have with respect to pain?

(c) What seems to be the role of the descending neural pathway that appears to originate in the periaqueductual gray (PAG) area in the midbrain?

Answers: 25-1. (a) Why the perception of pain is so subjective. (b) An analgesic, or pain-relieving, effect. (c) It mediates the suppression of pain.

OUR OTHER SENSES

26. Describe the perceptual experiences mediated by the kinesthetic and vestibular senses.

26-1. The system that monitors the positions of various parts of the body is called the _____ system. This system sends information to the brain about body position and movement obtained from receptors located in the joints and _____.

26-2. The system that monitors the body's location in space is called the _____ system. The receptors for the vestibular system are primarily hair cells contained within the _____ canals in the inner ear.

26-3. What point does the text make about the kinesthetic and vestibular systems, and indeed all sensory systems, in carrying out their tasks?

Answers: 26-1. kinesthetic, muscles **26-2.** vestibular, semicircular **26-3.** They integrate information from other senses (in carrying out their tasks).

REFLECTING ON THE CHAPTER'S THEMES

27. Explain how this chapter highlighted three of the text's unifying themes.

27-1. The fact that competing theories of both color vision and pitch were eventually reconciled attests to the value of theoretical diversity. Why is this?

27-2. Why must our experience of the world always be highly subjective?

27-3. What do cultural variations in depth perception, taste preferences, and pain tolerance tell us about the physiological basis of perception?

Answers: 27-1. They drove and guided the research that resolved the conflicts. **27-2.** The perceptual processes themselves are inherently subjective. **27-3.** That it is subject to cultural influences.

28. **Discuss how the Impressionists, Cubists, and Surrealists used various principles of visual perception.**

28-1.   After reading the Application section in your text, try and answer the following questions by only looking at the paintings:

_____ (a) Which cubist painting depends particularly on the Gestalt principles of proximity and similarity for its effect?

_____ (b) Which surrealist painting makes use of a reversible figure to enhance a feeling of fantasy?

_____ (c) Which two impressionist paintings make use of color mixing to illustrate how different spots of colors can be blended into a picture that is more than the sum of its parts?

_____ (d) Which cubist painting uses proximity, similarity, and closure to allow you to see its abstract subject (feature analysis applied to canvas)?

Answers: **28-1.** (a) Figure 4.60, (b) Figure 4.61, (c) Figures 4.56 and 4.57, (d) Figure 4.58.

29. **Discuss how Escher, Vasarely, and Magritte used various principles of visual perception.**

29-1.   After reading the Application section in your text, try and answer the following questions by only looking at the paintings.

_____ (a) Which painting uses variations in context to make identical triangles appear very different?

_____ (b) Which two paintings incorporate impossible figures to achieve their effect?

_____ (c) Which painting makes particular use of texture gradient and light and dark shadow to convey the impression of depth?

Answers: **29-1.** (a) Figure 4.65 (b) Figures 4.62, 4.63, (c) Figure 4.64.

30. **Explain how contrast effects can be manipulated to influence or distort judgments.**

30-1.   Which of the following contrast strategies, the door in the face technique or employing comparitors, is being illustrated in the following situations:

(a) You want to hit the Florida beaches for Spring Break, but you need extra money from home. Realizing this is going to be a hard sell, you first ask for a week in Paris and then try and settle for the beaches.

(b) When your lover catches you in an indiscretion, you quickly point out many more serious infractions by friends and acquaintances.

30-2.   Both of these strategies illustrate the point that our perceptions and judgments are _____.

Answers: **30-1.** (a) the foot in the door technique (b) employing comparitors **30-2.** subjective.

Review of Key Terms

Absolute threshold
Additive color mixing
Afterimage
Auditory localization
Basilar membrane
Binocular depth cues
Bottom-up processing
Cochlea
Color blindness
Comparitors
Complimentary colors
Cones
Convergence
Dark adaptation
Depth perception
Distal stimuli
Door-in-the-face technique
Farsightedness
Feature analysis
Feature detectors
Fovea
Frequency theory

Gate-control theory
Gustatory system
Impossible figures
Inattentional blindness
Just noticeable difference (JND)
Kinesthetic system
Lateral antagonism
Lens
Light adaptation
Monocular depth cues
Motion parallax
Nearsightedness
Olfactory system
Opponent process theory
Optic chiasm
Optic disk
Parallel processing
Perception
Perceptual constancy
Perceptual hypothesis
Perceptual set
Phi phenomenon

Pictorial depth cues
Place theory
Proximal stimuli
Psychophysics
Pupil
Receptive field of a visual cell
Retina
Retinal disparity
Reversible figure
Rods
Sensation
Sensory adaptation
Signal-detection theory
Subjective contours
Subliminal perception
Subtractive color mixing
Top-down processing
Trichromatic theory
Vestibular system
Visual illusion
Volley principle
Weber's law

_____ 1. The stimulation of sense organs.

_____ 2. The selection, organization, and interpretation of sensory input.

_____ 3. The study of how physical stimuli are translated into psychological (sensory) experience.

_____ 4. The failure to see fully visible objects or events because our attention is focused elsewhere.

_____ 5. The minimum amount of stimulation that can be detected by an organism for a specific type of sensory input

_____ 6. The smallest amount of difference in the amount of stimulation that can be detected in a sense.

_____ 7. States that the size of a just noticeable difference is a constant proportion of the size of the initial stimulus.

_____ 8. Proposes that sensory sensitivity depends on a variety of factors besides the physical intensity of the stimulus.

_____ 9. Involves a gradual decline in sensitivity to prolonged stimulation.

_____ 10. Our sense of smell.

_____ 11. The transparent eye structure that focuses the light rays falling on the retina.

_____ 12. The opening in the center of the iris that helps regulate the amount of light passing into the rear chamber of the eye.

_____ 13. The neural tissue lining the inside back surface of the eye that absorbs light, processes images, and sends visual information to the brain.

_____ 14. Specialized receptors that play a key role in daylight vision and color vision.

_____ 15. Specialized receptors that play a key role in night vision and peripheral vision.

_____ 16. A tiny spot in the center of the retina that contains only cones, where visual acuity is greatest.

_____ 17. The process in which the eyes become more sensitive to light in low illumination.

_____ 18. The process in which the eyes become less sensitive to light in high illumination.

_____ 19. A variety of deficiencies in the ability to distinguish among colors.

_____ 20. The retinal area that, when stimulated, affects the firing of a particular cell.

_____ 21. A hole in the retina where the optic nerve fibers exit the eye (the blind spot).

_____ 22. Neurons that respond selectively to very specific features of more complex stimuli.

_____ 23. Works by removing some wavelengths of light, leaving less light than was originally there.

_____ 24. Works by superimposing lights, leaving more light in the mixture than in any one light by itself.

_____ 25. Proposes that the human eye has three types of receptors with differing sensitivities to different wavelengths.

_____ 26. Pairs of colors that can be added together to produce gray tones.

_____ 27. A visual image that persists after a stimulus is removed.

_____ 28. Proposes that color is perceived in three channels, where an either-or response is made to pairs of antagonistic colors.

_____ 29. A drawing compatible with two different interpretations that can shift back and forth.

_____ 30. A readiness to perceive a stimulus in a particular way.

_____ 31. A process in which we detect specific elements in visual input and assemble these elements into a more complex form.

_____ 32. A progression from individual elements to the whole.

_____ 33. A progression from the whole to the individual elements.

_____ 34. An inexplicable discrepancy between the appearance of a visual stimulus and its physical reality.

_____ 35. The illusion of movement created by presenting visual stimuli in rapid succession.

_____ 36. Stimuli that lie in the distance (in the world outside us).

_____ 37. The stimulus energies that impinge directly on our sensory receptors.

_____ 38. An inference about what distal stimuli could be responsible for the proximal stimuli sensed.

_____ 39. Involves our interpretation of visual cues that tell us how near or far away objects are.

_____ 40. Clues about distance that are obtained by comparing the differing views of two eyes.

_____ 41. Clues about distance that are obtained from the image in either eye alone.

_____ 42. A tendency to experience a stable perception in the face of constantly changing sensory input.

_____ 43. Locating the source of a sound in space.

_____ 44. A fluid-filled, coiled tunnel that makes up the largest part of the inner ear.

_____ **45.** A membrane running the length of the cochlea that holds the actual auditory receptors, called hair cells.

_____ **46.** Holds that our perception of pitch corresponds to the vibration of different portions, or places, along the basilar membrane.

_____ **47.** Holds that our perception of pitch corresponds to the rate, or frequency, at which the entire basilar membrane vibrates.

_____ **48.** Holds that groups of auditory nerve fibers fire neural impulses in rapid succession, creating volleys of impulses.

_____ **49.** Our sense of taste.

_____ **50.** Occurs when neural activity in a cell opposes activity in surrounding cells.

_____ **51.** Objects that can be represented in two-dimensional figures but cannot exist in three-dimensional space.

_____ **52.** Holds that incoming pain sensations pass through a "gate" in the spinal cord that can be opened or closed.

_____ **53.** The sense that monitors the positions of the various parts of the body.

_____ **54.** The system that provides the sense of balance.

_____ **55.** The point at which the optic nerves from the inside half of each eye cross over and then project to the opposite half of the brain.

_____ **56.** Clues about distance that can be given in a flat picture.

_____ **57.** The registration of sensory input without conscious awareness.

_____ **58.** Involves simultaneously extracting different kinds of information from the same input.

_____ **59.** A case in which close objects are seen clearly but distant objects appear blurry.

_____ **60.** A case in which distant objects are seen clearly but close objects are blurry.

_____ **61.** A depth cue which refers to the fact that objects within 25 feet project images to slightly different locations on your right and left retinas, so the right and left eyes see slightly different images.

_____ **62.** A binocular cue which involves sensing the eyes converging toward each other as they focus on closer objects.

_____ **63.** A monocular depth cue which involves images of objects at different distances moving across the retina at different rates.

_____ **64.** The perception of contours where none actually exist.

_____ **65.** People, objects, events, and other standards that are used as a baseline for comparitors in judgments.

_____ **66.** Involves making a very large request that is likely to be turned down to increase the chances that people will agree to a smaller request.

Answers: 1. sensation **2.** perception **3.** psychophysics **4.** inattentional blindness **5.** absolute threshold **6.** just noticeable difference (JND) **7.** Weber's law **8.** signal detection theory **9.** sensory adaptation **10.** olfactory system **11.** lens **12.** pupil **13.** retina **14.** cones **15.** rods **16.** fovea **17.** dark adaptation **18.** light adaptation **19.** color blindness **20.** receptive field of a visual cell **21.** optic disk **22.** feature detectors **23.** subtractive color mixing **24.** additive color mixing **25.** trichromatic theory of color vision **26.** complementary colors **27.** afterimage **28.** opponent process theory of color vision **29.** reversible figure **30.** perceptual set **31.** feature analysis **32.** bottom-up processing **33.** top-down processing **34.** visual illusion **35.** phi phenomenon **36.** distal stimuli **37.** proximal stimuli **38.** perceptual hypothesis **39.** depth perception **40.** binocular cues **41.** monocular cues **42.** perceptual constancy **43.** auditory localization **44.** cochlea **45.** basilar membrane **46.** place theory **47.** frequency theory **48.** volley principle **49.** gustatory system **50.** lateral antagonism **51.** impossible figures **52.** gate-control theory **53.** kinesthetic sense **54.** vestibular system **55.** optic chiasm **56.** pictorial depth cues **57.** subliminal perception **58.** parallel processing **59.** nearsightedness **60.** farsightedness

61. retinal disparity **62**. convergence **63**. motion parallax **64**. subjective contours **65**. comparitors **66**. door-in-the-face technique

Review of Key People

Linda Bartoshuk
Gustav Fechner

Herman von Helmholtz
David Hubel and Torston Wiesel

Ronald Melzack and Patrick Wall
Max Wertheimer

_____   **1.**   Pioneered the early work in the detection of thresholds.

_____   **2.**   These two men won the Nobel prize for their discovery of feature detector cells in the retina.

_____   **3.**   One of the originators of the trichromatic theory of color vision.

_____   **4.**   Made use of the phi phenomenon to illustrate some of the basic principles of Gestalt psychology.

_____   **5.**   A leading authority on taste research.

_____   **6.**   Proposed a gate-control theory of pain.

Answers: 1. Fechner **2.** Hubel and Wiesel **3.** Helmholtz **4.** Wertheimer **5.** Bartoshuk **6.** Melzack and Wall.

Self-Quiz

1. We have gathered 50 people together to determine the absolute threshold on a particular tone. The absolute threshold will have been reached when:
    a. the first person reports hearing the tone
    b. all persons report hearing the tone
    c. 25 persons report hearing the tone
    d. no persons are able to hear the tone

2. Research shows that subliminal perception:
    a. cannot be reliably demonstrated
    b. produces only moderate persuasive effects
    c. can exert powerful persuasive effects
    d. does not show adaptation effects

3. Which of the following places a major emphasis on decision-making processes in the perception of thresholds?
    a. Weber's law
    b. Fechner's law
    c. Steven's power factor
    d. signal detection theory

4. The receiving area of a retinal cell is called the:
    a. cone
    b. fovial field
    c. rod
    d. receptive field

5. The fact that we are generally much more aware of the changes in our sensory environments rather than the constants is the general idea behind:
   a. signal detection theory
   b. sensory adaptation
   c. the method of constant stimuli
   d. sensory equalization

6. The major difference between a green light and a blue light is the:
   a. wave frequency
   b. wave purity
   c. wavelength
   d. wave saturation

7. Which theory of color vision best explains why the color of an afterimage is the complement of the original color?
   a. the trichromatic theory
   b. the opponent process theory
   c. both theories explain this phenomenon equally well
   d. neither theory adequately explains this phenomenon

8. When watching a wild car chase scene in a movie we can be thankful for:
   a. chunking
   b. lateral processing
   c. bottom-up processing
   d. the phi phenomenon

9. Which of the following is not one of the pictorial depth cues?
   a. convergence
   b. linear perspective
   c. relative height
   d. texture gradients

10. Which of the following is an example of what is meant by perceptual constancy?
    a. Moths are always attracted to light.
    b. A round pie tin always appears to us as round.
    c. Proximal and distal stimuli are always identical.
    d. Absolute thresholds always remain the same.

11. Gate-control theory is an attempt to explain:
    a. why the perception of pain is so subjective
    b. how subliminal perception works
    c. how receptive fields influence one another
    d. how the optic chiasm directs visual information

12. Research has shown that the perception of pitch depends on:
    a. the area stimulated on the basilar membrane
    b. the frequency at which the basilar membrane vibrates
    c. both the area stimulated and the frequency at which the basilar membrane vibrates
    d. the frequency at which the ossicles vibrate

13. You are sitting in an arena watching the end of a very close basketball game and you fail to notice that one of the referees has removed his shirt. This an example of:
    a. a visual illusion.
    b. inattentional blindness.
    c. retinal disparity.
    d. attentional blindness.

14. Our sense of balance depends upon:
    a. the semicircular canals
    b. the kinesthetic senses
    c. visual cues
    d. all of the above are involved in our sense of balance

15. Which of the following terms perhaps best describes human perception?
    a. accurate
    b. objective
    c. subjective
    d. unknowable

16. When judging the steepness of a hill, human beings:
    a. are rather accurate
    b. tend to underestimate the steepness
    c. tend to overestimate the steepness
    d. are better when making visual judgments of steepness than judgments based on touch

17. When politicians point out that their misdeeds are only miniscule when judged against their competitors, they are making use of:
    a. the door-in-the-face technique
    b. comparitors
    c. bottom-up processing
    d. top-down processing

Answers: 1. c **2.** b **3.** d **4.** d **5.** b **6.** c **7.** b **8.** d **9.** a **10.** b **11.** a **12.** c **13.** bc **14.** d **15.** c **16.** c **17.** b.

InfoTrac Keywords

Dark Adaptation
Depth Perception

Optical Illusions

Reversible Figure

Chapter Five
VARIATIONS IN CONSCIOUSNESS

Review of Key Ideas

ON THE NATURE OF CONSCIOUSNESS

1. **Discuss the nature and evolution of consciousness.**

   1-1. The personal awareness of internal and external events is how psychologists define _____.
   Consciousness is like a moving stream in that it is constantly_____.

   1-2. Not only is consciousness constantly changing, it also exists at different levels. Freud believed that at its
   deepest level we would find the _____. Moreover, there is a _____ of
   levels of awareness from the conscious to the unconscious. There (is/is not) some awareness during sleep
   and even while under anesthesia.

   1-3. Consciousness must have evolved because it increased the likelihood of survival and reproductive
   success, perhaps because it allowed for forethought and _____. Several other equally plausible explanations have also been offered, but as of now (only one/none) has been supported by empirical
   evidence.

   Answers: 1-1. consciousness, changing **1-2.** unconscious, continuum, is **1-3.** planning, none.

2. **Discuss the relationship between consciousness and EEG activity.**

   2-1. EEG recordings reveal that there (is/is not) some relationship between brain waves and levels of consciousness. There are four principal bands of brain wave activity, based on the frequency of the wave
   patterns, these are alpha, beta, delta, and theta. Identify these wave patterns from their descriptions given
   below.

   _____ (a) alert (13-24 cps)   _____ (c) deep sleep (4-7 cps)

   _____ (b) relaxed (8-12 cps)   _____ (d) deepest sleep (1-4 cps)

2-2. While variations in consciousness are correlated with variations in brain activity, the causal basis of this relationship remains _____.

Answers: **2-1.** is (a) beta (b) alpha (c) theta (d) delta **2-2.** unknown.

BIOLOGICAL RHYTHMS AND SLEEP

3. **Summarize what is known about our biological clocks and their relationship to sleep.**

3-1. One of the biological rhythms, the daily or 24-hour circadian rhythm, is influential in the regulation of sleep and wakefulness. This is accomplished through the regulation of several bodily processes, including body temperature. Describe below what happens to body temperature when we:

(a) begin to fall asleep.

(b) continue into deeper sleep.

(c) begin to awaken.

3-2. There is evidence that exposure to _____ is responsible for regulating the 24-hour circadian clock. Sunlight affects the suprachiasmatic nucleus in the hypothalamus, which in turn signals the _____ gland. The pineal gland then secretes the hormone melatonin, which is a major player in adjusting biological clocks. Getting out of sync with the circadian rhythm is more likely to occur when the days are (shortened/lengthened).

Answers: **3-1.** (a) temperature decreases (b) temperature continues to decrease (c) temperature begins to increase **3-2.** light (or sunlight), pineal, shortened.

4. **Discuss various methods of helping people to realign their circadian rhythms.**

4-1. One method for realigning circadian rhythms is to take small doses of the hormone _____. Research results using this method produce (consistent/inconsistent) results.

4-2. Researchers have also tried carefully timed exposure to bright _____. The effects using this technique have been modest and (consistent/inconsistent).

4-3. Another strategy to help rotating shift workers involves gradually changing their rotation schedules by moving through progressively (earlier/later) starting times.

Answers: **4-1.** melatonin, inconsistent. **4-2.** light, inconsistent **4-3.** later.

5. Describe how sleep research is conducted.

5-1. Sleep research is conducted by electronically monitoring various bodily activities such as brain waves, muscular activity, eye movements, and so on, while persons actually _____ in a specially prepared laboratory setting. Through the use of a television camera or a window, researchers also _____ the subjects during sleep.

Answers: **5-1.** sleep, observe (watch).

6. Describe how the sleep cycle evolves through the night.

6-1. Answer the following questions regarding the sleep cycle.

(a) How many stages are there in one sleep cycle?

(b) Which two stages make up slow-wave sleep?

(c) Which brain waves are prominent during slow-wave sleep?

Answers: **6-1.** (a) four (or five if you've included REM sleep) (b) 3 and 4 (c) delta.

7. Compare and contrast REM and NREM sleep.

7-1. What particularly differentiates NREM sleep from rapid eye movement sleep, or _____ sleep, is that during REM sleep the brain wave pattern resembles that of a person who is wide _____. However, REM sleep is actually a fifth stage of sleep in which the muscle tone is extremely relaxed, and the sleeper is virtually _____. It is also during REM sleep that vivid _____ is most likely to occur.

7-2. The sleep cycle is repeated approximately _____ times during an average night of sleep. NREM sleep dominates the early part of the sleep period, but _____ sleep and dreaming dominate the later stages of sleep. As one progresses through the night, the depth of NREM sleep tends to progressively (increase/decrease).

Answers: **7-1.** REM, awake, paralyzed, dreaming **7-2.** four, REM, decrease.

8. Summarize age trends in patterns of sleep.

8-1. Not only do newborns sleep more frequently and for more total hours during a day than do adults, they also spend a greater proportion of time in _____ sleep. As they grow older, children move toward longer but (more/less) frequent sleep periods, and the total proportion of REM sleep declines from about 50 percent to the adult level of about _____ percent. During adulthood there is a gradual shift towards the (lighter/deeper) stages of sleep.

Answers: **8-1.** REM, less, 20, lighter.

9. **Summarize how culture influences sleep patterns.**

9-1.   Answer the following questions regarding sleeping patterns across cultures.

(a)   Which pattern, children sleeping with their parents (co-sleeping) or children sleeping alone, is the most widely practiced?

(b)   Where are the "siesta" cultures generally located?

(c)   What is the effect of industrialization on the practice of siestas?

Answers: 9-1. (a) co-sleeping (b) tropical regions (c) The practice declines.

10. **Discuss the neural and evolutionary basis of sleep.**

10-1.   Sleep and wakefulness is apparently under the control of several neural structures, but one that appears to be particularly essential for both sleep and wakefulness is the reticular _____. When a part of this system, called the ascending _____ _____ system (ARAS), is severed in cats, the cats remain in continuous _____. When the ARAS is stimulated in normal cats, they act _____.

10-2.   However, many other brain structures and at least five neurotransmitters are also involved in the regulation of sleep. There (is/is not) a "sleep center" in the brain, nor is there any one neurotransmitter that serves as a _____ chemical.

10-3.   At least three hypotheses attempt to account for the evolutionary (adaptive) basis of sleep: sleep evolved to conserve energy, it reduces exposure to many sources of danger, and it helps to restore body resources. Which hypothesis has the greater empirical support?

Answers: 10-1. formation, reticular activating, sleep, alert or awake **10-2.** is not, sleep **10-3.** Sleep evolved to conserve energy.

11. **Summarize evidence on the effects of complete and partial sleep deprivation, including the chapter's Featured Study.**

11-1.   Answer the following questions regarding the effects of different kinds of sleep deprivation.

(a)   While both complete and partial sleep deprivation have a negative effect on mood and also on performance on both cognitive and perceptual-motor tasks, what is rather surprising about the degree of these negative effects?

(b)   In what way might increased sleepiness be a major problem with respect to the workplace?

11-2. In the Featured Study it was observed that sleep deprived students performed substantially worse on a cognitive task than non-deprived students. How did the sleep-deprived students rate their own effort, concentration, and performance?

Answers: 11-1. (a) The effects tend to be modest. (b) It can lead to increased accidents. **11-2.** They were unaware of these deficits.

12. Discuss the effects of selective deprivation of REM sleep and slow-wave sleep.

12-1. Studies in which subjects were selectively deprived of REM sleep, leaving NREM sleep undisturbed, found (substantial/little) negative effects from REM deprivation. One curious effect that has been noted from selective REM deprivation is that subjects tend to increase their amount of (NREM/REM) sleep when given the first opportunity to do so. This same rebound effect has also been found with stages 3 and 4, or _____-_____ sleep.

Answers: 12-1. little, REM, slow-wave.

13. Discuss the prevalence, causes, and treatments of insomnia.

13-1. While practically everybody will suffer from occasional bouts of insomnia, it is estimated that about _____ of adults will suffer from occasional insomnia, and of these about _____ will suffer from chronic problems with insomnia. There are three basic types of insomnia, which are easily remembered because one type occurs at the beginning of sleep, one type during sleep, and the third type at the end of sleep. Thus, one type involves difficulty in initially _____ asleep; one type involves difficulty in _____ asleep; and one type involves persistent _____ awakening.

13-2. While there are a number of different causes of insomnia, most of them appear to revolve around the anxiety and emotional reactions that result from the _____ of everyday living. Also health problems and taking certain _____ can be a factor.

13-3. As there are many different causes of insomnia, it seems reasonable that there (is/is not) a single form of treatment. However, researchers agree that the most commonly used form of treatment, using sedatives, or _____ pills, is not the treatment of choice. Evidence shows that while sleeping pills do promote sleep, they also interfere with both the slow-wave and _____ part of the sleep cycle.

Answers: 13-1. 34%-35%, 15%-17%, falling, remaining, early **13-2.** stress (or problems), drugs **13-3.** is not, sleeping, REM.

14. Describe the symptoms of narcolepsy, sleep apnea, night terrors, nightmares, and somnambulism.

14-1. Described below are five different case histories of persons suffering from five different sleep disorders. Make the appropriate diagnosis for each one.

(a) Throckmorton is a young child who frequently wakes up during the night with a loud piercing cry, but cannot describe what happened to him; he usually returns quickly to sleep. A night spent at the sleep clinic discloses that the episodes generally occur during NREM sleep. Throckmorton is most likely suffering from _____ _____.

(b) Gazelda reports that occasionally, even when typing a term paper or driving a car, she will quickly drop into a deep sleep. The sleep is often accompanied by dreams, which indicates REM sleep. Gazelda is most likely suffering from _____.

(c) Ajax is a young child who frequently wakes up terrified and relates vivid dreams to his parents who rush to comfort him. The family physician tells the parents there is probably nothing to worry about, unless these episodes persist, and that the child will most likely outgrow this problem. The diagnosis here is probably _____.

(d) Mr. Whistletoe will occasionally get up late at night and walk around the house. Unfortunately, Mr. Whistletoe is completely unaware of this behavior and usually returns to bed without awakening. Upon awakening the next morning he is surprised by a new bruise on his leg, and he wonders how the chair in the living room got tipped over. Mr. Whistletoe would be diagnosed as suffering from _____, or sleepwalking.

(e) Henrietta complains that during a night's sleep, she frequently wakes up gasping for breath. A visit to the sleep clinic discloses that, indeed, she does stop breathing for brief periods all through the night. Henrietta undoubtedly suffers from _____ _____.

Answers: 14-1. (a) night terrors (b) narcolepsy (c) nightmares (d) somnambulism (e) sleep apnea.

THE WORLD OF DREAMS

15. Discuss the nature of dreams.

15-1. The conventional view of dreams is that they are mental experiences during REM sleep and often have a bizarre story like quality and vivid imagery. What do many theorists now think of this view?

15-2. In what way do non-REM dreams appear to differ from REM dreams?

Answers: 15-1. They question many aspects of this view. 15-2. They are less vivid and less story like.

16. Summarize findings on dream content.

16-1. Calvin Hall, who analyzed the contents of more than 10,000 dreams, concluded that the content of most dreams is (exotic/mundane). Moreover, he found that dreams seldom involve events that are not centered on _____. Hall also found that dreams tend to be like soap operas in that they revolve around such common themes as misfortune, _____, and _____.

16-2. Answer the following questions regarding the differences in dream content between men and women. Which sex is more likely to dream about:

_____ (a) acting aggressively

_____ (b) sex with strangers

_____ (c) children

16-3. What did Freud mean when he stated that our dreams reflect day residue?

16-4. What other factor has an inconsistent effect on our dreams?

Answers: 16-1. mundane, ourselves, sex, aggression **16-2.** (a) men (b) men (c) women **16-3.** They are influenced by what happens to us in our daily lives. **16-4.** external stimuli (dripping water, ringing phones, etc.).

17. Describe some cultural variations in beliefs about the nature and importance of dreams.

17-1. Say which of the following statements about dreams is more characteristic of Western cultures (W) or non-Western cultures (NW).

_____ (a) Little significance paid to the meaning of dreams.

_____ (b) Remembering dreams is important.

_____ (c) Believe that dreams may provide information about the future.

_____ (d) Are likely to report frequent dreams involving food.

Answers: 17-1. (a) W (b) NW (c) NW (d) Persons from any culture who are chronically hungry.

18. Describe the three theories of dreaming covered in the chapter.

18-1. The text mentions three theories as to why we need to dream. Tell what cognitive purpose, if any, each of these theories proposes as to the purpose of dreaming.

(a) This was Sigmund Freud's theory about the need to dream.

(b) This theory proposed by Rosalind Cartwright is cognizant of the fact that dreams are not restricted by logic or reality.

(c) The activation-synthesis theory of Hobson and McCarley proposes that dreams occur as side effects of neural activation of the cortex by lower brain centers.

Answers: 18-1. (a) Dreams serve the purpose of wish fulfillment. (b) Dreams allow for creative problem solving. (c) Dreams serve no cognitive purpose.

HYPNOSIS: ALTERED CONSCIOUSNESS OR ROLE PLAYING?

19. Discuss hypnotic susceptibility, and list some prominent effects of hypnosis.

19-1. While there are many different hypnotic induction techniques, they all lead to a heightened state of _____. Research shows that individuals (do/do not) vary in their susceptibility to hypnotic induction. In fact, approximately _____ percent of the population does not respond at all, and approximately _____ percent are highly susceptible to hypnotic induction. People who are highly susceptible to suggestions under hypnosis are also responsive to suggestions without being hypnotized. These people appear to have a trait characterized as _____ suggestibility.

19-2. The text lists several of the more prominent effects that can be produced by hypnosis. Identify these effects from their descriptions given below.

(a) Reducing awareness of pain. _____

(b) Engaging in acts one would not ordinarily do. _____

(c) Perceiving things that do not exist or failing to perceive things that do exist. _____

(d) Claiming that sour foods taste sweet. _____ _____

(e) Carrying out suggestions following the hypnotic induction session. _____ _____

(f) Claiming to forget what occurred during the induction session. _____

Answers: 19-1. suggestibility, do, 10, 10, imaginative **19-2.** (a) anesthetic (b) disinhibition (c) hallucinations
(d) sensory distortions (e) posthypnotic suggestions (f) amnesia.

20. Explain the role-playing and altered-states theories of hypnosis.

20-1. A theory of hypnosis proposed by Barber and Orne is that hypnosis is really a form of acting or role-playing in which the subjects are simply playing as if they are hypnotized. What two lines of evidence support this theory?

20-2. A theory of hypnosis proposed by Hilgard is that hypnosis does in fact result in an altered state of consciousness. This theory holds that hypnosis results in a dissociation or _____ of consciousness into two parts. One half of the divided consciousness communicates with the hypnotist while the other half remains _____, even from the hypnotized subject. In this case, pain perceived by the "hidden" part of the consciousness (is/is not) reported to the "aware" part of consciousness. The divided state of consciousness proposed by Hilgard (is/is not) a common experience in everyday life. One such example of this commonly experienced state is appropriately called highway _____.

Answers: 20-1. Nonhypnotized subjects can duplicate the feats of hypnotized subjects and it has been shown that hypnotized subjects are often merely acting out their expectations of how hypnotized subjects should act.
20-2. splitting or dividing, hidden, is not, is, hypnosis.

MEDITATION: PURE CONSCIOUSNESS OR RELAXATION?

21. Summarize the evidence on the physiological correlates and long-term benefits of meditation.

21-1. Certain short-term physiological changes may occur during meditation. One of the most prominent of these changes is that EEG brain waves change from the rapid beta waves to the slower _____ and theta waves. This change to slower waves is accompanied by (an increase/a decrease) in metabolic activity such as heart rate, oxygen consumption, etc. All of these physiological changes are characteristic of a normal state of _____. This state of relaxation (is/is not) unique to meditation.

21-2. Some recent brain imaging techniques have shown that experienced meditators (do/do not) show high activity in the prefrontal cortex (indicating focused attention) and low activity in an area in the parietal lobe (indicating lowered body awareness).

21-3. The claims made for the long-term effects of meditation may have some merit in that some studies have shown that subjects had lower levels of some stress hormones, improved mental health, and reduced anxiety and drug abuse. These changes can (<u>also/not</u>) be induced by other commonly used methods for inducing relaxation. The claim that meditation can produce a unique state of pure consciousness (<u>has/has not</u>) been conclusively proven.

Answers: 21-1. alpha, a decrease, relaxation, is not **21-2.** do **21-3.** also, has not.

ALTERING CONSCIOUSNESS WITH DRUGS

22. List and describe the major types of abused drugs and their effects.

22-1. The text list six different categories of psychoactive drugs; identify these drugs from the descriptions given below.

(a) This drug is the most widely used, and abused, of all psychoactive drugs and produces a relaxed euphoria that temporarily boosts self-esteem. Wine and beer are both examples of the drug _____.

(b) While this class of drugs derived from opium is effective at relieving pain, it can also produce a state of euphoria, which is the principal reason that opiates, or _____, are attractive to recreational users.

(c) The drugs in this class, such as LSD, mescaline and psilocybin, are known for their ability to distort sensory and perceptual experiences, which is why they are given the collective name of _____.

(d) The drugs in this class include marijuana, hashish, and THC. Although they vary in potency, each of them can produce a mild and easygoing state of euphoria along with enhanced sensory awareness and a distorted sense of time. This class of drugs gets its name from the hemp plant _____ from which they are all derived.

(e) This class of drugs is known for its sleep inducing (sedation) and behavioral depression effects, resulting in tension reduction and a relaxed state of intoxication. While there are several different drugs in this class, the barbiturates are the most widely abused. Commonly known as "downers", they are more properly called _____.

(f) This class of drugs produces arousal in the central nervous system and ranges from mildly arousing drugs like caffeine and nicotine, to strongly arousing drugs like cocaine and the amphetamines. Known for their ability to produce an energetic euphoria, the drugs in this class go by the name of _____.

(g) This drug, also known as ecstacy, is a compound related to both amphetamines and mescaline and other hallucinogens. It produces a short-lived high.

Answers: 22-1. (a) alcohol (b) narcotics (c) hallucinogens (d) cannabis (e) sedatives (f) stimulants (g) MDMA.

23. **Summarize which drugs carry the greatest risk of tolerance, physical dependence, and psychological dependence.**

23-1.   When a person must continue taking a drug to avoid withdrawal illness or addiction, _____ dependence is said to occur. When a person must continue taking a drug to satisfy intense emotional craving for the drug, then _____ dependence is said to occur.

23-2.   As can be seen in Table 5.5 in the text, the three riskiest drugs in terms of tolerance and physical and psychological dependence are:

23-3.   What physiological change in the brain appears to facilitate both physical and psychological dependence?

Answers: 23-1. physical, psychological **23-2.** narcotics/opiates, sedatives, stimulants **23-3.** alterations in synaptic transmission.

24. **Explain how psychoactive drugs exert their effects on the brain.**

24-1.   Psychoactive drugs work primarily by altering neurotransmitter activity between neurons at junctions called _____. For example, amphetamines increase the release of DA and NE and they also slow reuptake at DA and NE synapses. Similarly, the drug _____ mainly blocks reuptake at DA, NE, and serotonin synapses.

24-2.   Endorphins, produced naturally by the body, produce an effect very similar to that produced by _____ drugs.

24-3.   Virtually all abused drugs increase activity in the (mesolimbic) pathway, which has been characterized as a "_____ pathway."

Answers: 24-1. synapses, cocaine **24-2.** narcotic **24-3.** reward.

25. **Summarize evidence on the major physical health risks associated with drug abuse.**

25-1.   What two physical effects were found in the study in which rats were allowed unlimited access to heroin or cocaine, and which drug was the most deadly?

25-2.   There are three major ways in which drugs may affect physical health. The most dramatic way is when a person takes too much of a drug, or drugs, and dies of an _____. Another way is when drug usage directly damages bodily tissue; this is referred to as a _____ effect. The third way is when drug usage results in accidents, improper eating and sleeping habits, infections, etc. These effects are collectively called _____ effects.

Answers: 25-1. loss of body weight and death, cocaine **25-2.** overdose, direct, indirect.

26. **Discuss controversies about marijuana's health risks and preliminary evidence on the risks associated with MDMA use.**

26-1.   Say whether the following statements concerning marijuana are true or false.

_____ (a) Marijuana produces only a slight and insignificant decrease in the immune response.

_____ (b) Marijuana can have lasting effects on a male-smoker's sexual functioning.

_____ (c) Heavy use of marijuana can produce measurable impairments in attention and memory.

26-2.   Say whether the following statements regarding the long-term use of MDMA are true or false.

_____ (a) There is evidence linking heavy MDMA use with sleep disorders, depression, anxiety, or hostility.

_____ (b) There is no evidence linking MDMA use with subtle effects on cognitive function and memory deficits.

Answers: **26-1.** (a) true (b) false (c) true **26-2.** (a) true (b) false.

REFLECTING ON THE CHAPTER'S THEMES

27. **Explain how the chapter highlighted four of the text's unifying themes.**

27-1.   Identify which of the underlying themes (psychology evolves in a sociohistorical context, experience is subjective, cultures mold some aspects of behavior, and psychology is theoretically diverse) is illustrated by the following statements.

(a) Psychologists have followed many different approaches and developed many different theories in their attempt to understand consciousness.

(b) The study of consciousness by psychologists followed rather than preceded renewed public interest in this topic.

(c) There are striking individual differences in the way people respond to hypnosis, meditation, and drugs.

(d) The significance given to dreams and sleep patterns can be influenced by this factor.

Answers: **27-1.** (a) Psychology is theoretically diverse. (b) Psychology evolves in a sociohistorical context. (c) Experience is subjective. (d) Culture molds some aspects of behavior.

APPLICATION: ADDRESSING PRACTICAL QUESTIONS ABOUT SLEEP AND DREAMS

28. **Summarize evidence on common questions about sleep discussed in the Application.**

28-1.   Answer the following questions about sleep and napping.

(a) How much sleep do we require?

(b) While napping can be refreshing for most people, in what way can it prove inefficient?

(c) Why are drugs such as sedatives and alcohol likely to interfere with refreshing sleep?

(d) What does evidence show about the effectiveness of attempting to learn complex material, such as a foreign language, during deep sleep?

28-2. In addition to developing sensible daytime habits to combat insomnia, there are numerous methods for facilitating actually going to sleep. A common feature in all of them is that they generate a feeling of _____. Some methods generate a feeling of boredom, which is akin to relaxation. The important point here is that one (does/does not) ruminate on the heavy events in life when attempting to go to sleep.

Answers: 28-1. (a) It varies across individuals. (b) Insufficient time is spent in deeper sleep. (c) They interfere with REM and slow-wave sleep. (d) It is very ineffective. **28-2.** relaxation or calmness, does not.

29. Summarize evidence on the common questions about dreams discussed in the Application.

29-1. While there are some persons who claim they never dream, what is really happening is that they cannot _____ their dreams. Dreams are best recalled when waking occurs during or immediately following (REM/NREM) sleep. Determination and practice (can/cannot) improve one's ability to recall dreams. A dream whose action takes place over a 20-minute period will actually last for approximately _____ minutes.

29-2. Freud believed that dreams do require interpretation because their true meaning, which he called the _____ content, is symbolically encoded in the obvious plot of the dream, which he called the _____ content. Freud's theory that dreams carry hidden symbolic meaning would mean that dream interpretation (is/is not) a very complicated affair. More recent researchers now believe that dreams are (more/less) complicated than Freud believed. Calvin Hall makes the point that dreams require some interpretation simply because they are mostly (visual/verbal).

29-3. In what way does lucid dreaming differ from regular dreaming?

29-4. Indicate whether the following statements are "true" or "false".

_____ (a) Evidence shows that some control over one's dreams is possible, but it is not easy and results are not always consistent.

_____ (b) There have been several reported cases of persons reporting their own deaths as the result of fatal dreams.

_____ (c) It has been shown that subjects can communicate with researches using prearranged eye signals during lucid dreaming.

Answers: 29-1. remember (or recall), REM, can, 20 **29-2.** latent, manifest, is, less, visual **29-3.** In lucid dreaming one is aware that one is dreaming. **29-4.** (a) true (b) false (c) true.

CRITICAL THINKING APPLICATION

30. Discuss the influence of definitions and how they are sometimes misused as explanations for the phenomena they describe.

30-1. Whether alcoholism is a disease or a result of personal failure depends on _____ gets to make up the definition. In fact, there is (only one/no) conclusive way to determine if alcoholism is a disease.

30-2. To say that someone drinks too much because she is alcoholic is an example of _____ reasoning. Definitions can never serve as _____ of the thing they are defining.

Answers: **30-1.** who, no **30-2.** circular, explanations.

Review of Key Terms

Alcohol
Ascending reticular activating
    system (ARAS)
Biological rhythms
Cannabis
Circadian rhythms
Dissociation
Electroencephalograph (EEG)
Electromyograph (EMG)
Electrooculograph (EOG)
Hallucinogens

Hypnosis
Insomnia
Latent content
Lucid dreams
Manifest content
MDMA
Meditation
Narcolepsy
Narcotics or opiates
Nightmares
Night terrors

Non-REM (NREM) sleep
Physical dependence
Psychoactive drugs
Psychological dependence
REM sleep
Sedatives
Sleep apnea
Slow-wave sleep (SWS)
Somnambulism
Stimulants
Tolerance

_____ 1. A device that monitors the electrical activity of the brain.

_____ 2. A device that records muscle activity and tension.

_____ 3. A device that records eye movements.

_____ 4. Periodic fluctuations in physiological functioning.

_____ 5. The 24-hour biological cycles found in humans and many other species.

_____ 6. Sleep involving rapid eye movements.

_____ 7. Sleep stages 1 through 4, which are marked by an absence of rapid eye movements.

_____ 8. Consists of the afferent fibers running through the reticular formation that influence physiological arousal.

_____ 9. Drugs that are derived from opium that are capable of relieving pain. These drugs are also called narcotics.

_____ 10. Involves chronic problems in getting adequate sleep.

_____ 11. A disease marked by sudden and irresistible onsets of sleep during normal waking hours.

_____ 12. Reflexive grasping for air that awakens a person and disrupts sleep.

_____ 13. Abrupt awakenings from NREM sleep accompanied by intense autonomic arousal and feelings of panic.

_____ 14. Anxiety arousing dreams that lead to awakening, usually from REM sleep.

_____ 15. Occurs when a sleeping person arises and wanders about in deep NREM sleep.

_____ 16. A systematic procedure that typically produces a heightened state of suggestibility.

_____ 17. Involves a splitting off of mental processes into two separate, simultaneous streams of awareness.

_____ 18. A family of medical exercises in which a conscious attempt is made to focus attention in a nonanalytical way.

_____ 19. Chemical substances that modify mental, emotional, or behavioral functioning.

_____ 20. Sleep stages 3 and 4, in which low-frequency delta waves become prominent in EEG recordings.

_____ 21. Drugs that have sleep-inducing and behavioral depression effects.

_____ 22. Drugs that tend to increase central nervous system activation and behavioral activity.

_____ 23. A diverse group of drugs that have powerful effects on mental and emotional functioning, marked most prominently by distortions in sensory and perceptual experience.

_____ 24. The hemp plant from which marijuana, hashish, and THC are derived.

_____ 25. A variety of beverages containing ethyl alcohol.

_____ 26. A progressive decrease in a person's responsiveness to a drug.

_____ 27. A condition that exists when a person must continue to take a drug to avoid withdrawal illness.

_____ 28. A condition that exists when a person must continue to take a drug to satisfy mental and emotional craving for the drug.

_____ 29. Freud's term that refers to the plot of a dream at the surface level.

_____ 30. Freud's term that refers to the hidden or disguised meaning of events in a dream.

_____ 31. Dreams in which persons are aware that they are dreaming.

_____ 32. A drug, also known as ecstacy, compounded from both amphetamine and hallucinogens that produces a short-lived high.

Answers: 1. electroencephalograph (EEG) **2**. electromyograph (EMG) **3**. electrooculograph (EOG) **4**. biological rhythms **5**. circadian rhythms **6**. REM sleep **7**. non-REM sleep **8**. ascending reticular activating system (ARAS) **9**. narcotics or opiates **10**. insomnia **11**. narcolepsy **12**. sleep apnea **13**. night terrors **14**. nightmares **15**. somnambulism **16**. hypnosis **17**. dissociation **18**. meditation **19**. psychoactive drugs **20**. slow-wave sleep (SWS) **21**. sedatives **22**. stimulants **23**. hallucinogens **24**. cannabis **25**. alcohol **26**. tolerance **27**. physical dependence **28**. psychological dependence **29**. manifest content **30**. latent content **31**. lucid dreams **32**. MDMA.

Review of Key People

Theodore Barber   Sigmund Freud   J. Alan Hobson
Rosalind Cartwright   Calvin Hall   William James
William Dement   Ernest Hilgard

_____ 1. Originated the term, "the stream of consciousness".

_____ 2. Argued for the existence of the unconscious and the hidden meaning of dreams.

_____ 3. As one of the pioneers in early sleep research, he coined the term REM sleep.

_____ 4. After analyzing thousands of dreams, he concluded that their contents are generally quite mundane.

_____ 5. Proposes a problem-solving view as a reason for dreaming.

_____ 6. One of the authors of the role-playing theory of hypnosis.

_____ 7. A proponent of the altered state (divided consciousness) theory of hypnosis.

8. His activation-synthesis model proposes that dreams are only side effects of neural activation.

Answers: 1. James **2.** Freud **3.** Dement **4.** Hall **5.** Cartwright **6.** Barber **7.** Hilgard **8.** Hobson.

Self-Quiz

1. Which brain wave is probably operating while you are taking this quiz?
   a. alpha
   b. beta
   c. theta
   d. delta

2. What did William James mean by his tern "the stream of consciousness"?
   a. consciousness always remains at the same level
   b. consciousness never stops
   c. consciousness is constantly changing
   d. consciousness is beyond personal control

3. The circadian rhythm operates around a:
   a. 1-year cycle
   b. 28-day cycle
   c. 24-hour cycle
   d. 90-minute cycle

4. The most vivid dreams generally occur during:
   a. REM sleep
   b. NREM sleep
   c. the early hours of sleep
   d. when alpha brain waves are present

5. What appears to be responsible for regulating the circadian rhythm?
   a. amount of time spent sleeping
   b. amount of time spent awake
   c. cultural practices
   d. exposure to light

6. Severing the ascending reticular activating system in cats caused them to:
   a. become very aggressive
   b. become very fearful
   c. remain in continuous wakefulness
   d. remain in continuous sleep

7. The content of most dreams is usually:
   a. mundane
   b. exotic
   c. exciting
   d. erotic

8. Which of the following sleep disorders is most life threatening?
   a. nightmares
   b. narcolepsy
   c. sleep apnea
   d. somnambulism

9. Persons can be made to act as if they are hypnotized even without the use of hypnotic induction. This statement is:
   a. true
   b. false

10. Which of the following physiological changes is unique to meditation?
    a. increased alpha rhythms
    b. decreased heart rate
    c. decreased oxygen consumption
    d. All of these thing are common to many form of relaxation.

11. Psychoactive drugs exert their effect on the brain by:
    a. decreasing blood supply to the brain
    b. altering neurotransmitter activity
    c. breaking down essential brain amino acids
    d. penetrating the nucleus of the neurons

12. The most widely abused drug in the United States is:
    a. alcohol
    b. cocaine
    c. heroin
    d. hallucinogens

13. Which of the following is likely to produce highly subjective events?
    a. hypnosis
    b. meditation
    c. psychoactive drugs
    d. All of the above can produce highly subjective events.

14. Which of the following statements is correct?
    a. Most people do not dream in color.
    b. Practice will not improve the ability to recall dreams.
    c. From birth until death, everyone dreams.
    d. Dreams generally last only one or two minutes.

15. What was found in the Featured Study regarding the effects of sleep deprivation in college students?
    a. sleep deprivation had little effect on their ability to perform cognitive tasks
    b. sleep deprivation had a substantial negative effect on their mood
    c. sleep deprivation had a substantial positive effect on their ability to perform cognitive tasks because the students compensated by increasing their effort
    d. the students were unaware of the actual negative effect of the deprivation

   Answers: 1. b 2. c 3. c 4. a 5. d 6. d 7. a 8. b 9. a 10. d 11. b 12. a 13. d 14. c 15. d.

InfoTrac Keywords

Biological Rhythms   Meditation   REM Sleep
Hallucinogens

Chapter Six
LEARNING

Review of Key Ideas

CLASSICAL CONDITIONING

1. Describe Pavlov's demonstration of classical conditioning and the key elements in this form of learning.

1-1.   Classical conditioning is a type of learning that occurs when two stimuli are paired or associated closely in time. In Pavlov's initial demonstration, the two stimuli were a bell and _____.

1-2.   The response to one of the two stimuli occurs naturally and does not have to be learned or acquired through conditioning. This "unlearned" stimulus, in this case the food, is technically known as the _____ stimulus.

1-3.   The other stimulus is said to be neutral in the sense that it does not initially produce a response. When a response to this neutral stimulus is *acquired* or *learned*, the technical name for it is the _____ stimulus. In Pavlov's initial study the conditioned stimulus was the sound of a _____.

1-4.   The unconditioned stimulus in Pavlov's original study was the _____ and the conditioned stimulus was the _____. Salivation to the meat powder is known as the _____ response; salivation to the bell is termed the _____ response.

1-5.   Label the parts of the classical conditioning sequence. Place the commonly used abbreviations for these terms in the parentheses.

(a) meat: _____ (   )

(b) salivation to meat: _____ (   )

(c) bell: _____ (   )

(d) salivation to bell: _____ (   )

2. **Discuss how classical conditioning may shape phobias and physiological processes, including sexual arousal.**

2-1.   The kids in the neighborhood where I (R.S.) grew up used to dig tunnels in a neighbor's backyard. One day someone got stuck in the tunnel and couldn't get out. Eventually he got out, but after that he didn't want to play in tunnels again. To this day that person still has an intense fear not only of tunnels but of closed-in spaces in general. Label the parts of the classical conditioning process involved in the acquisition of the phobia of closed-in spaces. Use the abbreviations CS, CR, UCS, and UCR. (Hint: Even though "getting stuck" involves a behavior or response, it also has stimulus components.)

_____ getting stuck

_____ fear produced by getting stuck

_____ tunnels and closed-in spaces

_____ fear of tunnels and closed-in spaces

2-2.   The individual described above had developed an intense fear or phobia, acquired in part through the process of _____ conditioning. Other emotions can be conditioned as well. For example, the smell of smoke and Beemans' gum described in your text, the playing of "our song," and the sight of one's home after a long absence could all produce a pleasant emotional response (or perhaps a slightly weepy, sentimental feeling). The emotional responses to such smells, sounds, or sights are learned, so the stimuli that produce these responses would be considered _____ stimuli.

2-3.   Similarly, certain physiological responses can be conditioned. Label the parts of the conditioning process in the study on immunosuppression in rats described in the text. (Use the abbreviations CS, CR, UCS, and UCR.)

_____ the immunosuppressive drug

_____ unusual taste

_____ decreased antibody production produced by the drug

_____ decreased antibody production produced by the taste

2-4.   Sexual arousal can be classically conditioned as well. In quail as in humans, stimuli routinely paired with sex (e.g., red lights in the quail study; lingerie, mood music, etc. in humans) evidently become _____ stimuli for sexual arousal.

2-5.   In one variation of Domjan's studies with quail the conditioned stimuli even produced an increased release of _____ in males, a conditioned response with a clear evolutionary advantage. One implication of this study for evolutionary theory, then, is that the capacity for classical conditioning, in this case conditioning of sexual arousal, has _____ value for a species.

3. **Describe the classical conditioning phenomena of acquisition, extinction, and spontaneous recovery.**

3-1. *Acquisition* of a conditioned response occurs when the CS and UCS are contiguous, or paired. Not all pairings result in conditioning, however. What characteristics of a CS are more likely to produce acquisition of a CR?

3-2. Acquisition refers to the formation of a conditioned response. What is the term that refers to the weakening or disappearance of a CR? _____

3-3. Extinction in classical conditioning occurs when the _____ stimulus is presented *alone*, without the _____ stimulus.

3-4. After CRs are extinguished they may reappear, even without further conditioning.

   (a) For example, after extinction of a response, a dog may again show the conditioned response (e.g., salivation to a bell) when returned to the apparatus in which it was originally conditioned. What is the name of this type of "reappearance" of the CR? _____ _____

   (b) When, or under what circumstance, is spontaneous recovery likely to occur?

   (c) If an animal is extinguished in a different environment from the one in which conditioning took place, it is likely to again show a CR when returned to the original environment. What is the name of this effect? _____ _____

Answers: **3-1.** A novel or particularly intense CS is more likely to produce conditioning. **3-2.** extinction **3-3.** conditioned, unconditioned **3-4.** (a) spontaneous recovery (b) after extinction, following a period of nonexposure to the CS (c) the renewal effect.

4. **Describe the processes of generalization and discrimination and summarize the classic study of Little Albert.**

4-1. With regard to the case of Little Albert:

   (a) What was the CS?

   (b) The UCS?

4-2. Albert was also afraid of white dogs and white rabbits. What is the name of the process that resulted in his acquisition of these additional fear responses? _____

4-3. Why would Albert be more likely to develop a fear of a white rabbit, say, than a white car or a dark horse?

4-4. The more similar stimuli are to the CS, the more likely the organism will _____ from the CS to the other stimuli. The less similar stimuli are to the CS, the more likely the organism is to _____ them from the CS.

4-5. Casey (R.S.'s cat, now deceased) salivated when she heard the sound of food being dumped into her bowl. The process by which this salivary response was learned is _____ conditioning. The food is a(an) (CS/UCS/CR/UCR). The sound of the food is a(an) (CS/UCS/CR/UCR). Salivation to the sound is a(an) (CS/UCS/CR/UCR).

4-6. Pets are also likely to salivate when they hear other, similar sounds, like bags rustling in the kitchen or dishes being pulled from the cupboard. Salivation to these other sounds represents stimulus

_____.

4-7. With continued training, in which food is paired only with the sound of food entering the bowl and not with the other sounds, the animal will learn to salivate only to the rattling bowl. The process of learning to respond only to one particular stimulus and not to a range of similar stimuli is termed

_____.

Answers: **4-1.** (a) a white rat (b) a loud noise **4-2.** generalization **4-3.** Because of similarity. The more similar the other stimuli to the CS, the more likely generalization is to occur. **4-4.** generalize, discriminate **4-5.** classical, UCS, CS, CR **4-6.** generalization **4-7.** discrimination.

5. Explain what happens in higher-order conditioning.

5-1. Suppose that a *bell* and *meat powder* are paired, as in the original Pavlovian study. At some point a conditioned salivary response will occur to the bell. Suppose that in a new series of trials a *clicking sound* (a new, neutral stimulus) is paired with the bell. Assuming that the stimuli are potent enough, that the timing is right, and so on, a _____ response will occur to the clicking sound.

5-2. This process, in which a stimulus that previously functioned as a "learned" or *conditioned* stimulus is used as an *unconditioned* stimulus, is known as _____ conditioning.

5-3. In our example, in which the clicking sound and bell were paired, which stimulus acted as the UCS?

_____

Answers: **5-1.** conditioned **5-2.** higher-order **5-3.** the bell.

OPERANT CONDITIONING

6. Discuss the nature of operant responding in comparison to the types of responding typically governed by classical conditioning.

6-1. A major feature of Pavlovian or classical conditioning is that conditioned responses occur when two stimuli are paired or associated. For example, when a sound and food are paired together, a conditioned salivary response occurs to the _____.

6-2. In contrast, in operant conditioning, learning or conditioning occurs from stimuli that (precede/follow) the response, the stimuli that are the "payoff" or _____ of that particular behavior.

6-3. Learning theorists originally supposed that the two types of conditioning controlled different types of responses, that classical conditioning controlled reflexive or (voluntary/involuntary) responses (such as salivation or leg flexion) while operant conditioning controlled voluntary responses. While this distinction holds up (all of the time/much of the time), it is now clear that the only absolute distinction is in terms of procedure.

7. **Describe Thorndike's work and explain his law of effect.**

7-1.   E. L. Thorndike's pioneering work on what he referred to as _____ learning provided the foundation for Skinner's _____ conditioning.

7-2.   According to Thorndike's law of _____, if a response leads to a *satisfying effect* in the presence of a stimulus, the association between the stimulus and response is strengthened. Thorndike's law of effect is similar to Skinner's concept of reinforcement: both emphasize the _____ of behavior.

8. **Describe Skinner's principle of reinforcement and the prototype experimental procedures used in studies of operant conditioning.**

8-1.   A reinforcer is a stimulus or event that (1) is presented *after* a response and that (2) increases the tendency for the response to be repeated. Apply that definition to this example: Grundoon, a captive monkey, occasionally swings on a bar in his cage. Suppose that at some point Grundoon's trainers decide to give him a spoonful of applesauce whenever he swings. Is the applesauce a reinforcer? In terms of the definition above, how do you know that applesauce is a reinforcer?

8-2.   The trainers switch to vinegar. Grundoon, an unusual primate, swings quite frequently when this behavior is followed by vinegar. Is vinegar a reinforcer here? How do you know?

8-3.   The trainers try another approach. They present Grundoon with fresh fruit *just before* they think he is likely to jump. It so happens that Grundoon's rate of jumping does increase. Is the fruit a reinforcer here? Why or why not?

8-4.   The prototypic apparatus used in operant conditioning studies is the operant chamber, better known as the _____. On one wall of the chamber is mounted a manipulandum, a device that makes for an easily discernible response. For rats, the manipulandum is usually a small _____; for pigeons, the device is a _____ that the bird learns to peck.

8-5.   A press of the lever or peck at the disk may produce a reinforcer, generally a small bit of food dispensed into the food cup mounted to one side or below the manipulandum. Each of these responses is recorded on a _____ _____, a device that creates a graphic record of the number of responses per unit time.

8-6. The cumulative recorder records the *rate* of the behavior, that is, the number of _____ made per unit _____.

8-7. Below is a highly stylized version of a cumulative record. About how many responses were made during the first 40 seconds? _____ Which section of the graph (a, b, c, d, or e) has the steepest slope? _____ Which section of the graph illustrates the fastest rate of responding? _____ About how many responses were made between the 40th and 70th seconds? _____

Answers: **8-1.** Yes. If the animal's rate of swinging increases when followed by applesauce, then applesauce is a reinforcer. **8-2.** Yes. Because the vinegar is presented *after the response*, and because the *response rate increases.* (Note that this is an imaginary example to illustrate the point that reinforcement is not defined in terms of "pleasantness" and "unpleasantness," which are unobservable subjective judgments. Instead, reinforcement is defined in terms of *strengthening* of a response tendency *by the events that follow* the responses. I don't know of any monkeys that will respond for vinegar. I doubt that there are any.) **8-3.** No. Reinforcing stimuli, by definition, *follow* the response. (Again, this is a contrived example just to illustrate the definition.) **8-4.** Skinner box, lever (or bar), disk **8-5.** cumulative recorder **8-6.** responses, time **8-7.** 10, d, d, 20.

9. Describe the operant conditioning phenomena of acquisition, shaping, and extinction.

9-1. Acquisition refers to the formation of new responses. In classical conditioning, acquisition occurs through a simple pairing of the CS and UCS. In operant conditioning, acquisition usually involves the procedure known as _____.

9-2. What is shaping? When is it used?

9-3. Extinction in classical conditioning involves removing the UCS while still presenting the CS.

(a) What is the extinction procedure in operant conditioning?

(b) What is the effect of extinction on behavior (response rate)?

(c) What does the term *resistance to extinction* mean?

Answers: 9-1. shaping **9-2.** Shaping is the process of reinforcing closer and closer approximations to the desired behavior. It is used in the formation of a new response. **9-3.** (a) No longer presenting the reinforcers after a response. (b) Response rate decreases and may eventually stop. (c) Animals may continue to respond, for a period of time, even when reinforcers are no longer presented. The extent to which they will *continue to respond during extinction* is referred to as *resistance* to extinction.

10. Explain how stimuli govern operant behavior and how generalization and discrimination occur in operant conditioning.

10-1. Suppose that a rat has been shaped so that when it presses a lever it receives a food pellet. With further training, the rat may respond only when a light (or sound, etc.) in the chamber is on and not when it is off. The food pellet (which follows the response) is a _____. The light (which precedes the response) is a _____ stimulus.

10-2. Reinforcers occur (<u>after/before</u>) the response occurs. Discriminative stimuli occur _____ the response occurs.

10-3. To create a discriminative stimulus, one reinforces a response only in the presence of a particular stimulus and not in its absence. In time that stimulus will gain control of the response: Animals will tend to emit the response only if the discriminative stimulus is (<u>present/absent</u>) and not if it is _____.

10-4. For example, rats can be trained to press a lever when a light comes on and not to press when the light is off. Lever presses that occur when the light is on are followed by a food pellet; those that occur in the dark are not. Label each component of this operant-conditioning process by placing the appropriate letters in the blanks below.

_____ light	a. discriminative stimulus
_____ lever press	b. response
_____ food	c. reinforcer

10-5. "Heel Fido!" says Ralph. Fido runs to Ralph's side. Fido gets a pat on the head. Label the parts of the operant conditioning sequence by placing the appropriate letters in the blanks. (To avoid confusion, the behavior or response of interest in this example is already labeled.)

_____ "Heel Fido!"	a. discriminative stimulus
_____ Fido gets a pat on the head.	b. response
__b__ Fido runs to Ralph's side.	c. reinforcer

10-6. Phyllis will lend money to Ralph, but only after Ralph promises to pay her back. Ralph is also careful to thank Phyllis for her help. The behavior we are looking at here is Phyllis's lending behavior.

_____ "Thank you very much, Phyllis."	a. discriminative stimulus
__b__ Phyllis lends.	b. response
_____ "I promise I'll pay you back."	c. reinforcer

10-7. Generalization occurs in operant as well as classical conditioning. For example, when I put dishes in the sink, our cat would *run to her bowl* looking for food. In technical terms, our cat _____ between the sound of food dropping in her bowl and the *similar* sound of dishes going into the sink. Despite the fact that food does not follow the sound of clattering dishes, our cat did *not* learn to _____ between the sounds in our kitchen.

Answers: **10-1.** reinforcer, discriminative **10-2.** after, before **10-3.** present, absent **10-4.** a, b, c **10-5.** a, c, (b) **10-6.** c, (b), a **10-7.** generalizes, discriminate.

11. Distinguish between primary and secondary reinforcers.

11-1. Define the following:

(a) Primary reinforcer:

(b) Secondary or conditioned reinforcer:

Answers: **11-1.** (a) A primary reinforcer satisfies biological needs, such as needs for food, water, warmth and sex. (b) A secondary, or conditioned, reinforcer is one that is learned or acquired through *association* with a primary reinforcer. For humans, secondary reinforcers may include praise, attention, and money.

12. Identify various types of schedules of reinforcement and discuss their typical effects on responding.

12-1. Schedules of reinforcement are either continuous or intermittent. If reinforcers follow each response, the schedule is referred to as a/an _____-reinforcement schedule, abbreviated CRF. If reinforcers only follow some responses and not others (e.g., FR, VR), or occur as a function of the passage of time (e.g., FI, VI), the schedule is referred to as a/an _____ schedule.

12-2. Identify the following schedules of reinforcement by placing the appropriate abbreviations in the blanks: continuous reinforcement (CRF), fixed ratio (FR), variable ratio (VR), fixed interval (FI), variable interval (VI).

_____ A pigeon is reinforced whenever it has pecked a disk exactly 20 times.

_____ A pigeon is reinforced for pecking a disk, on the average, 20 times.

_____ A rat is always reinforced for the first response that follows a two-minute interval.

_____ A slot machine delivers a payoff, on the average, after every 10th pull of the lever.

_____ Every time the pigeon pecks a disk, it receives a pellet of food.

_____ A rat is reinforced, on the average, for the first response following a two-minute interval.

_____ A pig is reinforced for the first response after 30 seconds, then for the first response after 42 seconds, then for the first response after five seconds, and so on.

_____ Every two weeks Ralph picks up his payroll check at the office.

_____ A rat is reinforced after the 73rd response, then after the 22nd response, then after the 51st response, and so on.

12-3. Resistance to extinction refers to the extent to which responses occur during a period of extinction. What is the general effect of the intermittent schedules of reinforcement on resistance to extinction?

12-4. In terms of the effect on *rate* of responding, what is the general difference between the *ratio* schedules (FR and VR) and the *interval* schedules (FI and VI)?

12-5. In terms of the effect on *pattern* of responding, what is the general difference between *fixed* schedules and *variable* schedules?

Answers: 12-1. continuous, intermittent (or partial) **12-2.** FR, VR, FI, VR, CRF, VI, VI, FI, VR **12-3.** The intermittent schedules increase resistance to extinction. **12-4.** Ratio schedules tend to produce more rapid responding than the interval schedules. **12-5.** Variable schedules tend to produce more regular patterns of responding, without pauses or scalloping, than do their fixed counterparts. They also result in more resistance to extinction.

13. Explain the distinction between positive and negative reinforcement.

13-1. Some Skinner boxes may be set up so that a mild electric shock can be delivered to the feet of the animal through the floor of the box. Suppose that whenever the animal presses the bar, the shock is turned *off* for a period of time. Will the lever-pressing behavior be *strengthened* or *weakened*? _____

13-2. By definition, what effect does reinforcement have on behavior? What is the effect of positive reinforcement on behavior? Negative reinforcement?

13-3. With positive reinforcement, a stimulus is *presented* after the response. What is the procedure with negative reinforcement?

Answers: 13-1. strengthened **13-2.** Reinforcement strengthens (increases the frequency of) behavior. Both positive and negative reinforcement strengthen behavior. **13-3.** The stimulus (an aversive stimulus) is *removed* after the response.

14. Describe and distinguish between escape learning and avoidance learning.

14-1. Review the section on escape and avoidance learning. In escape learning the animal first experiences the aversive stimulus and then makes a response that escapes it. In avoidance learning the animal responds to a cue that permits it to respond *before* the aversive stimulus is delivered, thereby avoiding it altogether. Label the following examples E for escape and A for avoidance.

_____ The weather has changed and Fred is getting cold. He goes inside.

_____ Little Sandra rapidly removes her hand from the hot stove.

_____ A cue light comes on in the dog's shuttle box. It jumps the hurdle to the other side.

_____ Randolph has been told that he will be mugged if he goes outside, so he stays inside.

_____ Sue has learned some new verbal behavior. If she simply says, "No, I don't want that" shortly after a salesman starts his pitch, the salesman will stop bothering her.

_____ Alice sees Ruppert in the distance. If Ruppert sees her he will ask for her course notes, which she doesn't want to lend him. She heads in the other direction.

14-2. What is the major difference between escape learning and avoidance learning?

Answers: 14-1. E, E, A, A, E, A **14-2.** The major difference is that with escape learning there is no cue stimulus, so that the animal must first experience the aversive stimulus and then *escape* it. In the case of avoidance learning, a cue preceding the aversive stimulus permits the animal to *avoid* the aversive event altogether.

15. Describe punishment and its effects.

15-1. Punishment involves *weakening* a response by presenting an aversive stimulus after the response has occurred. Review the concepts of reinforcement and punishment by labeling each of the following with one of these terms: *positive reinforcement, negative reinforcement,* or *punishment.*

(a) A stimulus is *presented* after the response; response rate *increases:* _____

(b) A stimulus is *presented* after the response; response rate *decreases:* _____

(c) A stimulus is *removed* after the response; response rate *increases:* _____

15-2. Response rate *increases*. Which of the following procedures may have been used?

a. positive reinforcement

b. negative reinforcement

c. punishment

d. either a or b above

15-3. Response rate *decreases*. Which of the following procedures may have been used?

a. positive reinforcement

b. negative reinforcement

c. punishment

d. either *b* or *c* above

15-4. When a rat presses a bar in an operant chamber, the electric shock stops. Bar pressing increases. What procedure has been used?

a. positive reinforcement

b. negative reinforcement

c. punishment

d. extinction

15-5. When the dog ran after the car, his master immediately threw a bucket of water on him. This sequence of events was repeated only twice, and the dog stopped running after the car. What has occurred?

    a. positive reinforcement

    b. negative reinforcement

    c. punishment

    d. extinction

15-6. When Randolph stepped out in his new outfit, everyone stared. If Randolph tends *not* to wear this outfit in the future, what has occurred?

    a. positive reinforcement

    b. negative reinforcement

    c. punishment

    d. extinction

15-7. In the space below list three negative side effects of punishment.

Answers: 15-1. (a) positive reinforcement (b) punishment (c) negative reinforcement **15-2.** d, because if response rate increases, *either* positive *or* negative reinforcement may be involved **15-3.** c. Not d, because negative reinforcement *increases* response rate. **15-4.** b **15-5.** c **15-6.** c **15-7.** Punishment may (1) suppress responses in general rather than just the response punished, (2) produce unwanted emotional responses, including fear and anger, and (3) increase aggressive behavior.

16. Discuss research on the side effects of punishment as a disciplinary procedure.

16-1. A recent comprehensive review of research on punishment of children concluded that (<u>physical punishment</u>/time out) is associated with increased aggression and, in adulthood, criminal and other undesirable behaviors.

16-2. Critics have raised questions about these conclusions. For example, it is possible that punishment does not cause aggression in children but that aggression in children causes them to be punished. The studies are, after all, (experimental/<u>correlational</u>), so cause-effect conclusions are difficult to make.

16-3. Critics also point out that the review (<u>did/did not</u>) distinguish between occasional mild physical punishment and harsh abusive punishment. Experts are unanimously opposed to harsh physical punishment, but judicious use of occasional mild spanking (is known to/<u>may not</u>) have negative effects.

16-4. The text suggests the following guidelines for use of punishment: (a) Apply punishment (<u>immediately</u>/after a delay). (b) Use a level of punishment that is the (most/<u>least</u>) severe to be effective. (c) When administering punishment (<u>explain</u>/do not explain) why it is being given. (e) In general, when employing punishment try to use (physical punishment/<u>withdrawal of privileges</u>).

Answers: 16-1. physical punishment **16-2.** correlational **16-3.** did not, may not **16-4.** (a) immediately (b) least (c) explain (d) withdrawal of privileges.

17. **Discuss the phenomena of instinctive drift and conditioned taste aversion.**

    17-1.   What is instinctive drift?

    17-2.   Why was the occurrence of instinctive drift surprising to operant psychologists? Discuss this question in terms of the supposed *generality* of the laws of learning.

    17-3.   What is conditioned taste aversion?

    17-4.   Why is the occurrence of conditioned taste aversion surprising? Discuss this question in terms of classical conditioning relating to (1) CS-UCS delays and (2) the sense of taste compared with other senses.

Answers: 17-1. It is the tendency for instinctive or innate behavior to interfere with the process of conditioning. **17-2.** Before the 1960s, operant psychologists assumed that any response that animals could emit could readily be conditioned. This did not turn out to be true. Animals may exhibit instinctive drift, the tendency to respond with certain innate behaviors that actually interfere with the process of conditioning. **17-3.** It refers to the somewhat unusual conditioning involving taste and nausea. If the distinctive taste of a particular food is followed some hours later by sickness (nausea, vomiting, etc.), that taste will become aversive and will itself come to elicit the response of nausea. **17-4.** It is surprising because (1) classical conditioning generally does not occur if there are long CS-UCS delays, and (2) taste is only one of several senses stimulated in this situation. Garcia concluded that the tendency for animals to fairly easily associate taste (as opposed to sight, sound, etc.) with sickness has survival value for a species in that it helps them avoid poisonous food in the future.

18. **Explain Domjan's ideas on the importance of ecologically relevant conditioned stimuli and discuss the evolutionary perspective on learning.**

    18-1.   Domjan (2005) proposes that taste aversion is not a unique phenomenon but represents the rapid conditioning that may occur when the CS is (neutral/<u>ecologically relevant</u>) with regard to the UCS. Such a CS-UCS relationship generally occurs in (the laboratory/<u>natural environment</u>).

    18-2.   In a traditional laboratory conditioning experiment, the CS is an arbitrary or _____ stimulus. For example, a tone or clicking sound may be artificially paired with food. In the natural environment, the CS is not "neutral" but is generally _____ relevant to the UCS. For example, in the natural environment food is not preceded by a bell but by specific smells or tastes; copulation by specific mating signals; danger from animals by specific sounds or smells, etc.

    18-3.   For Domjan species-specific differences in conditioning are the norm rather than the exception, and he urges researchers to shift their focus from the study of neutral to ecologically relevant CS-UCS pairings. When more naturally related CS-UCS associations are used, several differences are likely to occur: conditioning may occur (<u>more</u>/less) rapidly, may be more resistant to extinction, etc.

18-4. While most learning psychologists currently agree that differing evolutionary demands have produced differences in conditioning across species, they still maintain that there are highly general or _____ laws of learning. Taking a more radical view, some evolutionary psychologists propose that learning in different species has evolved along different paths; they assert that there (are/are not) universal principles of learning.

Answers: **18-1.** ecologically relevant, natural environment **18-2.** neutral, ecologically **18-3.** more **18-4.** universal, are not.

19. Describe research on latent learning, signal relations, and response-outcome relations, and explain their theoretical importance.

19-1. Is reinforcement really needed for learning, as traditional learning theorists have contended? In the 1940s Edward C. Tolman, an early dissenter from conventional learning theory, found that rats allowed to wander a complicated maze without reinforcement learned to get to the goal box rapidly once food was presented. In fact, they learned as rapidly as another group of rats reinforced on every trial. What does this prove? First, rats appeared to learn the complicated series of left and right turns without _____; second, they appeared to learn something about the layout of the maze, what Tolman termed a _____ map.

19-2. Tolman referred to this type of learning as _____ learning. Latent learning is not apparent from behavior when it first occurs, but it appears later if the incentive is present. Tolman was prophetic, in a sense, well ahead of his time. His views were rejected by mainstream theorists for the next several decades but, as this chapter makes clear, current models of conditioning (include/do not include) cognition as a factor in conditioning.

19-3. In the example of a signal relations study described, the number of conditioning trials in which CS and UCS were paired was the same for two groups, 20 trials. The difference between the two treatment groups was that for one group the (CS/UCS) was presented *alone* for an additional series of 20 trials.

19-4. Theorists originally assumed that classical conditioning is an automatic, reflexive phenomenon that does not depend at all on higher mental processes. If that actually were true, then what should have been the effect of presenting the UCS alone for additional trials? Remember that both groups received exactly the same number of conditioning trials (CS-UCS pairings).

a. Extinction would occur.

b. The UCS-alone trials would weaken conditioning.

c. The UCS-alone trials would have no effect on conditioning.

19-5. In fact, what did occur in the signal relations studies?

a. Extinction.

b. The UCS-alone trials weakened conditioning.

c. The UCS-alone trials had no effect on conditioning.

19-6. These results suggest that the CS *signals* the occurrence of the UCS and that additional trials with the UCS alone weaken the _____ value of the CS. What is surprising about these results? Rather than being an automatic, mechanical process, these studies suggest that classical conditioning involves _____ processes.

19-7. Response-outcome relations refers to the connection between an operant response and its consequences. For example, for a rat in a Skinner box the relationship between the lever press (the response) and the food pellet (the outcome) is this: the rat gets the food *only if* it presses the lever. In other words, the reinforcer is (contingent/not contingent) on the response.

19-8. But does the animal "know" the connection between the response and reinforcer, or is the connection stamped in automatically? That is the crux of the response-outcome relations issue. Evidence suggests that

a. reinforcement and punishment are relatively automatic, mindless processes.

b. cognition is not involved in an organism's responding in an operant chamber.

c. humans and other animals actively try to figure out the contingencies, the relationship between response and outcome.

19-9. Thus, research on signal relations and response-outcome relations has forced the development of new theories that emphasize a much more _____ explanation of conditioning, an explanation in which organisms actively attempt to detect the *relationship* between their behaviors and environmental events.

19-10. Why are the latent learning, signal relations (in classical conditioning) and response-outcome relations (in operant conditioning) studies surprising and of theoretical importance?

Answers: **19-1.** reinforcement, cognitive **19-2.** latent, include **19-3.** UCS! (If the CS were presented alone, it would be extinction.) **19-4.** c **19-5.** b **19-6.** signaling, cognitive (higher mental) **19-7.** contingent **19-8.** c **19-9.** cognitive **19-10.** These studies indicate that conditioning is not, as assumed earlier, an automatic process but instead depends to a considerable degree on higher mental (cognitive) processes.

OBSERVATIONAL LEARNING

20. Discuss the nature and importance of observational learning.

20-1. Observational learning occurs when an organism learns by observing others, who are called _____. This type of learning occurs in (humans/animals/both).

20-2. Why is the concept of observational learning so important? For one thing the idea was surprising to theorists who assumed that all learning could be accounted for by operant and classical conditioning. For another, it extends classical and operant conditioning to include not only *direct* experience but _____ or vicarious experience. We learn not only when we behave but when we _____ the behavior of others.

20-3. Bandura's theory has helped explain some puzzling aspects of conditioning in human behavior. For example, what happens when parents punish aggressive behavior in their children? While punishment by definition (increases/decreases) the behavior it follows, a parent using punishment also serves as a _____ for aggressiveness. In this way events intended to decrease aggression may, in the longer run, _____ aggression through the process of _____ learning.

21. **List the basic processes in observational learning and discuss Bandura's view on whether reinforcement affects learning or performance.**

21-1.   In the space below list and define the four processes that Bandura has identified as crucial components of observational learning. The first letter of each concept is listed at the left.

A_____:

R_____:

R_____:

M_____:

21-2.   Bandura asked the question that Tolman asked decades earlier: Is reinforcement essential for learning? Many learning theorists used to think so, but in Bandura's view reinforcement is essential only for (learning/performance). Bandura asserts that we may learn without being reinforced simply by _____ the behavior of a model, but we are unlikely to perform the response unless we are _____ for doing so.

Answers: **21-1.** Attention: Paying attention to a model's behavior and consequences. Retention: Retaining in memory a mental representation of what one has observed. Reproduction: Having the ability to reproduce what one sees, to convert the image to behavior. Motivation: Having the inclination, based on one's assessment of the likely payoff, to reproduce the observed behavior. **21-2.** performance, observing, reinforced.

22. **Discuss research on observational learning as it relates to the controversy about the effects of media violence.**

22-1.   Young children are exposed to an enormous amount of violence on T.V. Does televised violence increase the likelihood that they will engage in aggressive acts? Is it a *causal* factor in aggression? In hundreds of experimental laboratory studies, the answer is clearly (yes/no/maybe). Individuals exposed to media violence, even for short periods of time in a laboratory setting, are both verbally and physically more _____ immediately after the exposure.

22-2.   What are the longer-term effects? In the real world, several studies have found that the more violence children watch on television, the more aggressive they are at home and at school. These are _____ studies, not experiments, and the opposite causal relationship could be inferred: children who are violent in the first place may like to watch violent T.V.

22-3.   There is, however, particularly convincing evidence in long-term studies of the same individuals: the more televised violence individuals watch as children, the more likely they are to be _____ as adolescents and young adults. Since media aggression (follows/precedes) the aggressive behavior that occurs much later, these studies, when considered with the laboratory experiments, make alternative explanations unlikely.

22-4.   Thus, watching televised violence seems to cause aggressive behavior. Since most of us have been exposed to media violence, why aren't we all violent? The reason is that aggression is influenced by a (few/large number) of factors, so the resulting increase may be relatively modest. Still, a modest effect multiplied by millions of people can have big repercussions.

REFLECTING ON THE CHAPTER'S THEMES

23. Explain how the chapter highlighted two of the text's unifying themes.

23-1. Skinner's view is that behavior is in large part determined by the environment. One of our unifying themes, however, is that environment doesn't act alone – environment _____ with heredity. What two phenomena discussed in the chapter illustrate the powerful effect that biology has on conditioning? _____ and _____

23-2. The second theme well illustrated in this chapter is that psychology evolves in a sociohistorical context. Skinner's _____ psychology, for example, with its emphasis on _____ reinforcement, has clearly influenced trends in education, child rearing, and management styles in business.

PERSONAL APPLICATION • ACHIEVING SELF-CONTROL THROUGH BEHAVIOR MODIFICATION

24. Describe how to specify your target behavior and gather baseline data for a self-modification program.

24-1. What behavior do you want to change? The question sounds simple, but the task of defining a _____ behavior is frequently quite tricky.

24-2. The behavior that you select must be defined in terms of observable events so that you will know if and when it changes. For example, for the problem of anger control, which of the following would be the most *directly observable* definition of "anger"?
a. inner turmoil
b. intense hostility
c. loud voice and clenched fists

24-3. Once you specify the target behavior you must gather _____ data on your behavior prior to the intervention. At this time you should also keep track of events that precede the target behavior, the _____ events, and also the positive and negative reinforcers that follow it, the _____ of your behavior.

25. Discuss how to design, execute, evaluate, and end a self-modification program.

25-1. To increase a target behavior you would use _____. The reinforcer (can/can not) be something that you already are receiving. For example, you probably already watch TV, go to movies, or buy things for yourself, so you could make one of these events _____ on an increased frequency of the target behavior.

25-2. You would specify exactly what behavioral goals must be met before you receive the reinforcer; that is, you would arrange the _____. If your goal is to increase studying, you might specify that TV watching for one hour is _____ on having studied for two hours.

25-3. Or, you might specify that for each hour you studied you would earn points that could be "spent" for watching TV, or going to movies, or talking with friends, and so on. This type of arrangement is referred to as a _____ economy.

25-4. A fairly obvious way to decrease a target behavior is to use _____. The problem with this approach is that it is difficult to follow through with self-punishment. So, there are two guidelines to keep in mind when using punishment in a self-control program: (1) Use punishment only in conjunction with _____ reinforcement; and (2) use a relatively _____ punishment that you, or perhaps a third party, will be able to administer.

25-5. It is also possible to use reinforcement to decrease behavior. For example, if you want to gradually reduce the amount that you smoke, you could reinforce yourself whenever you smoke fewer than a particular number of cigarettes per day. Paradoxically, you are using _____ to decrease behavior.

25-6. For some situations you may be able to identify events that reliably precede the behaviors you are trying to stop. For example, for some people smoking is at least under partial control of certain types of social events. So, one strategy for decreasing a behavior is to identify, and then avoid, the (antecedent/consequent) events that may control the behavior.

25-7. Successful execution of the program depends on several factors. To avoid cheating try creating a formal written behavioral _____. Or, make an arrangement so that (only you/someone else) delivers the reinforcers and punishments.

25-8. If your program isn't working, some small revision may turn it around. Try increasing the strength of the reinforcer or else try _____ the delay between the behavior and delivery of the reinforcer.

25-9. It is generally a good idea to specify in advance the conditions under which you would end the program. You may wish to phase it out by having a/an (gradual/immediate) reduction in the frequency or potency of reinforcers, although for some successful programs the new behaviors become self-maintaining on their own.

Answers: 25-1. reinforcement, can, contingent **25-2.** contingency, contingent **25-3.** token **25-4.** punishment, positive, mild **25-5.** reinforcement **25-6.** antecedent **25-7.** contract (agreement), someone else **25-8.** decreasing **25-9.** gradual.

CRITICAL THINKING APPLICATION • MANIPULATING EMOTIONS: PAVLOV AND PERSUASION

26. Describe how classical conditioning is used to manipulate emotions.

26-1. It is easy to forget that Pavlovian conditioning involves more than salivating dogs. It involves emotion and in that respect is important for a range of reactions—from phobias to sexual arousal to the effects of advertising. Manipulation employs a special subtype of classical conditioning in which the elicited responses are emotion-laden likes and dislikes. This type of conditioning, known as _____ conditioning, is especially resistant to extinction.

26-2. For practice with classical conditioning concepts, especially as they relate to evaluative conditioning, label each of the following:

(a) A glamorous woman is shown entering an automobile. Label each of the following with CS, UCS, CR, and UCR. (Assume, for the sake of this example, that the target audience is initially more attracted to the woman than the car. It could work the other way, too.)

_____ the woman

_____ the car

_____ attraction to the car

_____ attraction to the woman

(b) A politician stands in front of an American flag.

What is the CS? _____

The UCS? _____

(c) A salesman takes you to lunch.

What is the CS? _____

The UCS? _____

The CR? _____

26-3. Of course, there's more going on in these examples than just classical conditioning. When we receive a favor, we are not only being conditioned, but may feel obliged to pay back or _____ the person's favor.

26-4. While the examples we've used involve liking or attraction, other emotions may be conditioned as well—such as feelings of masculinity and femininity. Want to be more masculine? Smoke these cigarettes, ads may suggest. Not that we must be conscious of manipulation attempts, for conditioning (does/does not) seem to require our awareness.

26-5. How do we protect ourselves against attempts to manipulate our emotions? One suggestion from research on persuasion is that merely being _____ of the pervasiveness of conditioning will by itself provide some protections against manipulation strategies.

Answers: 26-1. evaluative **26-2.** (a) UCS, CS, CR, UCR (b) the politician, the flag (c) the salesman (or his product), the lunch, liking for the salesman (or his product) **26-3.** reciprocate **26-4.** does not **26-5.** forewarned (aware).

Review of Key Terms

Acquisition	Fixed-ratio (FR) schedule	Primary reinforcers
Antecedents	Higher-order conditioning	Punishment
Avoidance learning	Instinctive drift	Reinforcement
Behavior modification	Instrumental learning	Reinforcement contingencies
Behavioral contract	Intermittent reinforcement	Resistance to extinction
Classical conditioning	Latent learning	Schedule of reinforcement
Concurrent schedules of reinforcement	Law of effect	Secondary reinforcers
Conditioned reinforcers	Learning	Shaping

Conditioned response (CR)
Conditioned stimulus (CS)
Continuous reinforcement
Cumulative recorder
Discriminative stimuli
Elicit
Emit
Escape learning
Evaluative conditioning
Extinction
Fixed-interval (FI) schedule

Matching law
Negative reinforcement
Observational learning
Operant chamber
Operant conditioning
Optimal foraging theory
Partial reinforcement
Pavlovian conditioning
Phobias
Positive reinforcement
Preparedness

Skinner box
Spontaneous recovery
Stimulus discrimination
Stimulus generalization
Token economy
Trial
Unconditioned response (UCR)
Unconditioned stimulus (UCS)
Variable-interval (VI) schedule
Variable-ratio (VR) schedule

_____ 1. A relatively durable change in behavior or knowledge that is due to experience.

_____ 2. Irrational fears of specific objects or situations.

_____ 3. The most common name of a type of learning in which a neutral stimulus acquires the ability to evoke a response that was originally evoked by another stimulus.

_____ 4. Another name for classical conditioning derived from the name of the person who originally discovered the conditioning phenomenon.

_____ 5. A type of classical conditioning, especially resistant to extinction, in which responses involved are emotion-laden likes and dislike.

_____ 6. A stimulus that evokes an unconditioned response.

_____ 7. The response to an unconditioned stimulus.

_____ 8. A previously neutral stimulus that has acquired the capacity to evoke a conditioned response.

_____ 9. A learned reaction to a conditioned stimulus that occurs because of previous conditioning.

_____ 10. To draw out or bring forth, as in classical conditioning.

_____ 11. Any presentation of a stimulus or pair of stimuli in classical conditioning.

_____ 12. The formation of a new response tendency.

_____ 13. Learning without reinforcement that is not apparent from behavior when the learning first occurs.

_____ 14. The gradual weakening and disappearance of a conditioned response tendency.

_____ 15. The reappearance of an extinguished response after a period of nonexposure to the conditioned stimulus.

_____ 16. Occurs when an organism responds to new stimuli that are similar to the stimulus used in conditioning.

_____ 17. Occurs when an organism learns not to respond to stimuli that are similar to the stimulus used in conditioning.

_____ 18. Occurs when a conditioned stimulus functions as if it were an unconditioned stimulus.

_____ 19. This term, introduced by Skinner, refers to learning in which voluntary responses come to be controlled by their consequences.

_____ 20. Another name for operant conditioning, this term was introduced earlier by Edward L. Thorndike.

_____ 21. Law stating that if a response in the presence of a stimulus leads to satisfying effects, the association between the stimulus and the response is strengthened.

_____ 22. Occurs when an event following a response strengthens the tendency to make that response.

_____ 23. A standard operant chamber in which an animal's responses are controlled and recorded.

_____ 24. Production of voluntary responses in responding in operant conditioning.

_____ 25. The circumstances or rules that determine whether responses lead to presentation of reinforcers; or, the relationship between a response and positive consequences.

_____ 26. Device that creates a graphic record of operant responding as a function of time.

_____ 27. The reinforcement of closer and closer approximations of the desired response.

_____ 28. A small enclosure in which an animal's responses are recorded and followed by specified consequences; a Skinner box.

_____ 29. Occurs when an organism continues to make a response after delivery of the reinforcer for it has been terminated.

_____ 30. Cues that influence operant behavior by indicating the probable consequences (reinforcement or nonreinforcement) of a response.

_____ 31. Stimulus events that are inherently reinforcing because they satisfy biological needs.

_____ 32. Stimulus events that acquire reinforcing qualities by being associated with primary reinforcers.

_____ 33. A specific pattern of presentation of reinforcers over time.

_____ 34. Occurs when every instance of a designated response is reinforced.

_____ 35. The name for all schedules of reinforcement in which a designated response is reinforced only some of the time.

_____ 36. The schedule in which the reinforcer is given after a fixed number of nonreinforced responses.

_____ 37. The schedule in which the reinforcer is given after a variable number of nonreinforced responses.

_____ 38. The schedule in which the reinforcer is given for the first response that occurs after a fixed time interval has elapsed.

_____ 39. The schedule in which the reinforcer is given for the first response that occurs after a variable time interval has elapsed.

_____ 40. Occurs when a response is strengthened because it is followed by the arrival of a rewarding (presumably pleasant) stimulus.

_____ 41. Occurs when a response is strengthened because it is followed by the removal of an aversive (unpleasant) stimulus.

_____ 42. Occurs when an organism engages in a response that brings aversive stimulation to an end.

_____ 43. Occurs when an organism engages in a response that prevents aversive stimulation from occurring.

_____ 44. Occurs when an event that follows a response weakens or suppresses the tendency to make that response.

_____ 45. Occurs when an animal's innate response tendencies interfere with conditioning processes.

_____ **46.** Occurs when an organism's responding is influenced by the observation of others, who are called models.

_____ **47.** A systematic approach to changing behavior through the application of the principles of conditioning.

_____ **48.** When a designated response is reinforced only some of the time; another name for intermittent reinforcement.

_____ **49.** Another name for secondary reinforcers.

_____ **50.** A written agreement outlining a promise to adhere to the contingencies of a behavior-modification program.

Answers: 1. learning **2.** phobias **3.** classical conditioning **4.** Pavlovian conditioning **5.** evaluative conditioning **6.** unconditioned stimulus (UCS) **7.** unconditioned response (UCR) **8.** conditioned stimulus (CS) **9.** conditioned response (CR) **10.** elicit **11.** trial **12.** acquisition **13.** latent learning **14.** extinction **15.** spontaneous recovery **16.** stimulus generalization **17.** stimulus discrimination **18.** higher-order conditioning **19.** operant conditioning **20.** instrumental learning **21.** law of effect **22.** reinforcement **23.** Skinner box **24.** emit **25.** reinforcement contingencies **26.** cumulative recorder **27.** shaping **28.** operant chamber **29.** resistance to extinction **30.** discriminative stimuli **31.** primary reinforcers **32.** secondary reinforcers **33.** schedule of reinforcement **34.** continuous reinforcement **35.** intermittent reinforcement **36.** Fixed-ratio (FR) schedule **37.** variable-ratio (VR) schedule **38.** Fixed-interval (FI) schedule **39.** variable-interval (VI) schedule **40.** positive reinforcement **41.** negative reinforcement **42.** escape learning **43.** avoidance learning **44.** punishment **45.** instinctive drift **46.** observational learning **47.** behavior modification **48.** partial reinforcement **49.** conditioned reinforcers **50.** behavioral contract.

Review of Key People

Albert Bandura	Robert Rescorla	E. L. Thorndike
John Garcia	Martin Seligman	John B. Watson
Ivan Pavlov	B. F. Skinner	

_____ **1.** The first to describe the process of classical conditioning.

_____ **2.** Founded behaviorism; examined the generalization of conditioned fear in a boy known as "Little Albert."

_____ **3.** Developed a principle known as the law of effect; coined the term _instrumental learning_.

_____ **4.** Elaborated the learning process known as operant conditioning; investigated schedules of reinforcement; developed programmed learning.

_____ **5.** Asserted that environmental stimuli serve as signals and that some stimuli in classical conditioning are better signals than others.

_____ **6.** Described and extensively investigated the process of observational learning.

_____ **7.** Discovered that taste aversion was conditioned only through taste and nausea pairings and not through other stimulus pairings, such as taste and shock.

_____ **8.** Proposed the theory of preparedness, the notion that there are species-specific predispositions to condition to certain stimuli and not to others.

Answers: 1. Pavlov **2.** Watson **3.** Thorndike **4.** Skinner **5.** Rescorla **6.** Bandura **7.** Garcia **8.** Seligman.

Self-Quiz

1. In Pavlov's original demonstration of classical conditioning, salivation to the bell was the:
   a. conditioned stimulus
   b. conditioned response
   c. unconditioned stimulus
   d. unconditioned response

2. Sally developed a fear of balconies after almost falling from a balcony on a couple of occasions. What was the conditioned response?
   a. the balcony
   b. fear of the balcony
   c. almost falling
   d. fear resulting from almost falling

3. When the UCS is removed and the CS is presented alone for a period of time, what will occur?
   a. classical conditioning
   b. generalization
   c. acquisition
   d. extinction

4. Sally developed a fear of balconies from almost falling. Although she has had no dangerous experiences on bridges, cliffs, and the view from tall buildings, she now fears these stimuli as well. Which of the following is likely to have produced a fear of these other stimuli?
   a. instinctive drift
   b. spontaneous recovery
   c. generalization
   d. discrimination

5. A researcher reinforces closer and closer approximations to a target behavior. What is the name of the procedure she is using?
   a. shaping
   b. classical conditioning
   c. discrimination training
   d. extinction

6. John says, "Please pass the salt." Ralph passes the salt. "Thank you," says John. John's request precedes a behavior (salt passing) that is reinforced ("Thank you"). Thus, the request "Please pass the salt" is a _____ for passing the salt.
   a. discriminative stimulus
   b. response
   c. positive reinforcer
   d. conditioned stimulus (CS)

7. A rat is reinforced for the first lever-pressing response that occurs, *on the average*, after 60 seconds. Which schedule is the rat on?
   a. FR
   b. VR
   c. FI
   d. VI

8. When the rat presses a lever, the mild electric shock on the cage floor is turned off. What procedure is being used?
   a. punishment
   b. escape
   c. discrimination training
   d. avoidance

9. A cue light comes on in the dog's shuttle box. It jumps the hurdle to the other side. What procedure is being used?
   a. punishment
   b. escape
   c. discrimination training
   d. avoidance

10. In a signal relations study, CS-UCS trials are alternated with presentation of the UCS alone. What will occur?
    a. stronger conditioning than would have occurred without the UCS alone trials
    b. weaker conditioning than would have occurred without the UCS alone trials
    c. latent learning
    d. extinction

11. The contingencies are as follows: if the response occurs, a stimulus is *presented*; if the response does not occur, the stimulus is not presented. Under this procedure the strength of the response *decreases*. What procedure is being used?
    a. positive reinforcement
    b. negative reinforcement
    c. punishment
    d. avoidance training

12. In terms of the traditional view of conditioning, research on conditioned taste aversion was surprising because
    a. there was a very long delay between CS and UCS
    b. the dislike of a particular taste was operantly conditioned
    c. conditioning occurred to all stimuli present when the food was consumed
    d. the sense of taste seems to be relatively weak

13. Animal trainers (the Brelands) trained pigs to put coins in a piggy bank for a food reward. The animals learned the response but, instead of depositing the coins immediately in the bank, the pigs began to toss them in the air, drop them, push them on the ground, and so on. What had occurred that interfered with conditioning?
    a. conditioned taste aversion
    b. blocking
    c. instinctive drift
    d. S & L scandal

14. Which of the following produces strong resistance to extinction?
    a. a continuous reinforcement schedule
    b. an intermittent reinforcement schedule
    c. optimal foraging behavior
    d. discrimination and differentiation

15. Earlier learning viewpoints considered classical and operant conditioning to be automatic processes involving only environmental events that did not depend at all on biological or cognitive factors. Research on which of the following concepts cast doubt on this point of view?
    a. latent learning, signal relations, and instinctive drift
    b. extinction, discrimination, and generalization
    c. CRF, ratio, and interval schedules
    d. escape, avoidance, and spontaneous recovery

Answers: 1. b **2.** b **3.** d **4.** c **5.** a **6.** a **7.** d **8.** b **9.** d **10.** b **11.** c **12.** a **13.** c **14.** b **15.** d.

InfoTrac Keywords

Behavior Modification
Classical Conditioning

Intermittent Reinforcement

Operant Conditioning

Chapter Seven
HUMAN MEMORY

Review of Key Ideas

ENCODING: GETTING INFORMATION INTO MEMORY

1. **Describe the three basic human memory processes.**

    1-1. The three basic human memory processes are:

    (a) Putting the information in, a process called _____.

    (b) Holding onto the information, a process called _____.

    (c) Getting the information back out, a process called _____.

    Answers: **1-1.** (a) encoding (b) storage (c) retrieval.

2. **Discuss the role of attention in memory.**

    2-1. If you are being introduced to a new person and you want to remember her name, it is first necessary to give selective _____ to this information. This requires _____ out irrelevant sensory input. The debate between early and late selection theories of attention is an argument over when this filtering takes place, before or after _____ is given to the arriving material.

    2-2. Although there is ample evidence to support both early- and late-selection theories of attention, what conclusion have some been led to?

    2-3. What effect does divided attention have on memory and many other tasks, such as using a cellular telephone while driving?

    Answers: **2-1.** attention, filtering, meaning **2-2.** The location of the attention filter may be flexible rather than fixed. **2-3.** It decreases performance.

3. **Describe the three levels of information processing proposed by Craik and Lockhart and how processing relates to memory.**

3-1.   Craik and Lockhart proposed three levels for encoding incoming information, with ever increasing retention as the depth of processing increases. In their order of depth these three levels are:

(a) _____   (b) _____   (c) _____

3-2.   Below are three-word sequences. Tell which level of processing each sequence illustrates and why.

(a) cat   IN   tree   _____

(b) car   BAR   czar   _____

(c) CAN   CAP   CAR   _____

3-3.   If this theory is correct then we would expect most persons to best remember the sequence in _____. This is because the words in this sequence have greater_____ than do the other two sequences. It has been found that processing time (is/is not) a reliable index of depth of processing, and thus what constitutes "levels" remains vague.

Answers: 3-1. (a) structural (b) phonemic (c) semantic **3-2.** (a) Semantic because we immediately give meaning to the words. (b) Phonemic because the words sound alike. (c) Structural because the words look alike. **3-3.** (a) cat in tree, meaning, is not.

4. **Describe three techniques for enriching encoding and research on each.**

4-1.   Elaboration helps us to better remember the words RUN FAST CAT than the words WORK SLOW TREE. Why is this?

4-2.   According to Paivio's dual-coding theory, why is it easier to remember the word APPLE than the word PREVAIL?

4-3.   What is the general idea behind self-referent encoding?

Answers: 4-1. Because the words RUN FAST CAT allow us to make richer and more elaborate associations among them than do the other three words (for example you can imagine a cat running fast). **4-2.** Because it is easier to form a visual image of the word APPLE, thus allowing for storage of both the word and image. **4-3.** We are more likely to remember information when it is relevant to ourselves.

5. Describe the role of the sensory store in memory.

5-1. Sensory memory allows for retention of information for a very (brief/long) period of time. The retention time for sensory memory for both vision and audition is about _____. During this brief period the information (remains in/is changed from) its original sensory form.

Answers: 5-1. brief, 1/4 second, remains in.

6. Discuss the characteristics of short-term memory (STM).

6-1. Indicate whether the following statements regarding short-term memory are true or false.

_____ (a) Has a virtually unlimited storage capacity.

_____ (b) Has a storage capacity of seven, plus or minus two, items.

_____ (c) Requires continuous rehearsal to maintain information in store for more than 20 or 30 seconds.

_____ (d) Stores information more or less permanently.

_____ (e) Chunking can help to increase the capacity of this system.

Answers: 6-1. (a) false (b) true (c) true (d) false (e) true.

7. Discuss Baddeley's model of working memory and related research.

7-1. Say which component of Baddeley's working memory + phonological rehearsal loop, visuospatial sketchpad, executive control system, or episodic buffer + is operating in the following situations.

(a) You are mentally weighing the pros and cons of attending a particular university.

(b) You continue to recite a phone number as you walk towards the phone.

(c) You are describing the location of a restaurant to a friend.

(d) You are able to integrate information while performing the above tasks and interface it with long-term memory.

7-2. Research has shown that the separate modules (do/do not) work independently as hypothesized. Research has also shown that there are variations in people as to their ability to juggle information in their working memory. These variations correlate (positively/negatively) with measures of high-level cognitive abilities.

Answers: 7-1. (a) executive control system (b) phonological rehearsal loop (c) visuospatial sketchpad (d) episodic buffer. **7-2.** do, positively.

8. **Evaluate the hypothesis that all memories are stored permanently in long-term memory (LTM).**

8-1.   There are two views regarding the durability of information in LTM. One is that no information is ever

lost, and the other is that _____ information is lost. Those who favor the permanent view

explain forgetting as a failure of _____. The information is still there, we just cannot get it

out.

8-2.   How do those who doubt the permanency of long-term memory counter the following two lines of

evidence cited by the permanent proponents?

(a) Flashbulb memories of previous events?

(b) Penfield's electrically triggered memories?

Answers: 8-1. some, retrieval **8-2.** (a) They often tend to be inaccurate and less detailed with the passage of time.
(b) The memories were often incorrect and resembled dreams or hallucinations more than real events.

9. **Evaluate the issues in the debate about whether short-term and long-term memory are really separate.**

9-1.   The traditional view is that short-term memory differs from long-term memory in that it depends on

phonemic (sound) encoding while long-term memory depends on _____ (meaning) encoding.

These two systems are also said to differ in the manner in which forgetting occurs. The loss of memory in

STM is thought to result from time-related decay, while LTM forgetting is attributed to _____.

9-2.   What research findings undermine the traditional view?

9-3.   Which view, multiple stores or a single system, dominates at the present time?

Answers: 9-1. semantic, interference **9-2.** Semantic encoding and interference have also been found in short-term
memory. **9-3.** multiple stores.

10. **Describe conceptual hierarchies, schemas, and semantic networks, and their role in long-term memory.**

10-1.   Group the following words into two groups or categories:

rose   dog   grass   cat   tree   rat

You probably grouped the words into plants and animals, which is the general idea behind _____.

Thus, clustering leads to forming categories (concepts), and in turn the categories are organized into

_____ hierarchies. For example, the categories of plants and animals can be placed under the higher

category (hierarchy) of _____ things.

10-2. It also appears that LTM stores information in clusters of knowledge about particular objects or events, called _____. For example, in the study cited by the text, the subjects who falsely recalled seeing books did so because of their schema of what a professor's _____ looks like. Although people are (<u>more/less</u>) likely to remember things consistent with their schemas, this is not always true, particularly with objects that contrast (<u>dramatically/casually</u>) with their schema-based expectations.

10-3. In addition to conceptual categories, it appears that LTM also stores information in terms of semantic networks. If you understand the idea behind semantic networks and its related idea of spreading activation, you should be able to answer the questions below.

Person A attends an urban university and frequently studies while riding a bus to and from school.

Person B attends a university located in a rural area and frequently studies outside in one of the many park-like areas surrounding the school.

(a) When asked to think of words associated with the word STUDY, which of the students is most likely to think of the word GRASS?_____

(b) Which person is most likely to think of the word TRAFFIC?_____

(c) Which person is most likely to think of the word PEACEFUL?_____

Answers: 10-1. clustering, conceptual, living **10-2.** schemas, office, more, dramatically **10-3.** (a) person B (b) person A (c) person B.

11. Explain how parallel distributed processing (PDP) models view the representation of information in memory.

11-1. PDP models assume that a piece of knowledge is represented by a particular _____ of activation across an entire system of innerconnected neural networks. This approach is called "connectionism" because the information lies in the strengths of the _____.

11-2. The PDP approach has at least two strengths. First, it (<u>agrees/disagrees</u>) with the findings from neurophysiological research. Second, it can account for the (<u>slow/blazing</u>) speed of human's cognitive functioning.

Answers: 11-1. pattern, connections **11-2.** agrees, blazing.

RETRIEVAL: GETTING INFORMATION BACK OUT OF MEMORY

12. Explain how retrieval cues and context cues influence retrieval.

12-1. In the following examples, indicate whether retrieval cues or context cues are being used to retrieve information from long-term memory.

(a) In trying to recall the name of a high school classmate, you get the feeling that his first name began with an "L", and begin saying names like Larry, Leroy, Lionel, etc.

(b) Or you may attempt to recall the high school classmate by imagining the history class in which he sat in the row next to you.

Answers: 12-1. (a) retrieval cues (b) context cues.

13. **Discuss Bartlett's work, the misinformation effect, and imagination inflation.**

13-1. Bartlett's work with the "The War of the Ghosts", found that the subjects reconstructed the original tale to fit with their already established _____. Since we use schemas to move information in and out of long-term memory, it is not too surprising that these schemas may alter retrieved information.

13-2. For example, Elizabeth Loftus found that subjects who were originally asked, "How fast were the cars going when they (hit/smashed) into each other?" were much more likely to falsely recall having seen broken glass on a videotaped scene when tested at a later date. In this case the word "smashed" resulted in a different _____ than did the word "hit." The distortion of memory by the word "smashed" is an example of how post-event information can result in the _____ of an original memory.

13-3. Reaearch has also shown that a few moments of imagination can significantly increase many subjects' belief that they actually had an experience similar to the imagined event. This effect is called _____ _____.

Answers: 13-1. schemas **13-2.** smashed, schema, reconstruction **13-3.** imagination inflation.

14. **Discuss the implications of evidence on source monitoring and reality monitoring.**

14-1. A third explanation for distorted memory retrieval involves source monitoring. Both source monitoring and its subtype, reality monitoring, require us to make attributions about the _____ of memories. Errors in memory from both kinds of monitoring are (rare/common).

14-2. Say whether the situations below are examples of source monitoring (S) or reality monitoring (R).

_____ (a) You become convinced that you broke your arm when you were five years old, but your mother tells you that it never happened.

_____ (b) You attribute a funny story to your good friend Tom when in fact it was Fred, whom you don't really care for, who told you the story.

_____ (c) You believe that you received an "A" in high school algebra, but your transcript shows a "C".

Answers: 14-1. origins, common **14-2.** (a) R (b) S (c) R.

FORGETTING: WHEN MEMORY LAPSES

15. **Describe Ebbinghaus's forgetting curve and three measures of retention.**

15-1. Ebbinghaus's forgetting curve, using nonsense syllables and himself as the subject, showed that forgetting was most rapid in the (first/second) nine hours after learning the material. Later research has shown that the dramatic decline is (the same/much less) when more meaningful material is involved.

15-2. Which of the three different methods of measuring forgetting is illustrated in each of the following situations?

(a) You are asked to identify a suspect in a police lineup.

(b) You time yourself while learning 20 new French words. After a week you find you have forgotten some of the words, and you again time yourself while learning the list a second time.

(c) You are asked to draw a floor plan of your bedroom from memory.

Answers: **15-1.** first, much less **15-2.** (a) recognition (b) relearning (c) recall.

16. Explain how forgetting may be due to ineffective encoding.

16-1. Why are most people unable to recognize the correct penny shown at the beginning of this chapter in the text?

16-2. What is another name for information loss due to ineffective coding of this kind?

16-3. Why is semantic coding better than phonemic coding for enhancing future recall of written material?

Answers: **16-1.** They never encoded the correct figure in their memories. **16-2.** pseudoforgetting **16-3.** Semantic coding will lead to deeper processing and more elaborate associations.

17. Compare and contrast decay and interference as potential causes of forgetting.

17-1. Two other theories of forgetting propose additional factors that may be involved in retrieval failure. One theory holds that retrieval failure may be due to the impermanence of the memory storage itself. This is the notion behind the _____ theory of forgetting. Decay theory is best able to explain retrieval failure in _____ memory and to a lesser extent in (short-term/long-term) memory.

17-2. The other theory attributes retrieval failure to other information already in the memory or to information arriving at a later time. This is the notion behind the _____ theory of forgetting. According to interference theory, the failure may be caused by interference from information already in the memory, a phenomenon called _____ interference, or the failure may be caused by interference occurring after the original memory was stored, a phenomenon called _____ interference. Interference is most likely to occur when the materials being stored are very (similar/different).

Answers: **17-1.** decay, sensory store, short-term **17-2.** interference, proactive, retroactive, similar.

18. Explain how forgetting may be due to factors in the retrieval process.

18-1.   Breakdowns in the retrieval process can occur when the encoding specificity principle is violated. This means there has been a mismatch between the original memory code and the _____ cue being used to retrieve the information. A common instance of this violation is seen when one attempts to retrieve a semantically coded word with (<u>semantic/phonemic</u>) retrieval cues.

18-2.   Retrieval failure may also occur when there is a poor fit between initial encoding processing and the processing required by the measure of retention. In other words, the two kinds of processing are not transfer-_____.

18-3.   Sigmund Freud felt that some breakdowns in the retrieval process could be attributed to purposeful suppression of information by unconscious forces, a phenomenon called _____ forgetting. Freud called motivated forgetting _____.

Answers: **18-1.** retrieval, phonemic **18-2.** appropriate **18-3.** motivated, repression.

19. Summarize evidence for the view that most recovered memories of childhood sexual abuse are genuine.

19-1.   Those who argue that most of these recovered memories are genuine assert that the frequency of sexual abuse in childhood is (<u>less/more</u>) widespread than most people realize.

19-2.   What did the 17-year follow-up study find regarding 129 female children who had emergency treatment for sexual abuse?

Answers: **19-1.** more **19-2.** 38 percent failed to report the original incident.

20. Summarize evidence for the view that most recovered memories of childhood sexual abuse are inaccurate.

20-1.   How do the skeptics of these recovered memories of childhood sexual abuse explain their origin?

20-2.   What is the only way to tell for certain if a recovered memory is genuine or a pseudomemory?

Answers: **20-1.** Some suggestible people are convinced by persuasive therapists (that these events must have happened). **20-2.** through independent corroborative evidence.

21. Summarize evidence on the biochemistry and neural circuitry underlying memory.

21-1. Which of the following biochemical changes have been implicated in the physiology of memory?

(a) alterations in synaptic transmission at specific sites

(b) induced changes in RNA

(c) hormones that can either facilitate or impair memory storage

(d) interference with protein synthesis

21-2. Answer the following questions regarding the neural circuitry of memory.

(a) What caused a rabbit to lose its memory of a conditioned eye blink?

(b) What neural changes were found in rats that learned to run a series of mazes?

(c) What does research with long-term potentiation (LTP) and the demonstration of an increase in neuronal dendritic trees tell us about how memory is stored?

Answers: 21-1. a, c, d **21-2.** (a) Destruction of an area in the cerebellum. (b) Increased growth of neuronal dendritic trees. (c) Specific memories may have specific localized dedicated neural circuits.

22. Distinguish between two types of amnesia and identify the anatomical structures implicated in memory.

22-1. Amnesia cases due to head injury provide clues about the anatomical basis of memory. There are two basic types of head-injury amnesia. When the memory loss is for events prior to the injury, it is called _____ amnesia. When the memory loss is for events following the injury, it is called _____ amnesia.

22-2. What general region of the brain appears to play a major role in the consolidation of memories?

22-3. Consolidation is an hypothesized process which involves the gradual conversion of information into durable memory _____ stored in long-term memory. These memories are consolidated in the hippocampal region and then stored in the (hippocampus/all over the cortex).

22-4. Parallel distributed processing models of memory suggest that the hippocampal area serves to _____ together individual elements of a specific memory which are then stored in various areas of the cortex.

Answers: 22-1. retrograde, anterograde **22-2.** the entire hippocampal region **22-3.** codes, all over the cortex **22-4.** bind.

ARE THERE MULTIPLE MEMORY SYSTEMS?

23. Distinguish between declarative and nondeclarative (procedural) memory.

23-1. Label the two following situations as to whether they are examples of declarative or nondeclarative memory.

(a) This system allows you to drive a car or play a piano with minimal attention to the execution of movements that are required.

(b) This system allows you to explain how to drive a car or play a piano to a friend.

Answers: 23-1. (a) nondeclarative (b) declarative.

24. Explain the distinctions between episodic memory versus semantic memory and prospective versus retrospective memory.

24-1. It has also been hypothesized that declarative memory can be further subdivided into semantic and episodic memory. Identify these two kinds of memory from the following descriptions:

(a) This kind of memory acts like an encyclopedia, storing all of the factual information you possess.

(b) This kind of memory acts like an autobiography, storing all of your personal experiences.

24-2. Still another possibility is that we have separate memory systems for prospective and retrospective memory. The distinction here is between our ability to remember events from the past or previously learned information, _____ memory, and our ability to remember or perform actions in the future, _____ memory.

24-3. Which form of prospective memory appears to give us the most trouble when we try and retrieve it, memory of event-based tasks or memory of time-based tasks?

Answers: 24-1. (a) semantic (b) episodic **24-2.** retrospective, prospective **24-3.** time-based tasks.

REFLECTIONS ON THE CHAPTER'S THEMES

25. Explain how this chapter highlighted three of the text's unifying themes.

25-1. Three unifying themes were especially noteworthy in this chapter: the subjectivity of experience, psychology's theoretical diversity, and multifactorial causation. The text mentions two areas in which subjectivity may influence memory. Identify them below.

(a) We often see only that which gets the focus of our _____.

(b) Every time we tell about a particular experience, details are added or subtracted because of the _____ nature of memory.

25-2. The numerous debates about the nature of memory storage, the causes of forgetting, and the existence of multiple memory systems nicely illustrate psychology's _____ _____.

25-3. Since the memory of a specific event can be influenced by many factors, operating in each of the three memory stores, it is obvious that memory, like most behavior, has _____

_____.

Answers: **25-1.** (a) attention (b) reconstructive **25-2.** theoretical diversity **25-3.** multifactorial causation.

APPLICATION: IMPROVING EVERYDAY MEMORY

26. Discuss the importance of rehearsal, distributed practice, and interference in efforts to improve everyday memory.

26-1. The text lists three general strategies for improving everyday memory. Identify which strategy is being employed in the following examples.

(a) Most persons can remember their phone number because of extensive_____.

(b) Willie Nurd, the bookworm, always takes breaks between study periods when changing subject matter. Willie must realize the importance of _____ practice.

(c) Ajax never studies any other material besides mathematics on the day of his math exams in order to minimize _____.

26-2. The serial position effect means that words in the middle of a list will need (more/less) of our attention.

Answers: **26-1.** (a) rehearsal (b) distributed (c) interference **26-2.** more.

27. Discuss the value of deep processing and good organization in efforts to improve everyday memory.

27-1. Answering questions such as these is much better than simply underlining the same material in the text because it forces you to engage in _____ _____.

27-2. Outlining material from textbooks can enhance retention because it leads to better _____ of the material.

Answers: **27-1.** deep processing **27-2.** organization.

28. Describe some verbal and visual mnemonic devices that can be used to improve everyday memory.

28-1. Specific strategies for enhancing memory are called _____ devices. Examples of strategies which do not employ visual images are listed below. See if you can identify which strategy is being employed in each illustration.

(a) Using the phrase, "My Very Excellent Mother Just Sells Nuts Under Protest", to remember the names and positions of the planets illustrates the use of an _____.

(b) International Business Machines is easily identified by its _____, IBM.

(c) The phrase, "One two three four, I left my keys in the drawer," illustrates the use of _____.

(d) Since you are going to the store, your roommate asks you to bring her a bar of Ivory soap, a box of Kleenex, and a Snickers bar. You then make up a story which begins, "On my way to the Ivory Coast to check on the latest shipment of Kleenex, I ...." Here you're making use of a _____ method as a mnemonic device.

28-2. Three techniques involving visual imagery can also serve as helpful mnemonic devices: the link method, the method of loci, and the keyword method. Identify them in the examples below.

(a) You want to remember the name of your bus driver, Ray Blocker, who has especially large forearms. You form an image of a man using his large arms to block light rays from his face.

(b) You want to remember to buy bananas, eggs, milk, and bread. You visualize walking in your front door and tripping on a bunch of bananas. Stumbling forward into the hallway you notice broken eggs on the table, etc.

(c) You imagine yourself using a banana to break eggs, which you then pour into a bowl of milk and bread.

Answers: 28-1. mnemonic (a) acrostic (b) acronym (c) rhyming (d) narrative **28-2.** (a) keyword method (b) method of loci (c) link method.

CRITICAL THINKING APPLICATION

29. Explain how hindsight bias and overconfidence, contribute to the frequent inaccuracy of eye-witness testimony.

29-1. The frequent inaccuracy of eye-witness testimony is due in part to the reconstructive nature of memory, source monitoring, and the misinformation effect. In addition, the text points out that still another factor is our tendency to mold our interpretation of the past to fit how events actually turned out. This is called _____ _____.

29-2. The failure to seek disconfirming evidence can often lead to the _____ effect, which is still another reason for the frequent inaccuracy of eye-witness testimony.

Answers: 29-1. hindsight bias **29-2.** overconfidence.

Review of Key Terms

Anterograde amnesia	Decay theory	Episodic memory system
Attention	Declarative memory system	Flashbulb memories
Chunk	Dual-coding theory	Forgetting curve
Conceptual hierarchy	Elaboration	Hindsight bias
Connectionist models	Encoding	Interference theory
Consolidation	Encoding specificity principle	Levels of processing theory

Link method
Long-term memory (LTM)
Long-term potentiation (LTP)
Method of loci
Misinformation effect
Mnemonic devices
Nondeclarative memory system
Overlearning
Parallel distributed processing (PDP) models
Proactive interference
Prospective memory

Reality monitoring
Recall
Recognition
Rehearsal
Relearning
Repression
Retention
Retrieval
Retroactive interference
Retrograde amnesia
Retrospective memory
Schema

Self-referent encoding
Semantic memory system
Semantic networks
Sensory memory
Serial-position effect
Short-term memory
Source-monitoring
Source-monitoring error
Storage
Tip-of-the-tongue phenomenon
Transfer-appropriate processing

_____ **1.** Putting coded information into memory.

_____ **2.** Maintaining coded information in memory.

_____ **3.** Recovering information from memory stores.

_____ **4.** The process of focusing awareness on a narrowed range of stimuli or events.

_____ **5.** Involves remembering to perform actions in the future.

_____ **6.** Involves remembering events from the past or previously learned information.

_____ **7.** The initial processing of information is similar to the type of processing required by the subsequent measure of retention.

_____ **8.** Assumes that cognitive processes depend on patterns of activation in highly interconnected computational networks that resemble neural networks.

_____ **9.** Occurs when participants' recall of an event they witnesses is altered by introducing postevent information.

_____ **10.** A theory that proposes that deeper levels of processing result in longer lasting memory codes.

_____ **11.** Involves linking a stimulus to other information at the time of encoding.

_____ **12.** A theory that memory is enhanced by forming both semantic and visual codes since either can lead to recall.

_____ **13.** Preserves information in the original sensory form for a very brief time.

_____ **14.** A limited capacity memory store that can maintain unrehearsed information for 20 to 30 seconds.

_____ **15.** The process of repetitively verbalizing or thinking about new information.

_____ **16.** A group of familiar stimuli stored as a single unit.

_____ **17.** An unlimited capacity memory store that can hold information over lengthy periods of time.

_____ **18.** Unusually vivid and detailed recollections of momentous events.

_____ **19.** Occurs when subjects show better recall of items at the beginning and end of a list than for items in the middle.

_____ **20.** Memory for factual information.

_____ **21.** Strategies for enhancing memory.

_____ **22.** Memory made up of chronological, or temporally dated, recollections of personal experiences.

_____ **23.** Memory that contains general knowledge that is not tied to the time when the information was learned.

24. _____ These consist of concepts joined together by links that show how the concepts are related.

25. _____ A long lasting increase in neural excitability at synapses along a specific neural pathway.

26. _____ An organized cluster of knowledge about a particular object or sequence of events.

27. _____ The attempt to mold our interpretation of the past to fit how it actually turned out.

28. _____ A temporary inability to remember something you know accompanied by the feeling that it's just out of reach.

29. _____ A curve graphing retention and forgetting over time

30. _____ The proportion of material remembered.

31. _____ The ability to remember information without any cues.

32. _____ Requires the selection of previously learned information from an array of options (e.g., multiple-choice tests).

33. _____ Requires the memorization of information a second time to determine how much time or effort is saved.

34. _____ Attributes forgetting to the impermanence of memory storage.

35. _____ Attributes forgetting to competition from other material.

36. _____ Occurs when new information impairs the retention of previously learned information.

37. _____ Occurs when previously learned information impairs the retention of new information.

38. _____ States that the value of a retrieval cue depends on how well it corresponds to the memory code.

39. _____ Involves purposeful suppression of memories (motivated forgetting).

40. _____ A theoretical process involving the gradual conversion of information into durable memory codes stored in long-term memory.

41. _____ The loss of memory for events that occurred prior to a brain injury.

42. _____ The loss of memory for events that occur after a brain injury.

43. _____ Strategies for enhancing memory.

44. _____ The continued rehearsal of material after it has apparently been mastered.

45. _____ Involves forming a mental image of items to be remembered in a way that connects them together.

46. _____ A mnemonic device that involves taking an imaginary walk along a familiar path.

47. _____ A multi-level classification system based on common properties among items (e.g., cats, animals, living things).

48. _____ The process of deciding how or whether information is personally relevant.

49. _____ The process of making attributions about the origins of memories.

50. _____ The process of deciding whether memories are based on external or internal sources.

51. _____ An error that occurs when a memory derived from one source is attributed to another.

52. _____ Another term for the procedural memory system which houses memory for actions, skills, and operations.

Review of Key People

Alan Baddeley
Sir Fredrick Bartlett
Fergus Craik and Robert Lockhart
Herman Ebbinghaus

Eric Kandel
Marcia Johnson
Elizabeth Loftus
George Miller

Brenda Milner
Richard Thompson
Endel Tulving

_____ 1. Proposed three progressively deeper levels for processing incoming information.

_____ 2. Proposed the concept of a working memory that underlies human thought processes.

_____ 3. She, and her colleagues, proposed the notions of source and reality monitoring.

_____ 4. Demonstrated that the reconstructive nature of memory can distort eyewitness testimony.

_____ 5. Used nonsense syllables to become famous for his forgetting curve.

_____ 6. One of his many contributions was the encoding specificity principle.

_____ 7. Proposed the concept of chunking for storing information in short-term memory.

_____ 8. Followed the case of HM, who had his hippocampus removed.

_____ 9. Experimentally demonstrated the reconstructive nature of memory.

_____ 10. Showed reflex learning in the sea slub produces changes in the strength of specific synaptic connections.

_____ 11. Showed that specific memories may depend on localized neural circuits in the brain.

Self-Quiz

1. Which of the following is not one of the three basic human memory processes?
   a. storage
   b. retrieval
   c. decoding
   d. encoding

2. Which one of the three levels of processing would probably be employed when attempting to memorize the following three-letter sequences: WAB WAC WAD?
   a. structural
   b. semantic
   c. phonemic
   d. chunking

3. According to Paivio's dual-coding theory:
   a. words are easier to encode than images
   b. abstract words are easier to encode than concrete words
   c. visual imagery may hinder the retrieval of words
   d. it should be easier to remember the word banana than the word justice

4. Retrieval from long-term memory is usually best when the information has been stored at which level of processing?
   a. structural
   b. semantic
   c. phonemic
   d. chunking

5. Which of the memory stores can hold the least amount of information?
   a. sensory store
   b. short-term memory
   c. long-term memory
   d. declarative memory

6. Which of the following sequences of words would be most subject to a clustering effect?
   a. FAN HEAVEN JUSTICE CHAIR
   b. HOUSE VACATION MOUSE STATISTIC
   c. BLUE DOG CAMEL YELLOW
   d. CONVERSE ICICLE CONCEPT THINKING

7. Which word best describes the speed of human cognitive functioning?
   a. slow
   b. moderate
   c. rapid
   d. blazing

8. When you attempt to recall the name of a high school classmate by imagining yourself back in the English class with her, you are making use of:
   a. retrieval cues
   b. context cues
   c. schemas
   d. recognition cues

9. You recall being lost in a shopping mall at the age of five but your parents assure you that it never happened. Errors like this are most likely due to:
   a. ineffective encoding
   b. a reality monitoring error
   c. a source monitoring error
   d. the misinformation effect

10. Taking this particular self-test measures your:
    a. constructive errors
    b. reconstructive errors
    c. recall
    d. recognition

11. Ineffective encoding of information may result in:
    a. the primacy effect
    b. the recency effect
    c. pseudoforgetting
    d. chunking

12. Decay theory is best able to explain the loss of memory in
    a. sensory store
    b. long-term memory
    c. short-term memory
    d. repressed memory

13. When you violate the encoding specificity principle, you are likely to experience an inability to:
    a. encode information
    b. store information
    c. retrieve information
    d. form a visual image of the material you want to retrieve

14. Which of the following statements is the most accurate evaluation as to the authenticity of the recall of repressed memories?
    a. Research confirms that they are authentic.
    b. Research confirms that they are not authentic.
    c. Research cannot confirm or deny their authenticity.
    d. I have no idea what you're talking about.

15. It is very easy to recall the name of your high school because it has been subjected to extensive:
    a. deep processing
    b. clustering
    c. chunking
    d. rehearsal

16. The failure to seek out disconfirming evidence can often lead to:
    a. the overconfidence effect
    b. the reconstructive bias
    c. the hindsight bias
    d. a source monitoring error

Answers: 1. c **2.** a **3.** d **4.** b **5.** b **6.** c **7.** d **8.** b **9.** b **10.** d **11.** c **12.** a **13.** c **14.** c **15.** d **16.** a.

InfoTrac Keywords

Amnesia   Flashbulb Memories   Misinformation Effect

Chapter Eight
LANGUAGE AND THOUGHT

Review of Key Ideas

THE COGNITIVE REVOLUTION IN PSYCHOLOGY

1. Describe the "cognitive revolution" in psychology.

    1-1. Answer the following questions regarding the cognitive revolution in psychology.

        (a) In what decade did this revolution get underway?

        (b) Why were earlier cognitive approaches abandoned?

        (c) What theoretical school openly opposed the cognitive approach?

    Answers: 1-1. (a) The 1950s (b) They were too subjective (as opposed to being empirical or objective).
(c) Behaviorism.

LANGUAGE: TURNING THOUGHTS INTO WORDS

2. Outline the key properties of language.

    2-1. Language is characterized by four properties: it is symbolic, semantic, generative, and structured.
Identify each of these properties in the following statements.

        (a) Applying rules to arrange words into phrases and sentences illustrates the_____ property
of language.

        (b) Using words or geometric forms to represent objects, actions or events illustrates the
_____ property of language.

(c) Making different words out of the same letters, such as NOW and WON, illustrates the
_____ property of language.

(d) Giving the same meaning to different words, such as chat, katz, and cat, illustrates the
_____ aspect of language.

2-2.   Identify the following parts (units) of language.

(a) With around 40 of these basic sounds you can say all of the words in the English language.
_____

(b) Phonemes are combined into these smallest units of meaning in a language, which may include root
words as well as prefixes and suffixes. _____

(c) The component of language concerned with understanding the meaning of words and word combinations is called _____.

(d) These rules specify how words can be combined into phrases and sentences. _____

Answers: 2-1. (a) structured (b) symbolic (c) generative (d) semantic 2-2. (a) phonemes (b) morphemes (c) semantics
(d) syntax.

3. Outline the development of human language during the first year.

3-1.   Answer the following questions regarding the development of language during the first year of life.

(a) What are a child's three major vocalizations during the first six months of life?

(b) What is the range in months for the babbling stage of language development?

(c) What gradually occurs as the babbling stage progresses?

Answers: 3-1. (a) crying, laughing, and cooing (b) 6 to 18 months (c) The babbling increasingly resembles spoken
language.

4. Describe children's early use of single words and word combinations.

4-1.   What does the text mean when it states that the receptive vocabulary of toddlers is much larger than their
productive vocabulary?

4-2.   Identify the following phenomenon observed in children's early use of language.

(a)   What phenomenon is illustrated when a child calls all four-legged creatures "doggie"?_____

(b)   What phenomenon is illustrated when a child correctly communicates her desire to know where the family dog is simply by asking, "doggie"?_____

(c)   What phenomenon is illustrated when a child complains to her mother, "doggie eat cookie"?_____

(d)   What phenomenon is illustrated when a child says, "doggie runned away"?

(e)   What phenomenon is illustrated when a child puns, "I love your I's"?_____

(f)   Solve the following anagram which best describes how children acquire language skills. FWSYLIFT_____

Answers: 4-1. They can understand more spoken words than they can reproduce themselves. **4-2.** (a) overextensions (b) holophrases (c) telegraphic speech (d) overregularization (e) metalinguistic awareness (f) SWIFTLY.

5.   Summarize the effect of bilingualism on language and cognitive development and the factors that influence the learning of a second language.

5-1.   What does research comparing monolingual and bilingual children show with respect to their language and cognitive development?

5-2.   What two factors positively influence the learning of a second language?

Answers: 5-1. They are largely similar in their rate of development (in both areas). **5-2.** starting at an early age and becoming acculturated.

6.   Summarize evidence on language acquisition in animals.

6-1.   Indicate whether each of the following is true or false.

_____ (a)   Researchers have been able to teach chimpanzees to use symbols to communicate.

_____ (b)   Kanzi the chimp appears to comprehend both words and their relations to one another as specified by the structure.

_____ (c)   Language acquisition in chimpanzees appears to be very similar to language acquisition in children.

Answers: 6-1. (a) true (b) true (c) false.

7. **Discuss the possible evolutionary basis of language.**

   7-1.   What evolutionary advantage might language have given human populations when compared to the Neanderthals (whom many believe lacked the language capabilities found in human beings)?

   Answers: 7-1. The Neanderthals became extinct (and we're still here).

8. **Compare and contrast the behaviorist, nativist, and interactionist perspectives on the acquisition of language.**

   8-1.   Identify the following perspectives on the acquisition of language.

   (a) This perspective places great emphasis on the role of reinforcement and imitation._____

   (b) This perspective assumes that children make use of a language acquisition device (LAD) to acquire transformational rules which enable them to easily translate between surface structure and deep structure._____

   (c) This interactionist perspective argues that language development is tied to progress in thinking and general cognitive development. _____

   (d) This interactionist perspective argues that language development is directed to some extent by the social benefits children derive from interaction with mature language users._____ _____

   (e) This interactionist theory proposes that the neural circuits supporting language emerge gradually in response to language learning experiences._____

   8-2.   Which perspective places greatest emphasis on:

   (a) nurture _____

   (b) nature _____

   (c) nature interacting with nurture _____

   Answers: 8-1. (a) behaviorist (b) nativist (c) cognitive theories (d) social communication theories (e) emergentist theories 8-2. (a) behaviorist (b) nativist (c) interactionist.

9. **Discuss culture and language and the status of the linguistic relativity hypothesis.**

   9-1.   What is the major idea behind Benjamin Whorf's linguistic relativity hypothesis?

   9-2.   What did Eleanor Rosch's experiment show when she compared the color recognition ability of English-speaking people and Dani people, who have only two words for color?

   9-3.   While language does not appear to invariably determine thought, it might exert some influence over the way we approach an idea. In other words, one's language may make it either _____ or more _____ to think along certain lines.

PROBLEM SOLVING: IN SEARCH OF SOLUTIONS

10. List and describe the three types of problems proposed by Greeno.

10-1. Greeno has proposed three types of problems (arrangement, inducing structure, and transformation). Identify each of these types from descriptions given below.

(a) This type of problem requires the problem solver to discover the relations among the parts of the problem.

(b) This type of problem requires the problem solver to place the parts in a way that satisfies some specific criterion.

(c) This type of problem requires the problem solver to carry out a sequence of changes or rearrangements in order to reach a specific goal.

10-2. Which types of Greeno's problems are represented in the following situations?

(a) Which two three-letter English words can be made from the letters TBU?

(b) Fill in the missing word in, "Grass is to green as snow is to _____".

(c) You need to take your child to a pediatrician, your dog to the veterinarian, and your mother to the hairdresser, all within a limited time period. You think to yourself, "I'll take the kid and the dog and pick up Mom. Mom can stay with the kid at the doctor's office while I take the dog to the vet. Then I'll..."

10-3. Which type of problems are often solved in a sudden burst of insight?

11. **Explain how irrelevant information and functional fixedness can hinder problem solving.**

11-1.   Which of the barriers to effective problem solving, irrelevant information or functional fixedness, are you overcoming when you:

(a) make a financial decision without first consulting your horoscope?

(b) use a page of newspaper as a wedge to keep a door open?

Answers: 11-1. (a) irrelevant information (b) functional fixedness.

12. **Explain how mental set and unnecessary constraints can hinder problem solving.**

12-1.   Which of the barriers to effective problem solving, mental set or unnecessary constraints, are you overcoming when you:

(a) color outside the lines to create a more interesting picture?

(b) teach an old dog a new trick?

Answers: 12-1. (a) unnecessary constraints (b) mental set.

13. **Describe a variety of general problem-solving strategies.**

13-1.   The text describes a variety of different problem-solving techniques, or _____. Which of these heuristics (means/ends analysis, forming subgoals, working backward, searching for analogies, or changing the representation of the problem) would be most applicable in solving the following problems?

(a) While opening your car door you drop the keys. The keys hit your foot and bounce underneath the car, too far to reach. It has stopped raining, so you close your umbrella and ponder how to get your keys.

(b) You have accepted the responsibility for chairing the homecoming celebration at your school.

(c) Alone at night in the office, you observe that the ribbon is missing from a printer you want to use. After obtaining a new ribbon you can't figure out how to install it correctly. Glancing around, you see a similar printer with the ribbon installed.

(d) As an entering freshman in college, you have already chosen a field of study and a specific graduate school you wish to attend. Now all you have to do is accomplish this goal.

(e) You have agreed to become the campaign chairwoman for a friend who wants to run for student body president. Obviously, your goal is to make your friend look like a good choice to students, but which heuristic do politicians often employ here?

Answers: 13-1. heuristics (a) search for analogies (the umbrella can be used as a rake) (b) form subgoals (c) work backwards (see how the ribbon comes out) (d) means/ends analysis (e) change the representation of the problem (make the opponents look like a bad choice).

14. Discuss the distinction between field independence and dependence.

14-1. Answer the following true-false questions regarding the distinctions between field dependent and field independent persons.

_____ (a) Field dependent persons are more likely to use internal cues to orient themselves in space.

_____ (b) Field independent persons are more likely to recognize the component parts of a problem rather than just seeing it as a whole.

Answers: 14-1. (a) false (b) true.

15. Discuss cultural variations in cognitive style as they relate to problem solving.

15-1. Answer the following true-false questions regarding cultural variations in cognitive style.

_____ (a) Persons living in cultures that depend on hunting and gathering for their subsistence are generally more field dependent than persons living in more sedentary agricultural societies.

_____ (b) Persons raised in cultures with lenient child-rearing practices and an emphasis on personal autonomy tend to be more field independent.

15-2. Nisbett and others have proposed that East Asian cultures focus on context and relationships among elements in a field, which they call a _____ cognitive style, whereas people from Western cultures focus on objects and their properties, rather than context, which they call an _____ cognitive style. They conclude that these cultural disparities in cognitive style are (substantial/minimal).

Answers: 15-1. (a) false (b) true **15-2.** holistic, analytical, substantial.

16. **Compare the additive and elimination by aspects approaches to selecting an alternative.**

   16-1. Indicate which of these two approaches to decision making would be best when:

   (a) The task is complex and there are numerous alternatives to choose from.

   (b) You want to allow attractive attributes to compensate for unattractive attributes.

   Answers: **16-1.** (a) elimination by aspects (b) additive.

17. **Describe additional findings on factors that influence decisions about preferences.**

   17-1. When forced to choose between various options, people fluctuate (less/more) than assumed by most models of decision making. One reason for these fluctuations appears to be incidental _____ fluctuations.

   17-2. It has also been found that comparative and separate approaches to the evaluation of options yield (similar/different) results. While people often make decisions based on comparative evaluations, the chosen event or product is actually experienced in a _____, or isolated, evaluation.

   17-3. Another factor in decision making is the need to avoid _____ about making a bad decision. Research shows that people tend to (over-/under-) estimate how much regret they will experience as a result of poor decisions.

   Answers: **17-1.** more, emotional **17-2.** different, separate **17-3.** regret, over-estimate.

18. **Explain the factors that individuals typically consider in risky decision-making.**

   18-1. What differentiates risky decision-making from other kinds of decision making?

   18-2. What is the most you can know when making a risky decision?

   18-3. What two things must be known in order to calculate the expected value of making a risky decision when gambling with money?

   18-4. How does the concept of subjective utility explain why some persons still engage in risky decision-making when the expected value predicts a loss?

   Answers: **18-1.** The outcome is uncertain. **18-2.** the probability of a particular outcome **18-3.** the average amount of money you could expect to win or lose with each play and the probability of a win or loss **18-4.** The personal worth of the outcome may outweigh the probability of losing.

19. **Describe the availability and representativeness heuristics.**

19-1.   Estimating the probability of an event on the basis of how often one recalls it has been experienced in the past is what Tversky and Kahneman call a(an) _____ heuristic.

19-2.   When most people are asked if there are more words that begin with N or words that have N as the third letter, they apply the availability heuristic and guess incorrectly. Explain why they do this.

19-3.   Estimating the probability of an event on the basis of how similar it is to a particular model or stereotype of that event is what Tversky and Kahneman call a _____ heuristic.

19-4.   "Steve is very shy. He has a high need for structure and likes detail. Is Steve more likely to be a salesperson or a librarian?" When persons are given this problem, they usually guess that he is a librarian, even though there are many more salespersons than there are librarians. Explain why they do this.

Answers: **19-1.** availability **19-2.** Because they can immediately recall many more words that begin with N than words having N as the third letter. **19-3.** representativeness **19-4.** Because they employ the representativeness heuristic and Steve fits the stereotype of a librarian.

20. **Describe base rate neglect and the conjunction fallacy and their causes.**

20-1.   Identify which example of flawed reasoning, base rate neglect, or the conjunction fallacy, is being described below.

(a) Estimating that the odds of two uncertain events happening together are greater than the odds of either event happening alone.

(b) Guessing that "Steve" is a librarian and not a salesperson.

(c) Which one of these two errors in judgment is a misapplication of the representativeness heuristic?

Answers: **20-1.** (a) the conjunction fallacy (b) base rate neglect (c) base rate neglect.

21. **Summarize the research on the alternative outcomes effect.**

21-1.   Answer the following questions regarding the Featured Study.

(a) Was the objective probability of obtaining the focal outcome easy or difficult to calculate in these two studies?

(b) What happened when the objective probability of the focal outcome remained the same, but the distribution of alternative outcomes was narrowed (e.g., 2/9 versus 2/1-1-1-1-1-1)?

(c) What does this research tell us about the notion of objective probabilities?

Answers: 21-1. (a) easy (b) Subjective estimates of its likelihood decline. (c) They are ultimately very subjective.

22. **Explain evolutionary theorists' evaluation of cognitive research on flaws in human decision strategies.**

22-1. According to evolutionary theorists, is the human mind better wired to deal with:

(a) base rates and probabilities or raw frequencies?

(b) whole actions or parts of actions?

22-2. What happens when problems are reformulated in ways that resemble problems ancient humans had to face?

Answers: 22-1. raw frequencies (b) whole actions **22-2.** the irrationality decreases.

23. **Describe the nature of the fast and frugal heuristics.**

23-1. In going about our daily lives we are generally forced to make quick decisions (<u>with/without</u>) the relevant information. According to Gigerenzer, in these situations we usually employ _____ and _____ heuristics based on our own general knowledge. Research shows that these fast and frugal heuristics (<u>are/are not</u>) very effective.

Answers: 23-1. without, fast, frugal, are.

REFLECTING ON THE CHAPTER'S THEMES

24. **Explain how this chapter highlighted four of the text's themes.**

24-1. Indicate which one of the four unifying themes (the interaction of heredity and the environment, behavior is shaped by cultural heritage, the empirical nature of psychology, and the subjectivity of experience) are best represented by the following statements.

(a) Psychologists developed objective measures for higher mental processes thus bringing about the cognitive revolution.

(b) The manner in which questions are framed can influence cognitive appraisal of the questions.

(c) Neither pure nativist theories nor pure nurture theories appear to adequately explain the development of language.

(d) The ecological demands of one's environment appear to somewhat affect one's cognitive style.

Answers: 24-1. (a) the empirical nature of psychology (b) the subjectivity of experience (c) the interaction of heredity and the environment (d) Behavior is shaped by cultural heritage.

UNDERSTANDING PITFALLS IN DECISION MAKING

25. Explain what is meant by the gambler's fallacy.

    25-1.   A man walks into a gambling casino with a notepad and begins noting which numbers are coming up on a roulette wheel. After several hours, he notes that number 26 has never come up during this period. He then begins placing bets on 26. This man is falling for the _____ _____.

Answers: 25-1. (a) the gambler's fallacy.

26. Describe the propensity to overestimate the improbable and seek confirming evidence.

    26-1.   What flaw in reasoning often results from intense media coverage of dramatic, vivid, but infrequent events?

    26-2.   What omission leads to the confirmation bias when making decisions?

    26-3.   How is the confirmation bias related to belief perseverance?

Answers: 26-1. the propensity to overestimate the improbable **26-2.** failure to seek out disconfirming evidence
26-3. Disconfirming evidence is subjected to little or skeptical evaluation.

27. **Discuss the overconfidence effect and the effects of framing on decisions.**

27-1. Answer the following true/false questions regarding the overconfidence effect.

_____ (a) We are much less subject to this effect when making decisions about ourselves as opposed to more worldly matters.

_____ (b) Scientists are not generally prone to this effect when making decisions about information in their own fields.

_____ (c) In the study of college students cited by the text, it was observed that the gap between personal confidence and actual accuracy of decisions increased as the confidence level increased.

27-2. Asking persons if they would prefer their glass of wine to be half-full or half-empty illustrates the general idea behind the _____ of questions.

27-3. Are persons more likely to take risky options when the problem is framed so as to obtain gains, or when it is framed so as to cut losses?

Answers: 27-1. (a) false (b) false (c) true **27-2.** framing **27-3.** when it is framed so as to cut losses.

28. **Describe some language manipulation strategies that people use to shape others' thoughts.**

28-1. State which language manipulation strategy is being used in each of the following situations.

(a) A politician says that his opponent "has an IQ somewhat below room temperature."

(b) Pet owners have their pets "put to sleep" when they become terminally ill.

(c) Only someone unbelievably stupid would be against more gun control legislation.

(d) Insurance companies sell "life insurance" policies rather than "death benefits" policies.

28-2. Research examining semantic slanting shows that an organization is best advised to slant its objectives so as to be (for/against) something when attempting to accomplish its goal.

Answers: 28-1. (a) name calling (b) semantic slanting (c) anticipatory name calling (d) semantic slanting **28-2.** for.

Review of Key Terms

Acculturation
Algorithm
Alternative outcomes effect
Availability heuristic
Bilingualism
Cognition
Confirmation bias
Conjunction fallacy
Decision making
Fast mapping
Field dependence-independence
Framing

Functional fixedness
Gambler's fallacy
Heuristic
Insight
Language
Language acquisition device (LAD)
Linguistic relativity
Mean length of utterance (MLU)
Mental set
Metalinguistic awareness
Morphemes
Overextension

Overregularization
Phonemes
Problem solving
Problem space
Representativeness heuristic
Risky decision making
Semantics
Syntax
Telegraphic speech
Theory of bounded rationality
Trial and error
Underextention

_____ 1. The component of language concerned with understanding the meaning of words and word combinations.

_____ 2. A collection of symbols, and rules for combining those symbols, that can be used to create an infinite variety of messages.

_____ 3. The smallest units of sound in a spoken language.

_____ 4. The smallest units of meaning in a language.

_____ 5. The rules that specify how words can be combined into phrases and sentences.

_____ 6. Using a word incorrectly to describe a wider set of objects or actions than it is meant to.

_____ 7. Using a word to describe a narrower set of objects than it is meant to.

_____ 8. Single-word utterances that represent the meaning of several words.

_____ 9. The ability to reflect on the use of language.

_____ 10. Consists of the acquisition of two languages that employ different speech sounds, vocabulary, and grammatical rules.

_____ 11. The degree to which a person is socially and psychologically integrated into a new culture.

_____ 12. Basing the estimated probability of an event on the ease with which relevant instances come to mind.

_____ 13. Basing the estimated probability of an event on how similar it is to the typical prototype of that event.

_____ 14. The mental processes involved in acquiring knowledge.

_____ 15. The tendency to perceive an item only in terms of its most common use.

_____ 16. The sudden discovery of a correct solution to a problem following incorrect attempts.

_____ 17. A strategy for solving problems.

_____ 18. The process by which children map a word on an underlying concept after only one exposure to the word.

_____ 19. The average of youngsters' spoken statements (measured in morphemes).

_____ 20. Generalizing grammatical rules to irregular cases where they do not apply.

_____ 21. Making decisions under conditions of uncertainty.

_____ 22. A hypothetical innate mechanism or process that facilitates the learning of language.

_____ 23. Persisting in using problem-solving strategies that have worked in the past.

_____ 24. The theory that one's language determines one's thoughts.

_____ 25. The active efforts to discover what must be done to achieve a goal that is not readily attainable.

_____ 26. Trying possible solutions sequentially and discarding those that are in error until one works.

_____ 27. Evaluating alternatives and making choices among them.

_____ 28. How issues are posed or how choices are structured.

_____ 29. Occurs when peoples' belief about whether an outcome will occur changes depending on how alternative outcomes are distributed, even though the summed probability of the alternative outcomes is held constant.

_____ 30. A methodical, step-by-step procedure for trying all possible alternatives in searching for a solution to a problem.

_____ 31. The tendency to seek information that supports one's decisions and beliefs while ignoring disconfirming evidence.

_____ 32. Occurs when people estimate that the odds of two uncertain events happening are greater than the odds of either event happening alone.

_____ 33. Refers to individuals' tendency to rely primarily on either external or internal frames of reference when orienting themselves in space.

_____ 34. The belief that the odds of a chance event increase if the event hasn't occurred recently.

_____ 35. Refers to the set of possible pathways to a solution considered by the problem solver.

_____ 36. Asserts that people tend to use simple strategies in decision making that focus only on a few facets of available options and often result in "irrational" decisions that are less than optimal.

Answers: 1. semantics **2.** language **3.** phonemes **4.** morphemes **5.** syntax **6.** overextensions **7.** underextensions **8.** telegraphic speech **9.** metalinguistic awareness **10.** bilingualism **11.** acculturation **12.** availability heuristic **13.** representativeness heuristic **14.** cognition **15.** functional fixedness **16.** insight **17.** heuristic **18.** fast mapping **19.** mean length of utterances (MLU) **20.** overregularization **21.** risky decision-making **22.** language acquisition device (LAD) **23.** mental set **24.** linguistic relativity **25.** problem solving **26.** trial and error **27.** decision making **28.** framing **29.** alternative outcomes effect **30.** algorithm **31.** confirmation bias **32.** conjunction fallacy **33.** field dependence-independence **34.** gambler's fallacy **35.** problem space **36.** theory of bounded rationality.

Review of Key People

Noam Chomsky
Leda Cosmides & John Tooby
Gerd Gigerenzer

Daniel Kahneman
Steven Pinker
Sue Savage-Rumbaugh

Herbert Simon
B. F. Skinner
Amos Tversky

_____ 1. Won the Nobel Prize for his research on decision making and artificial intelligence.

	2.	Proposed that children learn language through the established principles of learning.
	3.	Proposed that children learn language through a biologically built-in language acquisition device.
	4.	One of the co-researchers who showed that people base probability estimates on heuristics that do not always yield reasonable estimates of success.
	5.	Along with her colleagues, she taught the chimp, Kanzi, to communicate in a way that made use of all the basic properties of language.
	6.	Argues that human language ability is a species-specific trait that is the product of natural selection.
	7.	Argue that the human mind has evolved to solve specific adaptive problems.
	8.	Conducted research that shows people often employ fast and frugal heuristics that can yield surprisingly effective results.

Answers: 1. Simon **2.** Skinner **3.** Chomsky **4.** Kahneman & Tversky **5.** Savage-Rumbaugh **6.** Pinker **7.** Cosmides & Tooby **8.** Gigerenzer.

Self-Quiz

1. Which of the following explanations best explains the success of the cognitive revolution in psychology?
   a. the refining of introspection as a research method
   b. the development of empirical methods
   c. the use of psychotherapy to explore the unconscious
   d. the success in teaching chimps to use language

2. Which of the following is not one of the basic properties of language?
   a. generative
   b. symbolic
   c. structured
   d. alphabetical

3. The word SLOWLY would be an example of a:
   a. metalinguistic
   b. phoneme
   c. syntactical unit
   d. morpheme

4. When a child says that TUB and BUT are constructed of the same three letters, she is showing an awareness of
   a. morphemes
   b. phonemes
   c. metalinguistics
   d. syntax

5. Which of the following statements is incorrect?
   a. A chimp has learned to sign (ASL) more than 150 words.
   b. Children and chimps appear to learn language in a similar manner.
   c. A chimp has shown comprehension for both words and their relation to one another.
   d. The ability to use language may not be unique to humans.

6. The fact that children appear to learn rules, rather than specific word combinations, when acquiring language skills argues most strongly against which theory of language development?
   a. cognitive
   b. behaviorist
   c. nativist
   d. social communication

7. Which one of Greeno's problems is exemplified by the anagram?
   a. arrangement
   b. inducing structure
   c. transformation
   d. chunking

8. Which barrier to problem solving are you overcoming when you use a piece of paperclip as a temporary replacement for the screw that fell out of your glasses?
   a. irrelevant information
   b. functional fixedness
   c. mental set
   d. unnecessary constraints

9. Which of the following heuristics would you probably employ if assigned the task of carrying out a school election?
   a. work backwards
   b. representativeness
   c. search for analogies
   d. form subgoals

10. Field independent persons are most likely to come from cultures that:
   a. encourage strict child-rearing practices
   b. have a stable agricultural base
   c. encourage lenient child-rearing practices
   d. stress conformity

11. When faced with having to choose among numerous alternatives, most persons will opt for
   a. an elimination by aspects approach
   b. an additive approach
   c. a means/end analysis
   d. a subjective-utility model

12. Most persons mistakenly believe that more people die from tornadoes than from asthma. This is because they mistakenly apply:
   a. the means/end analysis
   b. the compensatory decision model
   c. the availability heuristic
   d. the representativeness heuristic

13. Failure to actively seek out contrary evidence may lead to:
   a. overestimating the improbable
   b. the conjunction fallacy
   c. the gambler's fallacy
   d. the confirmation bias

14. People generally prefer a choice that provides an 80 percent chance of success over one that provides a 19 percent chance of failure. This illustrates the effect of:
    a. the availability heuristic
    b. the representativeness heuristic
    c. framing
    d. mental set

15. Owners of automobile junkyards prefer to use the term automobile recycling centers. This is an example of the use of:
    a. framing
    b. semantic slanting
    c. anticipatory name calling
    d. subjective utility

Answers: 1. b **2.** d **3.** d **4.** c **5.** b **6.** b **7.** a **8.** b **9.** d **10.** c **11.** a **12.** c **13.** d **14.** c **15.** b.

InfoTrac Keywords

Bilingualism   Mental Set   Risky Decision Making

Chapter Nine

INTELLIGENCE AND PSYCHOLOGICAL TESTING

Review of Key Ideas

KEY CONCEPTS IN PSYCHOLOGICAL TESTING

1. List and describe the principle categories of psychological tests.

1-1. Most psychological tests can be placed into one of two very broad categories. These two categories are: _____ tests and _____ tests.

1-2. There are three categories of mental abilities tests. Below are examples of each of these categories. Identify them.

(a) The ACT and SAT tests you may have taken before entering college are examples of _____ tests.

(b) The exams you frequently take in your introductory psychology class are examples of _____ tests.

(c) Tests used to demonstrate general intellectual giftedness are examples of _____ tests.

1-3. Personality tests allow an individual to compare himself or herself to other persons with respect to particular personality _____. Personality tests generally (do/do not) have right and wrong answers.

Answers: **1-1.** mental ability, personality (in either order) **1-2.** (a) aptitude (b) achievement (c) intelligence **1-3.** characteristics or traits, do not.

2. Explain the concepts of standardization and test norms.

2-1. Developing test norms and uniform procedures for use in the administration and scoring of a test is the general idea behind test _____.

2-2. In order to interpret a particular score on a test, it is necessary to know how other persons score on this test. This is the purpose of test _____. An easy method for providing comparisons of test scores is to convert the raw scores into _____ scores.

Answers: 2-1. standardization **2-2.** norms, percentile.

3. Explain the meaning of test reliability and how it is estimated.

3-1. The ability of a test to produce consistent results across subsequent measurements of the same persons, is known as its _____. Psychological tests (are/are not) perfectly reliable.

3-2. Readministering the same test to the same group of persons a week or two following the original testing (test-retest) allows one to estimate the _____ of a test. If a test is highly reliable, then a person's scores on the two different administrations will be very similar. The amount of similarity can be assessed by means of the _____ coefficient. The closer the correlation comes to 1.0 the (more/less) reliable the test is.

3-3. Another method for assessing reliability is to break the test into two halves and derive a correlation for the two halves. This method is called _____-_____ reliability.

Answers: 3-1. reliability, are not **3-2.** reliability, correlation, more **3-3.** split-half.

4. Explain the three types of validity and how they are assessed.

4-1. The ability of a test to actually measure what it claims to measure is known as its _____. The term "validity" is also used to refer to the accuracy or usefulness of the _____ based on a test.

4-2. There are three general kinds of validity. Identify each of these kinds from the descriptions given below.

(a) This kind of validity will tend to be high when, for example, scores on the ACT and SAT actually predict success in college. _____

(b) This kind of validity will be of particular importance to you when taking your exams for this class. It will be high if the exam sticks closely to the explicitly assigned material. _____

(c) This kind of validity is more vague than the other two kinds and refers to the ability of a test to measure abstract qualities, such as intelligence. _____

4-3. As with the estimation of reliability, the estimation of validity makes use of the _____ _____.

Answers: 4-1. validity, inferences or decisions **4-2.** (a) criterion-related validity, (b) content validity, (c) construct validity **4-3.** correlation coefficient.

THE EVOLUTION OF INTELLIGENCE TESTING

5. Summarize the contributions of Galton and Binet to the evolution of intelligence testing.

5-1. Identify each of the above men from the descriptions of their contributions given on the next page.

(a) This man developed the first useful intelligence test. His tests were used to predict success in school, and scores were expressed in terms of mental age. _____

(b) This man began the quest to measure intelligence. He assumed that intelligence was mainly inherited and could be measured by assessing sensory acuity. He also invented correlation and percentile test scores. _____

Answers: 5-1. (a) Binet (b) Galton.

6. Summarize the contributions of Terman and Wechsler to the evolution of intelligence testing.

6-1. Identify each of the above men from the descriptions of their contributions given below.

(a) This man revised Binet's tests to produce the Stanford-Binet Intelligence Scale, the standard for all future intelligence tests. He also introduced the intelligence quotient (IQ).

_____

(b) This man developed the first successful test of adult intelligence, the WAIS. He also developed new intelligence tests for children.

_____

(c) In developing his new intelligence tests, this man added many non-verbal items which allowed for the separate assessment of both verbal and non-verbal abilities. He also replaced the IQ score with one based on the normal distribution. _____

Answers: 6-1. (a) Terman (b) Wechsler (c) Wechsler.

BASIC QUESTIONS ABOUT INTELLIGENCE TESTING

7. Explain the meaning of an individual's score on a modern intelligence test.

7-1. Answer the following questions regarding intelligence test scores.

(a) In what manner is human intelligence assumed to be distributed?

(b) What percentage of people have an IQ score below 100?

(c) What percentage of persons would score two or more standard deviations above the mean? (see Fig. 9.7 in the text)

Answers: 7-1. (a) It forms a normal distribution. (b) 50% (c) 2%.

8. **Describe the reliability and validity of modern IQ test scores.**

   8-1.   Answer the following questions about the reliability of modern intelligence tests.

   (a) What are reliability estimates (correlation coefficients) are found for most modern intelligence tests?

   (b) What might be a problem here with respect to an individual's test score?

   8-2.   Answer the following questions with respect to the validity of modern intelligence tests.

   (a) What is the correlation between IQ tests and grades in school?

   (b) What is the correlation between IQ tests and the number of years of schooling that people complete?

   (c) What might be a general problem with assuming intelligence tests are a valid measure of general mental ability?

   Answers: 8-1. (a) They are in the low .90s. (b) Temporary conditions could lower the score. **8-2.** (a) .40s and .50s (b) .60 to .80 (c) They principally focus on mental abilities conducive to academic success and ignore other kinds of intelligence.

9. **Discuss how well intelligence tests predict vocational success.**

   9-1.   Is the ability of intelligence tests to predict vocational success much higher or much lower than their ability to predict academic success?

   9-2.   What do current court rulings and laws now require when using tests for purposes of hiring or promoting?

   Answers: 9-1. much lower **9-2.** The tests must measure specific abilities that are related to job performance.

10. **Discuss the use of IQ tests in non-Western cultures.**

   10-1.   Which of the following statements best summarizes the history of IQ testing in non-Western cultures?

   (a) Most Western and non-Western cultures have successfully adapted the IQ tests to their own cultures.

   (b) Many non-Western cultures have different conceptions of what intelligence is and do not necessarily accept Western notions as to how it can be measured.

10-2. What did Cole and his colleagues conclude regarding the ingredients of intelligence across cultures?

Answers: 10-1. b **10-2.** They are culture-specific.

EXTREMES OF INTELLIGENCE

11. Describe how mental retardation is defined and divided into various levels.

11-1. In addition to having subnormal mental abilities (IQ scores of less than 70 to 75), what else is included in the definition of mental retardation?

11-2. There are four levels of mental retardation: mild, moderate, severe, and profound. Identify each of these levels from the descriptions given below:

(a) These persons have IQ scores below 20 and require total care.

(b) These persons have IQ scores between 50 and 75 and may become self-supporting citizens after leaving school and becoming adults.

(c) These persons have IQ scores between 35 and 50 and can be semi-independent in a sheltered environment.

(d) These persons have IQ scores between 20 and 35 and can help to contribute to their self-support under total supervision.

Answers: 11-1. The individual must show deficiencies in adaptive (everyday living) skills originating before age 18. **11-2.** (a) profound (b) mild (c) moderate (d) severe.

12. Discuss what is known about the causes of mental retardation.

12-1. Although there are over 350 organic syndromes associated with retardation, including Down's syndrome, phenylketonuria, and hydrocephaly, organic causes only account for about _____ percent of retardation cases.

12-2. There are two general hypotheses as to the causes of the remaining 75 percent of retardation cases, most of which are diagnosed as mild. One theory is that retardation results from subtle _____ defects that are difficult to detect. The other theory suggests that retardation is caused by a variety of unfavorable _____ conditions.

Answers: 12-1. 25 **12-2.** physiological, environmental.

13. Discuss the role of IQ tests in the identification of gifted children.

    13-1.   Answer the following questions regarding gifted children:

        (a)   Although it is contrary to federal law, what method is used almost exclusively to identify gifted children?

        (b)   What is the lowest IQ score that is generally needed to qualify children as gifted?

Answers: 13-1. (a) scores on IQ tests (b) 130.

14. Describe the characteristics of the gifted and factors relating to adult achievements of the gifted.

    14-1.   Answer the following questions regarding the characteristics of the gifted.

        (a)   What did Terman's long-term study of gifted children show with respect to the physical, social, and emotional development of these children?

        (b)   Ellen Winner took a special look at profoundly (IQ above 180) gifted children. What did she estimate to be the incidence of interpersonal and emotional problems in these children when compared to other children?

        (c)   What three factors must interact and be present to an exceptional degree in order to produce the rarest form of giftedness, according to Renzulli?

        (d)   In addition to intensive training and hard work, what other factor may be necessary to achieve extraordinary achievement?

Answers: 14-1. (a) They were above average in all three areas. (b) It's about twice as high in the profoundly gifted children. (c) intelligence, motivation, creativity (in any order). (d) Rare, innate talent.

15. **Summarize the empirical evidence that heredity affects intelligence.**

   15-1. Below are the mean correlations for the intelligence of four different groups of children: *siblings reared together, fraternal twins reared together, identical twins reared apart*, and *identical twins reared together*. Match the group with the appropriate correlation.

   .86 _____   .60 _____

   .72 _____   .44 _____

   15-2. What do the above correlations tell us about the role of heredity on intelligence?

   Answers: 15-1. (.86) identical twins reared together (.72) identical twins reared apart (.60) fraternal twins reared together (.44) siblings reared together **15-2.** That heredity plays a significant role in intelligence.

16. **Discuss estimates of the heritability of intelligence and their limitations.**

   16-1. The consensus estimate of experts is that the heritability ratio for human intelligence hovers around 60 percent. What does this mean?

   16-2. Why can you not use a heritability ratio to explain a particular individual's intelligence?

   Answers: 16-1. The variation in intelligence in a particular group is estimated to be 60% due to heredity (leaving 40% for environmental factors). **16-2.** It is a group statistic and may give misleading results when applied to particular individuals.

17. **Describe various lines of research that indicate that environment affects intelligence.**

   17-1. What cumulative effects on intelligence have been found among children reared in deprived environments?

   17-2. What effects on intelligence have been found among children moved from deprived environments to more enriched environments?

   17-3. What relationship has been found between the intellectual quality of home environment and the intelligence of children?

17-4. Answer the following questions regarding the "Flynn effect."

(a) What did Flynn's research show with respect to generational changes in IQ scores since 1930 in the industrialized world?

(b) Can these generational changes be attributed to heredity?

Answers: 17-1. There is a gradual decrease in intelligence (across time). **17-2.** There is a gradual increase in intelligence (across time). **17-3.** They are significantly correlated. **17-4.** (a) Scores have been steadily rising. (b) no.

18. Explain how heredity and the environment interact to affect intelligence.

18-1. The notion behind the concept of reaction range is that heredity places an upper and lower _____ on how much an individual can vary, with respect to a characteristic such as intelligence. On the other hand, where an individual falls within these limits is determined by _____ factors.

18-2. The major point here is that the limits for intelligence are determined by _____ factors, and the movement within these limits is determined by _____ factors.

Answers: 18-1. limit, environmental **18-2.** genetic or hereditary, environmental.

19. Discuss alternative explanations for cultural differences in average IQ.

19-1. One of these explanations for the cultural differences in IQ score is Jensen's heritability argument that the differences are largely due to _____.

Another explanation is that the differences are due to _____ disadvantages.

Which of these two explanations is best supported by research?

19-2. Still another explanation is Steele's theory of stereotype vulnerability which holds that a widely held stereotype, that certain racial groups are mentally inferior, acts on the members of these groups so as to make them (more/less) vulnerable (they tend to under perform) when confronted with tests assessing intellectual ability. Steele believes that this same vulnerability (does/does not) exist for women entering domains dominated by men. Research so far (does/does not) support the theory of stereotype vulnerability.

19-3. A fourth explanation for the differences is that the IQ tests are culturally biased. What does the text conclude about the possible effects of cultural bias with respect to ethnic differences in IQ scores?

Answers: 19-1. heredity, socioeconomic, socioeconomic disadvantages **19-2.** more, does, does **19-3.** It produces weak and inconsistent effects.

20. **Discuss evidence on the biological correlates of intelligence.**

    21-1. Which biologically oriented approach to measuring intelligence, reaction time, or inspection time appears to be more promising?

    22-2. What correlation has been found between brain volume (as measured by MRI scans) IQ scores?

    22-3. There is a small (<u>negative/positive</u>) correlation between intelligence and longevity.

Answers: 20-1. inspection time **20-2.** .35 **20-3.** positive.

NEW DIRECTIONS IN THE ASSESSMENT AND STUDY OF INTELLIGENCE

21. **Describe Sternberg's and Gardner's theories of intelligence and the concept of emotional intelligence.**

    21-1. Sternberg's triarchic theory proposes that intelligence is composed of three basic parts. Match these parts with their individual functions:

SUBTHEORY	FUNCTION
____ Contextual	(a) Emphasizes the role played by society.
____ Experiential	(b) Emphasizes the cognitive processes underlying intelligence.
____ Componential	(c) Emphasizes the interplay between intelligence and experience.

    21-2. Which of these three sub-theories also contains three underlying subcomponents (metacomponents, performance components, and knowledge-acquisition components)?

    21-3. In a recent addition to his theory, Sternberg has proposed three facets of what he calls, "successful intelligence." Match these three facets with their respective descriptions.

FACETS (INTELLIGENCE)	DESCRIPTIONS
____ Analytical	(a) Ability to deal effectively with everyday problems.
____ Creative	(b) Ability to generate new ideas.
____ Practical	(c) Abstract reasoning, evaluation, and judgment.

    21-4. Gardner has proposed eight relatively distinct human intelligences. What does his research show with respect to a "g" factor among these separate intelligences?

    21-5. The ability to perceive and express emotion, assimilate emotion in thought, understand and reason with emotion, and regulate emotion is the general idea behind _____ intelligence.

REFLECTIONS ON THE CHAPTER'S THEMES

22. Discuss how the chapter highlighted three of the text's unifying themes.

    22-1.   Answer the following questions about the three unifying themes (cultural factors shape behavior, psychology evolves in a sociohistorical context, and heredity and environment jointly influence behavior).

        (a) What theme is exemplified by the controversy over the book *The Bell Curve*?

        (b) What theme is exemplified by the different views about the nature of intelligence held by Western and non-Western cultures?

        (c) What theme is exemplified by the extensive research using twin studies, adoption studies, and family studies?

APPLICATION: MEASURING AND UNDERSTANDING CREATIVITY

23. Discuss the role of insight and divergent thinking in creativity.

    23-1.   Which of the following statements best describes the role of insight in creativity?
        (a) Creativity usually involves sudden flashes of insight and great leaps of imagination.
        (b) Creativity usually involves logical extensions of existing ideas involving long, hard work, rather than insight.

    23-2.   Which of the following statements best describes the role of divergent thinking in creativity?
        (a) Research shows that divergent thinking contributed to creativity, but does not represent the true essence of creativity.
        (b) Research shows that divergent thinking is the essential ingredient of creativity.

24. Describe creativity tests, and summarize how well they predict creative achievement.

    24-1.   Most tests of creativity attempt to assess (<u>conventional/divergent</u>) thinking, such as: list as many uses as you can for a book. Creativity scores are based on the _____ of alternatives generated and the originality and _____ of the suggested alternatives.

24-2. Creativity tests are rather (good/mediocre) predictors of creativity in the real world. One reason for this is that they attempt to treat creativity as a (specific/general) trait, while research evidence seems to show it is related to quite _____ particular domains.

Answers: **24-1.** divergent, number, usefulness (utility) **24-2.** mediocre, general, specific.

25. Discuss associations between creativity and personality, intelligence, and mental illness.

25-1. What two traits appear to be at the core of the personality characteristics common to creative people?

25-2. What is the intelligence level of most highly creative people?

25-3. What form of mental illness appears to be associated with creative achievement?

Answers: **25-1.** independence and nonconformity **25-2.** average to above average **25-3.** mood disorders.

CRITICAL THINKING APPLICATION

26. Explain how appeals to ignorance and reification have cropped up in numerous debates about intelligence.

26-1. Tell whether the following statements represent examples of appeals to ignorance or to reification.

(a) He doesn't do very well in college because he's lacking in intelligence.

(b) If only 25% of the cases of mental retardation can be attributed to biological causes, the remaining 75% must be due to environmental factors.

(c) The down side to creativity is that it can lead to mood disorders.

(d) More money should be spent on research to find the accurate heritability co-efficient of intelligence.

Answers: **26-1.** (a) reification (b) appeals to ignorance (c) appeals to ignorance (d) reification.

Review of Key Terms

Achievement tests	Convergent thinking	Deviation IQ scores
Aptitude tests	Correlation coefficient	Divergent thinking
Construct validity	Creativity	Emotional intelligence
Content validity	Criterion-related validity	Heritability ratio

Intelligence quotient (IQ)
Intelligence tests
Mental age
Mental retardation
Normal distribution

Percentile score
Personality tests
Psychological test
Reaction range
Reification

Reliability
Standardization
Test norms
Validity

_____ 1. A standardized measure of a sample of a person's behavior.

_____ 2. Tests that measure general mental ability.

_____ 3. Tests that measure various personality traits.

_____ 4. Tests that assess talent for specific kinds of learning.

_____ 5. Tests that gauge the mastery and knowledge of various subject areas.

_____ 6. The development of uniform procedures for administering and scoring tests, including the development of test norms.

_____ 7. Data that provides information about the relative standing of a particular test score.

_____ 8. Number indicating the percentage of people who score above or below a particular test score.

_____ 9. The measurement consistency of a test.

_____ 10. The ability of a test to measure what it was designed to measure.

_____ 11. The degree to which the content of a test is representative of the domain it is supposed to measure.

_____ 12. The degree to which the scores on a particular test correlate with scores on an independent criterion (test).

_____ 13. The degree to which there is evidence that a test measures a hypothetical construct.

_____ 14. A score indicating the mental ability typical of a chronological age group.

_____ 15. Mental age divided by chronological age and multiplied by 100.

_____ 16. A symmetrical, bell-shaped curve that describes the distribution of many physical and psychological attributes.

_____ 17. Scores that translate raw scores into a precise location in the normal distribution.

_____ 18. Subnormal, general mental ability accompanied by deficiencies in everyday living skills originating prior to age 18.

_____ 19. An estimate of the percentage of variation in a trait determined by genetic inheritance.

_____ 20. Genetically determined limits on intelligence.

_____ 21. The generation of ideas that are original, novel, and useful.

_____ 22. Thinking that attempts to narrow down a list of alternatives to a single best solution.

_____ 23. Thinking that attempts to expand the range of alternatives by generating many possible solutions.

_____ 24. A numerical index of the degree of relationship between two variables.

_____ 25. Occurs when a hypothetical abstract concept is given a name and then treated as though it were a concrete, tangible object.

_____ 26. The ability to perceive and express emotion, assimilate emotion in thought, understand and reason with emotion, and regulate emotion.

Review of Key People

Alfred Binet
Sir Francis Galton
Howard Gardner
Arthur Jensen

Sandra Scarr
Claude Steele
Robert Sternberg

Lewis Terman
David Wechsler
Ellen Winner

_____ **1.** Developed the Stanford-Binet Intelligence Scale.

_____ **2.** Developed the first successful test of adult intelligence.

_____ **3.** Postulated a cognitive triarchic theory of intelligence.

_____ **4.** Proposed a reaction range model for human intelligence.

_____ **5.** Developed the first useful intelligence test.

_____ **6.** Postulated a heritability explanation for cultural differences in intelligence.

_____ **7.** Began the quest to measure intelligence.

_____ **8.** Proposed a stereotype vulnerability theory as an explanation for racial differences on IQ test scores.

_____ **9.** Has suggested the existence of a number of relatively autonomous human intelligences.

_____ **10.** Her research shows that profoundly gifted children suffer more emotional and social problems than do moderately gifted children.

Self-Quiz

1. This self-test you are now taking is an example of:
   a. an aptitude test
   b. an achievement test
   c. an intelligence test
   d. a criterion-related test

2. Which of the following statistics is generally used to estimate reliability and validity?
   a. the correlation coefficient
   b. the standard deviation
   c. the percentile score
   d. the median

3. What kind of validity do tests such as the SAT and ACT particularly strive for?
   a. content validity
   b. construct validity
   c. absolute validity
   d. criterion-related validity

4. With respect to modern intelligence tests:
   a. validity is generally higher than reliability
   b. reliability and validity are about the same
   c. reliability is generally higher than validity
   d. I have no idea what you're talking about.

5. Which of the following retarded groups can often pass for normal as adults?
   a. mild
   b. moderate
   c. profound
   d. both mild and moderate

6. What percentage of mental retardation cases have been definitely linked to organic causes?
   a. approximately 25%
   b. approximately 50%
   c. approximately 75%
   d. approximately 90%

7. Terman's long-term study of gifted children found that they tended to excel in:
   a. physical development
   b. social development
   c. emotional development
   d. they excelled in all three areas

8. Which of the following groups shows the lowest correlation with respect to intelligence?
   a. fraternal twins reared together
   b. fraternal twins reared apart
   c. identical twins reared apart
   d. siblings reared together

9. If the heritability ratio for intelligence is 80%, this means that for you, as an individual, heredity determines 80% of your intelligence and environment determines 20%. This statement is:
   a. true
   b. false

10. The "Flynn effect" arises from the observation that the general intelligence in industrialized societies:
    a. has been rising across time
    b. has been declining across time
    c. has remained steady across time
    d. is primarily effected by heredity and not environment

11. If the reaction range concept of human intelligence is correct, then a child with exactly normal intelligence will probably not get much higher than an IQ of:
    a. 107
    b. 112
    c. 122
    d. 130

12. Which of the following explanations for racial differences in intelligence is best supported by research evidence?
    a. Jensen's heritability theory
    b. cultural bias in IQ tests
    c. cultural disadvantage
    d. Watson's differential conditioning theory

13. Steele's theory of stereotype vulnerability is an attempt to explain:
    a. why Asian-Americans score higher than average on IQ tests
    b. why African-Americans score lower than average on IQ tests
    c. why cultural bias must necessarily be inherent in all intelligence tests
    d. why the general intelligence in a population declines across time

14. Most tests of creativity emphasize:
    a. convergent thinking
    b. divergent thinking
    c. bursts of insight
    d. getting at unconscious thought processes

15. What form of mental illness frequently has been found to be associated with outstanding creativity?
    a. anxiety disorders
    b. antisocial personality
    c. schizophrenia
    d. mood disorders

16. Which of the following statements is an example of reification?
    a. Birds of a feather flock together.
    b. Creative people are born, not raised.
    c. She gets good grades in school because she is intelligent.
    d. Intelligence tests are only moderate predictors of vocational success.

Answers: 1. b **2.** a **3.** d **4.** c **5.** a **6.** a **7.** d **8.** d **9.** b **10.** a **11.** b **12.** c **13.** b **14.** b **15.** d **16.** c **17.** c.

InfoTrac Keywords

Achievement Tests   Aptitude Tests   Intelligence Tests

Chapter Ten
MOTIVATION AND EMOTION

Review of Key Ideas

MOTIVATIONAL THEORIES AND CONCEPTS

1. Compare drive, incentive, and evolutionary approaches to understanding motivation.

1-1. Drive theories are based on the idea that organisms strive to maintain a a state of _____ or physiological equilibrium. For example, organisms are motivated to maintain water balance: when deprived of water they experience thirst. Thirst is a _____ to return to a state of water equilibrium.

1-2. A drive is a state of tension. According to drive theories organisms are motivated to seek drive or tension _____.

1-3. Theories that emphasize the pull from the external environment are known as _____ theories. For example, we may be motivated to eat not as a function of hunger (an internal drive) but as a result of the smell or appearance of food (an external cue). Incentive theories (operate/do not operate) according to the principle of homeostasis.

1-4. From the point of view of evolutionary theory all motivations, such as the needs for affiliation, dominance, achievement, and aggression, occur because they have _____ value for the species. Organisms with adaptive sets of motivational characteristics are more likely to pass their _____ on to the next generation.

1-5. Place the name of the theoretical approach described below (drive, incentive, or evolutionary) in the blanks.

_____ Emphasizes homeostasis, the pressure to return to a state of equilibrium.

_____ Actions result from attempts to reduce internal states of tension.

_____ Emphasizes "pull" from the environment (as opposed to "push" from internal states).

_____ Motivations arise as a function of their capacity to enhance reproductive success, to pass genes to the next generation.

Answers: 1-1. homeostasis (balance, equilibrium), drive **1-2.** reduction **1-3.** incentive, do not operate **1-4.** adaptive (survival, reproductive), genes **1-5.** drive, drive, incentive, evolutionary.

2. Distinguish between the two major categories of motives found in humans.

2-1. Most theories of motivation distinguish between _____ motives (e.g., for food, water, sex, warmth) and _____ motives. Biological needs are generally essential for the _____ of the group or individual.

2-2. Social motives (e.g., for achievement, autonomy, affiliation) are acquired as a result of people's experiences. While there are relatively few biological needs, people theoretically may acquire an unlimited number of _____ needs.

Answers: 2-1. biological, social, survival **2-2.** social.

THE MOTIVATION OF HUNGER AND EATING

3. Summarize evidence on the physiological factors implicated in the regulation of hunger.

3-1. Within the brain the major structure implicated in eating behavior is the _____.

3-2. Researchers used to think that eating was controlled by "on" and "off" centers in the hypothalamus. When the lateral hypothalamus (LH) was destroyed, animals stopped eating, as if hunger had been turned off like a switch. When the ventromedial hypothalamus (VMH) was destroyed, animals (started/stopped) eating.

3-3. Current thinking is that eating seems to be controlled more by (complex neural circuits/simple anatomical centers) that run through the hypothalamus rather than by on-off centers within the hypothalamus. While the LH and VMH are still factors in hunger regulation, researchers now think that another part of the hypothalamus, the paraventricular nucleus or _____, is more important.

3-4. Much of the food we consume is converted into _____, a simple sugar that is an important source of energy.

3-5. Based on research findings about glucose, Mayer proposed the theory that there are there are specialized neurons in the brain, which he called _____, that function to monitor blood glucose. Lower levels of glucose, for example, are associated with a(an) (increase/decrease) in hunger.

3-6. For cells to extract glucose from the blood, the hormone _____ must be present. Insulin will produce a(an) (increase/decrease) in the level of sugar in the blood, with the result that the person experiences a(an) (increase/decrease) in the sensation of hunger.

3-7. More recently a regulatory hormone called leptin has been discovered, a hormone produced by (fat cells/neurons) and circulated to the hypothalamus in the bloodstream. Higher levels of the hormone _____ reflect a higher level of fat in the body, which is associated with a (increase/decrease) in the sensation of hunger.

4. **Summarize evidence on how the availability of food, culture, learning, and stress influence hunger.**

   4-1.   Hunger is based not only on a physiological need but on external factors, such as the appearance, tastiness, and availability of food. Thus, some aspects of hunger motivation support the (drive/incentive) approach to motivation. Sometimes we eat, according to this research, simply because food is available and looks and tastes good.

   4-2.   Although we have some innate taste preferences (e.g., for fat), it is also clear that _____ affects what we eat. For example, taste preferences and aversions may be learned by pairing a taste with pleasant or unpleasant experiences, the process of _____ conditioning.

   4-3.   In addition, we are more likely to eat what we see others eating, so food preferences are acquired not only through conditioning but through the process of _____ learning.

   4-4.   Our environments also provide frustrating circumstances that create _____, a factor that may also triggers eating in many people. Although stress and increased eating are linked, it's not clear why the relationship occurs.

5. **Discuss the factors that contribute to the development of obesity.**

   5-1.   Evolutionary theorists propose that in our ancestral past, when faced with the likelihood of famine, people evolved a capacity to overeat. Overeating, as a hedge against food shortages, had _____ value. In the modern world food is no longer scarce, but our tendency to overeat remains.

   5-2.   It is clear that many factors affect body weight and that some of the most important are genetic. For example, Stunkard et al. (1986) found that adopted children were much more similar in BMI to their (biological/adoptive) parents than to their (biological/adoptive) parents, even though they were brought up by the latter.

   5-3.   The most striking finding of the Stunkard et al. (1990) study with twins was that (identical/fraternal) twins reared apart were more similar in BMI than (identical/fraternal twins reared in the same family environment. This research supports the idea that (genetics/environment) plays a major role in body weight.

   5-4.   The concept of set point may help explain why body weight remains so stable. The theory proposes that each individual has a "natural" body weight that is set, in large part, by the person's (genetics/environment). The body defends one particular weight.

   5-5.   According to _____ theory, individual differences in body weight are due in large part to differences in genetic makeup. This theory asserts that the body actively defends a (wide range/particular) body weight by, for example, increasing hunger or decreasing metabolism.

5-6. Settling-point theory is a bit more optimistic: individuals who make long-term changes in eating or exercise will drift downward to a lower _____ point without such active resistance. The settling-point view also asserts that this balance is achieved as a result of (<u>a wide variety of/genetic</u>) factors.

5-7. According to the dietary restraint concept, the world is divided into two types of people: unrestrained eaters, who eat as much as they want when they want; and _____ eaters, who closely monitor their food intake and frequently go hungry.

5-8. While restrained eaters are constantly on guard to control their eating, at times they may lose control and eat to excess. In other words, restraint may be disrupted or _____, with the result that people overeat. Paradoxically, then, restraint in eating may contribute to obesity.

Answers: **5-1.** survival (adaptive) **5-2.** biological, adoptive **5-3.** identical, fraternal, genetics **5-4.** genetics **5-5.** set-point, particular **5-6.** settling, a wide variety of **5-7.** restrained **5-8.** disinhibited.

SEXUAL MOTIVATION AND BEHAVIOR

6. **Describe the impact of hormones in regulating animal and human sexual behavior.**

6-1. The major female sex hormones are called _____ and the major male sex hormones _____. Both of these gonadal hormones occur in both sexes. The hormone testosterone is a key androgen.

6-2. While there is no one-to-one relationship, higher levels of the hormone _____, a key androgen, are related to higher levels of sexual activity in (<u>males only/females only/both sexes</u>).

Answers: **6-1.** estrogens, androgens **6-2.** testosterone, both sexes.

7. **Summarize evidence on the impact of erotic materials, including aggressive pornography, on human sexual behavior.**

7-1. What is the relationship between exposure to erotic materials and sexual activity? One fairly dependable finding has been that erotic materials tend to (<u>increase/decrease</u>) the likelihood of sexual activity for a few (<u>hours/weeks</u>) after exposure.

7-2. Another effect involves attitudes. In the Zillman and Bryant studies described, male and female under-graduate subjects exposed to heavy doses of pornography over a period of weeks developed *attitudes* about sexual practices that were more (<u>liberal/conventional</u>). Subjects also became (<u>more/less</u>) satisfied with their partners appearance and sexual performance.

7-3. In general researchers (<u>have/have not</u>) found a link between exposure to erotic materials and sex crimes. In addition, pornography appears to play a (<u>major/minor</u>) role in the commission of sexual offenses.

7-4. Some laboratory studies, however, have found that pornography depicting violence against women (<u>decreases/increases</u>) men's tendency to be aggressive toward women. In these studies aggression is defined as willingness to deliver (fake) electric shock to other subjects.

7-5.   In addition, some laboratory studies have found that exposure to aggressive pornography makes sexual coercion or rape seem (<u>less/more</u>) offensive to the participants, a troublesome finding in view of current information about the prevalence of rape.

Answers: **7-1.** increase, hours **7-2.** liberal, less **7-3.** have not, minor **7-4.** increases **7-5.** less.

8. Discuss parental investment theory and findings on human gender differences in sexual activity.

8-1.   Triver's parental investment theory is the idea that a species' mating patterns are determined by the *investment* each sex must make to produce and nurture offspring. Human females are the ones who are pregnant for nine months and subsequently breast feed their offspring. Therefore, according to this analysis, they have a greater _____ in the child than do males.

8-2.   Parental investment theory contends that the sex that makes the smaller investment will compete for mating opportunities, while the sex that makes the larger investment will be more selective of partners. Thus, males of many mammalian species will seek to mate with (<u>as many/as few</u>) females as possible, while females will optimize their reproductive potential by being (<u>selective/unrestricted</u>) in mating.

8-3.   In line with predictions from parental investment theory and evolutionary theory in general, several studies have found that in comparison to women, men will show (1) (<u>more/less</u>) interest in sexual activity in general, (2) desire for a greater _____ of sexual partners, and (3) more willingness to engage in (<u>casual/committed</u>) sex.

Answers: **8-1.** investment **8-2.** as many, selective **8-3.** more, variety (number), casual.

9. Describe the Featured Study on culture and mating preferences.

9-1.   According to evolutionary theories, what characteristics do human females look for in a male partner? What do males look for in a female partner?

9-2.   More than 10,000 people participated in Buss's study. The people surveyed were from (<u>the United States/ 37 different cultures</u>).

9-3.   In one or two sentences, summarize the results of Buss's study.

9-4.   What conclusions can reasonably be drawn from Buss's study? Place a T or F in the blanks.

_____   Some of the differences in mating preferences were universal across cultures.

_____   The data are consistent with evolutionary theories of sexual motivation.

_____   The data may be explained by alternative interpretations that do not derive from evolutionary theory.

_____ One possible alternative explanation of the data is that women value men's economic resources because their own potential has been restricted.

Answers: 9-1. According to the evolutionary theories, women want men who will be able to acquire resources (e.g., have education, money, status, ambition). Men want women who have good breeding potential (e.g., are beautiful, youthful, in good health). **9-2.** 37 different cultures **9-3.** Results supported predictions from the evolutionary theories: women placed more value than men on finding a partner with good financial prospects; men placed more value than women on the characteristics of youth and physical attractiveness (as summed up in the song Summertime from Gerschwin's Porgy and Bess, "Oh, your daddy's rich, and your mama's good looking.") **9-4.** All of these statements are true or represent reasonable inferences. Some differences were universal, and the data are consistent with evolutionary theories. At the same time there are alternative explanations involving the fact of discrimination against women in virtually all societies.

10. Summarize evidence on the nature of sexual orientation and on how common homosexuality is.

10-1. Sexual orientation refers to a person's preference for emotional and sexual relationships with individuals of the other sex, the same sex, or either sex. Those who prefer relationships with the other sex are termed _____, with the same sex _____, and with either sex _____.

10-2. Because people may have experienced homosexuality in varying degrees, it seems reasonable to consider sexual orientation as a(an) (continuum/all-or-none distinction). In part because of this definitional problem and in part due to prejudice against homosexuals, it is difficult to determine precisely the proportion of homosexuals in the population. A frequently cited statistics is 10%, but recent survey place the proportion somewhere between _____.

Answers: 10-1. heterosexuals (straights), homosexuals (gays or lesbians), bisexuals **10-2.** continuum, 5-8%.

11. Summarize evidence on the determinants of sexual orientation.

11-1. What factors determine sexual orientation? Psychoanalysts thought the answer involved some aspect of the parent-child relationship. Behaviorists assumed that it was due to the association of same-sex stimuli with sexual arousal. Thus, both psychoanalytic and behavioral theorists proposed (environmental/biological) explanations of homosexuality.

11-2. Extensive research on the upbringing of homosexuals has (supported/not supported) the idea that homosexuality is primarily explainable in terms of environmental factors.

11-3. Recent studies have produced evidence that homosexuality is in part genetic. Which of the following types of studies have supported this conclusion? (Place Y for yes or N for no in the blanks.)

_____ Studies of hormonal differences between heterosexuals and homosexuals.

_____ Studies of twins and adopted children.

_____ Autopsy studies of the hypothalamus.

11-4. Subjects in one of the studies described were gay men who had an identical twin brother, a fraternal twin brother, or an adopted brother. For each of the categories, what percent of the brothers of the subjects were also gay? Place the appropriate percentages in the blanks: 11%, 22%, 52%.

_____ Identical twins

_____ Fraternal twins

_____ Adopted brothers

11-5. LeVay (1991) has reported that a cluster of neurons in the anterior _____ is (smaller/larger) in gay men than in straight men. Since all of the gay men in this study had died of AIDS, which itself may produce changes in brain structure, these findings should be interpreted with caution. Nonetheless, these data support the idea that there are (environmental/biological) factors that are related to sexual orientation.

11-6. While most studies (have/have not) found a difference between gay and straight men in circulating hormones, many theorists do suspect that hormones in the *prenatal* environment are a factor. For example, researchers have found that offspring of women exposed, during pregnancy, to treatment with a synthetic _____ are more likely to be homosexual.

11-7. While much of the evidence points toward biological factors, the fact that identical twins turn out to share sexual orientation only half of the time suggests that _____ factors are involved in some way. What those factors might be remains unknown, however.

11-8. Homosexuality in men and women seems to follow somewhat different courses. Women's sexual orientation appears to be more malleable, or have greater _____, than men's. For example, women are more likely than men to change their sexual orientation in their adult years.

Answers: **11-1.** environmental **11-2.** not supported **11-3.** N, Y, Y **11-4.** 52%, 22%, 11%. Note that a companion study for lesbians found similar results. **11-5.** hypothalamus, smaller, biological **11-6.** hormone (androgen) **11-7.** environmental **11-8.** plasticity (fluidity, changeability).

12. Outline the four phases of the human sexual response.

12-1. Write the names of the four phases of the human sexual response in the order in which they occur. (Hint: I made up a mnemonic device that's hard to forget. The first letter of each phase name produces EPOR, which happens to be ROPE spelled backward.)

(a) _____

(b) _____

(c) _____

(d) _____

12-2. In the blanks below write the first letter of each phase name that correctly labels the descriptions below.

_____ Rapid increase in arousal (respiration, heart rate, blood pressure, etc.)

_____ Vasocongestion of blood vessels in sexual organs; lubrication in female

_____ Continued arousal, but at a slower place

_____ Tightening of the vaginal entrance

_____ Pulsating muscular contractions and ejaculation

_____ Physiological changes produced by arousal subside.

_____ Includes a refractory period for men

Answers: 12-1. (a) excitement (b) plateau (c) orgasm (d) resolution **12-2.** E, E, P, P, O, R, R.

ACHIEVEMENT: IN SEARCH OF EXCELLENCE

13. **Describe the achievement motive and how it is measured.**

    13-1. People with high achievement motivation have a need to:

        a. master difficult challenges

        b. outperform others

        c. meet high standards of excellence

        d. all of the above

    13-2. To measure need for achievement, researchers ask subjects to tell stories about a series of pictures (e.g., a man holding a violin). The test using pictures in this manner is known as the Thematic Apperception Test or _____.

Answers: 13-1. d **13-2.** TAT.

14. **Discuss how individual differences in the need for achievement influence behavior.**

    14-1. People who score high on need for achievement tend to differ from those who score low in the following ways (True/False):

       _____ They work harder and persist longer.

       _____ They are better able to handle negative feedback about performance.

       _____ They seek immediate gratification and sacrifice future goals.

       _____ They seek competitive, entrepreneurial occupations.

       _____ They select tasks of intermediate (not too hard, not too easy) difficulty.

Answers: 14-1. T, T, F, T, T.

15. **Explain how situational factors influence affect achievement strivings.**

    15-1. According to Atkinson's elaboration of McClelland's views, achievement-oriented behavior is determined not only by (1) achievement motivation but by (2) the _____ that success will occur and (3) the _____ value of success.

15-2. As the difficulty of a task increases, the _____ of success at the task decreases. At the same time, success at harder tasks may be more satisfying, so the _____ value of the task is likely to increase. When both the incentive value and probability of success are weighed together, people with a high need for achievement would tend to select tasks of (extreme/moderate) difficulty.

Answers: **15-1.** probability, incentive **15-2.** probability, incentive, moderate.

THE ELEMENTS OF EMOTIONAL EXPERIENCE

16. Describe the cognitive component of emotion.

16-1. The word *cognition* refers to thoughts, beliefs, or conscious experience. When faced with an ugly-looking insect (or, for some people, the edge of a cliff or making a speech in public), you might say to yourself, "This is terrifying (or maybe disgusting)." This thought or cognition has an evaluative aspect: we assess our emotions as pleasant or unpleasant. Thus, one component of emotion is the thinking or _____ component, which includes _____ in terms of pleasantness-unpleasantness.

Answers: **16-1.** cognitive, evaluation.

17. Describe the physiological and neural bases of emotion.

17-1. The second component of emotion is the _____ component, primarily actions of the _____ nervous system (responsible for flight or flight). Your encounter with the insect might be accompanied by changes in heart rate, breathing, or blood pressure—or by increased electrical conductivity of the skin, known as the _____ skin response (GSR).

17-2. Lie detectors don't actually detect lies, they detect _____ reflected by changes in heart rate, respiration, and GSR. Emotion does not necessarily reflect lying: some people can lie without showing emotional arousal and others show arousal when asked incriminating questions. Advocates claim that polygraphs are about 85% to 90% accurate; recent research (supports/does not support) this claim. In most courtrooms polygraph results (are/are not) considered reliable enough to be used as evidence.

17-3. Recent evidence suggests that the brain structure known as the _____ plays a central role in emotion. For example, research has found that animals that have their amygdalas destroyed cannot learn classically conditioned _____ responses.

17-4. The amygdala doesn't process emotion by itself but is at the core of a complex set of neural circuits. According to LeDoux, sensory information relating to fear arrives at the thalamus and from there is relayed along two pathways, to the nearby _____ and also to areas in the _____.

17-5. LeDoux's theory includes that idea that the amygdala processes information extremely rapidly, which has clear _____ value for the organism in threatening situations. The cortex responds more slowly but in greater detail and relays potentially moderating information to the amygdala. While the hub of this vigilance system seems to be the _____, both pathways are useful in assessing threat.

17-6. We step into an elevator and are immediately terrified, reflecting the pathway centered in the _____. After thinking about the situation for a while we calm down, a reaction likely to involve the _____.

Answers: **17-1.** physiological, autonomic, galvanic **17-2.** emotion (autonomic arousal), does not support, are not **17-3.** amygdala, fear **17-4.** amygdala, cortex **17-5.** survival (adaptive), amygdala **17-6.** amygdala, cortex.

18. Discuss how emotions are reflected in facial expressions and explain the facial feedback hypothesis.

18-1. We communicate emotions not only verbally but _____, through our postures, gestures, and, especially, in our facial _____.

18-2. Ekman and Friesen found that there are _____ fundamental facial expressions of emotion: happiness, sadness, anger, fear, surprise, and disgust.

18-3. According to some researchers facial expressions not only reflect emotions but help create them. This viewpoint, known as the _____ hypothesis, asserts that facial muscles send signals to the brain that help produce the subjective experience of emotion. For example, turning up the corners of your mouth and crinkling your eyes will tend to make you feel _____.

Answers: **18-1.** nonverbally (through body language), expressions **18-2.** six **18-3.** facial-feedback, happy.

19. Discuss cross-cultural similarities and variations in emotional experience.

19-1. Ekman and Friesen asked people in different cultures to label the emotion shown on photographs of faces. What did they find?

19-2. While there are considerable similarities in emotional expression across cultures, there are also striking differences. For example, word labels for sadness, anxiety, and remorse (occur/do not occur) in all cultures.

19-3. There are also cultural differences governing when people express particular emotions. For example, what emotions are you "supposed" to show at a funeral, or when watching a sporting event? The unwritten rules that regulate our display of emotion, known as _____ rules, vary considerably across cultures.

Answers: **19-1.** People from very different cultures show considerable agreement in labeling facial expressions. **19-2.** do not occur **19-3.** display.

THEORIES OF EMOTION

20. **Compare and contrast the James-Lange and Cannon-Bard theories of emotion and explain how Schachter reconciled these conflicting views in his two-factor theory.**

20-1. Suppose you saw a rat in your room (and assume that you are afraid of rats). Why would you be afraid? One would think that the process would be as follows: first you would be consciously aware of your fear of the rat, then you would experience the autonomic or visceral arousal that accompanies fear. The James-Lange theory reverses this process: we first experience the (visceral arousal/conscious fear) and then we experience (visceral arousal/conscious fear).

20-2. According to the James-Lange theory, then, fear and other emotions occur not as a result of different conscious experiences but as a result of different patterns of _____ activation.

20-3. The Cannon-Bard theory argued that a subcortical structure in the brain (they thought it was the thalamus) simultaneously sends signals to both the cortex and the autonomic nervous system. According to this theory:

　a. conscious fear would precede autonomic arousal

　b. autonomic arousal would precede conscious fear

　c. autonomic arousal and conscious fear would occur at the same time

20-4. According to Cannon-Bard, emotion originates in:

　a. subcortical structures

　b. the autonomic nervous sytem

　c. conscious awareness

20-5. The Cannon-Bard theory contends that different emotions (e.g., fear, joy, love, anger) are accompanied by:

　a. different patterns of autonomic arousal

　b. nearly identical patterns of autonomic arousal

　c. neither of the above

20-6. Schachter's two-factor view is similar to the James-Lange theory in that (visceral arousal/conscious experience) is thought to precede the mental awareness of an emotion. The theory is similar to the Cannon-Bard theory in that (general/differentiated) autonomic arousal is assumed to account for a wide variety of emotions.

20-7. According to Schachter, when we experience general arousal we experience difference emotions as a result of <u>inferences</u> we make from cues in the environment. Hence, the two factors in Schachter's theory are _____ (roughly the same for all emotions) and _____ (people's interpretation of the arousal based on the situation).

20-8. To review the three theories, label each of the following with the name of a theory:

　(a) _____ The subjective experience of emotion is caused by different patterns of autonomic arousal.

　(b) _____ Emotions cannot be distinguished on the basis of a autonomic arousal; general autonomic arousal causes one to look for an explanation or label.

(c) _____ Love is accompanied by a different autonomic pattern from hate.

(d) _____ The subjective experience of emotion is caused by two factors, arousal and cognition.

(e) _____ Emotions originate in subcortical brain structures; different emotions produce almost identical patterns of autonomic arousal.

(f) _____ Ralph observes that his heart pounds and that he becomes a little out of breath at times. He also notices that these signs of arousal occur whenever Mary is around, so he figures that he must be in love.

Answers: 20-1. visceral arousal, conscious fear **20-2.** autonomic (visceral) **20-3.** c **20-4.** a **20-5.** b **20-6.** visceral arousal, general **20-7.** arousal, cognition **20-8.** (a) James-Lange (b) Schachter's two-factor (c) James-Lange (d) Schachter's two-factor (e) Cannon-Bard (f) Schachter's two-factor.

21. **Summarize the evolutionary perspective on emotion.**

   21-1. By preparing an organism for aggression and defense, the emotion of anger helps an organism survive. From an evolutionary perspective, all emotions developed because of the _____ value they have for a species.

   21-2. Evolutionary theorists view emotions primarily as a group of (<u>innate/learned</u>) reactions that have been passed on because of their survival value. They also believe that emotions originate in subcortical areas, parts of the brain that evolved before the cortical structures associated with higher mental processes. In the view of evolutionary theorists, emotion evolved before thought and is largely (<u>dependent on/ independent of</u>) thought.

   21-3. How many basic, inherited emotions are there? The evolutionary writers assume that the wide range of emotions we experience are blends or variations in intensity of approximately _____ innate or prewired primary emotions.

   Answers: 21-1. survival (adaptive) **21-2.** innate, independent of **21-3.** eight to ten.

REFLECTING ON THE CHAPTER'S THEMES

22. **Explain how this chapter highlighted five of the text's unifying themes.**

   22-1. Five of the text's organizing themes were prominent in this chapter. Indicate which themes fit the following examples by writing the appropriate abbreviations in the blanks below: C for cultural contexts, SH for sociohistorical context, T for theoretical diversity, HE for heredity and environment, and MC for multiple causation.

   (a) Achievement behavior is affected by achievement motivation, the likelihood of success, the likelihood of failure, and so on. ____

   (b) Display rules in a culture tell us when and where to express an emotion. ____

(c) Changing attitudes about homosexuality have produced more research on sexual orientation; in turn, data from the research has affected societal attitudes. ____

(d) Body weight seems to be influenced by set point, blood glucose, and inherited metabolism. It is also affected by eating habits and acquired tastes, which vary across cultures. ____, ____, and ____

(e) The James-Lange theory proposed that different emotions reflected different patterns of physiological arousal; Cannon-Bard theory assumed that emotions originate in subcortical structures; Schachter viewed emotion as a combination of physiological arousal and cognition ____.

Answers: 22-1. (a) MC (b) C (c) SH (d) HE, MC, C (e) T.

PERSONAL APPLICATION • EXPLORING THE INGREDIENTS OF HAPPINESS

23. Summarize information on factors that do not predict happiness.

   23-1. Indicate whether each of the following statements is true or false.

      (a) ____ There is very little correlation between income and happiness.

      (b) ____ Younger people tend to be happier than older people.

      (c) ____ People who have children tend to be happier than those without children.

      (d) ____ People with high IQ scores tend to be happier than those with low IQ scores.

      (e) ____ There is a negligible correlation between physical attractiveness and happiness.

   23-2. List five factors discussed in your text that have little or no relationship to happiness.

Answers: 23-1. (a) T, (b) F, (c) F, (d) F, (e) T **23-2.** money (income), age, parenthood (either having or not having children), intelligence, physical attractiveness.

24. Summarize information on factors that are moderately or strongly correlated with happiness.

   24-1. Indicate whether each of the following statements is true or false.

      (a) ____ One of the strongest predictors of happiness is good health.

      (b) ____ Social support and friendship groups are moderately related to happiness.

      (c) ____ Religious people tend to be somewhat happier than nonreligious people.

      (d) ____ Marital status is strongly related to happiness; married people tend to be happier than single people.

      (e) ____ Job satisfaction tends to be strongly related to general happiness; people who like their jobs tend to be happy.

      (f) ____ Differences in personality have a negligible relationship to happiness; introverts, on the average, are just as happy as extraverts.

24-2. List three factors that are moderately correlated with happiness and three that are strongly correlated.

Answers: 24-1. (a) F (People adapt, so there is only a moderate relationship between health and happiness.), (b) T, (c) T, (d) T, (e) T, (f) F (People who are extraverted, optimistic, and have high self-esteem tend to be happier.)
24-2. Moderately related: health, social activity (friendship), and religion. Strongly related: marriage, work (job satisfaction), and personality.

25. Explain three conclusions that can be drawn about the dynamics of happiness.

25-1. One conclusion about happiness is that the objective realities of a situation are less important than our _____ reactions to it.

25-2. In addition, the extent of our happiness depends on the comparison group. Generally, people compare themselves to others who are similar in some dimension, such as friends or neighbors. In the final analysis, our happiness is relative to the _____ to which we compare ourselves.

25-3. A third conclusion is that our baseline for judging pleasantness and unpleasantness constantly changes. When good things happen, we shift our baselines (what we feel we "need" or want) upward; when bad things happen, we shift down. In other words, people _____ to changing circumstances by changing their baselines of comparison. This process is termed _____ adaptation.

Answers: 25-1. subjective **25-2.** group (people) **25-3.** adapt (adjust), hedonic.

CRITICAL THINKING APPLICATION • ANALYZING ARGUMENTS: MAKING SENSE OUT OF CONTROVERSY

26. Describe the key elements in arguments.

26-1. In logic, an *argument* is a series of statements that claims to prove something (whether it does or not). Arguments are comprised of two major parts, a *conclusion* and one or more *premises*. The _____ are statements intended to present evidence or proof. The _____ supposedly derives from or is proved by the premises.

26-2. Consider this logical argument: "Any field of study that uses the scientific method is a science. Psychology uses the scientific method. Thus, psychology is a science." Label the parts of the argument below (C for conclusion and P for premise).

_____ Any field of study that uses the scientific method is a science.

_____ Psychology uses the scientific method.

_____ Thus, psychology is a science.

Answers: 26-1. premises, conclusion **26-2.** P, P, C. Note that this is an example of a valid argument. One may or may not agree with the premises (e.g., they may define science differently), but the conclusion logically follows from the premises.

27. **Explain some common fallacies that often show up in arguments.**

27-1. Read over the section on common logical fallacies described in your text. Then match the examples with the appropriate terms. (Suggestion: Use the abbreviations in parentheses for matching. Note that there are five fallacies and nine examples; some fallacies are used more than once.)

irrelevant reasons (IR)

circular reasoning (CR)

slippery slope (SS)

weak analogies (WA)

false dichotomy (FD)

(a) _____ Trouble sleeping causes great difficulty in our lives because insomnia is a major problem for people. (Hint: Is the conclusion different from the premise?)

(b) _____ People with insomnia should use the herb melatonin because insomnia is an enormous problem in our country. (Hint: Is the premise really related to the conclusion?)

(c) _____ Vitamin C is extremely effective in slowing the aging process. I know it is effective because I have taken it for many years.

(d) _____ Vitamin C is extremely effective in slowing the aging process. Obviously, the reason I take Vitamin C is that it works to reduce aging.

(e) _____ An argument from the 1960s: If we don't stop communism in Vietnam now, it will spread next to Laos, then to Cambodia, and then to the entire Southeast Asian Peninsula.

(f) _____ An argument from the 1990s: We can fight in the Balkans now, or we can prepare for World War III. (Hint: Are these our only choices?)

(g) _____ From 2003: You are either with us, or you are with the terrorists.

(h) _____ From 2005: We can either fight them in Iraq, or we will have to fight them here.

(i) _____ Ralph bought a mixmaster on a Tuesday in Peoria and it lasted a long time. If I buy a mixmaster on a Tuesday in Peoria, it should also last a long time.

Answers: 27-1. (a) CR. The premise and conclusion are the same. (b) IR. Insomnia may be a problem but that does not lead to the conclusion that the herb melatonin should be taken. (c) IR. The conclusion, the first statement in this example, is not related to the premise. Taking it for many years is not related to the conclusion that it is effective. (d) CR. The conclusion, the first statement, is simply a restatement of the premise. (e) SS. The argument is that if you allow one thing to happen, then a series of other things will inevitably happen. In fact, there may be no necessary connection between the hypothetical events. (f) FD. The choice seems to be between the two options, but, logically, these are not the only choices. We could also do both, or neither. (g) FD. We may not be with either. (h) FD. The implication is that there are only two choices. (i) WA. While the situations share some elements in common, this does not mean that they share all elements or that some elements cause others.

Review of Key Terms

Achievement motive
Affiliation motive
Androgens
Argument
Assumptions
Bisexuals
Body Mass Index (BMI)
Collectivism
Display rules
Drive
Emotion

Estrogens
Galvanic skin response (GSR)
Glucose
Glucostats
Hedonic Adaptation
Heterosexuals
Homeostasis
Homosexuals
Incentive
Individualism
Lie detector

Motivation
Obesity
Orgasm
Polygraph
Premises
Refractory period
Set point theory
Settling-point theory
Sexual orientation
Subjective well-being
Vasocongestion

_____ 1. Goal-directed behavior that may be affected by needs, wants, interests, desires, and incentives.

_____ 2. Cultural norms that regulate the expression of emotions.

_____ 3. One or more premises that are used to provide support for a conclusion.

_____ 4. The reasons presented in an argument to persuade someone that a conclusion is true.

_____ 5. Premises in an argument which are assumed but for which no proof or evidence is offered.

_____ 6. A measure of weight that controls for variations in height; weight in kilograms divided by height in meters, squared.

_____ 7. Refers to cultures that put group goals ahead of personal goals and defines a person's identity in terms of the groups to which a person belongs.

_____ 8. Blood sugar.

_____ 9. Neurons that are sensitive to glucose.

_____ 10. A hormone secreted by the pancreas needed for extracting glucose from the blood.

_____ 11. Refers to cultures that put personal goals ahead of group goals and defines a person's identity in terms of the personal attributes.

_____ 12. The theoretical natural point of stability in body weight.

_____ 13. The condition of being overweight.

_____ 14. The principal class of female sex hormones.

_____ 15. The principal class of male sex hormones.

_____ 16. A state of balance or equilibrium in the body.

_____ 17. An internal state of tension that motivates an organism to reduce tension.

_____ 18. Engorgement of the blood vessels during the human sexual response.

_____ 19. An external goal that motivates behavior.

_____ 20. A time following orgasm during which males are unresponsive to sexual stimulation.

_____ 21. Whether a person prefers emotional-sexual relationships with members of the same sex, the other sex, or either sex.

_____ 22. People who seek emotional-sexual relationships with members of the same sex.

	23.	People who seek emotional-sexual relationships with members of the other sex.
_____	24.	People who seek emotional-sexual relationships with members of either sex.
_____	25.	The view that body weight is determined by a wide variety of factors and that the body does not defend a particular point.
_____	26.	Individuals' personal perceptions of their overall happiness and life satisfaction.
_____	27.	The need to master difficult challenges and to excel in competition with others.
_____	28.	An increase in the electrical conductivity of the skin related to an increase in sweat gland activity.
_____	29.	A reaction that includes cognitive, physiological, and behavioral components.
_____	30.	The technical name for the "lie detector."
_____	31.	The informal name for polygraph, an apparatus that monitors physiological aspects of arousal (e.g., heart rate, GSR).

Answers: 1. motivation **2.** display rules **3.** argument **4.** premises **5.** assumptions **6.** body mass index (BMI) **7.** collectivism **8.** glucose **9.** glucostats **10.** hedonic adaptation **11.** individualism **12.** set point theory **13.** obesity **14.** estrogens **15.** androgens **16.** homeostasis **17.** drive **18.** vasocongestion **19.** incentive **20.** refractory period **21.** sexual orientation **22.** homosexuals **23.** heterosexuals **24.** bisexuals **25.** settling-point theory **26.** subjective well-being **27.** achievement motive **28.** galvanic skin response (GSR) **29.** emotion **30.** polygraph **31.** lie detector.

Review of Key People

David Buss
Walter Cannon
Ekman & Wallace Friesen

William James
Joseph LeDoux
William Masters & Virginia Johnson

David McClelland
Stanley Schachter

_____	1.	Proposed that emotions arise in subcortical areas of the brain.
_____	2.	Prominent evolutionary theorist who explored, among many other topics, gender differences in human mate preferences.
_____	3.	Proposed the two-factor theory of emotion.
_____	4.	Proposed that the amygdala serves as a "hub" of rapid emotional response, especially to sensory input involving threat.
_____	5.	Did the ground-breaking work on the physiology of the human sexual response.
_____	6.	Is responsible for most of the early research on achievement motivation.
_____	7.	In a series of cross-cultural studies found that people can identify six or so basic emotions from facial expressions.
_____	8.	Thought that emotion arose from one's perception of variations in autonomic arousal.

Answers: 1. Cannon **2.** Buss **3.** Schachter **4.** LeDoux **5.** Masters & Johnson **6.** McClelland **7.** Ekman & Friesen **8.** James.

Self-Quiz

1. Which of the following are most likely to be similar in BMI (body mass)?
   a. identical twins brought up in different family environments
   b. fraternal twins brought up in the same family environment
   c. parents and their adopted children
   d. adopted siblings brought up in the same family environment

2. The subjective feeling of hunger is influenced by:
   a. the amount of glucose in the bloodstream
   b. secretion of insulin by the pancreas
   c. external cues, including odor and appearance of food
   d. all of the above

3. What is the effect of insulin on blood glucose?
   a. Glucose level increases.
   b. Glucose level decreases.
   c. Glucose changes to free fatty acids.
   d. CCK increases.

4. According to this theory, the sex that makes the larger investment in offspring (bearing, nursing, etc.) will be more selective of partners than the sex that makes the smaller investment.
   a. adaptation level theory
   b. parental investment theory
   c. investment differentiation theory
   d. social learning theory

5. Which of the following theories proposes that the body actively tries to defend a precise body weight by adjusting metabolism and hunger?
   a. set-point theory
   b. settling-point theory
   c. adaptation level theory
   d. parental investment theory

6. Which of the following would best reflect the James-Lange theory of emotion?
   a. Thinking about the cause of general autonomic arousal produces different emotions.
   b. Different patterns of autonomic activation produce different consiously experienced emotions.
   c. Emotion originates in subcortical structures, which send signals to both the cortex and autonomic nervous system.
   d. Cognitive awareness of emotion precedes autonomic arousal.

7. The fact that identical twins are more likely to share sexual orientation than fraternal twins suggests that sexual orientation is:
   a. due to the environment
   b. in part genetic
   c. largely chemical
   d. primarily hormonal

8. Cultural norms that indicate which facial expressions of emotion are appropriate on what occasions are termed:
   a. display rules
   b. parental investments
   c. investment differentiations
   d. social scripts

9. According to the evolutionary theories, men seek as partners women who:
   a. are similar to them in important attitudes
   b. have a good sense of humor
   c. are beautiful, youthful, and in good health
   d. have good financial prospects

10. What test is generally used to measure need for achievement?
    a. the TAT
    b. the GSR
    c. the Rorschach
    d. the MMPI

11. Evidence regarding facial expression in different cultures suggests that:
    a. two-factor theory accounts for nonverbal behavior
    b. facial expression of emotion is to some extent innate
    c. emotions originate in the cortex
    d. learning is the major factor in explaining basic facial expressions

12. Which of the following proposed that emotion arises from one's perception or interpretation of autonomic arousal?
    a. Schachter
    b. Cannon-Bard
    c. LeDoux
    d. McClelland

13. Which of the following theories asserts that thinking or cognition plays a relatively small role in emotion?
    a. two-factor theory
    b. James-Lange theory
    c. achievement theory
    d. evolutionary theory

14. Of the following, which has been found to be most strongly associated with happiness?
    a. physical attractiveness
    b. health
    c. job satisfaction
    d. general intelligence

15. Someone exhorts people to take action against company policy, as follows: "We can oppose these changes, or we can live out our lives in poverty." This type of argument reflects which of the following fallacies?
    a. slippery slope
    b. weak analogy
    c. false dichotomy
    d. circular reasoning

Answers: 1. a **2.** d **3.** b **4.** b **5.** a **6.** b **7.** b **8.** a **9.** c **10.** a **11.** b **12.** a **13.** d **14.** c **15.** c.

InfoTrac Keywords

Bisexuals	Display rules	Subjective well-being
Collectivism	Set point theory	

Chapter Eleven
HUMAN DEVELOPMENT ACROSS THE LIFE SPAN

Review of Key Ideas

PROGRESS BEFORE BIRTH: PRENATAL DEVELOPMENT

1. Outline the major events of the three phases of prenatal development.

   1-1.   Each box below represents one month in the typical pregnancy; each short line at the top of the boxes represents one week. Indicate the beginning and end of each phase of prenatal development by placing the appropriate capital letters from the diagram in the blanks after the descriptions below.

   a)   The germinal stage begins at conception, represented by point _____ in the diagram, and ends at point _____.

   (b) The embryonic stage begins at point _____ and ends at point _____.

   (c) The fetal stage begins at point _____ and ends at point _____.

   1-2.   List the names of the three phases of prenatal development in the order in which they occur. In the parentheses at the right indicate the age ranges encompassed by each stage.

1-3. Match each stage in the previous question with the descriptions below. Use the letters G, E, and F to represent the germinal, embryonic, and fetal stages.

_____ The placenta begins to form.

_____ At the end of this stage the organism begins to have a human appearance; it is about an inch in length.

_____ The zygote begins to implant in the uterine wall; about one in five are rejected.

_____ Muscles and bones develop and physical movements occur.

_____ Most major birth defects probably have their origins in this stage.

_____ The age of viability (about 22 to 26 weeks after conception) occurs during this stage.

Answers: 1-1. (a) G, E (b) E, F (c) F, N **1-2.** (a) germinal (birth to two weeks) (b) embryonic (two weeks to two months) (c) fetal (two months to nine months) **1-3.** G, E, G, F, E, F.

2. Summarize the impact of environmental factors on prenatal development.

2-1. Indicate whether the following statements concerning environmental factors and fetal development are true (T) or false (F).

_____ Severe malnutrition increases the risk of birth complications and neurological deficits.

_____ Few if any drugs consumed by a pregnant woman are able to pass through the placental barrier.

_____ Relative to its affluence the U. S. has a high infant mortality rate.

_____ Recent studies indicate that moderate drinking during pregnancy produces no risk for the developing fetus.

_____ Heavy drinking of alcohol by a pregnant woman may produce microencephaly, heart defects, and retardation in her child.

_____ Smoking during pregnancy is related to increased risk of miscarriage and other birth complications.

_____ The placenta screens out many but not all infectious diseases.

_____ Genital herpes is usually transmitted during the birth process, when newborns come into contact with their mothers' lesions.

_____ AIDS is transmitted primarily during the birth process, when newborns come into contact with their mothers' blood cells.

_____ Good quality prenatal care is associated with fewer premature births and higher infant survival rates.

Answers: 2-1. T, F, T, F, T, T, T, T, T, T.

THE WONDROUS YEARS OF CHILDHOOD

3. Describe general principals of motor development and cultural variations in motor development.

3-1. In the spaces below describe the two basic trends in motor development discussed in the text.

Cephalocaudal trend:

Proximodistal trend:

3-2. The average ages at which children display various behaviors and abilities are referred to as developmental _____. While these averages provide useful information they don't reflect variability, and the age at which children display certain behaviors or abilities varies (<u>enormously</u>/very little) across children.

3-3. With regard to the behavior of walking up steps, for example, which of the following is true?

a. children walk up steps at approximately the same age.

b. many normal children don't walk up steps until well after or well before the average age indicated.

3-4. Maturation refers to developmental changes that reflect (<u>genetic</u>/environmental) factors. Current thinking emphasizes not only maturation but children's active involvement in exploring their worlds.

3-5. While cross-cultural research has revealed some consistencies in maturation among cultures, the discussion of the Kipsis and Ache in your text makes clear that culture (<u>does</u>/does not) play a role in motor development.

3-6. In other words, cultural differences may _____ early motor development.
a. accelerate
b. delay
c. either accelerate or delay

Answers: 3-1. Head to foot: children tend to gain motor control of the upper body before the lower body. Center outward: the tendency to gain control of the torso before the limbs. **3-2.** norms, enormously **3-3.** b **3-4.** genetic **3-5.** does **3-6.** c.

4. Summarize the findings of Thomas and Chess's longitudinal study of infant temperament and Kagan's work on temperament.

4-1. Identify the following designs by indicating whether they are longitudinal or cross-sectional.

(a) _____ In this experimental design researchers compare groups of subjects of differing ages at a single point in time.

(b) _____ This design measures a single group of subjects over a period of time.

4-2. Using a longitudinal design Thomas and Chess identified three basic temperaments, described below. Place the names of these temperamental styles in the appropriate blanks: easy, slow-to-warm-up, difficult.

(a) _____ Happy, regular in sleep and eating, adaptable.

(b) _____ Less cheery, less regular in sleep and eating, more wary of new experiences.

(c) _____ Glum, erratic in sleep and eating, irritable.

4-3. By far the largest group of children (about 40%) was of the _____ temperament, another 15% were _____, and 10% were in the _____ category. The remaining 35% showed mixtures of these three temperaments.

4-4. The major conclusion from the Thomas and Chess study is that a child's temperament at three months tended to be a (<u>poor/fairly good</u>) predictor of temperament at age ten years.

4-5. Using direct observation, Kagan and his colleagues classified infants into two major categories: an _____ temperament (shy, timid) or an _____ temperament. About 15-20% of infants were in the former category and 25%-30% in the latter. As with the Thomas and Chess study, these classifications of infants (<u>were/were not</u>) predictive of later temperament, in this case 20 years later.

Answers: 4-1. (a) cross-sectional (b) longitudinal **4-2.** (a) easy (b) slow-to-warm-up (c) difficult **4-3.** easy, slow-to-warm-up, difficult **4-4.** fairly good **4-5.** inhibited, uninhibited, were. (While these studies suggest a genetic component to temperament, Kagan makes clear that temperament is not fixed in stone.)

5. Describe Harlow's and Bowlby's views on attachment.

5-1. Early behaviorists proposed that an infant's attraction to its mother occurred because the mother fed the baby, thereby forming an association with food. According to this point of view attachment was (<u>learned/innate</u>), and the mother functioned as a (<u>primary/conditioned</u>) reinforcer.

5-2. Doubts about the simple conditioning explanation of attachment occurred as a result of Harlow's famous studies with rhesus monkeys using. In these studies infant rhesus monkeys grew up with either "wire" and "cloth" substitute mothers. Although the infant monkeys had been fed (or reinforced) by the _____ monkeys, they clung to the _____ mothers when frightened. The infants had formed attachments to the mothers that provided contact comfort, not to those that had fed them.

5-3. Bowlby has proposed an evolutionary basis for mother-infant attachment, that infants emit certain behaviors that automatically trigger affectionate and protective responses in adults. What do infants do that make them so adorable to adults? Among the behaviors they emit are _____, cooing, clinging, and so on. The infant's behaviors, and the adult's responses to them, are assumed to be in large part (<u>learned/innate</u>). If smiling in infants causes adults to protect them, then smiling clearly has _____ value in an evolutionary sense.

Answers: 5-1. learned, conditioned **5-2.** wire, cloth **5-3.** smiling, adaptive (survival).

6. Summarize theories of attachment and research on patterns of attachment and their effects.

6-1. Ainsworth and her colleagues divide types of infant-mother attachment into three categories. Label each of the following with the pattern of attachment described: *secure, anxious-ambivalent,* or *avoidant.*

(a) _____ The infant is anxious even when the mother is near, becomes very agitated when she leaves, and is not comforted when the mother returns.

(b) _____ The infant seeks little contact with the mother and is not distressed when she leaves.

(c) _____ The infant plays comfortably when the mother is present, is upset when the mother leaves, but is quickly calmed by her when she returns.

6-2. Other researchers have added a fourth category of attachment, the disorganized-_____ attachment, in which children are confused about whether to approach or avoid their mothers.

6-3. Attachment appears to be related to behavior in later childhood and adulthood. For a number of desirable characteristics (e.g., persistence, curiosity, self-reliance) infants who experienced a _____ attachment seem to have the advantage. It is important to point out, however, that the relationship is correlational, so we (can/cannot) assume that secure attachment <u>causes</u> the favorable characteristics.

Answers: 6-1. (a) anxious-ambivalent (b) avoidant (c) secure **6-2.** disoriented **6-3.** secure, cannot.

7. Discuss cultural variations in attachment and explain Belsky's evolutionary perspective on attachment.

7-1. Especially between the ages of six months and a year and a half, infants show emotional distress or _____ anxiety when apart from their caregivers. Separation anxiety seems to be universal, occurring in all cultures.

7-2. There are slight differences in attachment patterns across cultures, however. For example, a study of German infants found a somewhat higher level of avoidant attachments. In all cultures studied, however, the _____ attachment is by far the predominant type.

7-3. Belsky proposed that in our evolutionary past the relative harshness of the environment affected parent-child attachment style, which in turn affected the later _____ strategy of the sexually mature offspring.

7-4. For example, a harsh, unsafe environment with scarce resources would cause parents to have little time for the child, which would produce a(an) (<u>secure/insecure</u>) attachment. When the child reached sexual maturity, the earlier attachment style would yield a sexually (<u>opportunistic/enduring</u>) mating strategy. Such a strategy would maximize reproductive potential in environments where long-term survival is (<u>ensured/precarious</u>).

7-5. In contrast, a safe environment rich in resources would allow parents the time and energy to be responsive to an infant's needs, which would produce a(an) _____ attachment. Belsky asserts that such an attachment is associated with (<u>quality/quantity</u>) in later mating relationships with relatively (<u>few/many</u>) sexual partners and a strong romantic bond.

7-6. In short, Belsky proposed that the local _____ affected parent-child _____ which influenced the child's later _____ strategy, which has significance for passing genes to the next generation.

8. **Outline the basic tenets of Erikson's theory and describe his stages of childhood personality development.**

8-1. Erikson's theory is derived from Freudian psychoanalytic theory. However, while Freud asserted that there are five childhood stages, Erikson proposed that there are a total of _____ stages and that these stages occur during an individual's (childhood/entire lifespan).

8-2. Erikson described four childhood stages and four adult stages. In the spaces below write the names of the crises that mark the four childhood stages, and indicate in the parentheses the approximate ages at which the crises are supposed to occur.

(a) _____ vs. _____   (   )

(b) _____ vs. _____   (   )

(c) _____ vs. _____   (   )

(d) _____ vs. _____   (   )

8-3. Below are descriptions of several individuals. In what childhood stage would they have acquired these characteristics, according to Erikson? Use the letters from the question above to indicate the stages.

_____ Jack has trouble functioning effectively in the world outside his family; he is unproductive, and he lacks a sense of competence.

_____ Kristi is insecure and suspicious of everyone.

_____ Larry was torn between being independent of his family and avoiding conflict; as an adult he feels guilty and lacks self-esteem.

_____ From an early age Maureen's parents never seemed satisfied with what she did. Maureen is plagued by a sense of shame and self-doubt.

8-4. As you may have noted in responding to the previous item, a weakness of Erikson's theory is that it attempts to account for very (few/many) aspects of personality. Thus, the theory cannot explain the enormous individual _____ between people.

9. **Outline Piaget's stages of cognitive development and discuss the strengths and weaknesses of Piaget's theory.**

9-1.   The diagram below represents Piaget's four main stages of development. Write the names of the stages in the appropriate blanks.

(d) _____

(c) _____

(b) _____

(a) _____

9-2.   The stages of development are marked by changes in children's thinking processes brought about by two major processes. If the child interprets a new experience in terms of an existing mental structure, then _____ is operating. On the other hand, if the child interprets an experience by changing his thinking strategy, then the child has used _____.

9-3.   Following is a list of characteristics of children's thinking during various stages. Identify the stage by placing the correct letter (from the diagram above) in the blanks.

_____ At the end of this stage the child is beginning to develop the capacity for symbolic thought (to think terms of mental images).

_____ At the beginning of this stage the child's behavior is dominated by reflexes and the ability to coordinate sensory input and movement.

_____ The child understands conservation and can handle hierarchical classification but tends not to use abstractions.

_____ The child's thought processes are abstract and systematic.

_____ Object permanence occurs toward the end of this stage.

_____ During the first part of this stage, "out of sight, out of mind" might describe the child's reaction to hidden objects.

_____ When water is poured from a wide beaker into a taller beaker, children say there is now more water in the taller beaker.

_____ The child demonstrates a lack of understanding of conservation.

_____ The child shows the shortcomings of centration, irreversibility, egocentrism, and animism.

_____ For the first time the child in this stage is mentally able to undo an action and also is able focus on more than one feature of a problem at the same time.

9-4.   When my (R. S.) daughter Vanessa was about five, I placed two rows of stones on the grass, as illustrated below. Each row contained the same number of stones.

Row A: • • • • • • • •

Row B: • • • • • • • •

I then spread out one row so that it took up more space:

Row A: • • • • • • • •

Row B: • • • • • • • •

(a) I then asked Vanessa to point to the row that now had more stones. If Vanessa behaved like other preoperational children, which row would she point to? _____

(b) The preoperational child has not yet mastered the principle that physical quantities remain constant in spite of changes in their shape or, in this case, arrangement. What is the name of this principle? _____

9-5.   Some research has demonstrated that certain aspects of Piaget's theory may be incorrect in detail. For example, there is some evidence that object permanence and some aspects of conservation may develop (earlier/later) than Piaget had thought.

9-6.   Piaget also had little to say about individual _____ in development or about so-called _____ of stages in which elements of an earlier stage may appear in a later one.

9-7.   Piaget thought that people of all cultures would pass through the stages at the same time; subsequent research has found that this (is/is not) the case. While the sequence of stages appears to be relatively invariant across cultures, the _____ that children follow in passing through these stages varies considerably across cultures. Nonetheless, Piaget's brilliance, the novelty of his approach, and the wealth of research that his theory inspired assure his place in history.

Answers: 9-1. (a) sensorimotor (b) preoperational (c) concrete operations (d) formal operations 9-2. assimilation, accommodation 9-3. a, a, c, d, a, a, b, b, b, c 9-4. (a) Row A (at which point Samantha, then eight and in the stage of concrete operations, was astonished by her sister's choice and informed her that there were the same number in both!) (b) conservation 9-5. earlier 9-6. differences, mixing 9-7. is not, timetable (age, time).

10. Describe Vygotsky's sociocultural theory of cognitive development.

10-1.   Vygotsky's theory of cognitive development differs from Piaget's in three major respects. First, while Piaget emphasized the child as active agent exploring the world around him, Vygotsky emphasized social _____ as a key factor in cognitive development. Second, Piaget viewed the stages of development as relatively universal across cultures; in contrast, Vygotsky asserted that _____ played a differentiating role in cognitive development. Third, for Piaget language was just one expression of a stage of cognitive development; for Vygotsky, language was a _____ factor in organizing the child's world.

10-2. Match the following with the emphasis in either Piaget's or Vygotsky's theories.

_____ The literacy and language in a culture is a crucial factor in cognitive development.

_____ The interaction between children and their teachers, peers, and parents is critical in cognitive development.

_____ Language occurs as a result of reaching a particular stage of development.

10-3. Label the following descriptions with major concepts from Vygotsky's theory.

_____ There is a gap between what a child can achieve alone versus what they could achieve with guidance from more skilled members of a society.

_____ The tutor (or teacher, parent, peer, etc.) helps bridge the gap, and the amount of help is adjusted as the child's competence at a task increases.

Answers: 10-1. interaction, culture, central (major) **10-2.** Vygotsky, Vygotsky, Piaget **10-3.** zone of proximal development (ZPD), scaffolding.

11. Summarize evidence which suggests that some cognitive abilities could be innate.

11-1. When infants look at a stimulus that is presented repeatedly, the strength of their responses gradually decreases. They spend less and less time looking at the stimulus, and their heart and respiration rates decrease. This reduction in response strength is known as _____. When a new stimulus is presented, response strength increases, a process known as _____.

11-2. By using the habituation-dishabituation technique, researchers can tell when a child is able to discriminate between different events. For example, at three to four months of age, infants understand that (write T or F for each of the following):

_____ Objects on slopes roll down rather than up.

_____ One solid object cannot pass through another.

_____ Objects move in continuous paths.

11-3. In another demonstration of the cognitive abilities of young children, five-month-old infants were shown a display in which an object was added to or subtracted from others behind a screen. Remarkably, the children exhibited surprise, indicated by the response of (habituation/dishabituation), when the expected number of objects was not there.

11-4. This result suggests that infants have some rudimentary understanding of arithmetic—at least that they can _____ and _____ small numbers (e.g., 1 + 1, 3-1). More recently (see the Featured Study) the same authors found that nine-month-old infants seem to understand even larger numbers (e.g., 5 + 5).

11-5. Because these cognitive abilities occur at such an early age, before infants would have had much chance to learn them, some theorists have concluded that these capacities are largely (<u>acquired/innate</u>).

11-6. Two groups of theorists favor the innate explanation: nativists and evolutionary psychologists. Of these it is primarily the (<u>nativists/evolutionary theorists</u>) who are interested in explaining why we would be pre-wired with certain cognitive abilities. They assert that basic addition and subtraction abilities, for example, had clear _____ value in a hunting, foraging, and social-bargaining society.

Answers: 11-1. habituation, dishabituation **11-2.** T, T, T **11-3.** dishabituation **11-4.** add, subtract **11-5.** innate
11-6. evolutionary theorists, survival (adaptive).

12. Outline Kohlberg's stages of moral development and summarize the strengths and weaknesses of Kohlberg's theory.

12-1. Kohlberg's theory includes three moral levels, each with two stages for a total of six stages. Indicate which of the three moral levels is described in each of the following statements.

    (a) Acts are considered wrong because they are punished or right because they lead to positive consequences. _____

    (b) Individuals at this level conform very strictly to society's rules, which they accept as absolute and inviolable. _____

    (c) This level is characterized by situational or conditional morality, such that stealing might be considered wrong in one circumstance but permissible in another. _____

12-2. The central ideas of Kohlberg's theory have received a fair amount of support. Research has found that children (<u>do/do not</u>) tend to progress through Kohlberg's stages in the order that he indicated. As children get older, stages 1 and 2 reasoning tend to decrease while stages 3 and 4 reasoning tend to _____.

12-3. There have also been several criticisms of Kohlberg's theory. First, individuals may show characteristics of several different stages at the same time. In other words, as was true of other stage theories, there tends to be a "_____" of stages.

12-4. Second, researchers have focused too heavily on (<u>Kohlberg's/newly created</u>) dilemmas, which tends to narrow the scope of research on moral reasoning.

12-5. Third, it may be the case that Kohlberg's theory is much more (<u>value-free/culture-specific</u>) than he had supposed. For example, subjects from small, technologically unsophisticated village societies (<u>usually/rarely</u>) show reasoning beyond stage 3.

Answers: 12-1. (a) preconventional (b) conventional (c) postconventional **12-2.** do, increase **12-3.** mixing
12-4. Kohlberg's **12-5.** culture-specific, rarely.

THE TRANSITION OF ADOLESCENCE

13. Describe the physiological changes of puberty and research on neural development in adolescence.

13-1. Read over the section on <u>Puberty and the Growth Spurt</u> in your text. Then fill in the blanks below with the appropriate concepts: adolescent growth spurt, secondary sex characteristics, puberty, menarche, primary sex characteristics.

(a) _____ Rapid growth in height and weight in the two-year span preceding puberty.

(b) _____ The period of time during which secondary sex characteristics appear.

(c) _____ Physical features that distinguish one sex from another but that are not essential for reproduction (e.g., facial hair in males, breasts in females).

(d) _____ The sexual structures essential for reproduction develop fully.

(e) _____ The stage that includes menarche in females and the first production of sperm in males.

(f) _____ The first occurrence of menstruation.

(g) _____ The first occurrence of ejaculation.

13-2. Girls who mature (<u>early/late</u>) and boys who mature (<u>early/late</u>) may be subject to greater emotional distress during adolescence. In both sexes, early maturation is associated with difficulties (e.g., alcohol use, trouble with the law), but the problems encountered by early-maturing (<u>females/males</u>) are likely to be more severe.

13-3. Indicate true or false for the following:

_____ The overall size of the human brain increases significantly during adolescence.

_____ White matter (myelin) in the brain increases during adolescence.

_____ Gray matter decreases in adolescence due to synaptic pruning and formation of neural networks.

_____ Maturation of the brain is not complete until late adolescence or early adulthood.

_____ The prefrontal cortex matures last, which may account for increased risky behavior during adolescence.

Answers: 13-1. (a) adolescent growth spurt (b) puberty (c) secondary sex characteristics (d) primary sex characteristics (e) puberty (f) menarche (g) spermarche **13-2.** early, late, females **13-3.** F, T, T, T, T.

14. Evaluate the assertion that adolescence is a time of turmoil.

14-1. How tumultuous is adolescence? With regard to suicide and other indicants of stress, current data indicate that: (Mark T or F for each of the following statements.)

_____ Suicide among adolescents is higher than for any other age group.

_____ The ratio of attempted to completed suicides is much higher for adolescents than for any other age group.

_____ Adolescence brings an increase in conflicts between parents and their children.

_____ Adolescents engage in more risky behaviors and are more prone to negative emotions than are other age groups.

_____ In general, adolescents encounter somewhat more storm and stress than do people in other periods of life.

14-2. Violence (<u>is/is not</u>) higher during the adolescent years than during other age periods. Arrests for violent crimes increases up to about age _____ and then gradually decline. While school shootings are highly publicized, almost all of adolescent violence occurs (<u>within/outside</u>) school settings.

Answers: 14-1. F, T, T, T, T **14-2.** is, 18, outside.

15. Discuss some common patterns of identity formation in adolescence.

15-1. Adolescence is a period of change, so it is readily understandable that adolescents tend to focus on the struggle for _____, the question of "Who am I?"

15-2. Recall that Erik Erikson described four crises that mark childhood. What is the crisis that marks the fifth stage, adolescence, according to Erikson? _____ vs. _____

15-3. Marcia (1966, 1980) has described four orientations or statuses that individuals may adopt in attempting to resolve identity: identity diffusion, identity foreclosure, identity moratorium, and identity achievement.

   (a) One possible status is simply to take on the values and roles prescribed by one's parents, the status of identity _____. While this may temporarily resolve the crisis, in the long run the individual may not be comfortable with the adopted identity.

   (b) Another status involves a period of experimentation with various ideologies and careers and a delay in commitment to any one, termed identity _____.

   (c) If the experimentation and lack of commitment become permanent, the individual is said to be in a status of identity _____.

   (d) On the other hand, if the consideration of alternatives leads to conviction about a sense of self, one takes on the status referred to as identity _____.

15-4. Although identity achievement is the most mature status and diffusion the least, adolescents do not pass through the statuses in an orderly manner. In fact, recent research has found that (<u>very few/most</u>) adolescents shift back and forth among the four identity statuses. In addition, most individuals reach the most mature stage, identity _____ at a later age than Marcia had supposed.

Answers: 15-1. identity **15-2.** identity, confusion **15-3.** foreclosure, moratorium, diffusion, achievement **15-4.** most, achievement.

16. Summarize evidence on the stability of personality and the prevalence of the midlife crisis.

16-1. Do people change throughout their lifetimes, or does personality tend to remain the same? Research evidence supports the conclusion that:

    a. personality is stable across one's lifetime

    b. personality changes across one's lifetime

    c. both of the above

    d. neither of the above

16-2. The explanation for these apparently contradictory findings is that some personality traits do appear to _____ as people grow older while others remain _____.

16-3. Two influential studies conducted in the 1970s asserted that people experience a period of emotional turmoil some time between ages 35 and 45, a transitional phase known as the _____ _____.

16-4. The mid-life crisis, described as a period of reappraisal and assessment of time left, was thought by Gould and Levinson to be a transitional phase that affected (<u>very few/most</u>) adults. Recent studies have caste doubt on the conclusion that a midlife crisis is a normal part of aging. Using more objective methods, a large number of investigators have found that (<u>very few/most</u>) people go through a midlife crisis.

Answers: 16-1. c **16-2.** change, stable (the same) **16-3.** midlife crisis **16-4.** most, very few.

17. Outline Erikson's stages of development in adulthood.

17-1. In the spaces below write the names of the crises that mark Erikson's three stages of adulthood. In the parentheses indicate the approximate period of adulthood during which the crises are supposed to occur.

    (a)_____ vs. _____   (   )

    (b)_____ vs. _____   (   )

    (c)_____ vs. _____   (   )

17-2. Following are descriptions of the crises occurring in each of the above stages. Indicate the stages by placing the appropriate letters (a, b, or c from the previous question) in the blanks.

_____ Concern for helping future generations versus a self-indulgent concern for meeting one's own desires.

_____ Concern to find meaning in the remainder of one's life versus a preoccupation with earlier failures and eventual death.

_____ Concern for developing a capacity for intimacy with others versus a strategy in which others are manipulated as a means to an end.

Answers: 17-1. (a) intimacy vs. isolation (early adulthood) (b) generativity vs. self-absorption (middle adulthood) (c) integrity vs. despair (aging years) **17-2.** b, c, a.

18. **Describe typical transitions in family relations during the adult years.**

18-1. In part due to shifting social and economic trends, remaining single or postponing marriage is a much more acceptable option today than it was a few decades ago. Nonetheless, over _____ percent of adults eventually marry.

18-2. In general the level of happiness in marriage tends to be U-shaped. That is, spouses overall satisfaction with marital life tends to be highest at both the beginning and end and reach a low point toward the _____ of the family cycle.

18-3. What causes the drop in marital satisfaction during the middle years? To some degree it coincides with the burdens of child rearing. The decline begins to occur (only after/even before) the first child is born, however, so other factors appear to be involved as well.

18-4. Although most couples rate parenthood as a very positive experience, the birth of a child is frequently quite stressful. Adolescence, while not as contentious a period as previously believed, (does/does not) bring an increase in parent-child conflict. The effects of this conflict appear to be more adverse for the (children/parents).

18-5. Marital satisfaction tends to (decrease/increase) as the children grow up and leave home. Parent seem to adjust well to the "empty nest" and, in fact, are more likely to have problems if their children (return to/ stay away from) the home.

Answers: **18-1.** 90 **18-2.** middle **18-3.** even before **18-4.** parents **18-5.** increase, return to.

19. **Describe the physical changes associated with aging and the evidence on Ahzheimer's disease.**

19-1. As we age, our physical and cognitive characteristics change. Indicate which of the following physical traits increase and which decrease by placing checkmarks in the appropriate blanks.

	Increases	Decreases
Physical changes		
Proportion of body fat:	_____	_____
Overall weight:	_____	_____
Brain weight:	_____	_____
Visual acuity:	_____	_____
Ability to see close:	_____	_____
Hearing:	_____	_____

19-2. The ending of the menstrual cycle and loss of fertility among women is referred to as _____. Most women experience some physical discomfort during menopause (e.g., hot flashes), but the emotional distress (does/does not) appear to be especially severe.

19-3. Men (also/do not) go through a comparable experience. Testosterone levels begin to decline at middle age, and the eventual loss is (slight/substantial). The change occurs gradually, however, and is not comparable to the relatively sudden onset of menopause in women.

19-4. An abnormal condition marked by loss of memory and other cognitive abilities is termed a

_____. Dementia occurs in approximately _____% of individuals over age 65. Thus,

dementia (is/is not) a normal part of the aging process.

19-5. The disorder known as _____ disease accounts for approximately 70% of dementia.

This disease is accompanied by a (slight/widespread) loss of neurons, beginning in the hippocampus and

spreading to other areas of the brain.

19-6. Alzheimer's usually begins (before/after) age 65 and is initially marked by the rapid forgetting of newly

acquired information. Eventually, victims may fail to recognize familiar people and become disoriented

and unable to care for themselves. A cure for Alzheimer's (does/does not) appear to be close at hand.

Answers: **19-1.** Body fat and overall weight increase (except that overall weight may decrease somewhat after the mid-
50s); the rest decrease **19-2.** menopause, does not **19-3.** do not, substantial **19-4.** dementia, 15, is not **19-5.** Alzheimer's,
widespread **19-6.** after, does not.

20. Describe the cognitive changes associated with aging.

20-1. With regard to changes in cognitive ability that may accompany aging, which of the following is/are

true? (Mark T or F.)

_____ Average test scores in cognitive ability show some decline after age 60.

_____ For the majority of people the decline in general intelligence that occurs in later years appears to

be relatively slight.

_____ The major type of general cognitive loss that occurs with aging is thought to involve processing

speed.

_____ Problem solving ability generally remains unimpaired as people age if older people are given

additional time to compensate for reduced speed.

20-2. Are there sizeable declines in memory with age? While most researchers have concluded that memory

losses associated with aging are moderate, recent studies by Salthouse conclude that the decreases are

(minimal/substantial) and that they begin in (early/late) adulthood. Thus, the picture is mixed.

Answers: **20-1.** T, T, T, T **20-2.** substantial, early.

REFLECTIONS ON THE CHAPTER'S THEMES

21. Explain how this chapter highlighted the interaction of heredity and environment.

21-1. The behavior of a child is the result of the child's genetic inheritance and its environment, which includes

the behavior of the child's parents. In turn, the behavior of the parents toward the child is affected both

by their inherited characteristics and by the behavior of the child. Thus, behavior is the result not of

heredity or environment operating separately but of an _____ between the two factors.

21-2. To understand the concept of interaction consider this problem: There is a form of mental retardation that results from phenylketonuria, an inherited inability to metabolize a common amino acid in milk. When fed milk, children born with phenylketonuria become mentally retarded. Is this type of retardation an inherited disorder?

a. Yes, it's genetic.

b. No, it's caused by the environment.

c. A certain proportion of the causal factors are hereditary and the remainder are due to the environment.

d. The disorder results from heredity and environment operating jointly.

21-3. This chapter has been concerned with changes in human behavior across the life span. The theme being stressed here is that these changes result from an interaction of heredity and environment. In your own words, explain how the interaction operates.

Answers: 21-1. interaction **21-2.** d. (This disorder might at first seem to be inherited, since there is a genetic trait involved. But the retardation does not occur if the infant is not fed milk products, which involves the environment. The point is that this disorder, like behavior in general, cannot be attributed solely to nature or to nurture or even to relative weights of each; it is a function of an interaction between the two. **21-3.** The interaction of heredity and environment refers to the fact that we are a product of both factors. It means more than that, however. Heredity and environment don't operate separately. Interaction means that the genetic factors affect the operation of the environment and that environmental factors affect genetic predispositions. The influence of one factor depends on the effects of the other.

PERSONAL APPLICATION • UNDERSTANDING GENDER DIFFERENCES

22. Summarize evidence on gender differences in behavior and discuss the significance of these differences.

22-1. Which gender tends to show more of (or score higher on tests of) the following abilities or traits? Circle the correct answer at the right.

Cognitive

verbal skills	Males	Females	Neither
mathematical skills	Males	Females	Neither
visual-spatial skills	Males	Females	Neither

Social

physical aggression	Males	Females	Neither
sensitivity to nonverbal cues	Males	Females	Neither
sexually permissive attitudes	Males	Females	Neither

22-2. There is an enormous overlap between the genders with regard to these traits. There are, of course, females who are more aggressive than the average male and males who are more sensitive to nonverbal cues than the average female. Thus, it is important to note that the differences referred to in this section are differences between group _____ and that there is enormous variability within groups.

Answers: 22-1. cognitive: females, males, males; social: males, females, males **22-2.** averages (means).

23. Explain how biological factors are thought to contribute to gender differences.

23-1. For evolutionary theorists, the relative invariance of gender differences found across cultures reflects natural selection. From this perspective males are more sexually active and permissive than females because reproductive success for males is maximized by seeking (few/many) sexual partners. Greater aggressiveness has survival value for males because it enhances their ability to acquire material _____ sought by females selecting a mate.

23-2. Evolutionary theorists also assert that ability differences between the genders reflect the division of labor in our ancestral past. Males were primarily the hunters and females the gatherers, and the adaptive demands of hunting may have produced males' superiority at most _____ tasks.

23-3. The evolutionary view of gender is certainly an interesting and plausible explanation of the remarkable similarity in gender differences across cultures. The viewpoint has its critics, however. For one thing, there are reasonable _____ theories of gender differences; for another, the evolutionary explanation is relatively (easy/difficult) to test empirically.

23-4. Concerning other biological factors, several studies suggest that hormones contribute to shaping gender differences. For example, females exposed prenatally to high levels of an _____-like drug given their mothers during pregnancy tend to show more male-typical behavior than do other females.

23-5. Other biological evidence indicates that males depend more heavily on the left hemisphere for verbal processing and the right for spatial processing than is the case with females. That is, males may tend to exhibit more cerebral _____ than females.

23-6. The specialization finding has been linked to another finding, that females have larger _____ callosums (the connecting sheath of axons between hemispheres) than do males.

23-7. Results from studies of specialization and of gender differences in the corpus callosum have been (inconsistent/consistent), however. In addition, it would be difficult to see how gender differences in specialization could account for gender differences in ability.

Answers: **23-1.** many, resources **23-2.** spatial (visual-spatial) **23-3.** alternative, difficult **23-4.** androgen **23-5.** specialization **23-6.** corpus **23-7.** inconsistent.

24. Explain how environmental factors are thought to contribute to gender differences.

24-1. Many researchers remain convinced that gender differences are largely shaped by the environment. One of the ways that children learn gender roles is from the consequences for their behavior, the rewards and punishments that they receive in the process known as _____ conditioning.

24-2. Children also acquire information by seeing what others do, the process of _____ learning. While children imitate both males and females, they are more likely to imitate the behavior of (same-sex/opposite-sex) models.

24-3. In addition to operant conditioning and observational learning, children are active participants in their own gender-role socialization, the process referred to as _____-socialization. First, once they discover (at age five or six) that being a boy or girl is a permanent condition, they will then _____ themselves as boys or girls. Second, following classification in terms of gender children will _____ characteristics and behaviors associated with their gender. Third, they will bring their _____ in line with their values by engaging in "sex-appropriate" behaviors.

24-4. Whether through operant conditioning, observational learning, or self-socialization, the major forces for gender-role socialization occur in three main areas of the child's environment: in their _____, in _____, and in the _____.

Answers: **24-1.** operant **24-2.** observational (modeling), same-sex **24-3.** self, classify (categorize), value, behavior **24-4.** families, schools, media.

CRITICAL THINKING APPLICATION • ARE FATHERS ESSENTIAL TO CHILDREN'S WELL-BEING?

25. **Explain the argument that fathers are essential for healthy development and some criticism of this line of reasoning.**

25-1. Over the past several decades the percentage of children brought up without fathers in the home has steadily increased, from about 17% in 1960 to more than 35% today. During the same period there has also been a dramatic (decrease/increase) in teen pregnancy, juvenile delinquency, violent crime, drug abuse, eating disorders, and family dysfunction in general.

25-2. Further, fatherless children are two to three times more likely than fathered children to drop out of high school, become a teenage parent, or become a juvenile delinquent. In other words, father absence (causes/is correlated with) a host of unfortunate cultural trends.

25-3. Based on the association between father absence and social problems, some writers have asserted that the presence of a father is essential for a child's well-being. As you are by now well aware, however, one (can/cannot) infer causation on the basis of correlational data alone.

25-4. Among the reasonable alternative explanations for the correlational relationship described are the following. Father absence frequently occurs when the parents _____, so it is possible that this factor, rather than father absence, may cause the negative effects referred to.

25-5. Or, since father absence is much more frequent in (low-income/high-income) families, it is possible that poverty, rather than father absence, may cause some (or all) of the negative effects.

25-6. In your continued critical thinking about the assertions discussed, recall also the fallacies in reasoning introduced in Chapter 10: irrelevant reasons, circular reasoning, slippery slope, weak analogies, and false dichotomy. Which of these apply to the following assertions? Use the abbreviations IR, CR, SS, WA, or FD.

(a) ____ If present trends continue, our society could be on the verge of social suicide.

(b) ____ To tolerate the trend of fatherlessness is to accept the inevitability of continued societal recession.

Answers: 25-1. increase 25-2. is correlated with 25-3. cannot 25-4. divorce 25-5. low-income 25-6. (a) SS. The argument is that if we allow one event to happen, then other events will inevitably follow on this slippery slope that will lead to disaster (b) FD. The quote may have elements of more than one fallacy, but the author really is posing a dichotomy: Either we reduce father absence, or else we will face social decline. Of course, we could do both (reduce father absence and face social decline) or neither.

Review of Key Terms

Accomodation
Age of viability
Animism
Assimilation
Attachment
Centration
Cephalocaudal trend
Cognitive development
Conservation
Cross-sectional design
Dementia
Development
Developmental norms
Dishabituation
Egocentrism
Embryonic stage
Family life cycle

Fetal alcohol syndrome
Fetal stage
Gender
Gender differences
Gender roles
Gender stereotypes
Germinal stage
Habituation
Infantile amnesia
Irreversibility
Longitudinal design
Maturation
Menarche
Mentor
Meta-analysis
Mid-life crisis
Motor development

Object permanence
Placenta
Prenatal period
Primary sex characteristics
Proximodistal trend
Puberty
Pubescence
Secondary sex characteristics
Separation anxiety
Sex
Social clock
Socialization
Stage
Temperament
Zone of proximal development
Zygote

_____ 1. The sequence of age-related changes that occurs as a person progresses from conception to death.

_____ 2. The period of pregnancy, extending from conception to birth.

_____ 3. The first two weeks after conception.

_____ 4. The structure that connects the circulation of the fetus and the mother but that blocks passage of blood cells.

_____ 5. The second stage of prenatal development, lasting from two weeks after conception until the end of the second month.

_____ 6. The third stage of prenatal development, lasting from two months after conception through birth.

_____ 7. The age at which the baby can first survive in the event of a premature birth.

_____ 8. A collection of congenital problems associated with a mother's excessive use of alcohol during pregnancy.

_____ 9. Changing existing mental structures to explain new experiences, a concept from Piaget's theory of cognitive development.

_____ 10. Developmental changes in muscular coordination required for physical movement.

_____ 11. The head-to-foot direction of motor development.

_____ 12. The center-outward direction of motor development.

_____ 13. The average ages at which people display certain behaviors and abilities.

_____ 14. Characteristic mood, energy level, and reactivity.

_____ 15. One group of subjects is observed over a long period of time.

_____ 16. Investigators compare groups of subjects of differing ages at a single point in time.

_____ 17. A difficult, turbulent period of doubt and reappraisal of one's life that may occur at midlife.

_____ 18. Emotional distress displayed by an infant when separated from a person with whom it has formed an attachment.

_____ 19. Culturally constructed distinctions between femininity and masculinity.

_____ 20. Widely held beliefs about females' and males' abilities, personality traits, and social behavior.

_____ 21. Development of thinking, reasoning, remembering, and problem solving.

_____ 22. The gradual reduction in response strength that occurs when people are repeatedly exposed to some event.

_____ 23. The increase in response strength that occurs when people are exposed to a new stimulus event.

_____ 24. A mental capacity that involves recognizing that objects continue to exist even when they are no longer visible.

_____ 25. Piaget's term for the awareness that physical quantities remain constant in spite of changes in their shape or appearance.

_____ 26. The Piagetian term for the tendency to focus on just one feature of a problem and neglect other important features.

_____ 27. The inability to cognitively visualize reversing an action.

_____ 28. Thinking characterized by a limited ability to share another person's viewpoint.

_____ 29. A sequence of stages that families tend to progress through.

_____ 30. Interpreting new experiences in terms of mental structures already available, a concept from Piaget's theory of cognitive development.

_____ 31. The attribution of lifelike qualities to inanimate objects.

_____ 32. A developmental period during which certain behaviors and capacities occur.

_____ 33. The biologically based categories of male and female.

_____ 34. A close, emotional bond of affection between an infant and its caregiver.

_____ 35. Physical features associated with gender that are not directly needed for reproduction.

_____ 36. The physical structures necessary for reproduction.

_____ 37. The two-year span preceding puberty marked by the appearance of secondary sex characteristics and by rapid growth.

_____ 38. The first occurrence of menstruation.

_____ 39. The stage during which reproductive functions reach maturity.

_____ 40. An abnormal condition marked by multiple cognitive deficits; more prevalent in older adults but not a product of normal aging.

_____ 41. Developmental changes that reflect one's genetic blueprint rather than environment.

_____ 42. A one-celled organism created by the process of fertilization, the union of sperm and egg.

_____ 43. Behavioral differences between females and males.

_____ **44.** A term from Vygotsky's theory referring to the gradual adjustment in a helping structure as the child's competence increases.

_____ **45.** The acquisition of norms, roles, and behaviors expected of people in a particular group.

_____ **46.** Expectations concerning what is the appropriate behavior for each sex.

_____ **47.** Vygotsky's term for the gap between what the child can achieve alone versus with guidance from more skilled members of a society.

Answers: 1. development **2.** prenatal period **3.** germinal stage **4.** placena **5.** embryonic stage **6.** fetal stage **7.** age of viability **8.** fetal alcohol syndrome **9.** accomodation **10.** motor development **11.** cephalocaudal trend **12.** proximodistal trend **13.** developmental norms **14.** temperament **15.** longitudinal design **16.** cross-sectional design **17.** mid-life crisis **18.** separation anxiety **19.** gender **20.** gender stereotypes **21.** cognitive development **22.** habituation **23.** dishabituation **24.** object permanence **25.** conservation **26.** centration **27.** irreversibility **28.** egocentrism **29.** family life cycle **30.** assimilation **31.** animism **32.** stage **33.** sex **34.** attachment **35.** secondary sex characteristics **36.** primary sex characteristics **37.** pubescence **38.** menarche **39.** puberty **40.** dementia **41.** maturation **42.** zygote **43.** gender differences **44.** scaffolding **45.** socialization **46.** gender roles **47.** the zone of proximal development (ZPD).

Review of Key People

Mary Ainsworth
Jay Belsky
John Bowlby

Erik Erikson
Lawrence Kohlberg

Jean Piaget
Alexander Thomas & Stella Chess

_____ **1.** Conducted a major longitudinal study in which they identified three basic styles of children's temperament.

_____ **2.** Research on daycare; also, proposed the evolutionary view that early attachment is a determinant of later reproductive strategy.

_____ **3.** Theorized that there are critical periods in human infants' lives during which attachments must occur for normal development to take place.

_____ **4.** Partitioned the life span into eight stages, each accompanied by a psychosocial crisis.

_____ **5.** Pioneered the study of children's cognitive development.

_____ **6.** Developed a stage theory of moral development.

_____ **7.** Described three categories of infant-mother attachment.

Answers: 1. Thomas & Chess **2.** Belsky **3.** Bowlby **4.** Erikson **5.** Piaget **6.** Kohlberg **7.** Ainsworth.

Self-Quiz

1. Which prenatal period begins at the second week and ends at the second month of pregnancy?
   a. germinal stage
   b. embryonic stage
   c. fetal stage
   d. seminal stage

2. In which prenatal stage do most major birth defects probably have their origins?
   a. germinal stage
   b. embryonic stage
   c. fetal stage
   d. seminal stage

3. How does the brain change during adolescence?
   a. it becomes smaller
   b. it becomes larger
   c. white matter increases
   d. the prefrontal cortex becomes larger

4. According to Belsky's evolutionary viewpoint, the current harshness of an environment affects parent-child attachment, which in turn affects the offspring's later:
   a. accommodation and assimilation
   b. adaptation to traumatic events
   c. reproductive or mating strategy
   d. expression of discomfort and alienation

5. What is the major conclusion from Thomas and Chess's longitudinal study of temperament?
   a. Children's temperaments tend to go through predictable stages.
   b. The temperament of the child is not a good predictor of the temperament of the adult.
   c. Opposites attract.
   d. Children's temperaments tend to be consistent over the years.

6. The crisis occurring in the first year, according to Erikson, is one involving:
   a. trust versus mistrust
   b. initiative versus guilt
   c. industry versus inferiority
   d. identity versus conformity

7. During which stage in Piaget's system is the child first able to handle conservation problems and hierarchical classification problems?
   a. sensorimotor
   b. preoperational
   c. concrete operations
   d. formal operations

8. A child in the early sensorimotor period is shown a ball, which she watches intensely. The ball is then hidden under a pillow. What will the child do?
   a. ask, "Where is the pillow?"
   b. stare at the pillow but not pick it up
   c. move the pillow and pick up the ball
   d. ignore the pillow, as if the ball didn't exist

9. Who developed a stage theory of moral development?
   a. Piaget
   b. Kohlberg
   c. Gould
   d. Bowlby

10. Which of the following cognitive capacities is most likely to decline as a function of aging?
    a. speed of learning
    b. crystallized intelligence
    c. problem-solving ability
    d. specialized intelligence

11. Some researchers have found that very young children (e.g., five months old) appear to be aware of the addition or subtraction of objects from behind a screen. The technique used in these studies was:
    a. sensory preconditioning
    b. self-socialization
    c. classical conditioning
    d. habituation-dishabituation

12. Which of the following factors tends to be accompanied by a drop in ratings of marital satisfaction?
    a. childlessness during early married life
    b. the birth of the first child
    c. the first child's departure for college
    d. when the last child leaves home

13. Females tend to score slightly higher than males on tests of:
    a. verbal ability
    b. mathematical ability
    c. visual-spatial ability
    d. cerebral specialization

14. Females exposed to high levels of androgen during prenatal development tend to show:
    a. more male-typical behavior than other females
    b. more stereotypic female behavior than other females
    c. less cerebral specialization than other females
    d. a larger corpus collosum than other females

15. Once children discover that their gender is permanent, they are likely to want to engage in behavior that is "sex appropriate" as defined by their culture. This process is referred to as:
    a. operant conditioning
    b. observational learning
    c. self-socialization
    d. classical conditioning

    Answers: 1. b **2.** b **3.** c **4.** c **5.** d **6.** a **7.** c **8.** d **9.** b **10.** a **11.** d **12.** b **13.** a **14.** a **15.** c.

InfoTrac Keywords

Dementia	Gender Stereotypes	Temperament
Fetal Alcohol Syndrome	Puberty	

Chapter Twelve
PERSONALITY: THEORY, RESEARCH, AND ASSESSMENT

Review of Key Ideas

THE NATURE OF PERSONALITY

1. **Define the construct of personality in terms of consistency and distinctiveness.**

   1-1. I could always tell when my colleague across the hall (now retired) had finished for the day, because I could hear squeaking as he carefully moved his computer table under his bookcase. And I knew what followed: he closed and reshelved his books, sorted the papers on his desk into two piles, and slid the pens and pencils into his desk drawer bin. The fact that my colleague engaged in the *same behaviors* every day illustrates the feature of personality termed _____.

   1-2. When I'm done, on the other hand, I usually just stand up and walk out, leaving my somewhat (some would say very) messy desk behind. The fact that my colleague and I *differ* with respect to office neatness illustrates the feature of personality termed _____.

   Answers: 1-1. consistency (stability) **1-2.** distinctiveness (behavioral differences).

2. **Explain what is meant by a personality trait and describe the five-factor model of personality.**

   2-1. A consistent or durable disposition to behave in a particular way is referred to as a personality _____. Personality trait descriptions frequently consist of a series of _____, such as anxious, excitable, shy, aggressive, and so on.

   2-2. There are an enormous number of trait words that could be used to describe people. Gordon Allport, for example, listed several thousand. Raymond Cattell reduced Allport's list to just _____ traits. More recently, McCrae and Costa have described an even simpler model involving only _____ traits, the so-called Big Five theory.

   2-3. Some researchers maintain that more than five factors are needed to describe personality. Others contend that fewer than five factors are needed. Of the various models, however, the dominant conception of personality structure is currently the _____ theory.

2-4. Below are listed some of the adjectives that describe each of the five factors: neuroticism, extraversion, openness to experience, agreeableness, and conscientiousness. List the name of each of the factors next to the descriptions. (The five factors are relatively easy to remember if one thinks of NEO, which may mean "new," and adds AC: NEOAC.)

_____: outgoing, sociable

_____: imaginative, nonconforming

_____: anxious, insecure

_____: dependable, disciplined

_____: sympathetic, trusting

Answers: 2-1. trait, adjectives **2-2.** 16, five **2-3.** Big Five (five-factor) **2-4.** extraversion, openness to experience, neuroticism, conscientiousness, agreeableness.

PSYCHODYNAMIC PERSPECTIVES

3. **List and describe the three components into which Freud divided the personality and indicate how these are distributed across three levels of awareness.**

3-1. Below is a schematic illustration of the three Freudian structures of personality. Label each.

(b) _____   (c) _____

(a) _____

3-2. Freud superimposed levels of consciousness on the psychic structures. The following illustration makes clear that two of the structures exist at all three levels, while one is entirely unconscious. Label the levels.

(a) _____

(b) _____

(c) _____

4. **Explain the preeminence of sexual and aggressive conflicts in Freud's theory and describe the operation of defense mechanisms.**

4-1.   Freud believed that most of our conflicts arise from _____ and _____ urges. Conflicts relating to these areas were preeminent in his mind because (1) they are subject to subtle social _____ and, for that reason, are a source of confusion; and (2) they are less likely to be immediately gratified and more apt to be _____ than other urges.

4-2.   Following is a list of the defense mechanisms. Match each with the correct description by placing the appropriate letters in the blanks.

A. rationalization   D. displacement   F. regression

B. repression   E. reaction formation   G. identification

C. projection

_____   A return to an earlier, less mature stage of development.

_____   Forming an imaginary or real alliance with a person or group; becoming like them.

_____   Creating false but reasonable-sounding excuses.

_____   Pushing distressing thoughts into the unconscious.

_____   Attributing ones own thoughts, feelings, or conflicts to another.

_____   Expressing an emotion that is the exact opposite of the way one really, but unconsciously, feels.

_____   Diverting emotional feelings from their original source to a substitute target.

4-3.   Using the letters from the previous question, match the defense mechanisms with the following examples.

_____   After John and Marsha break up, John says he hates Marsha; this statement helps him defend against his real feelings of affection.

_____   "Society is filled with perverts," says the preacher; but later evidence suggests that he is the one with the sexual conflicts.

_____   In reaction to the stress of entering college, Alice starts acting like a grade-school kid.

_____   Bruce acts like John Wayne, and he owns tapes of all the Duke's movies.

_____   Mary is angry at her mother, so she kicks her baby brother.

5. **Outline Freud's psychosexual stages of development and their theorized relations to adult personality.**

5-1. List Freud's stages of psychosexual development, in the order in which they are supposed to occur, in the blanks below. Place the ages in the parentheses.

(a) _____ (   )

(b) _____ (   )

(c) _____ (   )

(d) _____ (   )

(e) _____ (   )

5-2. The following behaviors or personality characteristics are supposed to result from fixation at a particular psychosexual stage. Place the names of the correct stages in the blanks.

(a) She has problems with anger control, is hostile toward people in authority, and defies any attempt at regulation of her behavior. _____

(b) He eats too much, drinks too much, and smokes. _____

(c) He has occasional outbursts of hostility toward his father that he can't understand. In family arguments he sides with his mother. _____

5-3. The Oedipus complex occurs during the _____ stage, between the ages of _____ and _____. This complex theoretically involves an erotically tinged attraction toward the (same-sex/opposite-sex) parent and a strong hostility toward the (same-sex/opposite-sex) parent. Resolution of the Oedipus complex involves (increasing/stopping) both the child's erotic attraction and the child's hostility.

Answers: **5-1.** (a) oral (first year) (b) anal (second year) (c) phallic (ages 3 through 5) (d) latency (age 5 to puberty) (e) genital (puberty on) **5-2.** (a) anal (b) oral (c) phallic **5-3.** phallic, 3, 5, opposite-sex, same-sex, stopping.

6. **Summarize the revisions of Freud's theory proposed by Jung and Adler.**

6-1. Freud devised the theory and method of treatment termed *psychoanalysis*. To differentiate his approach from Freud's, Jung called his theory _____ _____. Like Freud, Jung emphasized the unconscious determinants of personality. Unlike Freud, he proposed that the unconscious consists of two layers, a _____ unconscious and a _____ unconscious. The personal unconscious is similar to Freud's unconscious, but it has less emphasis on sexuality. The collective unconscious is a repository of inherited, ancestral memories that Jung termed _____.

6-2. Jung's major contribution to psychology is considered by many to be his description of two major personality types: _____, reserved, contemplative people who tend to be concerned with their own internal world of thoughts, and _____, outgoing people who are more interested in the external world of others.

6-3. For Freud, the driving energy behind the human personality was sexuality; for Jung it may have been the collective unconscious. For Adler, it was striving for _____ and the attempt to overcome childhood feelings of inferiority. Efforts to overcome imagined or real inferiorities involve _____ through development of one's abilities. While Adler considered compensation to be a normal mechanism, he saw _____ as an abnormal attempt to conceal feelings of inferiority.

6-4. Adler is associated with the term _____ _____, an exaggerated feeling of inadequacy, supposedly caused by parental pampering or neglect in early childhood. Adler also thought that _____ _____ (that is, whether one is an only child, first-born, second-born, etc.) had a major effect on personality.

6-5. Adler's concept of birth order has created considerable interest. Initial data failed to support Adler's hypotheses, but Frank Sulloway's recent analyses of decades of research concludes that birth order (is/is not) a factor in personality. Referring to the _____ trait theory, Sulloway proposed, for example, that first-borns are more conscientious but less agreeable than later-borns. (Not all/All other) research on birth order has supported Sulloway's conclusions, and the topic is of current interest to many researchers.

Answers: 6-1. analytical psychology, personal, collective, archetypes **6-2.** introverts, extraverts **6-3.** superiority, compensation, overcompensation **6-4.** inferiority complex, birth order **6-5.** Big Five, Not all.

7. **Summarize the strengths and weaknesses of the psychodynamic approach to personality.**

7-1. Psychoanalytic formulations have had a major impact on the field of psychology. List the four contributions discussed in your text.

7-2. Psychoanalytic formulations have also been extensively criticized. After each of the following statements, list the particular criticism, from the discussion in your text, that the statement invites.

(a) Freud proposed that females develop weaker superegos and that they have a chronic sense of inferiority caused by penis envy. _____

(b) Although he discussed some characteristics associated with the psychosexual stages, Freud didn't really specify which events, occurring during which childhood stages, produce which sets of personality traits. _____

(c) Claims of support for the theories are based largely on clinical case studies and clinical intuition. _____

Answers: 7-1. the discovery that *unconscious forces* can influence behavior, that *internal conflict* may generate psychological distress, and that *early childhood experiences* influence the adult personality, and that people do use *defense mechanisms* **7-2.** (a) sexism (b) poor testability (vague ideas) (c) inadequate or weak evidence.

8. **Discuss how Skinner's principles of operant conditioning can be applied to the structure and development of personality.**

   8-1.   Which of the following processes plays an important part in Skinner's ideas about human behavior?

          a.   mental conflict

          b.   the mind

          c.   free will

          d.   none of the above

   8-2.   According to Skinner, much of our behavior is affected by reinforcement, punishment, or extinction—in other words, by the environmental _____ that follow our behavior. For example, if some individuals behave in a consistently aggressive manner (i.e., have aggressive personality traits), they do so because they have been _____ for behaving aggressively in the past.

   8-3.   Skinner recognized that there are differences between people and that people behave relatively consistently over time. Distinctiveness and consistency occur, however, not because of what's going on in an individual's *mind* but because of what has occurred previously in their _____.

   8-4.   Thus, for Skinner, personality is not mental, but environmental. People's minds don't change, their environment changes. Skinner makes a strong case for the point of view that our behavior is caused, or _____ rather than free, and that the determinants are largely _____ rather than genetic.

   Answers: **8-1.** d **8-2.** consequences (stimuli, events), reinforced **8-3.** environment **8-4.** determined, environmental.

9. **Describe Bandura's social cognitive theory and compare it to Skinner's viewpoint.**

   9-1.   In what respect is Bandura's point of view similar to Skinner's?

   9-2.   Three of the major differences between Bandura's and Skinner's viewpoints involve the concepts, listed below. Carefully define and explain these concepts and indicate how they represent a difference from Skinner's position.

          (a) reciprocal determinism:

          (b) observational learning:

          (c) self-efficacy:

9-3. We don't imitate everyone. We tend to imitate others whom we like, consider attractive, powerful, or observe being reinforced. In observational learning, the person whom we imitate is referred to as a

_____.

Answers: 9-1. Both Bandura and Skinner believed that personality is largely shaped through learning. **9-2.** (a) *Reciprocal determinism* refers to the point of view that not only does environment determine behavior, as Skinner asserted, but that behavior determines environment, and further, that behavior, environment, and mental processes all mutually affect one another. (b) *Observational learning* is the process through which we learn behaviors by observing the consequences of someone else's (i.e., a model's) behavior. For example, we learn not only by being reinforced, as Skinner proposed, but by observing someone else being reinforced. (c) *Self-efficacy* is a belief in our ability to perform certain behaviors. This belief affects whether we undertake those behaviors and how well we perform them. Skinner makes no allowance for mentalistic concepts such as self-efficacy. **9-3.** model.

10. Identify Mischel's major contribution to personality theory and indicate why his ideas have generated so much controversy.

10-1. Mischel's major contribution to personality theory is his contention that human behavior is not as consistent as had been supposed, that behavior is determined to a great extent by the

_____.

10-2. Why was Mischel's idea a provocative one for the field of personality? Because the definition of personality emphasizes *consistent differences*. Mischel's findings suggest that behavior (is/is not) as consistent across different situations as personality theorists had thought.

Answers: 10-1. situation (immediate environment) **10-2.** is not.

11. Summarize the strengths and weaknesses of the behavioral approach to personality.

11-1. The major strengths of the behavioral approach have been its commitment to empirical

_____ and its identification of important _____ determinants of behavior.

11-2. The major weaknesses of the behavioral approach, according to its critics, have been its overdependence on research involving _____ subjects, its denial of free will and of the importance of _____ processes, and its view of personality as nothing more than a collection of behaviors or _____ associations.

Answers: 11-1. research, environmental (empirical) **11-2.** animal, cognitive, stimulus-response.

HUMANISTIC PERSPECTIVES

12. Explain how humanism was a reaction against both the behavioral and psychodynamic approaches and discuss the assumptions of the humanistic view.

12-1. The humanistic movement reacted against the behavioral approach because of its mechanistic view of personality and its emphasis on _____ research, and against the psychoanalytic approach because of its emphasis on _____ drives.

12-2. The humanistic viewpoint found fault with both movements because they stressed

_____, or absolute causation. The humanists also thought that the behaviorists and the Freudians failed to recognize the (<u>unique/common</u>) qualities of human behavior.

12-3. Humanistic psychology emphasizes the (<u>similarities/differences</u>) between human beings and the other animal species, believes we (<u>are controlled by/can rise above</u>) our biological heritage, asserts that we are largely (<u>rational/irrational</u>) creatures, and maintains that a person's (<u>subjective/objective</u>) view of the world is more important than _____ reality.

Answers: 12-1. animal, primitive (animalistic) **12-2.** determinism, unique **12-3.** differences, can rise above, rational, subjective, objective.

13. Identify the single structural construct in Rogers's person-centered theory, and summarize his view of personality development.

13-1. Who are you? What are you like? What are your unique qualities? What is your typical behavior? Your answers to these questions are likely to reflect what Rogers called the _____.

13-2. Although Ralph tends to be a submissive and somewhat lazy person (and that is the way his friends, family, and co-workers describe him), he views himself as hard-working and dynamic, a leader both on the job and at home.

(a) What is Ralph's self-concept?

(b) Is his self-concept congruent or incongruent?

(c) According to Rogers, what parental behavior may have led to this incongruence?

(d) According to Rogers, what parental behavior would have resulted in Ralph's achieving congruence rather than incongruence?

13-3. Define the following Rogerian concepts.

(a) conditional love:

(b) unconditional love:

13-4. What is defensiveness for Rogers?

Answers: 13-1. self or self-concept **13-2.** (a) that he is hard-working, dynamic, and a leader (b) incongruent (c) conditional love or acceptance (d) unconditional love or acceptance **13-3.** (a) affection given conditionally, the condition being that the child or adult must live up to another's expectations (b) affection given without conditions, full acceptance of the person not dependent on what he or she is or does. **13-4.** Defensiveness is related to Roger's incongruence. As with Freud, people defend against anxiety by distorting or denying reality. For Rogers, defensiveness arises when people defend their self-concepts against inconsistent experiences.

14. Explain Maslow's hierarchy of needs, and summarize his findings on the characteristics of self-actualizing people.

14-1. Maslow proposed that human needs are arranged in a hierarchy, usually depicted as a pyramid, with the most basic, physiological needs at the _____ and higher-level needs closer to the _____.

14-2. The lower level needs would include needs for food, water, and factors related to survival and security. Next in the hierarchy would be a need for acceptance by others. Higher level needs, called _____ needs, would include the need for knowledge and aesthetic beauty. At the top of the pyramid is the need for _____, the need to express one's full potential.

14-3. A higher level need would be activated only after a lower level need is satisfied. For example, a need for knowledge would be activated (before/after) needs for esteem, belongingness, and several lower level needs had been reasonably well satisfied.

14-4. Maslow referred to a need to fulfill one's potential in his concept of _____. For example, if a woman had the talent and strong desire to become a mathematician, but followed the urging of others and became a nurse instead (or vice versa), she would not be _____.

14-5. Maslow proposed that people who are self-actualized have exceptionally healthy personalities. Which of the following, according to Maslow, are characteristic of self-actualized people? Place Y in the blank if the description applies, N if it does not.

_____ spontaneous

_____ has more profound emotional experiences than others

_____ uncomfortable being alone

_____ not dependent on others for approval

_____ thrive on their work

_____ extreme in personality (e.g., either conforming or rebellious)

Answers: 14-1. bottom, top **14-2.** growth, self-actualization **14-3.** after **14-4.** self-actualization, self-actualized **14-5.** Y, Y, N, Y, Y, N.

15. Summarize the strengths and weaknesses of the humanistic approach to personality.

15-1. To its credit, the humanistic movement called attention to the possibility that a person's _____ views may be more important than objective reality. The movement also emphasized the importance of the _____, or self-concept, and stressed the study of the (normal/abnormal) personality.

15-2. Critics have also identified several weaknesses of the humanistic formulations. Match the weaknesses listed below with the statements, by placing the appropriate letters in the blanks.

a. poor testability

b. unrealistic view of human nature

c. inadequate evidence

____ Humanistic psychologists tend to scorn research, so little experimental support for their views has emerged.

____ Even without research, some of the descriptions, such as of self-actualized personalities, have an idealized, perfectionistic ring.

____ Humanistic ideas are frequently difficult to define, so research on some concepts is difficult or impossible.

Answers: 15-1. subjective, self, normal **15-2.** c, b, a.

BIOLOGICAL PERSPECTIVES

16. Describe Eysenck's theory of personality.

16-1. According to Eysenck, individual differences in personality can be understood in terms of a hierarchy of traits. At the top of the hierarchy are three fundamental higher-order traits from which all other traits derive: _____, _____, and _____.

16-2. Eysenck asserted that a major factor in personality involves the ease with which people can be _____. Eysenck believed that differences in conditionability, like personality differences in general, are to a large extent (environmentally/genetically) determined.

16-3. Conditionability, in turn, is related to extraversion-introversion. According to Eysenck, (extraverts/introverts) have higher levels of physiological arousal, a characteristic that makes them (more/less) readily conditioned.

16-4. Why would conditionability be related to introversion? Because easily conditioned people could be readily conditioned to fear social situations. People who fear social situations may be classified as _____.

Answers: 16-1. extraversion, neuroticism, psychoticism **16-2.** conditioned, genetically **16-3.** introverts, more **16-4.** introverts.

17. Summarize behavioral genetics research on personality and its conclusions.

17-1. The most important and conclusive result from the various twin studies is the finding that the personalities of (identical/fraternal) twins reared (together/apart) were more similar than those of (identical/fraternal) twins reared (together/apart). This outcome has been found with several dependent measures, including the factors of the Big Five personality inventory as well as peer ratings.

17-2. Approximately what percentage of the variance in personality is assumed to be caused by genetic factors?

a. 10 to 20 percent

b. 20 to 40 percent

c. 40 to 60 percent

d. 60 to 80 percent

17-3. How important a determinant of personality is family environment, according to the results of these studies?

a. of very little importance

b. of about the same importance as heredity

c. more important than heredity

17-4. The twin studies have had a major impact on the way psychologists think about the causes of human behavior. Why are the results so important and so surprising?

17-5. Is the family environment an unimportant factor? Obviously, opinions still differ on this issue. For one thing, the family environment may not be as homogeneous as has been assumed. That is, children in the same family (may not be/are always) treated the same way. Research on this issue continues.

Answers: 17-1. identical, apart, fraternal, together. This is the most important comparison because, even though the fraternal twins shared the same environment, their common environment did not make them nearly as similar as twins who did not have a common environment *but who shared the same heredity.* **17-2.** c **17-3.** a **17-4.** Theories of development and personality have tended to stress the importance of the environment, especially the family environment; the recent twin studies find heredity to be very important and family environment to be of little importance. Thus, the results are contrary to the expectations of most of us and of much of the theorizing in the field of personality. **17-5.** may not be.

18. Outline Buss' explanation for why the Big Five traits are important.

18-1. As group animals, we gain an advantage by being able to predict the behavior of other human beings. That is, the ability to recognize the "Big Five" characteristics in others has _____ value for our species.

18-2. The big five traits are: neuroticism, extraversion, openness to experience, agreeableness, and conscientiousness. In terms of survival value, it is useful to know who in a group will fulfill their commitments, the trait of _____ ; who will fall apart under stress, the trait of _____ ; who will be a good problem solver, the trait of _____ , and so on.

18-3. The fact that these traits appear as dimensions across a variety of cultures attests to their importance. For Buss, our ability to _____ these traits in others also has adaptive significance. MacDonald, also an evolutionary theorist, asserts that it is the traits themselves, not just the ability to _____ them, that had adaptive value in our evolutionary past.

Answers: 18-1. adaptive (survival, evolutionary) **18-2.** conscientiousness, neuroticism, openness to experience **18-3.** recognize, recognize.

19. Summarize the strengths and weaknesses of the biological approach to personality.

19-1. People frequently blame parents for children's personalities. I recently asked a friend of mine why she thought a mutual acquaintance was so obnoxious. She said, "Well, raised with such crazy parents, what would you expect?" I asked, "Is that an argument for environment or heredity?" That is one of the benefits of the twin studies: they put data in place of speculation. But what are some of the weaknesses of the biological approach? First, heritability ratios should be regarded only as _____ that will vary depending on sampling and other procedures. In addition, there is not really a truly comprehensive biological _____ of personality.

Answers: 19-1. estimates, theory.

CONTEMPORARY EMPIRICAL APPROACHES TO PERSONALITY

20. Explain the chief concepts and hypotheses of terror management theory.

20-1. Human beings are keenly aware that _____ is inevitable, an awareness at odds with our drive for self-preservation. According to terror-management theory, people deal with this fear through the worldviews or traditions created by their _____ .

20-2. If we have a sense of worth, as defined by the standards of a culture, then we are able to manage our _____ relating to death. In other words, our cultures provide us an anxiety buffer in the form of self-_____ .

20-3. In summary, fear of death increases our valuation of culture and increases our desire for self-esteem, which serves as an _____ buffer.

Answers: 20-1. death, cultures **20-2.** terror (fear), esteem **20-3.** anxiety.

21. Describe how elevated mortality salience influences people's behavior.

21-1. According to terror management theory, situations that make our mortality *salient* cause us to attempt to bolster our self-esteem and, therefore, defend cultural values. Thus, terror management theory leads to several predictions. Which of the following appear to be true when situations cause us to ponder our mortality?

_____ We are more negative toward critics of our country.

_____ We show more respect for symbols of the country, such as the flag.

_____ We have more negative evaluations of people from different ethnic groups.

_____ We are more materialistic.

_____ We develop a stronger preference for charismatic leaders with a grand vision.

_____ We are more patriotic, less tolerant of those who question government policies.

_____ We tend to prefer mountain climbing to skydiving and scuba diving.

Answers: 21-1. All are true except the last one (which I just tossed in so that there would be at least one false).

22. Summarize research on culture and personality and on cultural variations in conceptions of self.

22-1. With the current increased attention to cultural factors, interest in the relationship between personality and culture has again surfaced, and the new data have revealed both cross-cultural similarities and differences. With regard to similarity, precisely the same "_____" personality factors tend to emerge in different cultures.

22-2. With regard to differences, research by Markus and Kitayama clearly indicates that the individualistic orientation characteristic of the West is not universal across cultures. While Americans tend to value (<u>independence/connectedness</u>), Asians value (<u>interdependence/uniqueness</u>) among people.

22-3. Similarly, while American parents encourage their children to (<u>stand out/blend in</u>), Asian parents emphasize taking pride in the accomplishments of (<u>each individual/the group</u>). Thus, Western cultures seem to be characterized by individualism and Asian cultures by _____.

Answers: 22-1. Big Five **22-2.** independence, interdependence **22-3.** stand out, the group, collectivism.

REFLECTING ON THE CHAPTER'S THEMES

23. Explain how the chapter highlighted three of the text's unifying themes.

23-1. We've just discussed one of the three themes emphasized in this chapter, that our behavior is influenced by our cultural heritage. Two other themes prominently demonstrated in the area of personality are that the field is theoretically _____ and that psychology evolves in a _____ context.

23-2. Freudian, behavioral, and biological perspectives of personality assume that behavior is determined; the _____ perspective does not. The biological perspective stresses genetic inheritance; the behavioral perspective stresses (<u>heredity/environment</u>). As these examples illustrate, the study of personality has produced an enormous amount of theoretical _____.

23-3. Concerning sociohistorical context, it is clear that theories of personality have strongly affected our culture. For example, the surrealist art movement, begun in the 1920s, derives directly from _____ psychology, as do other movements in literature and the arts. And the current debate on the effects of media violence is, to a large extent, a product of research in social _____ theory.

23-4. In turn, culture has affected psychology. For example, it seems quite likely that the sexually repressive climate of Victorian Vienna caused Freud to emphasize the _____ aspects of human behavior; and it is clear, from Freud's own description, that World War I influenced his development of the second Freudian instinct, the _____ instinct. Thus, psychology evolves in a _____ context.

Answers: **23-1.** diverse, sociohistorical **23-2.** humanistic, environment, diversity **23-3.** psychoanalytic (Freudian), learning **23-4.** sexual, aggression, sociohistorical.

PERSONAL APPLICATION • UNDERSTANDING PERSONALITY ASSESSMENT

24. Describe the MMPI, 16PF, and NEO Personality Inventory, and summarize the strengths and weaknesses of self-report inventories.

24-1. The MMPI, 16PF, and NEO Personality Inventories are (projective/self-report) tests. All three tests are also used to measure (single/multiple) traits.

24-2. Identify which tests (MMPI, 16PF, or NEO) are described by each of the following.

(a) _____ Measures the "Big Five" personality traits.

(b) _____ Originally designed to diagnose psychological disorders.

(c) _____ Contains 187 items assessing 16 personality traits.

24-3. The major strength of self-report inventories, in comparison with simply asking a person what they are like, is that they provide a more precise and more (objective/personal) measure of personality.

24-4. The major weakness of self-report inventories is that they are subject to several sources of error, including the possibility that test-takers: (1) may intentionally fake responses, that is, engage in deliberate _____; may answer questions in ways to make themselves "look good," the _____ _____ bias; may tend either to agree or to disagree with nearly every statement on a test, a source of error involving _____ sets.

Answers: **24-1.** self-report, multiple **24-2.** NEO, MMPI, 16PF, NEO **24-3.** objective **24-4.** deception (lying, faking), social desirability, response.

25. Describe the projective hypothesis and summarize the strengths and weaknesses of projective tests.

25-1. If you have ever looked at clouds and thought that the images you saw reflected something about your personality, then you accepted the *projective hypothesis*. The projective hypothesis is the idea that people will tend to _____ their characteristics onto ambiguous stimuli, which reveals something about their personalities and problems.

25-2. Two major projective tests are the Rorschach, a series of _____, and the TAT, a series of simple _____.

25-3. The advantages claimed for projective tests are that (1) since interpretations are not at all obvious, it is difficult for people to engage in intentional _____; and (2) projective tests may help tap problems or aspects of personality of which people are _____.

25-4. In fact, some evidence suggests that faking (especially faking bad) is possible with projective tests. In addition, the major weakness of projective tests concerns inadequate evidence that they are either _____ (consistent) or _____ (measure what they are intended to measure).

Answers: **25-1.** project **25-2.** inkblots, pictures (scenes) **25-3.** deception, unconscious (unaware) **25-4.** reliable, valid.

CRITICAL THINKING APPLICATION • HINDSIGHT IN EVERYDAY ANALYSES OF PERSONALITY

26. Discuss how hindsight bias affects everyday analyses of personality, as well as some theoretical analyses of personality.

26-1. I am writing this sentence several years after a very substantial decline in the stock market. Somewhat surprising, to me at least, is the fact that my colleagues say they saw "the bubble" coming. If everyone saw it coming, why didn't everyone sell before it occurred? Because we didn't see it coming. Rather, once exposed to information, we are inclined to believe that we knew it all along, the cognitive tendency known as the _____.

26-2. Suppose you meet someone who is achievement motivated and fiercely independent. You learn that this person was brought up by adoptive parents who were somewhat distant and undemonstrative. Would you think that the parent's child-rearing style accounted for their child's independence? Or, suppose that the person brought up by these parents is depressed and chronically unemployed. Would you connect the parenting and personality in this case, too? You might, because people tend to interpret _____ events in terms of _____ , which is a definition of the hindsight bias.

26-3. What is the hindsight bias? Write a definition in the space below.

26-4. In what way might psychoanalytic interpretations involve the hindsight bias?

26-5. How might evolutionary theory's account of the emergence of the Big Five traits reflect the hindsight bias?

Review of Key Terms

Archetypes
Behaviorism
Collective unconscious
Collectivism
Compensation
Conscious
Defense mechanisms
Displacement
Ego
Extraverts
Factor analysis
Fixation
Hierarchy of needs
Hindsight bias
Humanism
Id

Identification
Incongruence
Individualism
Introverts
Model
Need for self-actualization
Observational learning
Oedipal complex
Personal unconscious
Personality
Personality trait
Phenomenological approach
Pleasure principle
Preconscious
Projection
Projective tests

Psychodynamic theories
Psychosexual stages
Rationalization
Reaction formation
Reality principle
Reciprocal determinism
Regression
Repression
Self-actualizing persons
Self-concept
Self-efficacy
Self-enhancement
Self-report inventories
Striving for superiority
Superego
Unconscious

1. An individual's unique constellation of consistent behavioral traits.

2. A characteristic that represents a durable disposition to behave in a particular way in a variety of situations.

3. A systematic arrangement of needs, according to priority, in which basic, physiological needs must be met before social or growth needs are aroused.

4. All the diverse theories, descended from the work of Sigmund Freud, that focus on unconscious mental forces.

5. The primitive, instinctive component of personality that operates according to the pleasure principle.

6. The id's demands for immediate gratification of its urges.

7. The decision-making component of personality that operates according to the reality principle.

8. The ego's delay of gratification of the id's urges until appropriate outlets and situations can be found.

9. The moral component of personality that incorporates social standards about what represents right and wrong.

10. Consists of whatever you are aware of at a particular point in time.

11. Contains material just beneath the surface of awareness that can be easily retrieved.

12. Contains thoughts, memories, and desires that are well below the surface of conscious awareness.

_____ **13.** The series of largely unconscious Freudian reactions that protect a person from unpleasant emotions such as anxiety or guilt.

_____ **14.** The defense mechanism that pushes distressing thoughts and feelings into the unconscious or keeps them from emerging into consciousness.

_____ **15.** Attributing your own thoughts, feelings, or motives to another.

_____ **16.** Creating false but plausible excuses to justify unacceptable behavior.

_____ **17.** Diverting emotional feelings (usually anger) from their original source to a substitute target.

_____ **18.** Behaving in a way that is exactly the opposite of one's true (but unconscious) feelings.

_____ **19.** Reverting to immature patterns of behavior.

_____ **20.** Bolstering self-esteem by forming an imaginary or real alliance with some person or group.

_____ **21.** Developmental periods with a characteristic sexual focus that leave their mark on adult personality.

_____ **22.** A failure to move forward from one stage to another as expected.

_____ **23.** Characterized by erotically tinged desires for one's opposite-sex parent and hostility toward one's same-sex parent.

_____ **24.** Jungian concept referring to the structure holding material that is not in one's awareness because it has been repressed or forgotten.

_____ **25.** A storehouse of latent memory traces inherited from our ancestral past.

_____ **26.** Emotionally charged images and thought forms that have universal meaning.

_____ **27.** People who tend to be preoccupied with the internal world of their own thoughts, feelings, and experiences.

_____ **28.** People who tend to be interested in the external world of people and things.

_____ **29.** An Adlerian concept referring to a universal drive to adapt, to improve oneself, and to master life's challenges.

_____ **30.** Efforts to overcome imagined or real inferiorities by developing one's abilities.

_____ **31.** Personality tests that ask people a series of questions about their characteristic behavior.

_____ **32.** A statistical procedure that identifies clusters of variables that are highly correlated with one another.

_____ **33.** A theoretical orientation based on the premise that scientific psychology should study only observable behavior.

_____ **34.** The assumption that internal mental events, external environmental events, and overt behavior all influence one another.

_____ **35.** Learning that occurs when an organism's responding is influenced by the observation of others.

_____ **36.** A person whose behavior is observed by another.

_____ **37.** Our belief about our ability to perform behaviors that should lead to expected outcomes.

_____ **38.** A theoretical orientation that emphasizes the unique qualities of humans, especially their freedom and potential for personal growth.

_____ **39.** Approach that assumes we have to appreciate individuals' personal, subjective experiences to truly understand their behavior.

_____ 40. A collection of beliefs about one's own nature, unique qualities, and typical behavior.

_____ 41. A Rogerian concept referring to the degree of disparity between one's self-concept and one's actual experience.

_____ 42. The need to fulfill one's potential.

_____ 43. People with exceptionally healthy personalities, marked by continued personal growth.

_____ 44. The biased interpretation of past events in terms of present information.

_____ 45. Putting personal goals first and defining one's identity in terms of personal rather than group attributes.

_____ 46. Putting group goals ahead of personal ones and defining one's identity in terms of the group.

_____ 47. A person's overall assessment of her or his personal adequacy or worth.

_____ 48. The tendency to focus on positive feedback, exaggerate one's strengths, and see oneself as above average.

Answers: 1. personality **2.** personality trait **3.** hierarchy of needs **4.** psychodynamic theories **5.** id **6.** pleasure principle **7.** ego **8.** reality principle **9.** superego **10.** conscious **11.** preconscious **12.** unconscious **13.** defense mechanisms **14.** repression **15.** projection **16.** rationalization **17.** displacement **18.** reaction formation **19.** regression **20.** identification **21.** psychosexual stages **22.** fixation **23.** Oedipal complex **24.** personal unconscious **25.** collective unconscious **26.** archetypes **27.** introverts **28.** extraverts **29.** striving for superiority **30.** compensation **31.** self-report inventories **32.** factor analysis **33.** behaviorism **34.** reciprocal determinism **35.** observational learning **36.** model **37.** self-efficacy **38.** humanism **39.** phenomenological approach **40.** self-concept **41.** incongruence **42.** need for self-actualization **43.** self-actualizing persons **44.** hindsight bias **45.** individualism **46.** collectivism **47.** self-esteem **48.** self-enhancement.

Review of Key People

Alfred Adler	Carl Jung	Walter Mischel
Albert Bandura	Abraham Maslow	Carl Rogers
Hans Eysenck	Robert McCrae & Paul Costa	B. F. Skinner
Sigmund Freud		

_____ 1. The founder of psychoanalysis.

_____ 2. Developed the theory called analytical psychology; anticipated the humanists' emphasis on personal growth and self-actualization.

_____ 3. Founder of an approach to personality called individual psychology.

_____ 4. Modern behaviorism's most prominent theorist, recognized for his theories of operant conditioning.

_____ 5. A contemporary behavioral theorist who elaborated the concept of observational learning.

_____ 6. His chief contribution to personality theory has been to focus attention on the extent to which situational factors govern behavior.

_____ 7. One of the fathers of the human potential movement, he called his approach a person-centered theory.

_____ 8. The humanist who developed a theory of self-actualization.

_____ 9. Proposed that conditionability and introversion-extraversion are largely genetically determined.

10. Developed the NEO Personality Inventory to measure the Big Five traits.

Answers: 1. Freud **2.** Jung **3.** Adler **4.** Skinner **5.** Bandura **6.** Mischel **7.** Rogers **8.** Maslow **9.** Eysenck **10.** McCrae & Costa.

Self-Quiz

1. Personality traits are characterized by:
   a. consistency and distinctiveness
   b. charm and wit
   c. change as a function of the situation
   d. lack of individual differences

2. Someone attributes his thoughts or feelings or conflicts to someone else. For example, although he chronically interrupts people, he thinks that other people interrupt him. What Freudian defense mechanism is illustrated?
   a. rationalization
   b. reaction formation
   c. regression
   d. projection

3. Which of the following is entirely unconscious, according to Freud?
   a. the id
   b. the ego
   c. the superego
   d. the archetype

4. Although Osmo, at an unconscious level, has great hatred for Cosmo, he believes that he likes Cosmo and, to the outside world, gives all the appearance of liking him. Which defense mechanism is Osmo using?
   a. regression
   b. reaction formation
   c. projection
   d. rationalization

5. The Oedipal complex occurs during the:
   a. oral stage
   b. anal stage
   c. phallic stage
   d. genital stage

6. Which of the following concepts did Carl Jung originate?
   a. id
   b. superego
   c. inferiority complex
   d. introversion-extraversion

7. Which of the following did Adler emphasize in his theory of personality?
   a. striving for superiority
   b. castration anxiety
   c. introversion-extraversion
   d. the collective unconscious

8. Much of the behavior that we call personality results from reinforcement and observational learning, according to:
    a. Jung
    b. Skinner
    c. Bandura
    d. Adler

9. Which of the following tends to emphasize freedom and personal growth in its view of human behavior?
    a. the psychoanalytic approach
    b. the biological approach
    c. the behavioral approach
    d. the humanistic approach

10. According to Rogers, what causes incongruence?
    a. an inherited sense of irony
    b. conditional acceptance or affection
    c. unconditional acceptance or affection
    d. unconditioned stimuli

11. Herb had the desire and potential to be a violinist but became, instead, a trader in hog futures. He decided never to touch the violin again. What is going on with Herb, according to Maslow?
    a. He suffers from incontinence.
    b. He suffers from castration anxiety.
    c. He has not achieved self-actualization.
    d. He has an inferiority complex.

12. Which of the following views personality in terms of the adaptive significance of the Big Five traits?
    a. Abraham Maslow
    b. William James
    c. the behavioral approach
    d. the evolutionary approach

13. Your friend spends money like water. When you learn that he is from a poverty-stricken background, you attribute his spending patterns to his earlier deprivation. According to the critical thinking analysis, you are likely to do this because of:
    a. the hindsight bias
    b. a self-serving attribution
    c. the consistency and distinctiveness of personality
    d. circular reasoning

14. According to Mischel, which of the following is a major factor that predicts human behavior?
    a. childhood experience
    b. specifics of the situation
    c. extraversion and introversion
    d. central and peripheral traits

15. You are asked to tell stories about a series of pictures. Which test is being administered to you?
    a. Rorschach
    b. MMPI
    c. TAT
    d. 16PF

Answers: 1. a **2.** d **3.** a **4.** b **5.** c **6.** d **7.** a **8.** c **9.** d **10.** b **11.** c **12.** d **13.** a **14.** b **15.** c.

InfoTrac Keywords

Big Five Traits
Carl Rogers
Collectivism
Extraversion

Hindsight Bias
Introversion
Oedipus Complex
Personality Trait

Projective Tests
Psychoanalysis
Jungian

Chapter Thirteen
STRESS, COPING, AND HEALTH

Review of Key Ideas

THE NATURE OF STRESS

1. Discuss the impact of minor stressors.

    1-1. While some forms of stress arise from unusual, traumatic crises, most stress arises from (<u>infrequent/</u><u>everyday</u>) problems. These minor hassles appear to be detrimental to mental health because of the _____ nature of stress.

    Answers: **1-1.** everyday, cumulative.

2. Describe the nature or our appraisals of stress.

    2-1. The text defines stress as any circumstances that threaten or are perceived to threaten one's well being, and thereby they tax one's coping abilities. This definition would indicate that the sources of stress are quite (<u>subjective/objective</u>). Or to put it another way, stress lies in the mind of the _____.

    Answers: **2-1.** subjective, beholder or individual.

MAJOR TYPES OF STRESS

3. Distinguish between acute and chronic stress and describe frustration as a form of stress.

    3.1 Acute stressors (<u>do/do not</u>) have a relatively short duration and a clear endpoint, while chronic stressors (<u>do/not</u>).

    3.2. Which of the following three situations best illustrates what is meant by frustration?

    (a) Your family moves from a large city to a rather small, rural community.

(b) You are late for an appointment and stuck in a traffic jam.

(c) You are forced to choose between two good movies on television.

3-3. If you picked choice (b) then you have caught on that frustration always involves the _____ of the pursuit of some goal.

Answers: 3-1. do, do not b **3-2.** b **3-3.** thwarting or blocking.

4. **Identify the three basic types of conflict and discuss which types are most troublesome.**

4-1. Many persons do not want to pay their income taxes, but, on the other hand, they don't want to go to jail either. These persons are faced with an _____-_____ conflict.

4-2. Getting married has both positive and negative aspects that make it an excellent example of an _____-_____ conflict.

4-3. Consider the problem of the student who has to choose between scholarships for two different universities. Since he cannot accept both, he's faced with an _____-_____ conflict.

4-4. Now that you have correctly identified the three basic types of conflict, list them below in their order of troublesomeness, beginning with the least troublesome.

(a) _____

(b) _____

(c) _____

Answers: 4-1. avoidance-avoidance **4-2.** approach-avoidance **4-3.** approach-approach **4-4.** (a) approach-approach (b) approach-avoidance (c) avoidance-avoidance.

5. **Summarize evidence on life change and pressure as forms of stress.**

5-1. The Social Readjustment Rating Scale (SRRS) measures the stress induced by _____ in daily living routines. The developers of this scale theorized that all kinds of life changes, both pleasant and unpleasant, would induce stress. Early research showed that high scores on the SRRS were correlated with psychological disturbances and many kinds of physical _____.

5-2. Later research began to indicate that high scores on the SRRS were primarily the result of (pleasant/ unpleasant) events. At the present time, research seems to indicate that change by itself (is/is not) inevitably stressful.

5-3. There are two kinds of pressure. One is the pressure to get things accomplished, or the pressure to _____. The other is the pressure to abide by rules, or the pressure to _____.

5-4. Which appears to have the strongest influence on mental health, life changes or pressure?

Answers: 5-1. changes, illness **5-2.** unpleasant, is not **5-3.** perform, conform **5-4.** pressure.

6. Identify some common emotional responses to stress, and discuss the effects of emotional arousal.

6-1. The text describes three different dimensions of negative emotions that are particularly likely to be triggered by stress. Identify which of these dimensions is most likely to be present in the following situations.

(a) The emotions in this dimension are likely to be found as a person begins to feel more and more helpless and unable to cope (e.g., you detect signs that your lover is going to leave you).

(b) The emotions in this dimension are likely to be found as a person begins to feel increasingly put upon and treated unfairly (e.g., you are being falsely accused of a deed you didn't commit).

(c) The emotions in this dimension are likely to be found as a person faces increasing degrees of conflict or uncertainty (e.g., you're driving on a highway, and the fog is gradually becoming thicker).

6-2. What did the five year study of caregivers of AIDS patients find?

6-3. What does the inverted U hypothesis say about what happens to the optimal arousal level as tasks become more complex?

Answers: 6-1. (a) dejection, sadness, and grief (b) annoyance, anger, and rage (c) apprehension, anxiety, and fear **6-2.** The caregivers experienced many positive emotions (as well as negative ones). **6-3.** The optimal arousal level decreases.

7. Describe the fight-or-flight response and the three stages of the General Adaptation Syndrome.

7-1. What division of the autonomic nervous system mediates the fight-or-flight response?

7-2. Although the body's fight-or-flight response appears to be an evolutionary carry-over from our past, why is it perhaps of more harm than help to modern human beings?

7-3. Indicate which of the three stages of the General Adaptation Syndrome is being described in each of the following.

(a) This is the initial stage in which the body prepares for the fight-or-flight response.

(b) This is the second stage in which the body stabilizes its physiological changes as it begins to effectively cope with the stress.

(c) This is the third stage in which the body's coping resources are becoming depleted, and the resistance to many diseases declines.

Answers: **7-1.** sympathetic nervous system **7-2.** Because most stressful situations generally require a more complex response than simple fight or flight. **7-3.** (a) stage of alarm (b) stage of resistance (c) stage of exhaustion.

8. Discuss the two major pathways along which the brain sends signals to the endocrine system in response to stress.

8-1. Fill in the missing parts in the diagram below, detailing the two major pathways along which the brain sends signals to the endocrine system.

CEREBRAL CORTEX

(a) _____

SYMPATHETIC NS	PITUITARY GLAND
	ACTH
(b) _____ (GLAND)	(c) _____ (GLAND)
CATECHOLAMINES	CORTICOSTEROIDS
Increases heart rate & respiration, etc.	Increases energy, inhibits tissue inflammation, etc.

Answers: **8-1.** (a) hypothalamus (b) adrenal medulla (c) adrenal cortex.

9. Describe some relatively unhealthy coping responses that are common.

9-1. Answer the following questions regarding giving up and blaming oneself as responses to stress.

(a) What syndrome often results from giving-up in response to exposure to unavoidable stressful events?

(b) What phenomenon often accompanies blaming oneself in response to stress?

9-2. Answer the following questions regarding aggression and self-indulgence as responses to stress.

(a) Which of these responses is illustrated by the saying: "When the going gets tough, the tough go shopping?" _____

(b) Which of these responses is frequently, but not always, triggered by frustration? _____

(c) Which of these responses is linked to internet addiction? _____

9-3. What is a common fault with both of these behavioral responses to stress?

Answers: **9-1.** (a) learned helplessness (b) catastrophic thinking **9-2.** (a) self-indulgence (b) aggression (c) self-indulgence **9-3.** They divert effort away from solutions to problems.

10. Explain how defense mechanisms work, and discuss the value of defensive coping.

10-1. Indicate whether each of the following statements regarding defensive coping is true or false.

_____ (a) Although they are largely unconscious, defense mechanisms can operate at any level of consciousness.

_____ (b) Only neurotic persons use defensive mechanisms.

_____ (c) Defense mechanisms are used to shield against emotional discomfort that often occurs with stress, particularly anxiety.

10-2. One shortcoming of defensive coping is that it avoids the real problem. What other consequence might arise here?

10-3. What conclusion does the text draw regarding small versus extreme positive illusions?

Answers: **10-1.** (a) true (b) false (c) true **10-2.** health-related risks (poor health) **10-3.** Small positive illusions may be beneficial while extreme illusions may be harmful.

THE EFFECTS OF STRESS ON PSYCHOLOGICAL FUNCTIONING

11. Discuss the effects of stress on task performance and the burnout syndrome.

11-1. Baumeister's theory as to why stress affects task performance is that pressure to perform makes us self-conscious, and this elevated self-consciousness disrupts our _____. The term we commonly use for this is _____ under pressure. Research shows that this phenomenon is quite (<u>rare/common</u>) among normal persons.

11-2. Indicate whether each of the following statements regarding the burnout syndrome is true or false.

_____ (a) Burnout is related to only a few highly stressful occupations.

_____ (b) The onset of burnout is usually sudden.

Answers: 11-1. attention, choking, common **11-2.** (a) false (b) false.

12. List some psychological problems and disorders that may be stress related.

12-1. In addition to drug and alcohol abuse, what three other problems appear to be related to stress? (One of them has to do with school, one has to do with sleep, and one involves intimate relationships.)

12-2. Stress has also been implicated in the onset of serious psychological disorders. In addition to schizophrenia, what two other disorders are mentioned?

Answers: 12-1. poor academic performance, insomnia (and other sleep disorders), sexual difficulties **12-2.** depression and anxiety disorders.

THE EFFECTS OF STRESS ON PHYSICAL HEALTH

13. Describe the evidence linking personality factors to coronary heart disease.

13-1. What is the principal cause of coronary heart disorder?

13-2. Tell whether the following characteristics are found in Type A or Type B persons.

_____ (a) easygoing   _____ (d) amicable

_____ (b) competitive   _____ (e) hostile

_____ (c) impatient

13-3. Which aspect of the Type A behavior seems to be most highly related to coronary heart disorder?

Answers: 13-1. atheroclerosis **13-2.** (a) Type B (b) Type A (c) Type A (d) Type B (e) Type A **13-3.** hostility (anger).

14. Summarize the evidence linking emotional reactions and depression to heart disease.

14-1. Research has shown that negative emotions (can/cannot) trigger acute symptoms of heart disease. Once again, the most frequent emotional response that triggered participants' heart attacks was found to episodes of _____.

14-2. Which of the following statements appears to best reflect the causal relationship between depression and heart disease?

(a) Heart disease can lead to depression.

(b) Depression can lead to heart disease.

Answers: **14-1.** can, anger **14-2.** **(b)** Depression can lead to heart disease.

15. Discuss how stress affects immune functioning.

15-1. Research has found stress to be related to numerous diseases and disorders. What appears to be a common factor that relates stress to so many disorders?

15-2. A key factor in determining the impact of stress on immune function is the (<u>intensity/duration</u>) of the stressful event.

Answers: **15-1.** Stress appears to suppress the immune system temporarily. **15-2.** duration.

FACTORS MODERATING THE IMPACT OF STRESS

16. Discuss how social support moderates the impact of stress.

16-1. What two areas of our health appear to benefit from having strong social support groups?

16-2. What role does social support apparently play during times of high stress?

Answers: **16-1.** Both mental and physical health. **16-2.** It acts as a protective buffer.

17. Discuss how personality factors are related to stress resistance.

17-1. What difference was found between optimists and pessimists, with respect to good physical health?

17-2. What personality characteristic was found to be related to longevity in a recent study from a sample of Terman's gifted children?

Answers: **17-1.** Optimists were more likely to enjoy good physical health. **17-2.** conscientiousness.

18. **Explain the negative impact of smoking on health.**

    18-1.   Answer the following questions regarding the negative impact of smoking on physical health.

        (a) How much shorter is the life expectancy of an average smoker compared to a similar nonsmoker?

        (b) What are the two most frequent diseases that kill smokers?

        (c) What appears to happen with respect to readiness to give up as smokers cycle through periods of abstinence and relapse?

Answers: 18-1. (a) 13-14 years (b) lung cancer and heart disease (c) Readiness to quit smoking builds gradually.

19. **Discuss how poor nutrition and lack of exercise are related to health.**

    19-1.   Answer the following true-false questions related to nutrition and exercise.

    _____ (a) Vulnerability to cardiovascular diseases appear to be influenced by dietary factors.

    _____ (b) High consumption of salt invariably leads to hypertension.

    _____ (c) High fat diets have been linked to some forms of cancer.

    _____(d) Regular exercise will not increase longevity.

Answers: 19-1. (a) true (b) false (c) true (d) false.

20. **Discuss the relationship between behavioral styles and AIDS.**

    20-1.   What two bodily fluids are most likely to transmit AIDS?

    20-2.   What two general groups have the highest incidence of AIDS in the United States?

    20-3.   In the world as a whole, which form of transmission, gay and bisexual or heterosexual, is most common?

    20-4.   How can one virtually guarantee that he or she will not contact AIDS?

Answers: 20-1. blood and semen **20-2.** Gay & bisexual males and intravenous drug users. **20-3.** heterosexual transmission **20-4.** Stay with only one sexual partner (known to prefer this same lifestyle), and don't use intravenous drugs.

21. Explain how health-impairing lifestyles develop.

21-1. The text lists four complementary explanations as to why health-impairing lifestyles develop. Given the hints below, list these four reasons.

(a) slowly

(b) immediate

(c) delayed

(d) "not me"

Answers: 21-1. (a) They develop slowly. (b) The pleasure they provide is immediate. (c) The health-impairing consequences are delayed. (d) The consequences are likely to happen to others (but "not me").

REACTIONS TO ILLNESS

22. Discuss individual differences in willingness to seek medical treatment.

22-1. Indicate whether the following statements regarding individual differences in willingness to seek medical treatment are true or false.

_____ (a) Delay in seeking treatment is perhaps the biggest problem here.

_____ (b) The perception of pain and illness is very subjective.

Answers: 22-1. (a) true (b) true.

23. Describe some barriers to effective patient-provider communication and ways to overcome these problems.

23-1. Which of the following factors appears to be a barrier to effective patient-provider communication?

(a) economic realities   (d) patient evasiveness

(b) medical jargon   (e) patient passivity

(c) patient forgetfulness

23-2. What does the text recommend as the best way to improve patient-provider communication?

Answers: 23-1. all of these factors **23-2.** Don't be a passive consumer of medical advice.

24. **Discuss the extent to which people tend to adhere to medical advice.**

24-1. The text lists three reasons for failure to comply with medical advice. One is that patients often fail to completely _____ treatment instructions. A second is that the treatment may prove to be quite _____. The third reason is not directly related to either instructions or treatment, but rather to the attitude towards the _____. A negative attitude makes compliance (<u>more/less</u>) likely.

Answers: 24-1. understand, unpleasant (or aversive), physician or doctor, less.

REFLECTING ON THE CHAPTER'S THEMES

25. **Explain how this chapter highlighted two of the text's unifying themes.**

25-1. The fact that the amount of stress in any given situation primarily lies in the eyes of the beholder nicely illustrates the theme that experience is _____.

25-2. The fact that stress interacts with numerous other factors that affect health illustrates the theme of multifactorial _____.

Answers: 25-1. subjective **25-2.** causation.

APPLICATION: IMPROVING COPING AND STRESS MANAGEMENT

26. **Summarize Albert Ellis' ideas about controlling one's emotions.**

26-1. The main idea behind Albert Ellis' rational-emotive therapy is that stress is largely caused by _____ thinking. Therefore, by changing one's catastrophic thinking and taking a more rational approach, one can then reduce the amount of _____ being experienced.

26-2. Ellis illustrates this theory by postulating an A-B-C series of events. Describe below what is going on during each of these events.

(A) activating event:

(B) belief:

(C) consequence:

26-3. Since the emotional turmoil in the A-B-C sequence is caused by the B (Belief) sequence, effort must be directed towards changing irrational beliefs. Ellis proposed two techniques for doing this. One must first learn to _____ instances of irrational beliefs. Then one must learn to actively _____ these irrational beliefs.

Answers: 26-1. catastrophic, stress **26-2.** (A) the activating event that precedes the stress (B) one's belief about the event (C) the emotional consequences that result from the belief **26-3.** detect, dispute.

27. **Discuss the adaptive value of humor and releasing pent-up emotions.**

    27-1.   What dual role does humor appear to play in easing stress from difficult situations?

    27-2.   Why might writing or talking about a problem with a sympathetic friend prove useful when experiencing stress?

    27-3.   What two common benefits were found among people who learned to manage hostility and people who practiced forgiveness?

Answers: 27-1. It allows for both redefining the problem in a less threatening way and the releasing of tension. **27-2.** It may help to release pent-up tension. **27-3.** Both mental and physical health improved.

28. **Discuss the adaptive value of managing hostility and forgiving others.**

    28-1.   What is the goal of hostility management?

    28-2.   What does research suggest that forgiving is associated with?

Answers: 28-1. To reduce the frequency and intensity of one's hostile feelings. **28-2.** Better adjustment and well-being.

29. **Discuss the adaptive value of relaxation and exercise.**

    29-1.   Complete the following statements regarding the adaptive value of relaxation and exercise.

        (a) A quiet environment, a mental device, a passive attitude, and a comfortable position are conditions that facilitate:

        (b) Eating a balanced diet, getting adequate sleep and exercise, and staying away from overeating and harmful drugs can help to minimize:

Answers: 29-1. (a) learning to relax (b) physical vulnerability.

30. Describe some important considerations in evaluating health statistics and making health decisions.

30-1. Which kind of faulty statistical reasoning (correlation is no assurance of causation, statistical significance is not equivalent to practical significance, and failure to consider base rates) is illustrated by the following statements?

(a) Using cell phones may cause brain cancer.

(b) Since heart disease and depression are correlated, heart disease must cause depression.

(c) In a large sample population it was observed that the prevalence of hypertension was statistically significantly higher in higher sodium intake individuals. Therefore, everyone should reduce their sodium intake.

30-2. In addition to seeking information to reduce uncertainty, what other two basic principles of quantitative reasoning does the text suggest?

30-3. What should one do after reaching a decision and initiating action?

Answers: 30-1. (a) failure to consider base rates (and also forgetting that correlation is no assurance of causation) (b) correlation is no assurance of causation (c) statistical significance is not equivalent to practical significance **30-2.** Make risk-benefit assessments and list alternative courses of action **30-3.** Continue to reevaluate the decision (in light of treatment progress, new options, etc.).

Review of Key Terms

Acquired immune deficiency
 syndrome (AIDS)
Acute stressors
Aggression
Approach-approach conflict
Approach-avoidance conflict
Avoidance-avoidance conflict
Biopsychosocial model
Burnout
Catastrophic thinking
Catharsis

Chronic stressors
Conflict
Constructive coping
Coping
Defense mechanisms
Fight-or-flight response
Frustration
General adaptation syndrome
Health psychology
Immune response

Internet addiction
Learned helplessness
Life changes
Optimism
Pressure
Psychosomatic diseases
Rational-emotive therapy
Social support
Stress
Type A personality

_____ 1. Holds that physical illness is caused by a complex interaction of biological, psychological, and sociocultural factors.

_____ 2. Concerned with how psychosocial forces relate to the promotion and maintenance of health, and the causation, prevention and treatment of illness.

_____ 3. Any circumstances that threaten or are perceived to threaten our well-being and thereby tax our coping abilities.

_____ 4. A passive behavior produced by exposure to unavoidable aversive events.

_____ 5. Occurs in any situation in which the pursuit of some goal is thwarted.

_____ 6. Occurs when two or more incompatible motivations or behavioral impulses compete for expression.

_____ 7. Occurs when a choice must be made between two attractive goals.

_____ 8. Occurs when a choice must be made between two unattractive goals.

_____ 9. Occurs when a choice must be made whether to pursue a single goal that has both attractive and unattractive aspects.

_____ 10. Any noticeable alterations in one's living circumstances that require readjustment.

_____ 11. Expectations or demands that one should behave in a certain way.

_____ 12. A physiological reaction to threat in which the autonomic nervous system mobilizes an organism for either attacking or fleeing an enemy.

_____ 13. A model of the body's stress response consisting of three stages: alarm, resistance, and exhaustion.

_____ 14. An active effort to master, reduce, or tolerate the demands created by stress.

_____ 15. Involves any behavior that is intended to hurt someone, either physically or verbally.

_____ 16. Consists of spending an inordinate amount of time on the internet and the inability to control online use.

_____ 17. Largely unconscious reactions that protect a person from unpleasant emotions such as anxiety and guilt.

_____ 18. Relatively healthy efforts to deal with stressful events.

_____ 19. Involves physical, mental, and emotional exhaustion that is attributable to work-related stress.

_____ 20. Threatening events that have a relatively long duration and no readily apparent time limit.

_____ 21. A behavior pattern marked by competitive, aggressive, impatient, hostile behavior.

_____ 22. Threatening events that have a relatively short duration and a clear endpoint.

_____ 23. The body's defensive reaction to invasion by bacteria, viral agents, or other foreign substances.

_____ 24. Various types of aid and succor provided by members of one's social network.

_____ 25. A general tendency to expect good outcomes.

_____ 26. An approach to therapy that focuses on altering clients' patterns of irrational thinking to reduce maladaptive emotions and behavior.

_____ 27. The release of emotional tension.

_____ 28. Unrealistic and pessimistic appraisal of stress that exaggerates the magnitude of a problem.

29. Physical ailments caused, in part, by psychological factors, especially emotional distress.

30. A disorder in which the immune system is gradually weakened and eventually disabled by the human immunodeficiency virus (HIV).

Answers: 1. biopsychosocial model **2.** health psychology **3.** stress **4.** learned helplessness **5.** frustration **6.** conflict **7.** approach-approach conflict **8.** avoidance-avoidance conflict **9.** approach-avoidance conflict **10.** life changes **11.** pressure **12.** fight-or-flight response **13.** general adaptation syndrome **14.** coping **15.** aggression **16.** internet addiction **17.** defense mechanisms **18.** constructive coping **19.** burnout **20.** chronic stressors **21.** Type A personality **22.** acute stressors **23.** immune response **24.** social support **25.** optimism **26.** rational-emotive therapy **27.** catharsis **28.** catastrophic thinking **29.** psychosomatic diseases **30.** Acquired Immune Deficiency Syndrome (AIDS).

Review of Key People

Walter Cannon   Thomas Holmes & Richard Rahe   Neal Miller
Robin DiMatteo   Janice Kiecolt-Glaser   Hans Selye
Albert Ellis   Richard Lazarus   Shelley Taylor
Meyer Friedman & Ray Rosenman

1. Observed that minor hassles were more closely related to mental health than were major stressful events.

2. Noted for his extensive investigations of the three types of conflict.

3. These researchers developed the Social Readjustment Rating Scale.

4. One of the first theorists to describe the "fight-or-flight" response.

5. Coined the word "stress" and described the General Adaptation Syndrome.

6. These researchers found a connection between coronary risk and what they called Type A behavior.

7. Has conducted research on communication between health care providers and patients.

8. The developer of Rational-Emotive Therapy.

9. Showed that "positive illusions" may be adaptive for mental health and well-being.

10. Has conducted research linking streee to temporary suppression of the immune system.

Answers: 1. Lazarus **2.** Miller **3.** Holmes & Rahe **4.** Cannon **5.** Selye **6.** Friedman & Rosenman **7.** DiMatteo **8.** Ellis **9.** Taylor **10.** Kiecolt-Glaser.

Self-Quiz

1. Which of the following statements regarding stress is incorrect?
   a. Stress is a subjective experience.
   b. The effects of stress are cumulative.
   c. Minor hassles may prove more stressful than major ones.
   d. One should seek to avoid all stress.

2. You've been invited to dinner at a nice restaurant on the final night of a TV mini series you've been watching, and thus find yourself confronted with
   a. pressure
   b. frustration
   c. an approach-avoidance conflict
   d. an approach-approach conflict

3. The week of final exams subjects most students to what kind of stress?
   a. pressure
   b. change
   c. frustration
   d. conflict

4. High scores on the Social Readjustment Rating Scale were found to be correlated with psychological disturbances and
   a. type A behavior patterns
   b. physical illness
   c. pessimistic attitudes
   d. all of the above

5. According to optimal-arousal theories, which of the following situations would be least affected by a high optimal-arousal level?
   a. taking a psychology exam
   b. typing a term paper
   c. buttoning a shirt
   d. learning to drive a car

6. The General Adaptation Syndrome shows that the body
   a. gradually adapts to a particular stress
   b. gradually adapts to all form of stress
   c. may gradually weaken and die from continued stress
   d. can react rapidly to all forms of stress

7. Which of the following organs is involved in both of the body's two major stress pathways?
   a. the adrenal gland
   b. the sympathetic nervous system
   c. the pituitary gland
   d. the pineal gland

8. Aggression is frequently triggered by
   a. helplessness
   b. frustration
   c. loneliness
   d. change

9. Which of the following behavioral responses to stress may result in internet addiction?
   a. defensive coping
   b. self-indulgence
   c. positive illusions
   d. giving up

10. Which of the following situations is most likely to result in chronic stress?
   a. being diagnosed with AIDS
   b. preparing for final exams
   c. being late for an appointment and stuck in traffic
   d. being told that you need root canal work

11. Smoking is to lung cancer as Type A behavior is to
    a. coronary disease
    b. AIDS
    c. defensive coping
    d. mental disorders

12. One of the key links between stress and physical illness may be that the body's response to stress
    a. increases the optimal-arousal level
    b. suppresses the immune system
    c. decreases the optimal-arousal level
    d. suppresses the adrenal gland

13. Health-impairing life styles appear to develop
    a. rapidly
    b. unconsciously
    c. slowly
    d. as a defense against stress

14. A major idea behind Rational-Emotive Therapy is that stress is caused by
    a. conflict
    b. frustration
    c. pressure
    d. catastrophic thinking

15. Analyzing the possible gains and losses before undertaking a health-treatment program is an example of
    a. seeking information to reduce uncertainty
    b. listing alternative courses of action
    c. making a risk-benefit analysis
    d. analyzing base rates

Answers: 1. d **2.** d **3.** a **4.** b **5.** c **6.** c **7.** a **8.** b **9.** b **10.** a **11.** a **12.** b **13.** c **14.** d **15.** c.

InfoTrac Keywords

Constructive Coping   Internet Addiction   Type A Personality
Health Psychology

Chapter Fourteen
PSYCHOLOGICAL DISORDERS

Review of Key Ideas

ABNORMAL BEHAVIOR: MYTHS, REALITIES, AND CONTROVERSIES

1. **Describe the medical model of abnormal behavior.**

    1-1. A model is a metaphor or theory that is useful in describing some phenomenon. For example, the computer is frequently used as a model of thinking. The medical model uses physical illness as a model of psychological disorders. Under the medical model, maladaptive behavior is referred to as mental

    _____.

    1-2. The term "mental illness" is so familiar to all of us that we rarely think about the meaning of the concept and whether or not the analogy with disease is a good one. Among the model's critics, Thomas Szasz asserts that words such as *sickness*, *illness*, and *disease* are correctly used only in reference to the

    _____, and that it is more appropriate to view abnormal behavior as a deviation from accepted social _____ than as an illness.

    1-3. The text takes an intermediate position. The medical concepts of diagnosis, etiology, and prognosis have proven useful in treatment and study of psychological disorders, so while there are problems with the medical model, it may be of value as long as one understands that it is just a/an _____ and not a true explanation.

    Answers: 1-1. illness (disease, sickness) **1-2.** body, norms (behavior, standards) **1-3.** analogy (model).

2. **Explain the most commonly used criteria of abnormality.**

    2-1. What does abnormal mean? The three criteria most frequently used are *deviance*, *maladaptive behavior*, and *personal distress*.

    (a) _____: Does not *conform* to cultural norms or standards.

    (b) _____: Behavior that *interferes* with the individual's social or occupational functioning.

(c) _____: Intense *discomfort* produced by depression or anxiety.

2-2. Following are three statements that describe a person with a particular type of disorder. Which criterion of abnormal behavior is illustrated by each statement? Place the letters from the list above in the appropriate blanks.

_____ Ralph washes his hands several dozen times a day. His handwashing interferes with his work and prevents him from establishing normal friendships.

_____ Even if Ralph's handwashing compulsion did not interfere with his work and social life, his behavior still would be considered strange. That is, most people do not do what he does.

_____ It is also the case that Ralph's skin is very raw, and he becomes extremely anxious when he does not have immediate access to a sink.

2-3. While the three major categories of disorder are useful, assessments of abnormality are not entirely _____ -free. Cultural trends and political forces clearly influence these judgments. In addition, normality and abnormality are not either-or concepts but exist along a _____.

Answers: 2-1. (a) deviance (b) maladaptive behavior (c) personal distress **2-2.** b, a, c **2-3.** value (culture), continuum.

3. List three stereotypes of people with psychological disorders.

3-1. In the space below, list three stereotypes of people with psychological disorders:

(a) The disorders are _____.

(b) People with the disorders are _____ and dangerous.

(c) People with the disorders behave in a bizarre manner and are very _____ from normal people.

Answers: 3-1. (a) incurable (b) violent (c) different.

4. List the five diagnostic axes of DSM-IV.

4-1. Below are descriptions of the five axes of the DSM-IV classification system. Label each with the correct axis number (I through V).

_____ Notes concerning the severity of stress experienced by the individual in the past year

_____ Estimates of the individual's current level of adaptive functioning (social and occupational)

_____ Diagnosis of most types of mental disorders

_____ Diagnosis of long-running personality disorders or mental retardation

_____ Listing of physical disorders

Answers: 4-1. IV, V, I, II, III.

5. **Discuss estimates of the prevalence of psychological disorders.**

5-1.   Epidemiological studies assess the _____ of various disorders. Prevalence is the _____ of people who suffer from a disorder across a specific period of time. For our purposes, *lifetime* prevalence is most interesting.

5-2.   What percentage of people will exhibit a mental disorder at some point during their lifetime? If drug-related disorders are included, estimates range from one-third to, more recently, _____%. The estimates are complicated by several factors, but recent studies do suggest that there (has been/has not been) a genuine increase in lifetime prevalence.

5-3.   The most common disorders are *mood*, *anxiety*, and *substance use* disorders (including alcoholism). List these below in order of prevalence.

_____

_____

_____

Answers: 5-1. prevalence, percentage (proportion), the entire lifespan **5-2.** 44%, has been **5-3.** substance use, anxiety, mood.

ANXIETY DISORDERS

6. **List five types of anxiety disorders and describe the symptoms associated with each.**

6-1.   List the names of the four anxiety syndromes in the space below. As hints, the initial letters of some key words are listed at the left.

GAD: _____

PhD: _____

OCD: _____

PDA: _____ and _____

PTSD: _____

6-2.   Match the anxiety disorders with the symptoms that follow by placing the appropriate letters (from the previous question) in the blanks.

(a) _____   Sudden, unexpected, and paralyzing attacks of anxiety

(b) _____   Not tied to a specific object or event

(c) _____   Senseless, repetitive rituals

(d) _____   Brooding over decisions

(e) _____   Fear of specific objects or situations

(f) _____   Persistent intrusion of distressing and unwanted thoughts

(g) _____   Free-floating anxiety

(h) _____ Frequently includes fear of going out in public

(i) _____ Nightmare, flashbacks, and anxiety that may follow traumatic events

Answers: 6-1. generalized anxiety disorder, phobic disorder, obsessive-compulsive disorder, panic disorder and agoraphobia **6-2.** (a) PDA (in this example, panic attacks) (b) GAD (c) OCD (d) GAD (e) PhD (f) OCD (g) GAD (h) PDA (in this case, agoraphobia) (i) PTSD.

7. **Discuss the contribution of biological and cognitive factors, conditioning, and stress to the etiology of anxiety disorders.**

   7-1. Several types of studies suggest that there are inherited predispositions to anxiety disorders. For example, twin studies find higher concordance rates for anxiety among _____ twins than _____ twins.

   7-2. Other biological evidence implicates disturbances at the synapse. Therapeutic drugs taken for anxiety appear to affect the chemicals known as _____ (e.g., GABA, serotonin) that carry signals from one neuron to another.

   7-3. Conditioning, or learning clearly, plays a role as well. For example, if an individual is bitten by a dog, he or she may develop a fear of dogs through the process of _____ conditioning. The individual may then avoid dogs in the future, a response maintained by _____ conditioning.

   7-4. People are more likely to be afraid of snakes than of hot irons. Using Seligman's notion of preparedness, explain why.

   7-5. Critics note problems with the conditioning model. For example (answer true/false):

   ____ People with phobias frequently cannot recall the traumatic incident.

   ____ People who experience extreme traumas do not always develop phobias.

   7-6. As discussed in Chapter 6, the conditioning models are being extended to include a larger role for cognitive factors. For example, children probably acquire fears by _____ the behavior of anxious parents.

   7-7. Cognitive theorists indicate that certain *thinking styles* contribute to anxiety. For example, as indicated in your text, the sentence "The doctor examined little Emma's growth" could refer either to height or to a tumor. People who are high in anxiety will tend to perceive the (tumor/height) interpretation. People's readiness to perceive threat, in other words, appears to be related to their tendency to experience _____.

   7-8. Finally, *stress* is related to anxiety disorders. Studies described in your text indicate that stress is related both to _____ disorder and to the development of social _____.

Answers: 7-1. identical, fraternal **7-2.** neurotransmitters **7-3.** classical, operant **7-4.** Preparedness is Seligman's notion that human beings have evolved to be more prepared or more ready to be conditioned to some stimuli than to others. We have evolved to be more afraid of snakes than of hot irons, the latter having appeared only relatively recently in our evolutionary history. (As a whole, research has provided only modest support for the idea of preparedness in acquisition of phobias.) **7-5.** T, T **7-6.** observing (modeling) **7-7.** tumor, anxiety **7-8.** panic, phobia.

SOMATOFORM DISORDERS

8. Compare and contrast the three somatoform disorders and discuss their etiology.

8-1.   For each of the following symptoms, indicate which disorder is described by placing the appropriate letters in the blanks: S for somatization, C for conversion, and H for hypochondriasis.

_____ Serious disability that may include paralysis, loss of vision or hearing, loss of feeling, and so on.

_____ Many different minor physical ailments accompanied by a long history of medical treatment.

_____ Cannot believe the doctor's report that the person is not really ill.

_____ Symptoms that appear to be organic in origin but don't match underlying anatomical organization.

_____ Diverse complaints that implicate many different organ systems.

_____ Usually does not involve disability so much as overinterpreting slight, possible signs of illness.

_____ "Glove anesthesia;" seizures without loss of bladder control.

8-2.   In the film *Hannah and Her Sisters*, Woody Allen is convinced that certain minor physical changes are a sign of cancer. When tests eventually find no evidence of cancer, he is sure the tests have been done incorrectly. Which of the somatoform disorders does this seem to represent? _____

8-3.   The somatoform disorders are associated with certain personality types, with particular cognitive styles, and with learning. Among personality types, the _____ personality (self-centered, excitable, and overly dramatic) is implicated, as is the general trait of _____. Insecure attachment style relating to early experiences with care-givers may also be a factor.

8-4.   Another source of the somatoform disorders may involve _____ factors, the way people think about normal physiological processes. For example, some people may tend to (<u>catastrophize/ minimize</u>) minor bodily changes.

8-5.   In addition, the "sick role" may be positively reinforced through, for example _____ from others, or negatively reinforced by _____ certain of life's problems or unpleasant aspects.

Answers: 8-1. C, S, H, C, S, H, C **8-2.** hypochondriasis **8-3.** histrionic, neuroticism **8-4.** cognitive, catastrophize **8-5.** attention (kindness, etc.), avoiding (escaping).

DISSOCIATIVE DISORDERS

9. Describe three dissociative disorders.

9-1.   The three dissociative disorders involve memory and identity. Two of the disorders involve fairly massive amounts of forgetting, dissociative _____ and dissociative _____.

9-2. People who have been in serious accidents frequently can't remember the accident or events surrounding the accident. This type of memory loss, which involves specific traumatic events, is known as dissociative _____.

9-3. An even greater memory loss, in which people lose their memories for their entire lives along with their sense of identity, is termed dissociative _____.

9-4. You may have seen media characterizations of individuals who can't remember who they are—what their names are, where they live, who their family is, and so on. While popularly referred to as amnesia, this type of dissociative disorder is more correctly called dissociative _____.

9-5. A few years ago, there was a spate of appearances on talk shows by guests who claimed to have more than one identity or personality. This disorder is still widely known as _____-_____ disorder (MPD), but the formal name in the DSM-IV is _____ _____ disorder (DID). The disorder is also often (<u>correctly/mistakenly</u>) called schizophrenia.

Answers: **9-1.** amnesia, fugue **9-2.** amnesia **9-3.** fugue **9-4.** fugue **9-5.** multiple-personality, dissociative identity, mistakenly.

10. Discuss the etiology of dissociative identity disorder.

10-1. The diagnosis of dissociative identity disorder (DID) is controversial. Although many clinicians believe that the disorder is authentic, Spanos argues that it is the product of media attention and the misguided probings of a small minority of psychotherapists. In other words, Spanos believes that DID (or MPD) (<u>is/is not</u>) a genuine disorder.

10-2. While the majority of people with DID report having been emotionally and sexually _____ in childhood, the abuse has not been independently verified, and child abuse is related to a variety of disorders. Little else is known about the possible causes of this controversial diagnosis.

10-3. In a recent survey of American psychiatrists, a majority (i.e., three-fourths) of those polled indicated that there (<u>is/is not</u>) enough scientific evidence to warrant including DID as a valid diagnostic category.

Answers: **10-1.** is not **10-2.** abused **10-3.** is not.

MOOD DISORDERS

11. Describe the two major mood disorders.

11-1. The two major mood disorders are major _____ disorder (or unipolar disorer) and _____ disorder.

11-2. While the terms *manic* and *depressive* describe mood, they refer to a number of other characteristics as well, listed below. With one or two words for each characteristic describe the manic and depressive episodes. (Before you make the lists, it may be a good idea to review Table 14.1 and the sections on depressive and bipolar mood disorders.)

	Manic	*Depressive*
mood:	_____	_____
sleep:	_____	_____
activity:	_____	_____
sex drive:	_____	_____

Answers: **11-1.** depressive, bipolar **11-2.** mood: euphoric (elated, extremely happy, up, etc.) vs. depressed (blue, extremely sad, down); sleep: goes without or doesn't want to vs. can't (insomnia); activity: very active vs. sluggish, slow, inactive; sex drive: increased vs. decreased.

12. Explain how genetic, neurochemical, and neuroanatomical factors may be related to the development of mood disorders.

12-1. Twin studies implicate genetic factors in the development of mood disorders. In a sentence, summarize the results of these studies.

12-2. While the exact mechanism is not known, correlations have been found between mood disorders and abnormal levels of _____ in the brain, including norepinephrine and serotonin.

12-3. There may be an neuroanatomical basis for depression: the _____, known to be involved in memory consolidation, tends to be about 8%-10% smaller in depressed subjects.

12-4. Recent studies have found that the brain, and especially the hippocampus, tends to generate new neurons in adulthood, a process termed _____. The relevant new theory is that major life stress causes a suppression of this growth, and that suppression of neurogenesis is the central cause of _____.

12-5. According to this new theory, drugs that elevate serotonin relieve depression because serotonin promotes _____, the generation of new neurons. Research on this model continues.

Answers: **12-1.** For mood disorders, the concordance rate for identical twins is much higher than that for fraternal twins (about 67% for the former compared to 15% for the latter). **12-2.** neurotransmitters (neurochemicals) **12-3.** hippocampus **12-4.** neurogenesis, depression **12-5.** neurogenesis.

13. Explain how cognitive factors, interpersonal factors, and stress may be related to the development of mood disorders.

13-1. Martin Seligman's model of depression is referred to as the learned _____ model. While he originally based his theory of depression on an animal conditioning model involving exposure to unavoidable aversive stimuli, he has more recently emphasized (cognitive/behavioral) factors.

13-2. According to the revised version of learned helplessness, people with a _____ explanatory style are particularly prone to depression. For example, people who attribute obstacles to (situational factors/personal flaws) are more likely to experience depression.

13-3. In line with the cognitive explanation of depression, Susan Nolen-Hoeksema has found that people who repetitively focus or _____ about their depression are more likely to remain depressed.

13-4. Other researchers have also found that negative thinking to be a factor in depression. The featured study, for example, found that non-depressed first-year college students who score high on tests of _____ thinking have higher incidences of depressive episodes later, during a 2.5 year follow-up. An interesting aspect of the study is that it is _____ rather than retrospective.

13-5. With regard to interpersonal factors, depressed people tend to lack _____ skills. Lack of social skills diminishes people's capacities to obtain important _____, including good friends and desirable jobs.

13-6. Why do we tend to reject depressed people?

13-7. There is (very little/a moderately strong) link between stress and the onset of mood disorders.

Answers: 13-1. helplessness, cognitive **13-2.** pessimistic (negative), personal flaws **13-3.** ruminate **13-4.** negative, prospective **13-5.** social (interpersonal), reinforcers **13-6.** Because they are not pleasant to be around. Depressed people complain a lot, are irritable, and tend to pass their mood along to others. **13-7.** a moderately strong.

SCHIZOPHRENIC DISORDERS

14. Describe the general characteristics (symptoms) of schizophrenia.

14-1. Before we review the different types of schizophrenia, consider some general characteristics of the schizophrenic disorders, as follows.

(a) Irrational thought: Disturbed thought processes may include the false beliefs referred to as _____ (e.g., the idea that one is a famous political figure being pursued by secret agents, when that in fact is not true).

(b) Deterioration of adaptive behavior: The deterioration usually involves social relationships, work, and neglect of personal _____.

(c) Distorted perception: This category may include hearing (or sometimes seeing) things that aren't really there. These sensory experiences are known as _____.

(d) Disturbed emotion: Emotional responsiveness may be disturbed in a variety of ways. The person may have little or no responsiveness, referred to as _____ affect, or they may show _____ emotional responses, such as laughing at news of a tragic death.

Answers: 14-1. (a) delusions (b) hygiene (cleanliness) (c) hallucinations (d) flat (flattened, blunted), inappropriate (erratic, bizarre).

15. **Describe two classification systems for schizophrenic subtypes and discuss the course of schizophrenia.**

15-1.   Write the names of the four recognized subcategories of schizophrenia next to the descriptions that follow.

(a) _____ type: Particularly severe deterioration, incoherence, complete social withdrawal, aimless babbling and giggling, delusions centering on bodily functions.

(b) _____ type: Muscular rigidity and stupor at one extreme or random motor activity, hyperactivity, and incoherence at the other; now quite rare.

(c) _____ type: Delusions of persecution and grandeur.

(d) _____ type: Clearly schizophrenic but doesn't fit other three categories.

15-2.   Several critics have asserted that there are no meaningful differences among the categories listed above and have proposed an alternative classification system. Nancy Andreasen and others have described a classification system consisting of only two categories, one that consists of _____ symptoms and the other of _____ symptoms.

15-3.   In Andreasen's system, "positive" and "negative" do not mean pleasant and unpleasant. Positive symptoms add something to behavior (like chaotic speech), and negative symptoms *subtract* something (like social withdrawal). Indicate which of the following are positive and which negative, by placing a P or an N in the appropriate blanks.

_____ flattened emotions

_____ hallucinations

_____ bizarre behavior

_____ social withdrawal

_____ apathy

_____ nonstop babbling

_____ doesn't speak

15-4.   Theorists hoped that classification of schizophrenia into positive and negative symptoms would provide more meaningful categories in terms of etiology and prognosis. Some differentiation between the two types of symptoms has been found but, all in all, this system (has/has not) produced a classification that can replace the traditional subtypes.

15-5.   Mark the following T (true) or F (false).

_____ Schizophrenia tends to emerge in adolescence or early adulthood.

_____ Schizophrenia may have either a sudden or gradual onset.

_____ About 15-20% of schizophrenic patients experience a full recovery.

15-6. What characteristics tend to predict recovery from schizophrenia? In the list below, indicate the favorable and unfavorable prognostic indicators by placing a plus (+) or minus (-) in the appropriate blanks.

_____ Has a rapid onset

_____ Occurs at a young age

_____ Accompanied by good previous social and work adjustment

_____ Low proportion of negative symptoms

_____ A supportive family to return to

Answers: 15-1. (a) disorganized (b) catatonic (c) paranoid (d) undifferentiated **15-2.** positive, negative **15-3.** N, P, P, N, N, P, N **15-4.** has not **15-5.** T, T, T **15-6.** +, -, +, +, +.

16. Explain how genetic vulnerability, neurochemical factors, and structural abnormalities in the brain may contribute to the etiology of schizophrenia.

16-1. As with mood disorders, twin studies implicate genetic factors in the development of schizophrenia. In a sentence, summarize the general results of these studies.

16-2. As with mood disorders, neurotransmitter substances in the brain are implicated in the etiology of schizophrenia. Although the evidence is somewhat clouded, what is the name of the neurotransmitter thought to be involved? _____

16-3. In addition to possible neurochemical factors, certain differences in brain structure may be associated with schizophrenia. One of these differences involves enlarged brain _____, which are hollow, fluid-filled cavities in the brain. It is impossible to know at this point whether this brain abnormality is a cause of schizophrenia or a/an _____.

16-4. Recent brain-imaging studies have also found abnormal metabolic activity in both the frontal and _____ lobes of the cortex. In addition, the metabolic abnormalities in the prefrontal cortex coincide with a major pathway for the neurotransmitter dopamine. Since _____ is already implicated in schizophrenia, this finding supports the idea of a link between this area of the prefrontal cortex and schizophrenia.

Answers: 16-1. For schizophrenia, the concordance rate is higher for identical than for fraternal twins. (The actual concordance rates have been found to be about 48% for identical and 17% for fraternal twins. For comparison, the respective percentages found for mood disorders were about 67% and 15%.) **16-2.** dopamine (thought to be a factor, because most drugs useful in treating schizophrenia decrease dopamine activity in the brain) **16-3.** ventricles, effect (result, consequence) **16-4.** temporal, dopamine.

17. Summarize evidence on how neurodevelopmental processes, family dynamics, and stress may be related to the development of schizophrenia.

17-1. The _____ hypothesis of schizophrenia maintains that schizophrenia is caused, in part, by early neurological damage that occurs either prenatally or during the birth process.

17-2. Among the causes of neurological damage are _____ infections; _____, which may occur, for example, during famine; and complications that occur during _____.

17-3. Expressed emotion refers to the extent to which a patient's relatives are overly critical or protective or are in other ways overly emotionally involved with the patient. Patients returning to families that are high in expressed emotion have a relapse rate that is much (<u>higher</u>/<u>lower</u>) than that of families low in expressed emotion.

17-4. What role does stress play in the etiology of schizophrenia? Stress is a fact of life, and it is obvious that not everyone who experiences stress develops schizophrenia. Current thinking is that stress may be a precipitating factor for people who are biologically, or for other reasons, already _____ to schizophrenia.

Answers: **17-1.** neurodevelopmental **17-2.** viral (flu), malnutrition (starvation), delivery (birth, the birth process) **17-3.** higher **17-4.** vulnerable (predisposed).

PERSONALITY DISORDERS

18. Discuss the nature of personality disorders and problems with the diagnosis of such disorders.

18-1. The personality disorders, recorded on Axis II, are frequently (<u>less</u>/<u>more</u>) severe versions of disorders on Axis I. These disorders consist of relatively extreme and inflexible sets of _____ traits that cause subjective distress or impaired functioning.

18-2. A major problem with the classification of personality disorders is that there is an enormous overlap between the ten _____ disorders on Axis II and the disorders listed on Axis I. There is also considerable _____ among the personality disorders themselves.

18-3. For example, one study found that the majority of patients diagnosed with a histrionic personality disorder (<u>also</u>/<u>did not</u>) fit the descriptions of one or more other personality disorders. This blurring of the lines makes diagnosis difficult.

18-4. In hopes of remedying these problems, some theorists have suggested that rather than using non-overlapping *categories*, personality disorders should be described in terms of *continuous scores* on a set of personality _____. While this approach has advocates, psychologists are not in agreement about its potential utility.

Answers: **18-1.** less, personality **18-2.** personality, overlap **18-3.** also **18-4.** dimensions (factors, traits).

19. Describe the antisocial personality disorder, and discuss its etiology.

19-1. The *antisocial* personality disorder is more extensively researched than are the other personality disorders and is described in more detail in your text. Check the concepts from the following list that are likely to correctly describe this disorder.

_____ sexually promiscuous   _____ genuinely affectionate

_____ manipulative   _____ impulsive

_____ feels guilty   _____ lacks an adequate conscience

_____ much more likely to occur in males than females   _____ may appear charming

_____ may be a con-artist, thug, or unprincipled business executive

19-2. What types of studies support the idea that biological factors are involved in the etiology of the antisocial personality?

19-3. What environmental factors seem to be related to development of an antisocial personality?

Answers: 19-1. All the terms describe the antisocial personality except for _feels guilty_ and _genuinely affectionate_. **19-2.** Twin studies, in particular. The concordance rate is about 67% for identical twins and 31% for fraternal. (There also has been mixed support for Eysenck's idea that antisocial personalities are chronically lower in autonomic arousal and therefore less likely to develop conditioned inhibitions.) **19-3.** Studies suggest that erratic or ineffective parental discipline, abuse, or neglect may be involved. Since one or both parents may also exhibit antisocial characteristics, observational learning may also be a factor.

PSYCHOLOGICAL DISORDERS AND THE LAW

20. Explain the legal concept of insanity and discuss the grounds for involuntary commitment.

20-1. While the words _insane_ and _schizophrenic_ may in some cases apply to the same person, the terms do not mean the same thing. The term _____ is a legal term, while _____ is a descriptive term used in psychological diagnosis. For example, an individual troubled by hallucinations and delusions probably fits the category of _____. An individual who is judged by a court not to be responsible for his or her actions would be classified (under the M'naghten rule) as _____.

20-2. The following items concern the insanity defense. Mark True or False.

_____ The insanity defense is used in fewer than 1% of homicide cases.

_____ Available evidence suggests that in the majority of cases in which is it used, the insanity defense is a successful defense (i.e., wins the case).

20-3. Roughly, how is insanity defined under the M'naghten rule?

20-4. More frequent than judgments of insanity are proceedings related to _involuntary commitment_ to a psychiatric facility.

(a) What three criteria are used to determine whether an individual should be committed?

(b) What is required to temporarily commit an individual for one to three days?

(c) What is required for longer-term commitment?

20-5. What American ethical-cultural tradition is ignored in involuntary commitment?

CULTURE AND PATHOLOGY

21. Discuss the evidence on culture and pathology.

21-1. Your text divides viewpoints about culture and pathology into *relativists* and *panculturalists*. The
_____ believe that there are basic standards of mental health that are *universal* across

cultures. The _____ believe that psychological disorders *vary as a function of culture*.

21-2. Some data support the pancultural view. For example, most investigators agree that the three most serious categories of disorder, listed below, are universal:

_____

_____

_____

21-3. On the other hand, some cultures do not consider some milder disturbances, such as hypochondria, to be disorders; and, some cultures describe as abnormal certain syndromes that are unknown in other cultures. So, are psychological disorders universal, or do they vary across cultures?

a. There are some universal standards of normality and abnormality.

b. There are some disorders that are specific to particular cultures.

c. Both of the above: some aspects of psychopathology are universal, some vary as a function of culture.

REFLECTING ON THE CHAPTER'S THEMES

22. Explain how this chapter highlighted four of the text's organizing themes.

22-1. Below are examples of the highlighted themes. Indicate which theme fits each example by writing the appropriate abbreviations in the blanks: MC for multifactorial causation, HE for the interplay of heredity and environment, SH for sociohistorical context, and C for the influence of culture.

(a) Mood and schizophrenic disorders will occur if one has a genetic vulnerability to the disorder *and* if one experiences a considerable amount of stress. ____

(b) Psychological disorders are caused by neurochemical factors, brain abnormalities, styles of child rearing, life stress, and so on. ____

(c) Anorexia nervosa occurs almost exclusively in affluent Western societies. ____

(d) Decades ago, homosexuality was classified as a disorder; in recent DSMs it is not. ____ and ____

Answers: 22-1. (a) HE (b) MC (c) C (d) SH, C.

PERSONAL APPLICATION • UNDERSTANDING EATING DISORDERS

23. **Describe the symptoms and medical complications of anorexia nervosa and bulimia nervosa.**

23-1. What are the names of the two major categories of eating disorder? _____ and _____

23-2. The most obvious feature of anorexia nervosa is the drastic weight loss that accompanies the disorder. Other characteristics include an intense _____ of gaining weight, a disturbed _____ (they think they are fat, no matter how emaciated they become), and (struggling/ refusal) to maintain normal weight.

23-3. The two major subtypes of anorexia have in common a dangerous weight loss. In one case this is accompanied by _____ (severely limiting food eaten) and in the other by bingeing and then _____ (vomiting, using laxatives and diuretics) as well as excessive exercise.

23-4. The weight loss that accompanies anorexia nervosa is substantial, typically 25-30% below normal weight. A critical diagnostic criterion for anorexia nervosa in women is amenorrhea, the loss of the _____ cycle.

23-5. There are other consequences as well, including serious gastrointestinal difficulties, heart and circulatory problems, and osteoporosis, all of which may lead to death in approximately ____% of cases. Anorexia nervosa patients (usually/rarely) seek treatment on their own.

23-6. Bulimia nervosa shares many of the characteristics of the binge-eating/purging type of anorexia. Its main differentiating feature is the fact that people with bulimia maintain a (relatively normal/drastically decreased) body weight. They are also somewhat more likely to recognize that there is a problem and to cooperate with treatment.

Answers: **23-1.** anorexia nervosa, bulimia nervosa **23-2.** fear, body image, refusal **23-3.** restricting, purging **23-4.** menstrual **23-5.** 2-10%, rarely **23-6.** relatively normal.

24. **Discuss the history and prevalence of eating disorders.**

24-1. Anorexia nervosa and bulimia nervosa were extremely (common/rare) prior to the middle of the 20th century. Culture has a great deal to do with this disorder; the combination of abundant food and the desire for thinness seem to have been a major impetus. Thus, eating disorders are largely a product of (affluent/ developing) cultures, mostly in Western countries but more recently affluent non-Western as well.

24-2. Probably as a result of the greater pressure on women to fit the current fashion of thinness, about _____% of individuals with eating disorders are female. Studies suggest that about 1-1.5% of young women develop _____ nervosa and about 2-3% _____ nervosa. The typical age of onset of the disorders is about 14-18 for _____ nervosa and 15 to 21 for _____ nervosa.

Answers: **24-1.** rare, affluent **24-2.** 90-95%, anorexia, bulimia, anorexia, bulimia.

25. Explain how genetic factors, personality, and culture may contribute to eating disorders.

25-1. Data from _____ studies and studies of relatives of people with eating disorders suggest that there is some degree of genetic predisposition for the disorders.

25-2. There are also personality correlates of the disorders that may reflect an underlying vulnerability. For example, people who are impulsive, overly sensitive, and low in self-esteem are more likely to suffer from (bulimia/anorexia) nervosa. People characterized as neurotic, obsessive, and rigid are more likely to have (bulimia/anorexia) nervosa.

25-3. As mentioned previously, cultural values are clearly implicated as well. Over the last half of the 20th century, eating disorders (increased/decreased) in prevalence as the ideal body weight (increased/decreased). Although one cannot make causal conclusions, it seems likely that the cultural milieu is a major factor in eating disorders.

Answers: **25-1.** twin **25-2.** bulimia, anorexia **25-3.** increased, decreased

26. Explain how family dynamics and disturbed thinking may contribute to eating disorders.

26-1. It is very difficult to sort out cause and effect in case and informal studies, but some theorists contend that parents who are (under-involved/overly involved) in their children's lives unintentionally push their adolescent children to exert autonomy through pathological eating patterns. Other theorists contend that mothers pass along the thinness message by _____ unhealthy dieting practices.

26-2. Disturbed thinking seems to accompany eating disorders, but whether this is a cause or a result of the disorders is hard to say. (For example, studies of food deprivation in volunteer subjects also find disturbed thinking processes.) In any case, the type of thinking that leads one to think they are fat when they are actually _____ is clearly disturbed thinking. So is the thinking that may be described as rigid, all-or-_____ thinking (e.g., If I am not thin, I am worthless; if I eat, I am not in control of my life.).

Answers: **26-1.** overly involved, modeling (endorsing, agreeing with, passing on) **26-2.** thin (emaciated), none.

27. **Discuss how mental heuristics can distort estimates of cumulative and conjunctive probabilities.**

    27-1.   Basing an estimate of probability on the similarity of an event to a prototype (or mental representation) is a distortion in thinking referred to as the _____ heuristic.

    27-2.   Over a lifetime, what is the probability that someone will be afflicted with mental illness? Higher than most people think, about one chance in three. People underestimate this probability in part because when they think of mental illness, they think of severe disturbances, such as schizophrenia. When a _____ such as this comes to mind, people tend to ignore information about _____. This bias in our thinking is called the _____.

    27-3.   In fact, the lifetime mental illness referred to could be schizophrenia, or obsessive-compulsive disorder, or phobia, or substance abuse disorder, or any of an enormous number of other disorders. Each "or" in this instance should involve (adding/subtracting) estimates of the appropriate probabilities, an example of (conjunctive/cumulative) probabilities. The representativeness heuristic, however, results in our estimating probabilities based on similarity to a _____.

    27-4.   Here is another probability question: Which of the following is more likely (a or b)?

            a. having a phobia

            b. having a phobia and being obsessive-compulsive

            You don't have to know anything about these disorders or their actual probabilities to know that the answer is ____. In this example, you implicitly know that the likelihood of two events occurring together is less than that of either of these events occurring alone. This example illustrates "and" relationships or _____ probabilities.

    27-5.   Sometimes the answer is not so apparent. Consider this question: John was reported to have been brain damaged at birth. At age 14, John's IQ was measured as 70. Of the following, which is most likely? ____

            a. John wins a Nobel prize at age 40.

            b. John is given an experimental treatment for retardation; John wins a Nobel prize at age 40.

            c. John was mixed up with another baby; John's IQ test was scored incorrectly; John wins a Nobel prize at age 40.

    27-6.   The answer to the previous question is another example of _____ probabilities. If you, like most people that I have shown this problem, picked some answer other than "a," you made the error known as the _____ fallacy.

    27-7.   Why do we make the conjunction fallacy? In part, the mistake results, again, from our tendency to be influenced by prototypes, the _____ heuristic. Even though we know that, logically, the likelihood of two events occurring together is less than the probability of either occurring alone, the additional "explanation" makes the combined result seem more reasonable. In fact, it is just another example of _____ probabilities.

27-8. When you first read about mood disorders, or obsessive-compulsive disorder, or generalized anxiety disorder, or hypochondriasis, did you tend to think that each description might fit you or one of your friends? If so, you were probably influenced by the _____ heuristic.

27-9. The availability heuristic involves the ease with which we can bring something to _____. The more readily we can think of some event, the more likely it is to influence our judgment about its frequency or _____.

27-10. Review. If one estimates probability based on a mental image or prototype, one is using the _____. If we think that it is more likely that two events will occur together than that either will occur alone, we have made the error known as the _____ _____. If we base our estimate of probability on the ease with which something comes to mind, we are using the _____.

Answers: 27-1. representativeness **27-2.** prototype (mental representation), probability, representativeness heuristic **27-3.** adding, cumulative, prototype **27-4.** a, conjunctive **27-5.** a **27-6.** conjunctive, conjunction **27-7.** representativeness, conjunctive **27-8.** availability **27-9.** mind, probability **27-10.** representativeness heuristic, conjunction fallacy, availability heuristic.

Review of Key Terms

Agoraphobia
Anorexia nervosa
Antisocial personality disorder
Anxiety disorders
Availability heuristic
Bipolar disorders
Bulimia nervosa
Catatonic schizophrenia
Comorbidity
Concordance rate
Conjunction fallacy
Conversion disorder
Culture-bound disorders
Cyclothymic disorder
Delusions
Diagnosis
Disorganized schizophrenia

Dissociative amnesia
Dissociative disorders
Dissociative fugue
Dissociative identity disorder (DID)
Dysthymic disorder
Eating disorders
Epidemiology
Etiology
Generalized anxiety disorder
Hallucinations
Hypochondriasis
Insanity
Involuntary commitment
Major depressive disorder
Manic-depressive disorder
Medical model
Mood disorders

Multiple-personality disorder
Negative symptoms
Obsessive-compulsive disorder (OCD)
Panic disorder
Paranoid schizophrenia
Personality disorders
Phobic disorder
Positive symptoms
Posttraumatic stress disorder (PTSD)
Prevalence
Prognosis
Representativeness heuristic
Schizophrenic disorders
Somatization disorder
Somatoform disorders
Undifferentiated schizophrenia

_____ 1. Proposes that it is useful to think of abnormal behavior as a disease.

_____ 2. Involves distinguishing one illness from another.

_____ 3. Refers to the apparent causation and developmental history of an illness.

_____ 4. A forecast about the possible course of an illness.

_____ 5. An eating disorder characterized by fear of gaining weight, disturbed body image, refusal to maintain normal weight, and dangerous measures to lose weight.

_____ 6. The study of the distribution of mental or physical disorders in a population.

_____ 7. Refers to the percentage of a population that exhibits a disorder during a specified time period.

_____ 8. A class of disorders marked by feelings of excessive apprehension and anxiety.

_____ 9. Disorder marked by a chronic high level of anxiety which is not tied to any specific threat.

_____ 10. Disorder marked by a persistent and irrational fear of an object or situation that presents no realistic danger.

_____ 11. Disorder that involves recurrent attacks of overwhelming anxiety that usually occur suddenly and unexpectedly.

_____ 12. Disorder marked by persistent, uncontrollable intrusions of unwanted thoughts and urges to engage in senseless rituals.

_____ 13. A fear of going out in public places.

_____ 14. One part of a two-category classification system of schizophrenia that includes behavioral excesses such as hallucinations, delusions, and bizarre behavior.

_____ 15. A class of disorders involving physical ailments that have no authentic organic basis and are due to psychological factors.

_____ 16. Disorder marked by a history of diverse physical complaints that appear to be psychological in origin.

_____ 17. Disorder that involves a significant loss of physical function (with no apparent organic basis), usually in a single-organ system.

_____ 18. Disorder that involves excessive preoccupation with health concerns and incessant worrying about developing physical illnesses.

_____ 19. A class of disorders in which people lose contact with portions of their consciousness or memory, resulting in disruptions in their sense of identity.

_____ 20. A sudden loss of memory for important personal information that is too extensive to be due to normal forgetting.

_____ 21. The loss of memory of one's entire life along with one's sense of personal identity.

_____ 22. Older term, still widely used, that describes the coexistence in one person of two or more personalities.

_____ 23. The new term that replaced multiple-personality disorder in the DSM-IV.

_____ 24. A class of disorders marked by depressed or elevated mood disturbances that may spill over to disrupt physical, perceptual, social, and thought processes.

_____ 25. Severe disturbances in eating behavior, characterized by preoccupation with weight concerns and unhealthy efforts to control weight; includes the syndromes anorexia nervosa and bulimia nervosa.

_____ 26. A disorder marked by persistent feelings of sadness and despair and a loss of interest in previous sources of pleasure.

_____ 27. Disorders marked by the experience of both depressive and manic periods.

_____ 28. Statistic indicating the percentage of twin pairs or other pairs of relatives who exhibit the same disorder.

_____ 29. Estimating the probability of an event based on the ease with which relevant instances come to mind.

_____ 30. A class of disorders marked by disturbances in thought that spill over to affect perceptual, social, and emotional processes.

_____ 31. False beliefs that are maintained even though they clearly are out of touch with reality.

_____ 32. Sensory perceptions that occur in the absence of a real, external stimulus or gross distortions of perceptual input.

_____ 33. Type of schizophrenia dominated by delusions of persecution, along with delusions of grandeur.

_____ 34. Type of schizophrenia marked by striking motor disturbances, ranging from muscular rigidity to random motor activity.

_____ 35. Type of schizophrenia marked by a particularly severe deterioration of adaptive behavior.

_____ 36. Type of schizophrenia marked by idiosyncratic mixtures of schizophrenic symptoms.

_____ 37. A class of disorders marked by extreme, inflexible personality traits that cause subjective distress or impaired social and occupational functioning.

_____ 38. Disorder marked by impulsive, callous, manipulative, aggressive, and irresponsible behavior; reflects a failure to accept social norms.

_____ 39. A legal status indicating that a person cannot be held responsible for his or her actions because of mental illness.

_____ 40. A part of a two-category classification system of schizophrenia that includes behavioral deficits, such as flattened emotions, social withdrawal, and apathy.

_____ 41. Legal situation in which people are hospitalized in psychiatric facilities against their will.

_____ 42. Chronic but relatively mild symptoms of bipolar disturbance.

_____ 43. Abnormal syndromes found only in a few cultural groups.

_____ 44. Chronic depression that is insufficient in severity to merit diagnosis of a major depressive episode.

_____ 45. Estimating the probability of an event based on how similar the event is to a prototype.

_____ 46. An error in thinking that involves estimating that the odds of two uncertain events happening together are greater than the odds of either event happening alone.

_____ 47. An eating disorder that involves binge eating followed by unhealthy compensatory efforts such as vomiting, fasting, abuse of laxatives and diuretics, and excessive exercise.

_____ 48. The coexistence of two or more disorders in the same individual.

_____ 49. Older term used to refer to bipolar disorder.

_____ 50. Psychological disturbance due to the experience of a major traumatic event; may appear some time after the event.

Answers: 1. medical model **2.** diagnosis **3.** etiology **4.** prognosis **5.** anorexia nervosa **6.** epidemiology **7.** prevalence **8.** anxiety disorders **9.** generalized anxiety disorder **10.** phobic disorder **11.** panic disorder **12.** obsessive-compulsive disorder **13.** agoraphobia **14.** positive symptoms **15.** somatoform disorders **16.** somatization disorder **17.** conversion disorder **18.** hypochondriasis **19.** dissociative disorders **20.** dissociative amnesia **21.** dissociative fugue **22.** multiple-personality disorder **23.** dissociative identity disorder **24.** mood disorders **25.** eating disorders **26.** major depressive disorder **27.** bipolar disorders **28.** concordance rate **29.** availability heuristic **30.** schizophrenic disorders **31.** delusions **32.** hallucinations **33.** paranoid schizophrenia **34.** catatonic schizophrenia **35.** disorganized schizophrenia **36.** undifferentiated schizophrenia **37.** personality disorders **38.** antisocial personality disorder **39.** insanity **40.** negative symptoms **41.** involuntary commitment **42.** cyclothymia **43.** culture-bound disorders **44.** dysthymic disorder **45.** representativeness heuristic **46.** conjunction fallacy **47.** bulimia nervosa **48.** comorbidity **49.** manic-depressive disorder **50.** posttraumatic stress disorder (PTSD).

Review of Key People

Nancy Andreasen   David Rosenhan   Martin SeligmanThomas Szasz
Susan Nolen-Hoeksema

_____   **1.** Critic of the medical model; argues that abnormal behavior usually involves a deviation from social norms rather than an illness.

_____   **2.** Did a study on admission of pseudopatients to a mental hospital; concluded that our mental health system is biased toward seeing pathology where it doesn't exist.

_____   **3.** Proposed a classical conditioning explanation of phobias modified by "preparedness;" developed the learned helplessness model; modified learned helpless to include cognition (pessimistic explanatory style).

_____   **4.** Proposed an alternative approach to subtyping that divides schizophrenic disorders into just two categories, based on the presence of negative versus positive symptoms.

_____   **5.** Found that people who ruminate about their depression, by repetitively focusing on their sad feelings, tend to stay depressed longer that those who distract themselves.

Answers: 1. Szasz **2.** Rosenhan **3.** Seligman **4.** Andreasen **5.** Susan Nolen-Hoeksema.

Self-Quiz

1. Which of the following concepts or people asserts that abnormal behavior is best thought of as an illness?
    a. the behavioral model
    b. the medical model
    c. Thomas Szasz
    d. Arthur Staats

2. The concordance rate for mood disorders has been found to be about 67% among identical twins and 17% among fraternal twins. These data suggest that the mood disorders
    a. are caused primarily by stress
    b. have an onset at an early age
    c. are due primarily to family environment
    d. are caused in part by genetic factors

3. In Rosenhan's study involving admission of pseudopatients (i.e., normal individuals who said they heard voices) to psychiatric facilities, most of the pseudopatients were
    a. diagnosed as seriously disturbed
    b. diagnosed as suffering from a mild neurosis
    c. dismissed within two days
    d. misdiagnosed by the attendants but correctly diagnosed by psychiatrists

4. An individual gets sudden, paralyzing attacks of anxiety and also fears going out in public away from her house. Which anxiety disorder does this describe?
    a. generalized anxiety disorder
    b. phobic disorder
    c. obsessive-compulsive disorder
    d. panic attack and agoraphobia

5. Ralph cleans and scrubs the cupboards in his house seven times each day. Which anxiety disorder does this describe?
   a. generalized anxiety disorder
   b. phobic disorder
   c. obsessive-compulsive disorder
   d. panic disorder

6. Human beings may have evolved to be more easily conditioned to fear some stimuli than others. This is Seligman's notion of
   a. preparedness
   b. anxiety differentiation
   c. somatization
   d. learned helplessness

7. Delusions and hallucinations are likely to characterize
   a. major depressive disorder
   b. hypochondriasis
   c. phobias
   d. schizophrenia

8. Paralysis or loss of feeling that does not match underlying anatomical organization may be a symptom of
   a. somatization disorder
   b. conversion disorder
   c. hypochondriasis
   d. malingering

9. A disorder that was extremely rare prior to the last half of the 20th century is the syndrome
   a. manic-depressive disorder
   b. schizophrenia
   c. obsessive-compulsive disorder
   d. anorexia nervosa

10. The disorder marked by striking motor disturbances ranging from rigidity to random motor activity and incoherence is termed
    a. catatonic schizophrenia
    b. multiple personality
    c. dissociative disorder
    d. paranoid schizophrenia

11. Which of the following are disorders that occur in all cultures?
    a. generalized anxiety disorder and panic disorder
    b. hypochondriasis, somatization, conversion disorder
    c. schizophrenia, bipolar mood disorder, depression
    d. bulimia and anorexia nervosa

12. A disorder characterized by amenorrhea (loss of the menstrual cycle) in women is the syndrome termed
    a. generalized anxiety disorder
    b. bipolar mood disorder
    c. anorexia nervosa
    d. bulimia nervosa

13. An individual thinks he is Jesus Christ. He also believes that, because he is Christ, people are trying to kill him. Assume that this individual is not correct—he is not Christ, and people are not trying to kill him. Which of the following would be the most likely diagnosis?

a. multiple personality

b. paranoid schizophrenia

c. obsessive-compulsive disorder

d. catatonic schizophrenia

14. A court declares that, because of a mental illness, an individual is not responsible for his criminal actions (did not know right from wrong). The individual is

a. insane

b. psychopathic

c. psychotic

d. schizophrenic

15. Being careful not to make the conjunction fallacy, indicate which of the following is most probable

a. Ralph is an alcoholic; Ralph wins a major world tennis tournament.

b. Ralph is an alcoholic; Ralph enters a treatment program; Ralph wins a major world tennis tournament.

c. Ralph is an alcoholic; Ralph enters a treatment program; Ralph has been sober for a year; Ralph wins a major world tennis tournament.

d. Ralph is an alcoholic; Ralph enters a treatment program; Ralph has been sober for a year; Ralph practices tennis 50 hours a week; Ralph wins a major world tennis tournament.

Answers: 1. b **2.** d **3.** a **4.** d **5.** c **6.** a **7.** d **8.** b **9.** d **10.** a **11.** c **12.** c **13.** b **14.** a **15.** a.

InfoTrac Keywords

Agoraphobia	Conversion Disorder	Paranoid Schizophrenia
Anorexia Nervosa	Hypochondriasis (see hypochondria)	Somatization Disorder
Antisocial Personality Disorder	Major Depressive Disorder	Somatoform Disorders
Availability Heuristic	Obsessive-compulsive Disorder	

Chapter Fifteen
Treatment of Psychological Disorders

Review of Key Ideas

THE ELEMENTS OF THE TREATMENT PROCESS

1. **Identify the three major categories of therapy, and discuss how various demographic variables relate to the likelihood of treatment.**

   1-1.   Even though she already owns more than a thousand pairs of shoes, Imelba cannot resist the urge to buy more. She checks the Yellow Pages and calls three different psychotherapists regarding possible treatment for her compulsion.

   (a)   One therapist tells her that treatment will require her to talk with the therapist so as to develop a better understanding of her inner feelings. This therapist probably belongs to the _____ school of psychotherapy.

   (b)   Another therapist suggests that some form of medication may help alleviate her compulsion. This therapist probably pursues the _____ approach to psychotherapy.

   (c)   The third therapist is of the opinion that her urge to buy shoes results from learning, and correcting it requires that she unlearn this compulsion. This therapist probably pursues the _____ approach to psychotherapy.

   1-2.   Indicate whether the following statements about people who seek and choose not to seek psychotherapy are true or false.

   _____ Men are more likely than women to seek psychotherapy.

   _____ The two most common presenting symptoms are excessive anxiety and depression.

   _____ Persons seeking psychotherapy always have identifiable disorders.

   _____ Only a minority of persons needing psychotherapy actually receive treatment.

   _____ Many people feel that seeking psychotherapy is an admission of personal weakness.

Answers: 1-1. (a) insight (b) biomedical (c) behavioral **1-2.** false, true, false, true, true.

2. **Describe the various types of mental health professionals involved in the provision therapy.**

   2-1.   Identify the following kinds of mental health professionals:

   (a) Medically trained persons (physicians) who generally use biomedical and insight approaches to psychotherapy.

   (b) Persons with doctoral degrees who emphasize behavioral and insight approaches to psychotherapy in treating a full range of psychological problems (two types).

   (c) Nurses who usually work as part of the treatment team in a hospital setting.

   (d) These persons often work with both the patient and family to reintegrate the patient back into society.

   (e) Persons who usually specialize in particular types of problems, such as vocational, drug, or marital counseling.

   Answers: 2-1. (a) psychiatrists (b) clinical and counseling psychologists (c) psychiatric nurses (d) clinical social workers (e) counselors.

INSIGHT THERAPIES

3. **Explain the logic of psychoanalysis, and describe the techniques by which analysts probe the unconscious.**

   3-1.   Freud believed that psychological disturbances originate from unresolved conflicts deep in the unconscious levels of the mind. His theory of personality, which he called _____, would be classified as an _____ approach to psychotherapy. The psychoanalyst plays the role of psychological detective, seeking out problems thought to originate from conflicts left over from early _____.

   3-2.   The psychoanalyst employs two techniques to probe the unconscious. One technique requires the patient to tell whatever comes to mind, no matter how trivial. This technique is called _____ _____. The other technique requires the patient to learn to remember his or her dreams, which are then probed for their hidden meaning by the psychoanalyst. This technique is called _____ _____.

   Answers: 3-1. psychoanalysis, insight, childhood **3-2.** free association, dream analysis.

4. **Discuss resistance and transference in psychoanalysis.**

4-1.   Freud believed most people (<u>do/do not</u>) want to know the true nature of their inner conflicts and will employ various strategies so as to offer _____ to the progress of therapy. As therapy progresses, the patient often begins to relate to the therapist as though he or she was actually one of the significant persons (mother, father, spouse, etc.) in the patient's life. This phenomenon is called _____.

Answers: **4-1.** do not, resistance, transference.

5. **Identify the elements of therapeutic climate, and discuss therapeutic process in Rogers' client-centered therapy.**

5-1.   Client-centered therapy, as developed by Carl Rogers, holds that there are three important aspects necessary for a good therapeutic climate. These are genuineness, unconditional positive regard, and empathy. Match these terms with their correct definitions, as given below.

(a) The ability to truly see the world from the client's point of view and communicate this understanding to the client.

(b) The therapist's openness and honesty with the client.

(c) The complete and nonjudgmental acceptance of the client as a person, without necessarily agreeing with what the client has to say.

5-2.   The major emphasis for client-centered therapy is to provide feedback and _____ as the client expresses his or her thoughts and feelings. The idea here is that the client (<u>does/does not</u>) need direct advice. What is needed is help in sorting through personal confusion in order to gain greater _____ into true inner feelings.

Answers: **5-1.** (a) empathy (b) genuineness (c) unconditional positive regard **5-2.** clarification, does not, insight or understanding.

6. **Describe how group therapy is generally conducted, and identify some advantages of this approach.**

6-1.   When conducting group therapy, the therapist generally plays a/an (<u>active/subtle</u>) role, one that is primarily aimed at promoting _____ cohesiveness. Participants essentially function as _____ for each other, providing acceptance and emotional support.

6-2. Besides being less expensive, group therapy also has three other advantages: (1) the realization by the participants that their problems (are/are not) unique, (2) the opportunity to work in a safe environment to build _____ skills, and (3) the fact that group therapy is particularly appropriate for (all/certain) kinds of problems.

Answers: **6-1.** subtle, group, therapists **6-2.** are not, social, certain.

7. Discuss evidence on the efficacy of insight therapies and the role of common factors in therapy.

7-1. Evaluating the effectivensss of insight therapies (is/is not) especially complicated. For example, many problems simply clear up on their own, a condition called _____ *remission.*

7-2. Overall, research studies show that a clinically meaningful recovery within about 20 sessions occurs in about _____ percent of the patients. This number grows to about _____ percent after 45 sessions.

7-3. The benefits of therapy appear to represent the specific procedures employed by a given therapist and also to _____ factors employed by all therapists.

Answers: **7-1.** is, spontaneous **7-2.** 50, 75 **7-3.** common.

BEHAVIOR THERAPIES

8. Summarize the general principles underlying behavioral approaches to therapy.

8-1. In contrast to insight therapists, who believe that pathological symptoms are signs of an underlying problem, behavior therapists believe that the _____ are the problem. Thus, behavior therapists focus on employing the principles of learning to directly change maladaptive _____. The two general principles underlying this approach are (1) one's behavior is a product of _____, and (2) what has been learned can be _____.

Answers: **8-1.** symptoms, behavior, learning, unlearned.

9. Describe the goals and procedures of systematic desensitization and aversion therapy.

9-1. State whether the following situations would be most applicable to systematic desensitization or to aversion therapy.

(a) The treatment goal is to lessen the attractiveness of particular stimuli and behaviors that are personally or socially harmful.

(b) The treatment goal is to reduce irrational fears, such as found in phobias and other anxiety disorders.

(c) The three-step treatment involves pairing an imagined anxiety hierarchy with deep muscle relaxation.

(d) Treatment involves presenting an unpleasant stimulus, such as electric shock, while a person is engaged in performing a self-destructive, but personally appealing, acts.

(e) This would be the treatment of choice for students who are unduly anxious about public speaking.

Answers: 9-1. (a) aversion therapy (b) systematic desensitization (c) systematic desensitization (d) aversion therapy (e) systematic desensitization.

10. Describe the goals and techniques of social skills training.

10-1. As the name implies, social skills training is a behavior therapy designed to improve a clients social or _____ skills. Three different behavioral techniques are employed. First, one is required to watch closely the behavior of socially skilled persons, a technique called _____. Next, the client is expected to imitate and practice the behavior he or she has just witnessed, a technique called behavior _____. Finally, the client is expected to perform in social situations requiring increasingly more difficult social skills, a technique called _____.

Answers: 10-1. interpersonal, modeling, rehearsal.

11. Discuss the logic, goals, and techniques of cognitive therapy.

11-1. Answer the following questions regarding the logic, goals, and techniques of cognitive therapy.

(a) What is the basic logic behind cognitive therapy? Or, to put it another way, what is the origin of many psychological problems according to cognitive therapy?

(b) What is the primary goal of cognitive therapy?

(c) How do cognitive therapists go about changing a client's negative illogical thinking?

(d) What two therapy traditions did cognitive therapy emerge from?

Answers: 11-1. (a) negative illogical thinking (b) to change the client's negative illogical thinking (c) by having the client subject the automatic illogical thoughts to reality testing (d) insight therapy and behavior therapy.

12. Discuss evidence on the effectiveness of behavior therapies.

12-1. Compared to the evidence in support of insight therapies, the evidence in favor of behavior therapy is somewhat (weaker/stronger). It is important to remember, however, that behavior therapies are best suited for treating (specific/general) psychological disorders, and that all of the various behavioral techniques (are/are not) equally effective.

Answers: 12-1. stronger, specific, are not.

BIOMEDICAL THERAPIES

13. Describe the principal categories of drugs used in the treatment of psychological disorders.

13-1. Valium and Xanax, popularly called tranquilizers, are used to treat psychological disorders in which anxiety is a major feature. Thus, they are collectively called _____ drugs.

13-2. Another class of drugs is used to treat severe psychotic symptoms, such as hallucinations and confusion. These drugs are collectively called _____ drugs.

13-3. Three classes of drugs – tricyclics, MAO inhibitors, and selective serotonin reuptake inhibitors – have been found to be useful in alleviating depression. These drugs are collectively called _____ drugs.

13-4. A new class of drugs is replacing lithium for treating mood disorders. Valproic acid is the most popular of these new drugs, which are collectively known as _____ *stabilizers*.

Answers: 13-1. antianxiety **13-2.** antipsychotic **13-3.** antidepressant **13-4.** mood.

14. Discuss evidence on the effects and problems of drug treatments for psychological disorders.

14-1. Drug therapies have proven useful in the treatment of many psychological disorders. However, they remain controversial for at least three reasons. Use the hints below to describe these three reasons.

(a) resolve problems

(b) two areas having to do with excess

(c) cure is worse than the disease

14-2. What problem exists between drug companies and researchers that may influence results regarding the effectiveness and side effects of drugs?

Answers: 14-1. (a) They alleviate rather than solve psychological problems. (b) They are over-prescribed and patients are over-medicated. (c) The side effects may be worse than the disease. 14-2. The researchers are too financially dependent on the drug companies.

15. **Describe ECT, and discuss its therapeutic effects and its risks.**

   15-1.   Answer the following questions about the nature, therapeutic effects, and risks of ECT.

      (a) What is the physical effect of the electric shock on the patient?

      (b) What general class of disorders warrants conservative use of ECT as a treatment technique?

      (c) Why does ECT work?

      (d) What are some short-term side effects of ECT?

   Answers: 15-1. (a) It produces convulsive seizures. (b) severe mood disorders (depression and mania) (c) It is unknown at this time. (d) It can produce intellectual impairment.

16. **Summarize the concerns that have been expressed about the impact of managed care on the treatment of psychological disorders.**

   16-1.   Why might the impact on mental health care be more negative with managed health care than for other treatment specialties in carrying out medically necessary treatment programs?

   16-2.   What cost-cutting strategies, in addition to denial of treatment and prescribing older rather than newer drugs, are often employed by HMO's?

   Answers: 16-1. The question of what is medically necessary is more subjective (in the case of mental health treatment). 16-2. under-diagnosing conditions, failing to make needed referrals, limiting treatment times, rerouting patients to less highly trained professionals (in any order).

17. Discuss the merits of blending or combining different approaches to therapy.

17-1.   A significant trend in modern psychotherapy is to blend or combine many different treatment approaches. Psychologists who advocate and use this approach are said to be _____. One outcome study cited by the text suggests there may be merit to this approach. In this study, three different groups of depressed patients were treated by either insight therapy, drug therapy, or both. The greatest improvement was found in patients treated by _____.

Answers: 17-1. eclectic, both.

18. Discuss the barriers that lead to underutilization of mental health services by ethnic minorities and possible solutions to the problem.

18-1.   The text lists four general barriers (cultural, language, access, and institutional) to mental health services for ethnic minorities. Indicate which of these barriers is represented in the following statements.

_____ (a)   Many of the ethnic minorities are in low-paying jobs and without health insurance.

_____ (b)   Very few mental health facilities are equipped to provide culturally responsive services.

_____ (c)   There is a limited number of bilingual therapists.

_____ (d)   Psychotherapy was developed by whites in the Western world to treat whites in the Western world.

18-2.   What would be an optimal, but perhaps impractical, solution to the problems of language and cultural differences between therapists and clients?

18-3.   What kind of training was recommended for therapists?

18-4.   What suggestion was made with respect to traditional therapies?

Answers. 18-1. (a) access (b) institutional (c) language (d) cultural **18-2.** Ethnically match therapists and clients.
18-3. cultural sensitivity training **18-4.** That they be modified to be more compatible with specific ethnic groups.

INSTITUTIONAL TREATMENT IN TRANSITION

19. Explain why people grew disenchanted with mental hospitals and describe the community mental health movement.

19-1.   After more than a century of reliance on state mental hospitals, the evidence began to grow that these institutions were not helping the patients; rather, in many instances, they were worsening their condition. What condition, unrelated to funding, was said to be responsible for this state of affairs?

19-2. In order to correct for these shortcomings, the community mental health movement arose as an alternative treatment option. These community based facilities emphasize (<u>short-term/long-term</u>) therapy and getting patients stabilized and back into the community _____.

Answers: 19-1. The removal of patients from their communities separated them from essential support groups.
19-2. short-term, swiftly.

20. Describe the deinstitutionalization trend, and evaluate its effects.

20-1. The transferring of mental health care from large state institutions to community based facilities is what is meant by the term _____. As a result of deinstitutionalization, the number of mental patients in large institutional hospitals has _____ remarkably. The length of stay by patients in mental hospitals has also _____.

20-2. While deinstitutionalization has resulted in a decrease in the number of patients, as well as their length of stay, the number of admissions to psychiatric hospitals has actually _____. This is because of a large number of readmissions for short-term care, which the text calls "the _____ _____ problem." Another problem brought about by deinstitutionalization is that a large number of discharged patients who have meager job skills and no close support groups make up a substantial portion of the nation's _____ persons.

Answers: 20-1. deinstitutionalization, declined, declined **20-2.** increased, revolving door, homeless.

REFLECTING ON THE CHAPTER'S THEMES

21. Explain how this chapter highlighted two of the text's unifying themes.

21-1. What point does the text make about how theoretical diversity influenced the treatment techniques employed by psychotherapy?

21-2. The approaches to psychotherapy discussed in this chapter are not universally accepted or used, and some are actually counterproductive in many cultures. Why is this?

Answers: 21-1. It has resulted in better treatment techniques (because of the many diverse approaches). **21-2.** Cultural factors influence psychological processes.

APPLICATION: LOOKING FOR A THERAPIST

22. Discuss where to seek therapy, and the potential importance of a therapist's sex, professional background, and cost.

22-1. Most therapists (<u>are/are not</u>) in private practice. In addition to talking to friends and acquaintances, the text lists many places (Table 15.2) where one might seek psychotherapy. The general idea here is to _____ around when looking for a therapist.

22-2. The text concludes that the kind of degree held by the psychotherapist (is/is not) crucial, although a verifiable degree indicating some kind of professional training is important. The sex of the therapist should be chosen according to the feelings of the _____; it is unwise to engage a therapist whose sex makes the client feel uncomfortable.

22-3. Answer the following questions regarding the cost of psychotherapy.

(a) How does the cost of therapists involved in private practice compare with the fees charged by similar professional groups?

(b) Many community agencies use a sliding scale to assess therapy costs. What does this mean?

Answers: 22-1. are not, shop **22-2.** is not, client **22-3.** (a) The costs are similar. (b) Fees are assessed according to the ability to pay.

23. Discuss the importance of a therapist's theoretical approach.

23-1. Studies of the effectiveness of various theoretical approaches to therapy show they are (unequal/equal) in overall success. This equality of results among all theoretical approaches (does/does not) apply to all types of problems. The theoretical approach may make a difference for specific types of problems.

Answers: 23-1. equal, does not.

24. Summarize what one should look for in a prospective therapist and what one should expect out of therapy.

24-1. The text lists three areas to evaluate when looking for a therapist. Complete the following statements describing these areas.

(a) Can you talk to the therapist _____?

(b) Does the therapist appear to have empathy and _____?

(c) Does the therapist appear to be self-assured and _____?

24-2. What should one consider before terminating therapy because of lack of progress?

24-3. What did the Ehrenbergs say about what to expect from psychotherapy?

Answers: 24-1. (a) openly (in a candid, nondefensive manner) (b) understanding (c) confident **24-2.** The lack of progress may be due to resistance on the client's part. **24-3.** It takes time, effort, and courage.

25. **Explain how placebo effects and regression toward the mean can complicate the evaluation of therapy.**

   25-1.   In addition to therapy itself, what other two factors can influence the outcome of a treatment program?

   25-2.   Which of these two factors is least effected by having only a small sample?

   25-3.   Which of these factors leads us to predict that persons who score the healthiest on a mental health questionnaire will actually score lower on this questionnaire following a brief therapy intervention?

   Answers: 25-1. placebo effects and regression toward the mean **25-2.** placebo effects **25-3.** regression toward the mean.

Review of Key Terms

Antianxiety drugs
Antidepressant drugs
Antipsychotic drugs
Aversion therapy
Behavior therapies
Biomedical therapies
Client-centered therapy
Clinical psychologists
Cognitive-behavioral treatments
Cognitive therapy
Counseling psychologists

Deinstitutionalization
Dream analysis
Eclecticism
Electroconvulsive therapy (ECT)
Free association
Group therapy
Insight therapies
Interpretation
Mental hospitals
Mood stabalizers
Placebo effects

Psychiatrists
Psychoanalysis
Psychopharmacotherapy
Regression toward the mean
Resistance
Social skills training
Spontaneous remission
Systematic desensitization
Tardive dyskinesia
Transference

_____   1.   Psychologists who specialize in the treatment of full-fledged disorders.

_____   2.   Physicians who specialize in the treatment of psychological disorders.

_____   3.   Therapies that involve verbal interactions intended to enhance a client's self-knowledge and thus produce healthful changes in personality and behavior.

_____   4.   An insight therapy that emphasizes the recovery of unconscious conflicts, motives, and defenses through techniques such as free association and transference.

_____   5.   A technique in which clients are urged to spontaneously express their thoughts and feelings with as little personal censorship as possible.

_____   6.   A technique for interpreting the symbolic meaning of dreams.

_____   7.   A therapist's attempts to explain the inner significance of a client's thoughts, feelings, memories, and behavior.

_____   8.   A client's largely unconscious defensive maneuvers intended to hinder the progress of therapy.

_____ 9. A process that occurs when clients start relating to their therapist in ways that mimic critical relationships in their lives.

_____ 10. An insight therapy that emphasizes providing a supportive emotional climate for clients who play a major role in determining the pace and direction of their therapy.

_____ 11. An insight therapy that emphasizes recognizing and changing negative thoughts and maladaptive beliefs.

_____ 12. The simultaneous treatment of several clients.

_____ 13. Therapies that involve the application of learning principles to change a client's maladaptive behaviors.

_____ 14. A behavior therapy used to reduce anxiety responses through counterconditioning.

_____ 15. A behavior therapy in which an aversive stimulus is paired with a stimulus that elicits an undesirable response.

_____ 16. Recovery from a disorder that occurs without formal treatment.

_____ 17. A behavior therapy designed to improve interpersonal skills and which emphasizes shaping, modeling, and behavioral rehearsal.

_____ 18. Therapies that use physiological interventions intended to reduce symptoms associated with psychological disorders.

_____ 19. The treatment of mental disorders with drug therapy.

_____ 20. Drugs that relieve tension, apprehension, and nervousness.

_____ 21. Drugs that gradually reduce psychotic symptoms.

_____ 22. A neurological disorder marked by chronic tremors and involuntary spastic movements.

_____ 23. Drugs that gradually elevate mood and help bring people out of a depression.

_____ 24. Drugs used to control mood swings in patients with bipolar mood disorder.

_____ 25. A treatment in which electric shock is used to produce cortical seizure accompanied by convulsions.

_____ 26. A medical institution specializing in the provision of inpatient care for psychological disorders.

_____ 27. Involves drawing ideas from two or more systems of therapy, instead of just committing to one system.

_____ 28. Transferring the treatment of mental illness from inpatient institutions to community-based facilities that emphasize outpatient care.

_____ 29. Occur when people's expectations lead them to experience some change, even though they receive a fake treatment.

_____ 30. Occurs when people who score extremely high or low on some trait are measured a second time, and their new scores fall closer to the mean.

_____ 31. Psychologists who specialize in the treatment of everyday adjustment problems.

_____ 32. Employ varied combinations of verbal interventions and behavior modification techniques to help clients change maladaptive patterns of thinking.

Review of Key People

Aaron Beck

Dorthea Dix

Sigmund Freud

Carl Rogers

Joseph Wolpe

_____ **1.** Developed a systematic treatment procedure, which he called psychoanalysis.

_____ **2.** The developer of client-centered therapy.

_____ **3.** Noted for his work in the development of cognitive therapy.

_____ **4.** The developer of systematic desensitization.

_____ **5.** One of the early reformers who helped to establish state-funded mental hospitals.

Answers: 1. Freud **2.** Rogers **3.** Beck **4.** Wolpe **5.** Dix.

Self-Quiz

1. Which of the following is not a true statement?
   a. Women seek psychotherapy more than men.
   b. The two most common problems that lead to psychotherapy are sexual problems and depression.
   c. Persons seeking psychotherapy don't always have identifiable problems.
   d. Many people feel that seeking psychotherapy is an admission of personal weakness.

2. Which of the following mental health professionals must have a medical degree?
   a. psychiatric social workers
   b. clinical psychologists
   c. psychiatric nurses
   d. psychiatrists

3. Psychoanalysis is an example of what kind of approach to psychotherapy?
   a. insight
   b. learning
   c. biomedical
   d. a combination of learning and biomedical

4. When a client begins relating to his psychoanalyst as though she were his mother, we have an example of
   a. transference
   b. free association
   c. catharsis
   d. restructuring

5. The major emphasis in client-centered therapy is to provide the client with
   a. interpretation of unconscious thinking
   b. cognitive restructuring
   c. feedback and clarification
   d. good advice

6. Which of the following is likely to be found in cognitive therapy?
   a. searching for negative illogical thinking
   b. dream interpretation
   c. free association
   d. an emphasis on childhood conflicts

7. Which therapists are likely to play the least active (most subtle) role in conducting therapy?
   a. behavior therapists
   b. cognitive therapists
   c. group therapists
   d. pychoanalytic therapists

8. What percentage of patients show a meaningful recovery within about 20 sessions of insight therapies?
   a. 25
   b. 50
   c. 75
   d. 90

9. Which of the following therapies is most likely to see the symptom as the problem?
   a. psychoanalysis
   b. client-centered therapy
   c. cognitive therapy
   d. behavior therapy

10. Which of the following therapies would be most likely to employ aversive conditioning?
    a. psychoanalysis
    b. behavior therapy
    c. biomedical therapies
    d. client-centered therapy

11. Which of the following behavior therapy techniques would most likely be used to treat a fear of flying?
    a. systematic desensitization
    b. aversive conditioning
    c. modeling
    d. biofeedback

12. Electroconvulsive therapy (ECT) is now primarily used to treat patients suffering from
    a. anxiety
    b. phobias
    c. severe mood disorders
    d. psychosis

13 Psychotherapists who combine several different approaches in their approach to therapy are said to be
    a. enigmatic
    b. eclectic
    c. unspecific
    d. imaginative

14 The trend toward deinstitutionalization mainly came about because large state mental institutions:

a. were becoming too expensive

b. were actually worsening the condition of many patients

c. were overstaffed

d. were becoming too political

15 Which of the following factors can affect the outcome of a treatment program?

a. the efficacy of the treatment itself

b. regression toward the mean

c. placebo effects

d. all of these above

Answers: 1. b **2.** d **3.** a **4.** a **5.** c **6.** a **7.** c **8.** b **9.** d **10.** b **11.** a **12.** c **13.** b **14.** b **15.** d.

InfoTrac Keywords

Aversion Therapy   Electroconvulsive Therapy   Placebo Effects

Deinstitutionalization

Chapter Sixteen
SOCIAL BEHAVIOr

Review of Key Ideas

PERSON PERCEPTION: FORMING IMPRESSIONS OF OTHERS

1. **Describe how various aspects of physical appearance may influence our impressions of others.**

   1-1. In general, we attribute _____ personality characteristics to good-looking people. For example, we view attractive people as warmer, friendlier, better-adjusted, and more poised. We also tend to view attractive people as (less/more) *competent* than less attractive people.

   1-2. A recent review also indicates that we have a surprisingly strong tendency to view attractive people as (less/more) competent than less attractive people. Perhaps a result, attractive people tend to obtain better jobs and higher salaries.

   1-3. In addition, we make inferences about people based on their nonverbal behavior—how they move, talk, and gesture. For example, based on a 10-second videotape, participants in a recent study guessed others' sexual orientation with a relatively high degree of (accuracy/inaccuracy).

   Answers: **1-1.** positive (desirable, favorable) **1-2.** more **1-3.** accuracy (about 70%).

2. **Explain how schemas, stereotypes, and other factors contribute to subjectivity in person perception.**

   2-1. Briefly define the following:

   (a) schemas:

   (b) stereotypes:

2-2. Men are competitive, women are sensitive: these are stereotypes. Stereotypes are broad generalizations that tend to ignore the _____ within a group. People who hold stereotypes do not necessarily assume that all members of a particular group have the same characteristics, but merely that there is an increased _____ that they do.

2-3. Whether probabilistic or absolute, schemas in general and stereotypes in particular direct our perception, so that we tend to see the things we expect to see. Such selective perception results in an over-estimation of the degree to which our expectations match actual events, a phenomenon referred to as _____ correlation.

2-4. In one study, discussed in the text, subjects watched a videotape of a woman engaged in various activities (including drinking beer and listening to classical music). For one set of subjects she was described as a librarian and for another as a waitress. What effect did the occupational labels have on subjects' recall of the woman's *activities*? Which of the following is(are) true?

_____ Subjects in the "librarian" condition tended to recall her listening to classical music.

_____ Subjects in the "waitress" condition tended to recall her drinking beer.

2-5. The study just described illustrates subjectivity in person perception. The schemas, in this case the _____, that we have about categories of people, affect how we perceive and what we remember.

2-6. We think that when we make a blunder, people notice, and that when we do something right, people notice as well. We are correct: appearance and behavior do influence impressions. Recent research indicates, however, that we (overestimate/underestimate) the extent to which others pay attention to our appearance and our behavior.

2-7. Thus, people are (more/less) likely to notice our blunders than we think they will. And they are (more/less) likely to notice our successes than we think they will. This phenomenon is termed the _____ effect.

2-8. A related finding is that people think that they understand others (better/worse) than others understand them. For example, you might think that you understand your roommate better than your roommate understands you. This phenomenon is know as the illusion of _____ insight.

Answers: 2-1. (a) clusters of ideas about people and events (b) a type of schema; widely held beliefs about people based on group membership **2-2.** diversity (variability), probability **2-3.** illusory **2-4.** both are true **2-5.** stereotypes **2-6.** overestimate **2-7.** less, less, spotlight **2-8.** better, asymmetric.

3. Explain the evolutionary perspective on bias in person perception.

3-1. How does one explain bias or prejudice in terms of evolution? To explain anything in terms of evolution one assumes that the particular characteristic or trait had _____ value in our evolutionary past. For example, the bias in favor of physical attractiveness might have signaled health, associated with _____ potential in women and the ability to acquire _____ in men. The stereotype of _____ individuals as submissive and honest could simply result from our adaptive reaction to infants.

3-2. Evolutionary theorists also assert that we needed a quick way to categorize people as friend or enemy or, in more technical terms, as members of our _____ or members of the _____.

3-3. The question still remains: how could prejudice and bias be adaptive? It must be clear that what was adaptive in our evolutionary past (is also/may not be) adaptive now. Nonetheless, from the point of view of evolutionary theory, cognitive mechanisms involving bias have been shaped by natural _____.

Answers: **3-1.** adaptive, reproductive, resources, baby-faced **3-2.** ingroup, outgroup **3-3.** may not be, selection.

ATTRIBUTION PROCESSES: EXPLAINING BEHAVIOR

4. **Explain what attributions are and why we make them.**

4-1. Why are you reading this book? The search for causes of events and of our own and others' behavior is termed _____. For example, you might _____ your reading behavior to an upcoming test (or to personal interest, lust for knowledge, fear, etc.).

4-2. Attributions are inferences that people make about the _____ of events and about the their own and others' behavior.

4-3. Why do we make attributions? We seem to have a strong need to _____ our experiences.

Answers: **4-1.** attribution, attribute **4-2.** causes (origin, source, explanation) **4-3.** understand (explain).

5. **Describe the distinction between internal and external attributions.**

5-1. Which of the following involve internal and which external attributions? Label each sentence with an I or an E.

_____ He flunked because he's lazy.

_____ Our team lost because the officials were biased against us.

_____ The accident was caused by poor road conditions.

_____ He achieved by the sweat of his brow.

_____ Criminal behavior is caused by poverty.

_____ His success is directly derived from his parents' wealth and influence.

Answers: **5-1.** I, E, E, I, E, E.

6. **Summarize Weiner's theory of attribution.**

6-1. Weiner proposed that attributions are made, not only in terms of an internal-external dimension, but also in terms of a stable-unstable dimension. Suppose that Sally makes a high score on an exam. She could attribute her score to her ability, an (internal/external) factor that is also (stable/unstable). If she attributed her success to her good mood, the attribution would be (internal/external) and (stable/unstable).

6-2. Or, Sally may think she did well because these types of test are always easy, an (<u>internal/external</u>) and (<u>stable/unstable</u>) attribution. If she attributes her score to luck, the attribution would be (<u>internal/external</u>) and (<u>stable/unstable</u>).

Answers: **6-1.** internal, stable, internal, unstable **6-2.** external, stable, external, unstable.

7. **Describe several types of attributional bias and cultural variations in attributional tendencies.**

    7-1. Define or describe the following:

        (a) fundamental attribution error:

        (b) actor-observer bias:

        (c) defensive attribution:

        (d) self-serving bias:

    7-2. Recent research has indicated that the attributional biases described above may not apply to all cultures. Since collectivist societies emphasize accomplishing the goals of the group over individual achievement, collectivist cultures are (<u>less/more</u>) likely to attribute other's behavior to personal traits. In other words, people from collectivist cultures tend to be (<u>less/more</u>) prone to the fundamental attribution error.

    7-3. Some evidence also indicates that people from collectivist societies would be more likely to attribute their *successes* to (<u>the ease of a task/unusual ability</u>). Similarly, they would be more likely to attribute their *failures* to (<u>bad luck/lack of effort</u>). Thus, in contrast with people from individualistic societies, people from collectivist cultures appear to be (<u>less/more</u>) prone to the self-serving bias.

Answers: **7-1.** (a) the tendency for observers to attribute an individual's behavior to *internal* rather than *external* factors (b) the tendency for observers to attribute an actor's behavior to internal rather than external factors, *and the tendency for actors to attribute their own behavior to external causes* (Yes, there is overlap between these two concepts. The fundamental attribution error is part of the actor-observer bias.) (c) the tendency to attribute other people's misfortunes to internal causes, that is, the tendency to blame the victim (d) the tendency to attribute our *successes* to internal factors and our *failures* to situational factors **7-2.** less, less **7-3.** the ease of a task, lack of effort, less.

CLOSE RELATIONSHIPS: LIKING AND LOVING

8. **Summarize evidence on the role of physical attractiveness and similarity in attraction.**

    8-1. Physical attractiveness is the key determinant of romantic attraction for:
        a. males
        b. females
        c. both males and females

    8-2. The *matching hypothesis* asserts that people tend to date and marry others who are:
        a. similar to them in attitudes and personality
        b. are approximately equal to them in physical attractiveness
        c. both of the above

8-3. Do opposites really attract, or do we like people who are similar? An overwhelming amount of research supports the idea that we are attracted to people who are (similar to/different from) us on several dimensions, especially in terms of attitudes and personality.

8-4. The similarity-attraction relationship extends to:

a. friendship

b. romantic relationships

c. both of the above

8-5. It is clear that similarity causes attraction: people are attracted to others who are similar. Does attraction also cause similarity? Some studies (also/do not) support this causal direction as well.

Answers: 8-1. c **8-2.** b **8-3.** similar to **8-4.** c **8-5.** also.

9. Summarize evidence on the role of reciprocity and romantic ideals in attraction.

9-1. We tend to like people who like us. We also tend to think that if we like others, they will like us. This is the principle of _____ in attraction.

9-2. What do we get from reciprocal relationships? First, our friends frequently provide positive feedback that enhances the way we feel about ourselves, the self-_____ effect. Second, our friends may verify our own view of ourselves, the self-_____ effect.

9-3. In romantic relationships, people constantly evaluate their partners against various ideals. Studies have found that the *greater the difference* between people's perceptions of their partners and their ideals, the (more/less) satisfied they are with the relationship and the more likely it is to (continue/dissolve).

9-4. The perception of a partner is subjective, of course. People may exaggerate the good characteristics and overlook the bad. Some research has found that, among couples, individuals view their (more favorably/ less favorably) than their partners view themselves. For example, suppose Jeff and Mary are a couple. Who would have the more favorable evaluation of Jeff? (Jeff/Mary).

9-5. Positive illusions about one's partner may make for a better relationship than will a cold view of reality. The happiest couples seem to be those who hold a reciprocated and (accurate/idealized) view of their partners.

Answers: 9-1. reciprocity **9-2.** enhancement, verification **9-3.** less, dissolve **9-4.** idealized, Mary **9-5.** idealized.

10. Describe various distinctions regarding love described by Berscheid and Hatfield, and Sternberg.

10-1. Hatfield and Berscheid divide love into two types, the intense emotional and sexual feelings of _____ love and the warm and tolerant affection of _____ love.

10-2. Sternberg further divides companionate love into _____, characterized by closeness and sharing, and _____, an intention to maintain a relationship in the face of difficulties.

10-3. Thus, Sternberg lists three factors or types of love. Of these, _____ love appears to peak early and drop off rapidly, while _____ and _____ gradually increase over time.

10-4. Commitment seems to be a particularly important factor in determining the durability of a relationship. For example, in a study of dating couples, _____ was more predictive of whether or not the relationship would continue than was overall love.

Answers: 10-1. passionate, companionate **10-2.** intimacy, commitment **10-3.** passion, intimacy, commitment **10-4.** commitment.

11. Summarize the evidence on love as a form of attachment.

11-1. In Chapter 11 we discussed types of attachment styles between infants and their caregivers. What *general* conclusion did Hazen and Shaver reach concerning the association between types of infant attachment and the love relationships of adults?

11-2. Write the names of the three infant attachment styles next to the appropriate letters below.

S: _____

A-A: _____

A: _____

11-3. Using the letters from the previous question, identify the types of romantic relations predicted by the infant attachment styles.

_____ As adults, these individuals tend to use casual sex as a way of getting physically close without the vulnerability of genuine intimacy and commitment.

_____ These people experience more emotional highs and lows in their relationships, find conflict stressful, have more negative feelings after dealing with conflict.

_____ These individuals easily develop close, committed, well-adjusted, long-lasting relationships.

Answers: 11-1. The three types of infant-caretaker attachments (also described in Chapter 11) tend to predict the love relationships that children have as adults. **11-2.** secure, anxious-ambivalent, avoidant **11-3.** A, A-A, S.

12. Discuss cross-cultural research on romantic relationship and evolutionary analyses of mating patterns.

12-1. While there are cross-cultural similarities in what people look for in mates, there are differences as well. The idea that one should be in love in order to marry is in large part an 18th-century invention of (Eastern/Western) culture. Arranged marriages, in which romantic love is less important, tends to be characteristic of (collectivist/individualist) societies.

12-2. With regard to physical appearance, researchers have found some standards that appear to be consistent across cultures, such as facial _____ and men's preference for a moderately low _____ ratio.

12-3. What do the two sexes look for in potential mates? While both sexes value physical attractiveness, cross-cultural studies have found that _____ place greater emphasis on youth and beauty, while _____ look for mates who can acquire resources, which can be invested in children.

12-4. If men emphasize physical attractiveness and women resources, how does this affect *tactics* that the sexes use in pursuing the opposite sex? In support of the evolutionary perspective, Buss has found that men tend to use tactics that emphasize their (looks/resources) and, women use tactics that emphasize their (looks/resources). For example, _____ might talk about their jobs or display what they own while _____ would try to enhance their makeup or clothing.

12-5. Tactics may involve deception. Both sexes may lie about their income, careers, and past relationships. Females tend to be more upset when males lie about their _____ and also their commitment to the woman. Males tend to be more upset when females lie about previous _____.

12-6. Women tend to (exaggerate/underestimate) men's potential commitment, perhaps as an evolved strategy for protection against consenting to sex and being abandoned. Men tend to overestimate women's _____ interest, perhaps as an evolved tactic of not overlooking sexual opportunities.

12-7. Sometimes individuals may try to attract someone already in a relationship, a phenomenon referred to by evolutionary researchers as mate _____. According to Schmitt and Buss, about _____ % of undergraduates report having made an attempt to poach. Tactics are similar to other forms of attraction except that more secrecy is involved. One tactic is to attempt to entice the other person to poach them by complaining about their current _____ or asking for "advice."

Answers: **12-1.** Western, collectivist **12-2.** symmetry, waist-to-hip **12-3.** males, females **12-4.** resources, looks, men, women **12-5.** resources (wealth, status, careers), promiscuity (sexual relationships, affairs) **12-6.** underestimate, sexual **12-7.** poaching, 50-60%, relationship.

ATTITUDES: MAKING SOCIAL JUDGMENTS

13. Describe the components and dimensions of attitudes.

13-1. Do you favor gun control? Do you like expressionist art? Do you hate cottage cheese? Your answers would be *evaluations* and would also express your _____ toward these objects of thought.

13-2. Attitudes are positive or negative _____ of objects of thought. They may include three components: cognition (thought), affect (emotion), and behavioral predispositions. For example, people have attitudes toward cottage cheese. List the three possible components of attitudes next to the examples below.

_____ He likes cottage cheese.

_____ He eats cottage cheese.

_____ He thinks: "Cottage cheese seems kind of lumpy."

13-3. Attitudes also vary along various dimensions: strength, accessibility, and ambivalence. Place the appropriate words in the blanks.

_____ How easily does the attitude come to mind?

_____ How durable or firmly held is the attitude?

_____ To what degree does the attitude include both positive and negative aspects?

14. Discuss the relations between attitudes and behavior.

14-1. As LaPiere found in his travels with a Chinese couple, attitudes (<u>are/are not</u>) consistently good predictors of behavior. One reason involves a failure to account for the attitude dimensions just described, attitude _____, accessibility, and ambivalence. For example, the stronger the attitude, the better it will predict _____.

14-2. In addition, the actual situation is likely to present new information: possible embarrassment, pressure from others, the unanticipated pleasant or unpleasant aspects of the situation, and so on. In other words, the behavioral component is just a *predisposition* that may change as a function of norms or other constraints of the _____.

15. Summarize evidence on source factors, message factors, and receiver factors that influence the process of persuasion.

15-1. If you are the *source* of a communication, the message giver:

(a) What factors mentioned in your text would you use to make yourself more *credible*? _____ and _____

(b) What else would you hope to emphasize about yourself? _____

15-2. With regard to *message* factors:

(a) Which is generally more effective, a one-sided message or a two-sided message? _____

(b) In presenting your argument, should you use every argument that you can think of or emphasize just the stronger arguments? _____

(c) Is simple repetition a good strategy, or should you say something just once? _____

(d) If you repeat something often enough, people will come to believe it. What is the name of this effect? _____

(e) Do fear appeals tend to work? _____ When? _____

15-3. With regard to receiver *factors* in persuasive communications:

(a) If you know in advance that someone is going to attempt to persuade you on a particular topic, you will be (<u>harder/easier</u>) to persuade. This is the factor referred to as _____.

(b) Resistance to persuasion is greater when an audience holds an attitude incompatible with the one being presented. In this case, the receiver will also tend to scrutinize arguments longer and with more skepticism, an effect referred to as _____ bias.

(c) In addition, in part because they may be anchored in networks of other beliefs that may also require change, _____ attitudes are more resistant to change.

16. **Discuss how learning processes can contribute to attitudes.**

16-1.   Following are examples that relate learning theory to attitude change. Indicate which type of learning—classical conditioning, operant conditioning, or observational learning—matches the example.

_____ Ralph hears Bob express a particular political attitude that is followed by thunderous applause. Thereafter, Ralph tends to express the same attitude.

_____ Advertisers pair soft drinks (and just about any other product) with attractive models. The audience likes the models and develops a stronger liking for the product.

_____ If you express an attitude that I like, I will agree with you, nod, say "mm-hmm," and so on. This will tend to strengthen your expression of that attitude.

Answers: 16-1. observational learning, classical conditioning, operant conditioning.

17. **Explain how cognitive dissonance can account for the effects of counter-attitudinal behavior and effort justification.**

(Dissonance is a truly complicated theory, but the following exercise should help. First read over the text, then see how you do on these questions. Here's a hint: Both problems are contrary to common-sense ideas of reward and punishment. Dissonance theory prides itself on making predictions contrary to conventional wisdom. The first item, below, indicates that we like behaviors accompanied by less, not more, reward; the second item indicates that we like behaviors accompanied by more, not less, discomfort.)

17-1.   Ralph bought a used car. However, the car uses a lot of gas, which he doesn't like because he strongly supports conserving energy. He rapidly concludes that conserving fuel isn't so important after all.

(a) Ralph has engaged in counter-attitudinal behavior. What were the two contradictory cognitions? (One is a thought about his *behavior*. The other is a thought about an important *attitude*.)

(b) Suppose the car was a real beauty, a rare antique worth much more than the price paid. Alternatively, suppose that the car was only marginally worth what was paid for it. In which case would dissonance be stronger? In which case would the attitude about gas guzzling be more likely to change?

17-2.   Suppose Bruce decides to join a particular club. (1) One possible scenario is that he must travel a great distance to attend, the club is very expensive, and he must give up much of his free time to become a member. (2) Alternatively, suppose that the traveling time is short, the club is inexpensive, and he need not give up any free time. In which case (1 or 2) will he tend to value his membership more, according to dissonance theory? Briefly, why?

Answers: 17-1. (a) I know I bought the car. I'm against the purchase of cars that waste gas. (b) The additional reward in the first situation produces less dissonance and will tend to leave Ralph's original attitude about gas consumption intact. Ralph's attitude about gas consumption will change more when there is less justification (in terms of the value of the car) for his action. As described in your text, we tend to have greater dissonance, and greater attitude change, when less reward accompanies our counter-attitudinal behavior. **17-2.** According to dissonance theory, he will value the membership more under alternative 1, even if the benefits of membership are slight, because people attempt to *justify the effort* expended in terms of the benefits received. (While dissonance is a genuine phenomenon with many of the characteristics that Festinger described in 1957, several other variables are operating, so it is difficult to predict when dissonance will occur.)

18. Relate self-perception theory and the elaboration likelihood model to attitude change.

18-1. At a cocktail party Bruce eats caviar. When asked whether he likes caviar he responds, "I'm eating it, so I guess I must like it." This example illustrates _____ theory.

18-2. According to self-perception theory, people infer their attitudes by observing their own _____. Thus, if people engage in a behavior that is not accompanied by high rewards, they are likely to infer that they (<u>enjoy/do not enjoy</u>) the behavior.

18-3. To illustrate the elaboration likelihood model: Suppose that you are to travel in Europe and must decide between two options, renting a car or traveling by train (on a Eurailpass). In the blanks below, indicate which persuasive route, central (C) or peripheral (P), is referred to in these examples.

_____ On the basis of train brochures, showing apparently wealthy and dignified travelers dining in luxury on the train while viewing the Alps, you opt for the train.

_____ Your travel agent is an expert who has advised many of your friends, and she strongly recommends that you take the train. You decide on the train.

_____ A friend urges you to consider details you hadn't previously considered: traffic, waiting in line, additional cab fare, and so on. You seek additional information, and after weighing the relative expenses and conveniences for four traveling together, you decide to rent a car.

18-4. In the elaboration likelihood model, the route that is easier and that involves the least amount of thinking is the _____ route. The route in which relevant information is sought out and carefully pondered is the _____ route. Elaboration, which involves thinking about the various complexities of the situation, is more likely to occur when the _____ route is used.

18-5. Elaboration leads to (<u>more enduring/transient</u>) changes in attitudes. In addition, elaboration (i.e., the more central route) is (<u>more/less</u>) likely to predict behavior.

Answers: 18-1. self-perception **18-2.** behavior, enjoy **18-3.** P, P, C **18-4.** peripheral, central, central **18-5.** more enduring, more.

CONFORMITY AND OBEDIENCE: YIELDING TO OTHERS

19. Summarize research on the determinants of conformity.

19-1. Briefly summarize the general procedure and results of the Asch line-judging studies.

19-2. Suppose there are six accomplices, one real subject, and that one of the accomplices dissents from the majority. What effect will this "dissenter" have on conformity by the real subject?

19-3. Several factors affect conformity, as you may have observed. For example, people are more likely to conform in _____ situations, when the "correct" answer is very unclear.

Answers: 19-1. Subjects were asked to judge which of three lines matched a standard line, a judgment that was actually quite easy to make. Only one of the subjects was a real subject, however; the others were accomplices of the experimenter, who gave wrong answers on key trials. The result was that a majority of the real subjects tended to conform to the wrong judgments of the majority on at least some trials. **19-2.** Conformity will be dramatically reduced, to about one-fourth the frequency without a dissenter. **19-3.** ambiguous.

20. Describe the Featured Study on obedience to authority and the ensuing controversy generated by Milgram's research.

20-1. Two individuals at a time participated in Milgram's initial study, but only one was a real subject. The other "subject" was an accomplice of the experimenter, an actor. By a rigged drawing of slips of paper the real subject became the _____, and the accomplice became the _____. There were a total of _____ subjects, or teachers, in the initial study.

20-2. The experimenter strapped the learner into a chair and stationed the teacher at an apparatus from which he could, supposedly, deliver electric shocks to the learner. The teacher was to start at 15 volts, and each time the learner made a mistake, the teacher was supposed to _____ the level of shock by 15 volts—up to a level of 450 volts.

20-3. What percentage of the subjects continued to obey instructions, thereby increasing the shock all the way up to 450 volts? _____

20-4. What is the major conclusion to be drawn from this study? Why are the results of interest?

20-5. As you might imagine, Milgram's studies on obedience were controversial, producing both detractors and defenders. Following are summaries of the objections, involving both *generality* and *ethics*, followed by possible counter-arguments. Complete the counter-arguments by selecting the appropriate alternatives.

(a) "Subjects in an experiment expect to obey an experimenter, so the results don't generalize to the real world."

The flaw in this argument, according to Milgram's defenders, is that in many aspects of the real world, including the military and business worlds, obedience (is not/<u>is also</u>) considered appropriate. So, Milgram's results (<u>do</u>/do not) generalize to the real world.

(b) "Milgram's procedure, by which subjects were allowed to think that they had caved in to commands to harm an innocent victim, was potentially emotionally damaging to the subjects. Milgram's experiment was unethical."

Milgram's defenders assert that the brief distress experienced by the subjects was relatively (<u>slight</u>/ great), in comparison with the important insights that emerged.

Answers: 20-1. teacher, learner, 40 **20-2.** increase **20-3.** 65 percent **20-4.** The major conclusion is that ordinary people will tend to obey an authority, even when their obedience could result in considerable harm (and perhaps even death) to others. The result is of interest because it suggests that such obedience, as occurs in war atrocities (e.g., in World War II, at Mi Lai in Viet Nam, in Cambodia, Rwanda, Yugoslavia, and throughout history), may not be due so much to the evil *character* of the participants as to pressures in the situation. (Milgram's results are also of interest because most people would not expect them: even psychiatric experts predicted that fewer than 1% of the subjects would go all the way to 450 volts.) **20-5.** (a) is also, do (b) slight. (Many psychologists today share the critics' concerns, however, and the study has not been replicated in the United States since the 1970s.)

21. Discuss cultural variations in conformity and obedience.

21-1. As with other cross-cultural comparisons, replications in other countries yield some similarities and some differences. Indicate true (T) or false (F) for the following statements.

_____ The obedience effect found by Milgram seems to be a uniquely American phenomenon.

_____ In replications of the Milgram studies in several European countries, obedience levels were even higher than those in the United States.

_____ Replications of the Asch line-judging studies have found that cultures that emphasize collectivism are more conforming than are those that emphasize individualism.

Answers: 21-1. F, T, T.

BEHAVIOR IN GROUPS: JOINING WITH OTHERS

22. Describe the Stanford Prison Simulation and its implications.

22-1. The Stanford Prison study was conducted by Philip Zimbardo in the 1970s. A total of 24 undergraduate subjects were pre-screened and _____ assigned to be either guards or prisoners in a simulated prison on the campus at Stanford.

22-2. It is important to note that the participants were normal, psychologically healthy college students without obvious character flaws. Yet within a few days, subjects assigned to be _____ became sadistic and brutal, and subjects assigned to be the _____ became, for the most part, listless and apathetic. In other words, subjects tended to behave in line with the social _____ associated with the positions of guards and prisoners.

22-3. Although done more than 30 years ago, the study resonates with recent events involving American military personnel at Abu Ghraib prison in Iraq. While the government tended to blame character flaws (i.e., a few bad apples), Zimbardo would look for situational pressures. What would lead normal Americans to commit sadistic and brutal acts? Like the Milgram study, this simulation demonstrates once again the power of (personality differences/the situation).

22-4. How can we decrease the likelihood that prison guards will engage in torture or abuse? Zimbardo has several specific suggestions involving:

a. supervision of guards, sanctions for abuses, and accountability in the chain of command.

b. weeding out the individuals with moral issues.

c. counting on people's inherent good will.

23.   Discuss the nature of groups and the bystander effect.

23-1.   The word *group* doesn't have the same meaning for social psychologists that it does for everyone else. As I look out across my social psychology class on a Tuesday morning, I might say to myself, "Hm, quite a large group we have here today." Actually, my class is not a group in social psychological terms because it lacks one, and perhaps two, of the essential characteristics of a group. A group consists of two or more individuals who (a) _____ and (b) are _____ .

23-2.   Which of the following are groups, as defined by social psychologists?

_____ A husband and wife.

_____ The board of directors of a corporation.

_____ A sports team.

_____ Spectators at an athletic event.

_____ Shoppers at a mall.

23-3.   What is the bystander effect?

23-4.   Why does the bystander effect occur? In part because the presence of onlookers not doing anything produces an _____ situation (no one seems to be upset, so maybe it's not an emergency). In addition, the presence of others causes a _____ of responsibility (we're all responsible, or else someone else will do it).

Answers: **23-1.** (a) interact (b) interdependent **23-2.** The first three are groups, and the last two are not. **23-3.** When people are in groups (or at least in the presence of others), they are less likely to help than when they are alone. Or, the greater the number of onlookers in an emergency, the less likely any one of them is to assist the person in need. **23-4.** ambiguous, diffusion.

24.   Summarize evidence on group productivity, including social loafing.

24-1.   Individual productivity in large groups is frequently less than it is in small groups. Two factors contribute to this decreased productivity: a loss of _____ among workers in larger groups (e.g., efforts of one person interfere with those of another) and decreased _____ resulting from *social loafing*.

24-2.   Social loafing is the reduction in _____ expended by individuals working in groups compared to people working alone.

24-3.   In some situations in which members are convinced that individual performance is crucial and that excellent group performance will be rewarded, social loafing is (<u>less/more</u>) likely to occur. Social loafing is also less frequent in close-knit groups that emphasize group goals. Social loafing is less common in (<u>collectivist/individualistic</u>) societies, for example.

Answers: **24-1.** efficiency (coordination), effort **24-2.** effect **24-3.** less, collectivist.

25. **Describe group polarization and groupthink.**

25-1. This problem should help you understand the concept of group polarization. Suppose that a group of five corporate executives meet to decide whether, and by how much, to raise the cost of their product (between 0% and 20%). Before they meet as a group, the decisions of the five executives (expressed as a percentage) are as follows: +20%, +15%, +15%, +5%, and +5%. After they meet as a group, which of the following is most likely to be the result? Assume that group polarization occurs.

   a. +15%, +10%, +5%, +5%, and +0%

   b. +20%, +15%, +15%, +15%, and +10%

   c. +15%, +10%, +10%, +5%, and +5%

   d. +10%, +10%, +10%, +0%, and +0%

25-2. What is group polarization?

25-3. Have you ever been in a group when you thought to yourself, "This is a stupid idea, but my best friends seem to be going along with it, so I won't say anything." If so, you may have been in a group afflicted with groupthink. Groupthink is characterized by, among other things, an intense pressure to _____ to group opinions accompanied by very low tolerance for dissent.

25-4. Groups afflicted with groupthink tend to ignore important information. Members are under pressure to avoid presenting conflicting views, and they (underestimate/overestimate) the unanimity of the group.

25-5. Recent evidence has also found that group members tend not to pool information. That is, they tend to:

   a. discuss information that is commonly known among members.

   b. explore information that is unique to individual members.

25-6. According to Janis, the major cause of groupthink is high group _____, the group spirit or attraction that members have for the group. Other factors that may contribute to groupthink include *isolation*, (directive/nondirective) leadership, and *stress* accompanying the decision process.

25-7. Much of the support for groupthink consists of (laboratory studies/retrospective accounts). The theory is difficult to test in formal experiments, but it is a fascinating viewpoint that will undoubtedly inspire continued research.

Answers: 25-1. b **25-2.** Group polarization is the tendency for a group's decision to shift toward a more extreme position in the direction that individual members are *already leaning*. **25-3.** conform **25-4.** overestimate **25-5.** a **25-6.** cohesiveness, directive **25-7.** retrospective accounts.

26. **Explain how the chapter highlighted three of the text's unifying themes.**

26-1.   This chapter again illustrates psychology's commitment to empirical research. When people hear the results of psychological studies, they frequently conclude that the research just confirms common sense. Dispute this view by listing and describing *at least one study* with results that are not predictable from common sense assumptions.

26-2.   Cross-cultural differences and similarities also reflect one of the unifying themes. People conform, obey, attribute, and love throughout the world, but the manner and extent to which they do so are affected by cultural factors. Important among these factors is the degree to which a culture has an _____ or _____ orientation.

26-3.   Finally, the chapter provides several illustrations of the way in which our view of the world is highly subjective. For example, we tend to make ability and personality judgments based on people's physical _____; see what we expect to see as a result of the cognitive structures, termed social _____; distort judgments of physical lines based on pressures to _____; and make foolish decisions when we become enmeshed in the group phenom-enon, known as _____.

Answers: 26-1. This chapter has described at least three studies that defy the predictions of common sense or of experts. (1) Concerning *Milgram's studies*, psychiatrists incorrectly predicted that fewer than 1% of the subjects would go to 450 volts. (2) Results from *cognitive dissonance* studies are frequently the opposite of common sense. For example, common sense would suggest that the more people are paid, the more they would like the tasks for which they receive payment; dissonance researchers found that the opposite is true; people paid *more* liked the tasks *less*. (3) Common sense might predict that the larger the number of people who see someone in need of help, the more likely any one is to offer help. Research on the *bystander effect* consistently finds the opposite result. **26-2.** individualistic, collectivistic **26-3.** attractiveness (appearance), schemas, conform, groupthink.

PERSONAL APPLICATION • **UNDERSTANDING PREJUDICE**

27. **Relate person perception processes and attributional bias to prejudice.**

27-1.   Prejudice is a negative _____ toward others based on group membership. Like other attitudes, prejudice may include affective, _____, and behavioral components.

27-2.   The cognitive component of prejudice may be thought of as a schema about groups. This type of schema is frequently referred to as a _____.

27-3.   Stereotypes are part of the *subjectivity* of person perception. People tend to see what they expect to see, and when stereotypes are activated, people see and remember information that (is/is not) congruent with their stereotype.

27-4.   Stereotypes are highly accessible and frequently activated automatically, so that even though people reject prejudiced ideas, stereotypes (can not/may still) influence behavior.

27-5. Our *attributional biases* are also likely to maintain or augment prejudice. For example, observers tend to attribute success in men to (<u>ability/luck</u>) but success in women to (<u>ability/luck</u>).

27-6. People may also attribute other people's behavior to internal traits, the bias referred to as the _____ attribution error.

27-7. When people experience adversity such as prejudice, we are also likely to attribute their misfortune to character flaws, a predisposition referred to as defensive attribution or _____ blaming.

Answers: 27-1. attitude, cognitive **27-2.** stereotype **27-3.** is **27-4.** may still **27-5.** ability, luck **27-6.** fundamental **27-7.** victim.

28. Relate principles of attitude formation and intergroup competition to prejudice.

28-1. Attitudes are to a large extent learned. For example, if someone makes a disparaging remark about an ethnic group that is followed by approval, the approval is likely to function as a _____ that increases that person's tendency to make similar remarks in the future. This is the learning process known as _____. Or, if someone simply *observes* another person making such a remark, the observer may acquire the tendency to make similar remarks through the process known as _____.

28-2. Ingroup members view themselves as different from the outgroup in several ways. First, they tend to see their group as superior to outgroups, a tendency known as _____. In addition, they see themselves as relatively diverse or heterogeneous and outgroup members as relatively _____.

28-3. The tendency for ingroup members to see outgroup members as highly (<u>dissimilar/similar</u>) to one another is known as the illusion of outgroup _____.

28-4. Ingroup favoritism is something that doesn't go away. Prejudice clearly exists in modern societies, but it tends to be of the more (<u>subtle/blatant</u>) form. By one estimate, only about _____% of people display the more extreme form of prejudice involving intense hatred and aggression.

Answers: 28-1. reinforcer, operant conditioning, observational learning (modeling) **28-2.** ethnocentrism, homogeneous **28-3.** similar, homogeneity **28-4.** subtle, 10.

29. Relate ingroups, outgroups, and threats to social identity to prejudice.

29-1. People form into groups. The groups of which they are members of are called ingroups, and groups of which they are not members of are called outgroups. People tend to think that their ingroups are superior to _____. Thus, one source of hostility to outgroups is simply group formation.

29-2. People also tend to think that members of their ingroups are very different from one another (i.e., heterogeneous), and that members of outgroups are very similar to one another. In other words, in their perception of outgroups people experience the illusion of outgroup _____. This illusion makes it easier to sustain stereotypic beliefs about outgroups.

29-3. Hostility toward outgroups is also fostered both by threats to one's personal or social identity. For example, flunking a test may be a threat to your _____ identity; the low pass-rate of your social organization may be a threat to your _____ identity. Either threat may increase outgroup derogation.

Answers: **29-1.** outgroups **29-2.** homogeneity **29-3.** personal, social.

CRITICAL THINKING APPLICATION • WHOM CAN YOU TRUST? ANALYZING CREDIBILITY AND SOCIAL INFLUENCE TACTICS

30. **Discuss some useful criteria for evaluating credibility and some standard social influence strategies.**

30-1. We are constantly bombarded with information designed to persuade. Sometimes we are persuaded and happy about it, and sometimes we regret the outcome. How can we resist attempts at manipulation? Two tactics are discussed in this section: evaluating the _____ of the source, and learning about several widely-used social _____ strategies.

30-2. To assess credibility, consider these questions: Do they have a _____ interest? If so, information they provide may not be objective. What are the source's _____? Although degrees do not certify competence, they may indicate relevant training.

30-3. Is the information inconsistent with _____ views on the issue? If not, one should ponder why others haven't arrived at the same conclusion. Finally, what was the _____ of analysis used? One should be particularly skeptical if the source relies on anecdotes or focuses on small inconsistencies in accepted beliefs.

30-4. In addition, learn to recognize social influence strategies. Following are several scenarios. Identify each with one of the four strategies discussed: *foot-in-the-door*, *reciprocity*, *lowball*, and *scarcity*.

_____ Scenario 1: Mail solicitation for a magazine subscription. "Enclosed is a packet of seeds, free of charge, just for you. We hope you enjoy the beautiful flowers they produce! Also, you will benefit from subscribing to Outdoor Beauty magazine. We've enclosed a free copy."

_____ Scenario 2: Newspaper ad. "This weekend only—mammoth blowout car deals!! These beauties will go fast!!!! Don't miss this once-in-a-lifetime opportunity!!"

_____ Scenario 3: A college development office calling alumni. First week: "We don't care about the amount, perhaps $5, just so that we can ensure full participation." You commit to $5. Next week: "Would you become one of our member donors with a contribution of $100?"

Scenario 4: On the phone with a wholesale camera salesman. "Yes, we do have the XXY Camera at $499.00 plus tax. We'll ship that this afternoon. Now, did you want the new lens or the old lens with that? The new lens would be an additional $99. Did you want the carrying case also? " (Your assumption was that the so-called extras were included in the original price.)

Scenario 5: Mail solicitation. First week: "Would you answer this brief survey for us? There are only 12 questions." Next week: "Thanks for responding to our survey! We desperately need money for this worthwhile (candidate, school, charity, etc.)."

Scenario 6: At the car dealer. "Do we have a deal, then, at $22,800 plus tax? Great!! Let me check with my manager to see if that price includes dealer prep and the CD player." (Fifteen minutes pass while the salesman supposedly checks.) "Well, I tried, but the manager won't budge. Fortunately it's not much additional!"

Answers: 30-1. credibility, influence **30-2.** vested, credentials **30-3.** conventional, method **30-4.** reciprocity, scarcity, foot-in-the-door, lowball, foot-in-the-door, lowball.

Review of Key Terms

Attitudes	Group	Outgroup
Attributions	Group cohesiveness	Passionate love
Bystander effect	Group polarization	Person perception
Channel	Groupthink	Prejudice
Cognitive dissonance	Illusory correlation	Receiver
Collectivism	Individualism	Reciprocity
Commitment	Ingroup	Reciprocity norm
Companionate love	Internal attributions	Self-serving bias
Conformity	Interpersonal attraction	Social loafing
Defensive attribution	Intimacy	Social psychology
Discrimination	Lowball technique	Social roles
External attributions	Matching hypothesis	Social schemas
Foot-in-the-door technique	Message	Source
Fundamental attribution error	Obedience	Stereotypes

1. The branch of psychology concerned with the way individuals' thoughts, feelings, and behaviors are influenced by others.

2. The process of forming impressions of others.

3. Clusters of ideas about categories of social events and people, which we use to organize the world around us.

4. Widely held beliefs that people have certain characteristics because of their membership in a particular group.

5. Error that occurs when we thnk that two events are strongly associated even though they are not.

_____ 6. Inferences that people draw about the causes of events, others' behavior, and their own behavior.

_____ 7. Attributing the causes of behavior to personal dispositions, traits, abilities, and feelings.

_____ 8. Attributing the causes of behavior to situational demands and environmental constraints.

_____ 9. The tendency of an observer to favor internal attributions in explaining the behavior of an actor.

_____ 10. The tendency to blame victims for their misfortune so that we feel less likely to be victimized in a similar way.

_____ 11. The tendency to attribute our positive outcomes to personal factors and our negative outcomes to situational factors.

_____ 12. Liking or positive feelings toward another.

_____ 13. Getting people to agree to a small request to increase the chances that they will agree to a larger request later.

_____ 14. The observation that males and females of approximately equal physical attractiveness are likely to select each other as partners.

_____ 15. Liking those who show that they like us.

_____ 16. Widely shared expectations about how people in certain positions are supposed to behave.

_____ 17. A complete absorption in another person that includes tender sexual feelings and the agony and ecstasy of intense emotion.

_____ 18. A warm, trusting, tolerant affection for another whose life is deeply intertwined with one's own.

_____ 19. Warmth, closeness, and sharing in a relationship.

_____ 20. The intent to maintain a relationship in spite of the difficulties and costs that may arise.

_____ 21. Positive or negative evaluation of objects of thought; may include cognitive, behavioral, and emotional components.

_____ 22. The person who sends a communication.

_____ 23. The person to whom the message is sent.

_____ 24. The information transmitted by the source.

_____ 25. The medium through which the message is sent.

_____ 26. The rule that we should pay back when we receive something from others; may be used in an influence strategy.

_____ 27. Behaving differently, usually unfairly, toward the members of a group.

_____ 28. Situation that exists when related cognitions are inconsistent.

_____ 29. Yielding to real or imagined social pressure.

_____ 30. Involves getting someone to commit to an attractive deal before its hidden costs are revealed.

_____ 31. A form of compliance that occurs when people follow direct commands, usually from someone in a position of authority.

_____ 32. Involves putting group goals ahead of personal goals and defining one's identity in terms of the group one belongs to.

_____ 33. Involves putting personal goals ahead of group goals and defining one's identity in terms of personal attributes rather than group memberships.

_____ 34. Two or more individuals who interact and are interdependent.

_____ 35. The apparent paradox that people are less likely to provide needed help when they are in groups than when they are alone.

_____ 36. A reduction in effort by individuals when they work together, as compared to when they work by themselves.

_____ 37. Situation that occurs when group discussion strengthens a group's dominant point of view and produces a shift toward a more extreme decision in that direction.

_____ 38. Phenomenon that occurs when members of a cohesive group emphasize concurrence at the expense of critical thinking in arriving at a decision.

_____ 39. The group one belongs to and identifies with.

_____ 40. People who are not a part of the ingroup.

_____ 41. The strength of the liking relationships linking group members to each other and to the group itself.

_____ 42. A negative attitude held toward members of a group.

Answers: 1. social psychology **2.** person perception **3.** social schemas **4.** stereotypes **5.** illusory correlation **6.** attributions **7.** internal attributions **8.** external attributions **9.** fundamental attribution error **10.** defensive attribution **11.** self-serving bias **12.** interpersonal attraction **13.** foot-in-the-door technique **14.** matching hypothesis **15.** reciprocity **16.** social roles **17.** passionate love **18.** companionate love **19.** intimacy **20.** commitment **21.** attitudes **22.** source **23.** receiver **24.** message **25.** channel **26.** reciprocity norm **27.** discrimination **28.** cognitive dissonance **29.** conformity **30.** lowball technique **31.** obedience **32.** collectivism **33.** individualism **34.** group **35.** bystander effect **36.** social loafing **37.** group polarization **38.** groupthink **39.** ingroup **40.** outgroup **41.** group cohesiveness **42.** prejudice.

Review of Key People

Solomon Asch	Elaine Hatfield	Stanley Milgram
Ellen Berscheid	Cindy Hazen and Phillip Shaver	Bernard Weiner
David Buss	Fritz Heider	Philip Zimbardo
Leon Festinger	Irving Janis	

_____ 1. Was the first to describe the crucial dimension along which we make attributions; developed balance theory.

_____ 2. Did research on infant-caregiver attachment patterns as predictors of adult romantic relationships.

_____ 3. With Hatfield, did research describing two types of romantic love: passionate and companionate.

_____ 4. Originator of the theory of cognitive dissonance.

_____ 5. Devised the "line-judging" procedure in pioneering investigations of conformity.

_____ 6. In a series of "fake shock" experiments, studied the tendency to obey authority figures.

_____ 7. Developed the concept of groupthink.

_____ 8. Under the name of Walster, did early study on dating and physical attractiveness; with Berscheid, described types of romantic love.

_____ 9. Concluded that attribution has not only on internal-external dimension but a stable-unstable dimension.

10. Proposed an evolutionary view of attraction; did cross-cultural research on priorities in mate selection.

11. Well-known for the Stanford Prison Simulation.

Answers: 1. Heider **2.** Hazen & Shaver **3.** Berscheid **4.** Festinger **5.** Asch **6.** Milgram **7.** Janis **8.** Hatfield **9.** Weiner **10.** Buss **11.** Zimbardo.

Self-Quiz

1. Which of the following characteristics do we tend to attribute to physically attractive people?
   a. low intelligence
   b. friendliness
   c. unpleasantness
   d. coldness

2. Cognitive structures that guide our perceptions of people and events are termed
   a. attributions
   b. stigmata
   c. schemas
   d. denkmals

3. Inferences that we make about the causes of our own and others' behavior are termed
   a. attributions
   b. stigmata
   c. schemas
   d. denkmals

4. Bruce performed very well on the examination, which he attributed to native ability and hard work. Which attributional bias does this illustrate?
   a. the fundamental attribution error
   b. the actor-observer bias
   c. the self-serving bias
   d. illusory correlation

5. According to this viewpoint, men emphasize physical attractiveness in mate selection, while women emphasize the ability to acquire resources. Which theory does this describe?
   a. evolutionary theory
   b. cognitive dissonance
   c. sexual propensity theory
   d. attribution theory

6. Which of the following could be an example of the fundamental attribution error?
   a. Ralph described himself as a failure.
   b. Ralph thought that the reason he failed was that he was sick that day.
   c. Jayne said Ralph failed because the test was unfair.
   d. Sue explained Ralph's failure in terms of his incompetence and laziness.

7. Which influence technique involves asking for a small request in order to increase the likelihood of the target complying with a larger request later?
   a. foot-in-the-door
   b. feigned scarcity
   c. reciprocity norm
   d. lowball

8. Which of the following is, in general, likely to reduce the persuasiveness of a message?
   a. The receiver's viewpoint is already fairly close to that of the message.
   b. The receiver has been forewarned about the message.
   c. A two-sided appeal is used.
   d. The source is physically attractive.

9. Subjects in Group A are paid $1 for engaging in a dull task. Subjects in Group B are paid $20 for the same task. Which theory would predict that Group A subjects would enjoy the task more?
   a. balance
   b. cognitive dissonance
   c. reinforcement theory
   d. observational learning

10. In making a decision, you rely on the opinion of experts and the behavior of your best friends. According to the elaboration likelihood model, which route to persuasion have you used?
    a. central
    b. peripheral
    c. attributional
    d. 66

11. Which of the following is the best statement of conclusion concerning Milgram's classic study involving the learner, teacher, and ostensible shock?
    a. Under certain circumstances, people seem to enjoy the opportunity to be cruel to others.
    b. People have a strong tendency to obey an authority even if their actions may harm others.
    c. The more people there are who observe someone in need of help, the less likely any one is to help.
    d. Aggression seems to be a more potent force in human nature than had previously been suspected.

12. Which of the following is most likely to function as a group?
    a. shoppers at a mall
    b. the audience in a theater
    c. the board of trustees of a college
    d. passengers in an airplane

13. Someone witnesses a car accident. In which of the following cases is that individual most likely to stop and render assistance?
    a. Only she saw the accident.
    b. She and one other individual saw the accident.
    c. She and 18 others saw the accident.
    d. The other observers are pedestrians.

14. Suppose the original decisions of members of a group are represented by the following numbers in a group polarization study: 2, 3, 3, 4, 5. The range of numbers possible in the study is from 1 to 7. Which of the following possible shifts in decisions would demonstrate polarization?
    a. 1, 2, 3, 3, 4
    b. 3, 3, 4, 5, 5
    c. 4, 5, 6, 6, 7
    d. 3, 3, 6, 6, 6

15. According to Janis, what is the major cause of groupthink?
    a. strong group cohesion
    b. diffusion of responsibility
    c. the tendency of group members to grandstand
    d. group conflict

Answers: 1. b **2.** c **3.** a **4.** c **5.** a **6.** d **7.** a **8.** b **9.** b **10.** b **11.** b **12.** c **13.** a **14.** a **15.** a

InfoTrac Keywords

Attributions
Cognitive Dissonance
Group cohesiveness
Group polarization

Groupthink
Illusory correlation
Individualism and collectivism

Self-serving Bias
Social loafing
Stereotype and prejudice

Appendix B
STATISTICAL METHODS

Review of Key Ideas

1. **Describe several ways to use frequency distributions and graphs to organize numerical data.**

   1-1. Identify the following methods that are commonly used to present numerical data.

   (a) _____   (b) _____

   1-2. What data are usually plotted along the:

   (a) horizontal axis?

   (b) vertical axis?

   Answers: 1-1. (a) histogram (b) frequency polygram **1-2.** (a) the possible scores (b) the frequency of each score.

2. **Describe the measures of central tendency and variability discussed in the text.**

    2-1.   Tell which measure of central tendency–the mean, median, or mode–would be most useful in the following situations.

    (a) Which measure would be best for analyzing the salaries of all workers in a small, low-paying print shop that includes two high-salaried managers? Explain your answer.

    (b) Which measure would tell us the most common shoe size for men?

    (c) Which measure would be best for pairing players at a bowling match, using their individual past scores, so that equals play against equals?

    (d) Where do most of the scores pile up in a positively skewed distribution?

Answers: 2-1. (a) the median, because the high salaries of the two management persons would distort the mean (b) the mode (c) the mean (d) at the bottom end of the distribution.

3. **Describe the normal distribution and its use in psychological testing.**

    3-1.   Answer the following questions regarding the normal distribution.

    (a) Where do the mean, median, and mode fall in a normal distribution?

    (b) What is the unit of measurement in a normal distribution?

    (c) Where are most of the scores located in a normal distribution?

    (d) Approximately what percentage of scores falls above 2 standard deviations in a normal distribution?

(e) If your percentile ranking on the SAT was 84, what would your SAT score be (see Fig. B.7 in the text)?

Answers: 3-1. (a) at the center (b) the standard deviation (c) around the mean (plus or minus 1 standard deviation) (d) 2.3% (e) 600 (approximately).

4. **Explain how the magnitude and direction of a correlation is reflected in scatter diagrams and how correlation is related to predictive power.**

4-1. Answer the following questions about the magnitude and direction of a correlation, as reflected in scattergrams.

(a) Where do the data points fall in a scattergram that shows a perfect correlation?

(b) What happens to the data points in a scattergram when the magnitude of correlation decreases?

(c) What does a high negative correlation indicate?

4-2. Answer the following questions regarding the predictive power of correlations.

(a) How does one compute the coefficient of determination?

(b) What does the coefficient of determination tell us?

(c) What could we say if the sample study used in the text showed a correlation of -.50 between SAT scores and time watching television?

Answers: 4-1. (a) in a straight line (b) They scatter away from a straight line. (c) High scores on one variable (X) are accompanied by low scores on the other variable (Y). **4-2.** (a) by squaring the correlation coefficient (b) It indicates the percentage of variation in one variable that can be predicted based on the other variable. (c) Knowledge of TV viewing allows one to predict 25% of the variation on SAT scores (.50 x .50 = .25).

5. **Explain how the null hypothesis is used in hypothesis testing, and relate it to statistical significance.**

5-1. Answer the following questions regarding the null hypothesis and statistical significance.

(a) In the sample study correlating SAT scores and television viewing, the findings supported the null hypothesis. What does this mean?

(b) What level of significance do most researchers demand as a minimum before rejecting the null hypothesis?

(c) What is the probability of making an error when a researcher rejects the null hypothesis at the .01 level of significance?

Answers: 5-1. (a) We cannot conclude that there is a significant negative correlation between SAT scores and television viewing. (b) the .05 level (c) 1 in 100.

Review of Key Terms

Coefficient of determination
Correlation coefficient
Descriptive statistics
Frequency distribution
Frequency polygon
Histogram
Inferential statistics

Mean
Median
Mode
Negatively skewed distribution
Normal distribution
Null hypothesis
Percentile score

Positively skewed distribution
Scatter diagram
Standard deviation
Statistics
Statistical significance
Variability

_____ 1. The use of mathematics to organize, summarize, and interpret numerical data.

_____ 2. An orderly arrangement of scores indicating the frequency of each score or group of scores.

_____ 3. A bar graph that presents data from a frequency distribution.

_____ 4. A line figure used to present data from a frequency distribution.

_____ 5. Type of statistics used to organize and summarize data.

_____ 6. The arithmetic average of a group of scores.

_____ 7. The score that falls in the center of a group of scores.

_____ 8. The score that occurs most frequently in a group of scores.

_____ 9. A distribution in which most scores pile up at the high end of the scale.

_____ 10. A distribution in which most scores pile up at the low end of the scale.

_____ 11. The extent to which the scores in a distribution tend to vary or depart from the mean.

_____ 12. An index of the amount of variability in a set of data.

_____ 13. A bell-shaped curve that represents the pattern in which many human characteristics are dispersed in the population.

_____ 14. Figure representing the percentage of persons who score below (or above) any particular score.

_____ 15. A numerical index of the degree of relationship between two variables.

_____ 16. A graph in which paired X and Y scores for each subject are plotted as single points.

_____ 17. The percentage of variation in one variable that can be predicted based on another variable.

_____ 18. Statistics employed to interpret data and draw conclusions.

_____ 19. The hypothesis that there is no relationship between two variables.

_____ 20. Said to exist when the probability is very low that observed findings can be attributed to chance.

Answers: **1.** statistics **2.** frequency distribution **3.** histogram **4.** frequency polygon **5.** descriptive statistics **6.** mean **7.** median **8.** mode **9.** negatively skewed distribution **10.** positively skewed distribution **11.** variability **12.** standard deviation **13.** normal distribution **14.** percentile score **15.** correlation coefficient **16.** scatter diagram **17.** coefficient of determination **18.** inferential statistics **19.** null hypothesis **20.** statistical significance.

Appendix C

INDUSTRIAL/ORGANIZATIONAL PSYCHOLOGY

Review of Key Ideas

1. **Discuss the settings and content areas of I/O psychology.**

    1-1.   In a humorous commentary several years ago psychologist Jerry Burger said he longed to hear, just once, someone in a theater asking, "Is there a social psychologist in the house?" (Burger, 1986). Burger's comments reflect not only his wish that psychology be recognized outside academia but his desire for application. The field of _____ (I/O) psychology is an applied field, and in some respects it is the application of principles derived from social psychology, and a variety of other fields of psychology, to the world of _____.

    1-2.   The setting for the *practice* of I/O psychology is the workplace. The settings for research in I/O psychology include (<u>laboratory/field settings/both</u>).

    1-3.   There are three primary areas of interest for the I/O psychologists. Write the names of these subareas in the blanks below, next to the initial letters that represent them.

    P: _____ psychology

    O: _____ psychology

    HF: _____ _____ psychology

    1-4.   Following are descriptions of the three subareas of I/O psychology. Match the subareas with the descriptions by placing the letters from the previous question in the appropriate blanks.

    _____ Examines the way human beings fit the work environment; concerned with the interface between human beings and the tools and resources they use.

    _____ Tests and selects employees, tries to match the abilities of the person to the job requirements.

    _____ Concerned with job satisfaction, relationships among employees, social adaptation of the worker to the workplace.

1-5. Below are possible problems encountered in a workplace. Match the subareas with the problems (realizing that there may be overlap among these areas).

_____ The employees slow their pace of work and express dissatisfaction with leadership.

_____ Several employees unintentionally push the wrong buttons on the machines in their work environments.

_____ Ralph tests out poorly in accounting but has potential for working with the gyroplex machine.

Answers: 1-1. Industrial/organizational, work (the workplace, industry) **1-2.** both **1-3.** human factors (or human engineering), personnel, organizational **1-4.** HF, P, O **1-5.** O, HF, P.

2. Discuss how the systems approach relates to the subfields of I/O psychology.

2-1. The three subareas of I/O psychology generally do not operate independently. They are part of an overall sociotechnical _____, and changing one part affects the other parts.

2-2. For example, using email in place of meetings affects not only the way employees interface with machines (the _____ _____ subarea of I/O), but also the fit between employee characteristics and the job (the _____ subarea) as well as the way employees interact with one another (the _____ subarea).

2-3. Because the subareas of I/O are interdependent, the general approach of I/O psychology is termed a _____ approach.

Answers: 2-1. system **2-2.** human factors (human engineering), personnel, organizational **2-3.** systems.

3. Describe how the three subfields of I/O psychology emerged historically.

3-1. The first of the three subareas of I/O psychology to appear historically was _____ psychology. This field emerged as a result of several cultural influences. Sir Francis Galton, Darwin's cousin, developed the first psychological _____ of abilities; Binet developed the first recognized _____ test; and Munsterberg developed ability tests for a variety of applications (e.g., testing for ship captains, telephone operators, trolley drivers, etc.).

3-2. Two major historical events of the twentieth century spurred the use of ability testing on a massive scale and enhanced the importance of personnel psychology. What were these two events? _____ and _____.

3-3. Prior to 1930, the cost-benefit theories of Frederick _____ dominated industry's thinking about behavior in the workplace. Productivity was thought to be determined solely by identifying efficient movements, finding employees capable and willing to work, and paying amounts that were exactly proportionate to rate of _____.

3-4. In 1930 a now-famous study at a Western Electric plant near Chicago found that productivity appeared to be affected by workers' _____ toward their supervisors. This result was surprising because it had previously been thought that only physical factors, such as pay and working conditions, would affect productivity. This experiment marks the beginning of the human _____ movement in industrial psychology.

3-5. The subarea directed toward developing equipment with displays and controls suited to the human beings who use them is known as _____ _____ psychology.

3-6. Human factors developed in large part in response to the need to understand the best and safest ways for human beings to interact with airplanes and other weapons of war. What historical event marks the beginning of human factors psychology? _____.

Answers: 3-1. personnel, test, intelligence **3-2.** World War I and World War II **3-3.** Taylor, production (work) **3-4.** attitudes, relations **3-5.** human factors **3-6.** World War II.

4. Discuss how personnel psychologists go about the process of employee selection.

Job Analysis

4-1. Characteristics of a job are not always obvious. We know that accountants do accounting and managers do managing, but these rough descriptions are not specific enough to permit prediction from tests. A more precise description is provided by the process known as job _____, a method for breaking a job into its constituent parts.

4-2. Job analysis determines not only the constituent parts of a job but which of these are _____ to the job and which are not. Once the analysis has determined these components, the employer must decide on the human _____ needed to accomplish the job.

Answers: 4-1. analysis **4-2.** central, attributes (characteristics, abilities, traits, skills).

Test Administration and Interviewing

4-3. The next step is to determine whether or not job candidates have the characteristics needed for the job. To accomplish this, employers may administer psychological _____ purchased from test publishers or which they themselves develop.

4-4. Tests used must be both consistent (e.g., provide similar scores each time individuals are tested) and also measure what they are supposed to measure. That is, the tests must show appropriate levels of _____ and _____ (Chapter 9).

4-5. Tests of abilities or skills play a major role in this assessment. In addition, in part as a result of the popularity of the "_____" theory of personality, the last several years have seen renewed interest in using _____ tests (Chapter 12).

4-6. Although standardized tests are frequently used, the most widely used procedure in personnel selection is the _____. The _____ interview uses non-standardized questions with no clear right and wrong answers.

4-7. In contrast, the _____ interview uses standardized questions, asked of all candidates, which are scored for the adequacy of the answers. Of the two types of interview, only the _____ interview has been found to be reliable and valid.

Answers: 4-3. central, tests **4-4.** reliability, validity **4-5.** Big Five, personality **4-6.** interview, unstructured **4-7.** structured, structured.

Test Validity; Equal Employment Opportunity and Testing

4-8.   The process of demonstrating that a test is a good predictor of job performance involves

_____ of the test. If the test score has a strong positive _____ with a

reliable measure of job performance (e.g., supervisor rating), then the test may be described as having

validity.

4-9.   People of different races, ethnicities, ages, and genders (<u>always/may not</u>) perform at the same level on

personnel tests, so their use in employee selection creates controversy. For example, it is (<u>not uncommon/

unusual</u>) for minority applicants, on average, to have lower scores on standardized tests than white

applicants.

4-10.   Part of the controversy concerns the fairness or validity of the tests and part the use of a single measure

for selection. For example, some organizations test for only one attribute, such as general intelligence.

One possible solution is to administer a _____ of tests and allow relatively high

performance on one attribute (e.g., communication skills) to compensate for low performance on another.

Answers: **4-8.** validation, correlate **4-9.** may not, not uncommon **4-10.** battery (variety).

New Trends and Challenges

4-11.   Personnel psychology also includes *training and education* and *peformance assessment*. The question,

"What is the best way to provide instruction for the employee?" concerns the area of

_____. The question, "How well is the employee performing?" involves

_____.

4-12.   In recent years training and education policies within organizations have shifted, so that employers now

tend to provide:

a. routine and standardized training for all employees.

b. a user-friendly learning environment in which employees can seek new job skills.

4-13.   After the 2001 attack on the Twin Towers, I/O psychologists who had previously worked in different

federal agencies became part of a team under the Department of _____. Their charge

was to provide job analyses, personnel selection, training, and evaluation procedures for thousands of

new jobs and especially for _____ screeners. Not permitted the luxury of time, this

team accomplished their task with extraordinary speed.

Answers: **4-11.** training and education, performance assessment **4-12.** b **4-13.** Homeland Security, airport.

5. Summarize some major theories of work motivation.

5-1.   The two most popular theories of motivation of the 1960s are associated with Frederick Herzberg and B.

F. Skinner. Herzberg proposed that motivation in the workplace depends on the nature of (<u>the work itself/

extrinsic rewards</u>). Known as job _____ theory, Herzberg's viewpoint asserts that

workers are motivated, for example, by (<u>challenges/money</u>) associated with a particular job.

5-2. Skinner's reinforcement theory, as described here, maintains that job interest is created only when the work is followed by sufficient and meaningful _____, such as money or other extrinsic entities. Just as food creates interest in pressing the lever for the rat, so money maintains interest in work for the human.

5-3. Both theories apply to work motivation to some degree. However, (everyone/not everyone) wants a challenging job, and (everyone/not everyone) considers money the most important motivator in a job.

5-4. Two other theories of interest are *expectancy* theory and *self-efficacy* theory. Expectancy theory contends that people estimate the probability that a particular task will produce a desired _____. Under this theory, managers must make sure that workers understand the likelihood or _____ that particular rewards will follow particular types of work.

5-5. Work motivation may also depend on employees' confidence that they can accomplish the task, a point of view referred to as _____ theory. Implementation of this theory involves selecting workers who think they can do a job and providing conditions that will enhance this feeling.

5-6. Self-efficacy theory is currently considered under the broader model of _____ theory, which stresses the capacity of people to direct, control, and alter their behavior as they adjust to the requirements of the workplace.

5-7. Finally, the viewpoint know as _____ theory asserts that it is important to set specific, challenging training goals for workers.

Answers: 5-1. the work itself, enrichment, challenges **5-2.** reinforcers (rewards. consequences, outcomes) **5-3.** not everyone, not everyone **5-4.** reward, probability **5-5.** self-efficacy **5-6.** self-regulation **5-7.** goal setting.

6. Summarize research on job satisfaction.

6-1. What do people want in a job? Place checkmarks next to those items below that appear to be major factors associated with job satisfaction.

____ interesting and challenging work

____ pleasant co-workers

____ adequate salary

____ opportunities for advancement

____ effective and supportive supervisors

____ acceptable company policies

6-2. To assess job satisfaction most organizations distribute questionnaires that ask employees to rate their jobs. Most organizations assume that work satisfaction is related to three factors: absenteeism, turnover, and productivity. Research does, in fact, support the notion job satisfaction is related both to _____ and to _____. Employees who are happy with their jobs are absent less often, and they look for new jobs less frequently.

6-3. Managers might hope, and it would seem reasonable to expect, that job satisfaction would result in greater productivity. Decades of research (<u>have/have not</u>) found this to be the case. There is some evidence, however, that the reverse is true, that greater _____ leads to increased _____. If people are productive, they tend to like what they are doing.

Answers: 6-1. Thousands of studies have found that all of these are primary sources of job satisfaction! **6-2.** absenteeism, turnover **6-3.** have not, productivity, job satisfaction.

7. Discuss the concepts of work teams, leadership, and organizational culture.

7-1. The past 15 years or so has seen an increased use of work teams in American companies, an outcome of the downsizing of the 1980s. Which of the following has accompanied the emphasis on work teams? (Mark T or F.)

_____ Fewer people are expected to do more work with less supervision.

_____ Feelings of accountability and ownership increased at lower levels.

_____ Work motivation and job satisfaction increased.

7-2. With the emergence of the internet, I/O psychologists have been asked to facilitate development of _____ work teams. While there are clear advantages to virtual teams, there are some disadvantages as well: virtual teams may be separated by _____ zones, _____ differences, and inadequate face-to-face _____.

7-3. In recent years I/O psychologists have been particularly interested in the *transformational* and *charismatic* leadership styles. Differentiate between these somewhat overlapping concepts by indicating which style is described in each of the following. (Use T or C.)

_____ Succeeds through a vision of what should be accomplished, how the company should change.

_____ Succeeds through the sheer force of the leader's personality.

_____ Makes clear to employees the importance of what they are doing and persuades them to put the organization ahead of self-interest,

_____ Appeals to achievement and mastery (self-efficacy) needs of employees.

_____ Are particularly sensitive to others' needs.

_____ Are able to get followers to accept challenges they would normally reject.

7-4. Even more recently I/O psychologists have become interested in a style of leadership that assures that those affected by a decision play a role in its creation and implementation. This leadership style is known as _____ leadership, in part because it strives to emancipate or empower employees rather than rule them.

7-5. Another leadership style emphasizes understanding and managing moods, in oneself as well as in others. How does one deal with disappointment in the workplace? A leader who uses what is referred to as _____ intelligence might help the person to productively use their emotions for analysis and change.

7-6. Companies, like people, have differentiating characteristics or personalities. A company might emphasize innovation, or quality, or time urgency. In current I/O psychology jargon, these company norms or traditions or characteristics are referred to as the organizational _____.

7-7. Since the organizational culture impacts the relationships and work patterns among employees, I/O psychologists are particularly interested in the way (<u>employees/customers</u>) experience the culture. Employees' perception of specific aspects of an organizational culture is referred to as an organizational _____. (The major difference between culture and climate seems to be point of view: the company has a culture, the employees perceive a climate.)

7-8. An emerging interest in organizational psychology concerns the manner in which employees balance their work obligations and personal lives. A major focus of this research is to examine programs intended to reduce _____ at work and to find means for enhancing an employee's _____ life.

Answers: 7-1. T, T, T **7-2.** virtual, time, cultural (local/cultural), interaction (contact) **7-3.** T, C, T, T, C, C **7-4.** emancipatory **7-5.** emotional **7-6.** culture **7-7.** employees, climate **7-8.** stress, family.

8. Discuss how human engineering can enhance work environments.

8-1. Human factors or human engineering is the study of the interaction or _____ between humans and machines. There are two parts of this system, the _____ part, which conveys information to the operator, and the _____ part, which involves action or inaction by the human operator.

8-2. For example, dashboards in cars provide the _____ part of the system. Based on that information, the human being operates the pedals and knobs that provide the _____ part of the system, which changes the display, which in turn may affect the control.

8-3. To reduce interface problems, human factors specialists design display panels that are easily understood at a glance or control components shaped like the functions they control. For example, after World War II the knobs that operated the flaps on airplanes were redesigned to be shaped like _____.

8-4. Most people have certain expectations about the way things work. For example, people generally expect to unscrew things in a counterclockwise direction. Thus, a major design principle is to build controls that take into account response _____, people's natural expectations about the way controls work.

8-5. As I sit here writing the last paragraph of this study guide, my new laptop is behaving nicely. I am interfacing easily with the _____ and _____ parts of my system. How can human engineering enhance work environments? The simple answer is that well-designed machines reduce _____ in the human operator, a potential cause of health problems and accidents. I have pushed no wrong buttons, nothing has crashed, my stress-level is low, and for that I am grateful.

Answers 8-1. interface, display, control **8-2.** display, control **8-3.** display, control, flaps **8-4.** stereotype **8-5.** display, control, stress.

Reference: Burger, J. M. (1986). Is there a Ph.D. in the house? *APA Monitor, 17*, 4.

Appendix D
CAREERS IN PSYCHOLOGY

Review of Key Ideas

1. **What are the entry level options for psychology majors?**

    1-1.   Answer the following true-false questions regarding entry-level options for psychology majors.

    (a) You can get a job as a psychologist with a bachelor's degree.

    (b) You can get a good entry-level job with a bachelor's degree in psychology.

    (c) A recent survey found that "enjoying what I do" is more important than a high starting salary for graduates seeking an entry-level job.

    Answers: 1-1. (a) false (b) true (c) true.

2. **What are the keys to success in the entry-level job market?**

    2-1.   The test mentions three keys to a successful entry-level job search. The first is to have accurate _____ about the knowledge, skills, and values that are required for occupations that interest you. The second key is to _____ the skills that are prized by employers. The third key is to assemble convincing _____ that you possess these skills and values.

    2-2.   What three excellent skill-building vehicles are available to college students?

    Answers: 2-1. information, acquire, documentation **2-2.** College courses, relevant work experience, extra-curricular activities.

3. **What are the career options at the master's level?**

    3-1.   What are the three career options in the mental health area?

3-2.   What other area in psychology offers career options at the master's level?

Answers: 3-1. Clinical, clinical social work, agency counseling **3-2.** industrial/organizational.

4.   What are the career options at the doctoral level?

4-1.   What are the two broad areas for careers in psychology at the doctoral level?

4-2.   Answer the following true-false questions regarding career options at the doctoral level:

(a)   Teaching psychology in a university setting requires a Ph.D. in psychology.

(b)   Teaching in a university setting generally requires conducting research as well as teaching.

(c)   If you want to focus entirely on teaching, then you should consider a job in a two-year college.

Answers: 4-1. teaching and research, applied work **4-2.** (a) true (b) true (c) true.

5.   How should an undergraduate student prepare for admission to graduate school?

5-1.   There are three points to keep in mind when preparing for admission to graduate school. One is to begin _____ to develop the appropriate knowledge and skills graduate programs seek. Another is to keep your _____ up. Finally, position yourself to obtain strong _____ of recommendation from _____ faculty members.

Answers: 5-1. early, grades, letters, three.

Self-Quiz

1. Where should college students begin their career planning?
   a. at the beginning of their junior year in college
   b. when they finally decide on a career choice
   c. at the end of their freshman year
   d. immediately

2. Active career planning may actually help to guide an undecided person to a potential career choice.
   a. true
   b. false

Answers: 1. immediately **2.** true.